Advance Praise page for A New Lens on Emerging Adulthood

"Shulman beautifully extends the developmental systems perspective to provide a fresh, positive view of the struggles in the transition to adulthood. This book is at once scholarly, insightful, and lucid."
—**L. Alan Sroufe**, PhD, Professor Emeritus, Institute of Child Development, University of Minnesota and author of award-winning The Development of the Person

"Practitioners and researchers will be richly informed by Professor Shulman's masterful integration of the quantitative and qualitative findings from his seminal twelve-year study and new understandings of the transition to adulthood."
—**David Reiss**, MD, Professor of Clinical Child Psychiatry, Yale Child Study Center

"Professor Shulman's newest book presents a brilliant reworking of the psychological underpinnings of the emerging adulthood. He skillfully integrates his experiences as a clinical psychologist with findings from his ground-breaking study of the lived experiences of young adults and proposes that resolving personal, vocational, and relational uncertainty is central to these years. This book is a must-read for students and researchers as well as clinicians working with emerging adults."
—**Jennifer Connolly**, PhD, Professor, Department of Psychology and LaMarsh Centre for Child & Youth Research, York University, Toronto

EMERGING ADULTHOOD SERIES

Series Editor
Larry J. Nelson

Advisory Board
Elisabetta Crocetti
Shagufa Kapadia
Koen Luyckx
Laura Padilla-Walker
Jennifer L. Tanner

Books in the Series

Emerging Adults' Religiousness and Spirituality: Meaning-Making in an Age of Transition
Edited by Carolyn McNamara Barry and Mona M. Abo-Zena

Flourishing in Emerging Adulthood: Positive Development During the Third Decade of Life
Edited by Laura M. Padilla-Walker and Larry J. Nelson

The Marriage Paradox: Why Emerging Adults Love Marriage Yet Push It Aside
Brian J. Willoughby and Spencer L. James

The Life Story, Domains of Identity, and Personality Development in Emerging Adulthood: Integrating Narrative and Traditional Approaches
Michael W. Pratt and M. Kyle Matsuba

The Romantic Lives of Emerging Adults: Getting From I to We
Varda Konstam

Leaving Care and the Transition to Adulthood: International Contributions to Theory, Research, and Practice
Edited by Varda R. Mann-Feder and Martin Goyette

Young Adult Development at the School-to-Work Transition: International Pathways and Processes
Edited by E. Anne Marshall and Jennifer E. Symonds

The Experience of Emerging Adulthood Among Street-Involved Youth
Doug Magnuson, Mikael Jansson, and Cecilia Benoit

Sexuality in Emerging Adulthood
Edited by Elizabeth M. Morgan and Manfred H. M. van Dulmen

Generation Disaster: Coming of Age Post-9/11
Karla Vermeulen

A New Lens on Emerging Adulthood: Fluidity as the Path to Settling Down
Shmuel Shulman

A New Lens on Emerging Adulthood

Fluidity as the Path to Settling Down

SHMUEL SHULMAN

OXFORD
UNIVERSITY PRESS

Oxford University Press is a department of the University of Oxford. It furthers the University's objective of excellence in research, scholarship, and education by publishing worldwide. Oxford is a registered trade mark of Oxford University Press in the UK and certain other countries.

Published in the United States of America by Oxford University Press
198 Madison Avenue, New York, NY 10016, United States of America.

© Oxford University Press 2024

All rights reserved. No part of this publication may be reproduced, stored in a retrieval system, or transmitted, in any form or by any means, without the prior permission in writing of Oxford University Press, or as expressly permitted by law, by license, or under terms agreed with the appropriate reproduction rights organization. Inquiries concerning reproduction outside the scope of the above should be sent to the Rights Department, Oxford University Press, at the address above.

You must not circulate this work in any other form
and you must impose this same condition on any acquirer.

Library of Congress Cataloging-in-Publication Data
Names: Shulman, Shmuel, author.
Title: A new lens on emerging adulthood : fluidity as the path to
settling down / Shmuel Shulman.
Description: New York, NY : Oxford University Press, [2024] |
Includes bibliographical references and index.
Identifiers: LCCN 2023017748 (print) | LCCN 2023017749 (ebook) |
ISBN 9780190841836 (paperback) | ISBN 9780190841850 (epub) | ISBN 9780190841867
Subjects: LCSH: Adulthood. | Interpersonal relations.
Classification: LCC HQ799.95 .S485 2024 (print) | LCC HQ799.95 (ebook) |
DDC 305.24—dc23/eng/20230426
LC record available at https://lccn.loc.gov/2023017748
LC ebook record available at https://lccn.loc.gov/2023017749

DOI: 10.1093/oso/9780190841836.001.0001

Printed by Marquis Book Printing, Canada

*To Chava
and to Nadav, Yael, Ben, Roni, Itamar, Tom, Noa, Healy, and Daphna*

Contents

Acknowledgments		ix
	Introduction: The Conceptual Challenge of Emerging Adulthood and the Need for New Understandings	1
1	Relevant Theoretical and Research Frameworks for Understanding Emerging Adulthood and the Development of the Current Study	9
2	Developmental Goals During Emerging Adulthood: Constellations of Goal Coordination and Their Sequence Over Time	27
3	Pathways of Career Pursuit—Consistency, Detours, Disappointments: Finding One's Way or Getting Lost	46
4	Aspirations, Flourishing, and Compromises: Career Pursuit Pathways and Settling Down	62
5	Romantic Pathways Among Emerging Adults: Between Fluidity and Progression	79
6	Romantic Intimacy Statuses and Progress Toward the Future: There Is Hope for Change	96
7	Career Pursuit and Romantic Investment: How Do They Go Together?	115
8	Achieving Life Authorship: The Psychological Challenge of Emerging Adulthood	131
9	Gendered Pathways in Career Pursuit and Romantic Development	147
10	Personality Assets and Developmental Outcomes	164
11	Support Systems and Their Role in Developmental Processes During Emerging Adulthood	186
12	Patterns of Mental Health During Emerging Adulthood and Their Association With the Success or Failure to Attain Developmental Tasks	208
13	Developmental Pathways During Emerging Adulthood: A Cross-Cultural Perspective	230

14 Emerging Adulthood Revisited: A New Conceptualization for
    Understanding Fluctuations, Changes, and Processes   248

References   265
Index   291

Acknowledgments

This book is based on a comprehensive study that followed emerging adults for almost 15 years and could not have been carried out without a great deal of help. First, I would like to thank our faithful participants who were ready time and again to share their personal stories with us, the challenges with which they coped, the challenges they were able to overcome, and those that were more of a struggle. Your stories touched and inspired me and led me to new understandings. I greatly appreciate your commitment to this study over the years.

The conceptual seeds of this project were planted during the time I spent at the Institute of Child Development at the University of Minnesota, where I was exposed to the Minnesota Parent–Child Study. I am thankful to L. Alan Sroufe for his mentorship, insights, and friendship. I also remember fondly the late Sidney Blatt, whose ideas and insights were a source of inspiration and growth during the time I spent at Yale University and later. I fondly remember Jari-Erik Nurmi, University of Jyvaskyla, a friend and a colleague who passed away untimely; Jari's understandings and conceptualization contributed to the development and progress of this study.

I am also thankful to our graduate students who contributed their efforts and creativity to this project: Esther Kalniztky, Tamuz Barr, Yaara Livneh, Yossi Michaeli, Maor Hakhmigari-Kalfon, and Ornella Silberberg. I also want to thank Daniel Dickson for his important contribution during the years; Michael Pratt for his comments and suggestions, which made the outlay of the book clearer; and Jennifer Connolly for our discussions. Special thanks to Rivka Tuval-Mashiach who introduced me to the rich world of qualitative studies, which is a central pillar of this book.

This study could not have been accomplished without the financial support of the Israeli Science Foundation, whose support allowed us to launch this study. Later the study was generously supported by the Ben Dov Foundation at Bar Ilan University, which allowed us to repeat assessments.

Thanks to Debbie Werbeloff, my English editor, whose support and comments have accompanied me faithfully for many years. Thanks to Andrea Zekus, senior editor at Oxford University Press, who during the earlier stages of the book proposal was helpful in setting the path of the book. And last but not least, I am grateful to Hayley Singer, the editor whose assistance, questions, comments, and suggestions made this book better. It was a pleasure to work with you, Hayley.

Introduction

The Conceptual Challenge of Emerging Adulthood and the Need for New Understandings

In recent years, fewer young people make a smooth and linear transition to adulthood. The age of marriage has increased, and the lives of many young people are characterized by instabilities in both their careers and their romantic lives. These changes have been conceptualized as an extension of adolescence, with some arguing that this reflects the increased narcissism and self-absorption of "Generation me." However, when approaching the age of 30, the vast majority of young people are likely to have settled down. More than 80% have started a career or have a steady job (Organisation for Economic Co-operation and Development, 2022), and more than two thirds are married or involved in a stable and intimate romantic relationship (US Census Bureau, 2021). How is this gap between the instabilities and fluctuations of the 20s and the settling down when approaching the 30s bridged? The main purpose of this volume is to address this challenge and understand the developmental journey taken by young people during their 20s.

We propose a new conceptualization for understanding the major processes through which emerging adults make their way toward a successful transition to adulthood. We argue that fluidity does not have to be perceived as a setback. It instead can be understood as a mode of exploration, a way to find one's niche in an unstable cultural and economic environment. Our suggestions are based on a 12-year study during which we followed emerging adults from the age of 23 to the age of 35 who were living in Israel. Our study emerged from the common conception of emerging adulthood as a period of extended exploration. During the course of the study, we realized that this conceptualization might not capture the complexity of the processes taking place during these years. Thus, in Chapter 1 we describe the conceptual journey that *we* also took in our search and struggle to understand what emerging adulthood entails: our efforts to better understand what takes place during the emerging adult years and the search for a more comprehensive understanding of the meaning and purposes of emerging adults' behaviors. Relatedly, we describe how our research project evolved in order to better capture and understand the developmental processes that take place during these years. In our search to understand what could

A New Lens on Emerging Adulthood. Shmuel Shulman, Oxford University Press. © Oxford University Press 2024.
DOI: 10.1093/oso/9780190841836.003.0001

explain successful settling down, we first explored the factors that are associated with future adaptive (or less adaptive) outcomes. This led us to adopt a longitudinal design and to assess participants multiple times throughout their 20s. By adopting a longitudinal study, new insights were learned along the way, which led to refinement of the project. These included intensive interviews with our participants in addition to the periodic assessments.

The following chapters, as outlined below, describe the journey we took. The chapters start with a review of the current understandings of emerging adulthood and the questions that these understandings raise. Subsequently, we describe the methodological and conceptual underpinnings of the journey over a period of 12 years. Based on our findings and the insights we gained, we outline the new understanding and conceptualization of emerging adulthood that has developed through this journey.

We focused on understanding emerging adulthood through the lens of the two major tasks, career and romantic development, as told in the life stories of participants. While our study focused primarily on career and romantic development, we also discuss issues of personality development, the role of the family during emerging adulthood, psychopathology, and the role of cultural contexts.

Outlining the chapters of the book

Chapter 1 starts with a short review of current descriptions of the fluidity in emerging adult behavior, as well as the demographics of emerging adulthood as portrayed in the last three decades of literature. We then present the ways scholars have tried to understand and conceptualize emerging adulthood. Psychological studies tend to portray the emerging adulthood years as a period of confusion, exploration, and elevated narcissism. In contrast, sociological studies attribute settling down at a later age to economic and social uncertainty. In either case, these two bodies of research do not explain how, in spite of these obstacles, the majority of young people do settle down. In order to understand the connection between emerging adulthood behavior and future outcomes, we discuss the ideas inspired by a life course development perspective that led to the conceptualization and launching of our project. We describe the initial stages of our project, what we have learned from the preliminary findings, and our decision to develop the project over the course of 12 years. During this 12-year period, participants were assessed five times, to allow for the detection of developmental trajectories.

Chapter 2 focuses on the development and changes of personal goals across the years of emerging adulthood. Personal goals and plans were shown to direct individual life paths by regulating behavior (Haase et al., 2008) and leading individuals through their own development. Existing research often assessed the contribution of the presence or absence of an age-appropriate goal to developmental outcomes. In line with the dynamic understanding of emerging adulthood, we suggest in Chapter 2 that goals are not necessarily stable and might change across development. We show that across emerging adulthood, individuals may construct a variety of goal patterns, some of which might characterize a capacity to navigate one's course of development competently by setting consistently clear goals that evolve over time. In contrast, there are goal patterns that are characterized rather by difficulty setting a clear route, lead to floundering, and are associated with less adaptive developmental outcomes. Within this "goal pattern" framework we also learned that the lives and aspirations of emerging adults are mostly focused on two major goals, work and love. This led us to focus our understanding of emerging adulthood through the lens of work and love goals.

Chapters 3 and 4 discuss the career pursuit pathways we found in our project. In Chapter 3, we describe the four pathways found in our project, encompassing a variety of routes that individuals take in their career development. We show that, although it is quite common among individuals to lose their way, many are capable of finding an alternative route. Overall, most of our participants successfully met their original goals or the new goals they adopted over the years. Conceptually, we argue that the different pathways found in our project point to their inherent complexity. Thus, disruptions, fluidity, and changes can be understood as part of an adaptation process. In Chapter 4, based on the information gained from following our participants until the age of 35, we show that the process of adaptation continues even after the age of 30. We speculate that career adaptation might consist of two stages. First, during the earlier years of emerging adulthood, among those who lost their way, a substantial number were able to find a new way and to be invested in their new goal (career). Among those who were not successful in setting a clear goal or achieving the goal to which they aspired at first, a substantial number still found a stable job, made compromises, and settled down. We show that even among those who made compromises, the process of adaptation continues into the 30s. Individuals continued to readapt or found meaning in what they had attained and led more satisfactory lives.

Guided by the dynamic understanding of emerging adulthood, Chapters 5 and 6 aim to understand the meaning of the different romantic experiences observed during emerging adulthood. By following the development of the romantic history of our participants, we learned that casual romantic encounters do not necessarily represent instabilities and floundering but can rather serve as an arena for learning how to handle and master romantic relationships and progress toward commitment. In Chapter 6 we further show how the different romantic pathways taken during emerging adulthood are associated with future outcomes. In addition, as with career development, the pattern of romantic life that characterized the emerging adulthood years might also continue to change and develop. Some individuals who were involved only in sporadic encounters were found to progress toward commitment in their early 30s. The rich interviews helped us present examples, in each of the four chapters, of the different pathways as described by participants themselves. Furthermore, reading the detailed, rich developmental stories helped us to learn and shed light on the mechanisms that led to the changes over time.

Following the stories of the temporal developments within the domains of career and romantic relationships, Chapter 7 examines how young people address these two main developmental tasks—career and romance—simultaneously. We found a clear tendency to prioritize career development over romantic development. Yet, following our sample through their 20s and into their mid-30s taught us that over the years the patterns of balancing career and family do evolve and might be differently expressed. In addition, different reasons for the ways work and family are balanced can be found. Finally, in this chapter we show that in following the participants for a 12-year span we learned that, despite the initial priority of career, over time an increasing number of young people, both women and men, described not only the centrality of career but also the importance of family in their lives.

Chapter 8 examines how patterns of progress made during emerging adulthood might serve as models for, or guide future navigation through, life. Put differently, Chapter 8 explores the psychological assets a young person should acquire during the emerging adulthood years that could affect future behavior and outcomes. Guided by the conceptual work of McAdams (2013a, 2013b) on authorship, in this chapter we show that progress in career and romantic development is characterized by an ability to draw lessons from past experiences, learn how to overcome difficulties, and grow out of earlier difficulties. We further show that achievement of authorship is the mechanism that is expected to be attained during emerging adulthood and that this attained authorship is likely to shape future outcomes. Accordingly, we define and describe what achievement of authorship is in the domain of career and in the domain of romantic relationships. In addition, we show that achievement of authorship in one domain does not necessarily correspond with achievement of authorship in the other domain. For example, there are young men who achieved career authorship but not romantic authorship. The chapter concludes with findings that demonstrate the extent to which achievement of authorship associates with psychological well-being at age 35, thus suggesting the achievement of authorship as a psychological asset that can serve as the basis for future outcomes.

Chapter 9 examines the gendered pathways in career and romance that emerged in our study, among women and men during emerging adulthood. We show that, compared to women, men are more likely to embark on focused career pathways and to be able to readapt and competently pursue a new goal. In contrast, women were more likely to be involved in stable relationships, while young men were more frequently observed in sporadic relationships. This distinction recalls the gender-stereotyped attitudes toward work and family. Emerging adult men prioritize career over romantic investment. Emerging adult women tend to become more involved in stable relationships and, therefore, might feel more pressure to invest in their romantic relationships and less pressure to stay focused on their careers. We further show in Chapter 9 that the data collected at age 35 suggests that the issue of gendered pathways is more complex. Interviews at age 35 showed that motherhood is a significant part of their identity for these women, and they attribute high valence to motherhood despite having career aspirations. As a result, women employ a variety of modes to reconcile their family/motherhood and career aspirations. Chapter 9 concludes that the gendered pathways in career pursuit, as well as in romantic development, should not suggest that women are less driven to pursue a career. We should rather become aware of the greater family–career conflict which women have to endure. We suggest that a better understanding of the greater complexity of tasks that women need to address during the transition to adulthood could help in understanding how women succeed in modern society.

In Chapter 4, we showed that personality attributes, such as low self-criticism, associated with future level of goal attainment. Extending these findings in Chapter 10, we show that personality attributes associate with pattern of career or romantic pathway as well. We describe how personal capacities such as being efficacious, more inwardly motivated, and less self-critical facilitated successful navigation in the journey toward career development. Similarly, less dependent individuals progressed more competently toward intimate and committed relationships. As in the previous chapters, narrative accounts are presented and help shed further light on the quantitative findings. Personality development, which has gained interest in recent years, is also discussed in Chapter 10. Following our sample through the emerging adulthood years, we present and discuss the significant decrease in self-criticism and its meaning. We contend and show that this increase in personality "positivity" is aimed toward facilitating a smoother transition to adulthood and the assumption of adult career and family roles. Overall, Chapter 10 emphasizes the role of personality attributes in moderating the nature and capacity to navigate successfully toward adulthood. Furthermore, changes in personality documented during this stage of life are tuned to further facilitate a smoother transition.

The role of parental support for adaptive child developmental is a basic tenet in developmental psychology. Chapter 11 examines and discusses the role of parental support (and additional support systems) in the development of emerging adults. Based on our longitudinal data, we first describe the amount of support that young adults reported receiving from their parents and friends over the period of 12 years. We show that despite the changes in parent–child relationships during emerging adulthood, parents still are considered a primary source of support. Furthermore, we show that availability of parental support contributed to affiliation with more adaptive developmental pathways in both career and romantic development. These findings are supported by the narrative accounts of our participants describing their relationship with their parents across the years and the ways their parents provided (or did not provide) support. From careful reading of these interviews we learned that over the years emerging adults tended to develop a more mature and reflective understanding of their parents. Relatedly, we show that a more mature understanding of one's parents at age 29 is associated with better developmental and psychological outcomes at age 35, suggesting that the ability to perceive parents in a mature manner is also a source of strength for further development. Finally, the chapter examines the role of mentors in emerging adults' success at meeting developmental tasks.

Chapter 12 summarizes existing research showing conflicting trends with regard to the frequency and changes in mental health among emerging adults. To address this question, we first embed the understanding of mental health in emerging adulthood and its manifestations and changes over time within a developmental psychopathology perspective. We suggest that failure to achieve the developmental tasks of emerging adulthood (such as career development or romantic relationships) will associate with the expression of psychological problems. We present data from our longitudinal study demonstrating the interplay between success or failure to attain developmental tasks and the increase or decrease in depressive affect over a period of 12 years. Qualitative data is additionally presented to better demonstrate and understand associations between career and romantic developmental pathways and the developmental course of depressive affect. Applying the *scar* model of psychopathology (Durbin & Hicks, 2014; Klimstra & Denissen, 2017) and an individual differences perspective, we use our 12-year-long accumulated data and show the existence of different trajectories of depressive affect across the emerging adulthood years, their antecedents, and their impact on psychological well-being at age 35. The chapter concludes with a summary of a more comprehensive approach for understanding mental health during emerging adulthood.

There is an ongoing debate questioning the relevance of the emerging adulthood theory to non-Western cultures (Côté, 2006, 2014). Chapter 13 focuses on a cross-cultural perspective of emerging adulthood. In line with the main tenets of our book, we claim, as we did with our Israeli sample—a Western society—that it is important to listen to the life histories of young people from non-Western societies in order to learn about their lives and development. To become more acquainted with non-Western societies, the chapter first reviews the work and marital statuses of young people in societies across the globe. This review shows that postponement of the transition to adulthood has become a worldwide phenomenon. Instead of summarizing the existing studies of young people in non-Western societies within the framework of emerging adulthood theory, we rather focus on two "case stories" that richly document and describe the current lives of young people in two different societies. First, we present the "story" of young people on the island of Sardinia. Second, we focus on the Arab world, North Africa and Africa at large, which together represent societies that have been harshly affected economically and politically in recent years and where young people face a high level of uncertainty. For this purpose, we examine sociological, historical, and political processes that take place in these societies and their significant impact on the lives of young people. We closely examine the lives of emerging adults who live under enormous hardships as reported in the media and personal accounts. We describe that despite the difficult conditions, many emerging adults in these societies have not lost hope. Although some might regress into a condition of *waithood*, many others act differently. They mobilize their inner strengths either for daily survival or to search for creative ways to exit the misery. We thus use these accounts to further support our contention that emerging adulthood is a dynamic period of life during which young people actively pursue their developmental goals.

Chapter 14 first summarizes the major findings of the project and embeds these within theoretical frameworks. First, and in line with dynamic systems theory, we show how the different and seemingly unstable and inconsistent behaviors can be understood as the underlying mechanisms guiding progression to the assumption of adult roles. We describe the back-and-forth movements as being helpful for exploring and finding one's niche and assuming an adult role. Contingent upon this understanding, we discuss our findings with reference to the process of personality maturation that takes place during the years of emerging adulthood. Relatedly, we also emphasize that progression is not limited to the attainment of developmental tasks but leads to the achievement of a consolidated personal authorship that lays the ground for development in later adulthood. Considered together, in Chapter 14 we propose understanding emerging adulthood as a period of dynamic processes aimed at progression toward the *assumption of adulthood*. Furthermore, we suggest that the back-and-forth movements observed nowadays among emerging adults can be understood as a reflection of evolutionary efforts in adapting to a changing world.

We contend that adopting an evolutionary perspective can further be helpful in understanding the functional role of the processes and mechanisms employed by emerging adults today on their journey to adulthood. We conclude with a call to better understand the difficulties that emerging adults face today and the efforts they make to find their niche, rather than perceiving emerging adulthood merely as an extension of adolescence.

1
Relevant Theoretical and Research Frameworks for Understanding Emerging Adulthood and the Development of the Current Study

Research from industrialized countries shows that the period during which young people assume adult responsibilities and gain economic independence has moved to the later phase of the third decade of life (Arnett, 2000; Shulman & Ben Artzi, 2003). For example, the mean age for marriage is approaching 30. This change is, however, more substantial and is not only reflected by the postponement of career development and marriage. It is now common to find young people who do not have clearly defined occupational goals and have unfocused strategies for negotiating the transition from emerging adulthood to adulthood (K. Evans & Heinz, 1994; Shulman & Nurmi, 2010a). Observations also show that young people might oscillate between transitory and inconsistent states. For example, they may find a job, decide on and later renounce an occupation, return to some kind of training, and then pursue a different occupation. Others might oscillate between periods of work and unemployment, living independently at times and then returning to live with their parents (Arnett, 2000, 2007). Members of the European Group for Integrated Social Research (EGRIS, 2001) coined the term *divided lives*, characterizing the simultaneous experience of aspects of adolescent and adult life among young people, leading to their feeling that they are "nowhere" (Bynner et al., 1997) or that they are marginalized (Heinz, 1999). This led to the current description of young adults' transitions as a "yo-yo" structure (EGRIS, 2001). Furthermore, even emerging adults who seem to be committed to an occupation and to have an active life were found to not truly identify with their decisions and status, and the disparity between external behavior and internal feelings masked internal tensions and unexpressed dissatisfactions (Shulman et al., 2005, 2006). Thus, what may appear to be a successful transition might actually be unstable after a period of time.

There have been similar observations relating to the romantic lives of young people. As the age at which unions are formed has been postponed (Meier & Allen, 2009), a substantial number of emerging adults have been shown to engage in more casual sexual encounters (Claxton & van Dulmen, 2013). While in some cases sexual encounters might be motivated by the hope of starting a relationship (Owen & Fincham, 2011), in the majority of cases there was no expectation of a continued romantic relationship (Bogle, 2008). Emerging adults were quite often observed to be involved in a variety of non-committed sexual encounters ranging from one-night stands and hook-ups to friends with benefits (Claxton & van Dulmen, 2013; Puentes et al., 2008). Even when in a steady relationship, many might not be committed or have plans for the future with their partner. Furthermore, cohabitation, which in the past often led to commitment and marriage, has become merely another form of non-stable relational pattern for many young people (Manning & Smock, 2005).

Considered together, the lives of emerging adults seem to be characterized by lack of commitment to a current job or relationship and lack of long-term articulated goals, and to some extent their behavior appears to resemble that of adolescents. This pattern of life is characterized by an extended period of freedom during which young people allow themselves to make changes from one day to the next (EGRIS, 2001). Furthermore, these patterns of life are less in line with social and economic requirements and raise questions about whether the current generation of youth is preparing itself for the future in a way that guarantees secure employment opportunities. These observations have increasingly led to the popular view (that has been accepted to some extent by a number of scholars) that the younger generation wants everything given to them without having to earn it through hard work and perseverance, as was done by former generations (CBS News, 2008).

Conceptualization and research on the lives of emerging adults in the last two decades

In their book *Lost in Transition* Christian Smith and his colleagues (2011) assert "We have found five trends among emerging adults that are both hurtful for themselves and ultimately hurtful to a civil society." In particular, they emphasize the inability of the younger generation to think morally. Jean Twenge (2013) observed Millennials to be a highly individualistic generation, individualism that has started to increase in recent years. To better understand the current generation of young adults, she administered the Narcissistic Personality Inventory to a sample of young adults. She found a higher level of narcissism than was found in earlier surveys. Based on a comparison to earlier surveys, Twenge suggested that the current younger generation is becoming more narcissistic and more focused on their immediate needs and wishes, and she coined the term "Generation Me." Of note, scholars have criticized Twenge's conclusions and pointed to methodological flaws and misinterpretation of the data (see Jeffrey Arnett's criticism in an interview in the *New York Times*; Quenqua, 2013).

Jacob Paulsen and colleagues (2016) argue that anxiety regarding the next generation is not limited to a number of scholars or the current popular media. In the past the media lamented about the hippies in the 1960s and the flappers in the 1920s. In Chapter 13 we mention that similar concerns have been raised by the older generation and establishment in Egypt, complaining about the idleness of the younger generation and their unwillingness to accept responsibilities. Interestingly, Paulsen and colleagues (2016) mention that Aristotle characterized the young generation in a similar way. He described young people as thinking that they know everything and acting carelessly, while being full of confidence. An Acadian clay tablet dating back approximately 5000 years also raised similar concerns.

Observation of the fluid lives of young people led Jeffrey J. Arnett (2000, 2004, 2007) to propose a new theory through which to understand the behavior of young people. Arnett coined the term emerging adulthood to characterize the period between adolescence and adulthood. Emerging adulthood, which spans the ages from 18 to 29, has five defining features: *identity exploration*, *instability*, *possibilities* (capturing an optimistic approach to life), *self-focus*, and *feeling-in between*. Conceptually, the theory suggests that nowadays young people need an extended period of time in their lives, in fact an additional decade, to prepare for a successful transition to adulthood. During this period emerging adults continue to explore their identity, and until this process is complete they are self-focused and unstable. Conceptually, these different observations and understandings of emerging adults perceive the third decade of life from a *deficit* model. Indeed, James Côté (2000) referred to these years as a time of arrested development, during which young people delay the assumption of responsibilities typical of adulthood and, instead, engage in behaviors they feel they will not be able to enjoy once they become adults (Ravert, 2009). Although Arnett's theory provides an accurate description of the lives of emerging adults, there is no indication of whether the long-term outcomes are more beneficial to those who have been involved in identity exploration for many years (Hendry & Kloep, 2007), questioning the developmental function of emerging adulthood.

Reviewing the literature on narcissism, Paulsen and colleagues (2016) question the extent to which young people today are indeed more narcissistic or unprepared compared to earlier generations. Sociologists and labor market experts claim that the pace of transition to adulthood is affected rather by economic factors. For example, the Great Depression slowed down the timing of family formation, whereas the post–World War II economic boom led to earlier marriage, almost following high school graduation (Settersten & Ray, 2010). Similarly, John Bynner (2005) demonstrated that the 1958 British cohort who matured into a period of economic stability made a smoother transition to adulthood compared to the 1970 cohort who matured into an economic recession. Moreover, Côté (2000, p. 194) suggested that the behavior of emerging adults might be in reaction to current market conditions. He added that in order to succeed under current conditions, a high degree of overt narcissism can be helpful. Considered together, it is possible that the level of labor market certainty is a factor affecting the pace and nature of generational transitions into stability, commitment, and assumption of adult responsibility (Heinz, 2002).

Bynner claims that scholars who suggest that the current generation of young people is not prepared to make the transition to adulthood overlook the rich European youth studies in this field that followed youth for a substantial number of years (see, e.g., Heinz, 2002). First, the European studies show that contextual factors, such as labor market certainty, facilitate or slow the pace and quality of a person's transition. Second, this body of research has shown that there is no one path to adulthood. Individuals may embark on different pathways considering their background and personal assets. Some pathways are more successful, while others result in failure. Furthermore, changes in paths can be found along the way. Therefore, Bynner suggests that in order to capture and understand the complexity of making the transition to adulthood, a life-span (Lerner, 1998) or life-course (Elder, 1998) approach should be taken. Assessment of individuals at one point in time cannot provide the full picture of the ways emerging adults cope nowadays with the transition to adulthood. A more comprehensive and lasting assessment that could better inform us about the conditions and factors that may associate with either success or failure is discussed and outlined in the following sections.

What can be learned about career transitions from earlier youth studies

Closer examination of the European youth studies outlines the comprehensive approach undertaken in studying the ways that young Europeans take in their career pursuit. These studies contend that both the context (e.g., the labor market) and the individual's personality play a role in the selection of an occupational pathway and the quality of outcomes (Heinz, 2001). According to Walter Heinz (2002), life-course transitions are linked to *processes of self-socialization*, which shape vocational choice and decisions about occupational options. Thus, unlike earlier research that emphasized the context such as the nature of the labor market or economic certainty or uncertainty (Heinz, 1999; Mortimer & Johnson, 1998), more recent research has been concerned with determining to what extent the person–environment fit affects future outcomes (e.g., Heckhausen, 1999). For example, to what extent do labor market structure, job tasks, and economic certainty influence the process of career development; and, relatedly, what individual capacities and preferences play a role in shaping a person's career development under particular circumstances?

Developmental psychologists have studied the role of personal capacities in outcome behaviors extensively and found that planful behaviors are important in people's lives as they guide the actions a person takes (e.g., Freund & Baltes, 2002; Gollwitzer, 1999; Heckhausen et al., 2010; Koestner et al., 2008). For example, it is argued that people who competently pursue goals related to the developmental tasks of their age are more likely to attain their goals and experience high levels of well-being (Heckhausen et al., 2010; Nurmi, 2004; Salmela-Aro, 2010; see Dietrich et al., 2012, for a review).

Additional insights can be drawn from sociological and social-psychological conceptualizations of the school-to-work transition (STW) body of research and its personal and social capital models. Research on the STW transition grew predominantly out of the emerging trend of youth unemployment and declining wages in the early 1970s (Blustein et al., 2000). The STW body of research posits that successful transitions are facilitated by two constructs: The first, located within the individual, includes an array of basic vocation-relevant skills and a particular array of psychological characteristics such as self-initiative, purposefulness, flexibility, and agency; the second, related to the person's environment, includes a supportive family and supportive and engaged peers, teachers, counselors, and supervisors.

These constructs of personal skills and support systems resemble the personal capital and social capital models that were formulated in the study of transitions. Specifically, Côté (2002) proposed that several personal resources are crucially important for effective functioning within and between institutions (Morch, 1997) and for developing the necessary means for "fitting in" and "becoming" part of a workplace or community. This requires empowerment of oneself based on one's resources (attained education, agentic personality, advanced forms of psychological development) and meeting the environment in such a way as to benefit from what it has to offer (family support, peer support, etc.). Similar notions are found within the conceptual framework of resilience. In their seminal works on resilience, both Ann Masten and colleagues (1999) and Suniya Luthar and colleagues (2000) described individual capacities combined with available support as necessary for laying the foundation for the development of resilience.

Considered together with the earlier research on youth employment and the STW transition, it is suggested that personal capacity and availability of support systems have the potential to affect the success or failure of making a smooth transition to adulthood. These two resources should have the potential to contribute to a better person–environment fit and facilitate a smoother transition. We planned the initial stages of our project based on these understandings.

The role of personality and social resources in successfully meeting developmental challenges during emerging adulthood—The inception of the first stages of our project

In planning our project, we first had to consider what constituted a successful transition to adulthood. For one individual it might be completing studies, for another developing a career, and for a third just having stable employment. Taking a developmental psychology perspective, we defined developmental success as the attainment of aspired goals, which is also considered an indicator of well-being (Heckhausen et al., 2010; Nurmi, 2004; Salmela-Aro, 2010; see Dietrich et al., 2012, for a review). Within this conceptual framework, we planned to assess the extent to which age-related goals are attained over time. We focused on goal investment (the degree of importance of and commitment toward a goal), goal progress (the extent to which a goal is attained or likely to be attained), and goal stress (feelings of stress and interference between goals).

In order to assess the contribution of personal resources in goal attainment, we considered Sidney Blatt's (2008) theory of personality development and psychopathology and Richard Ryan's and Edward Deci (2000) self-determination theory (SDT). Blatt's (2008) theory of personality and psychopathology focuses on personality characteristics that are considered relevant for optimal development and well-being throughout the life span. Blatt argues that individuals need to negotiate two developmental processes successfully. First and central to our study is self-definition, which means establishing a coherent, realistic, and positive sense of self; and second is establishing close and stable relationships. For example, positive self-definition, such as high dispositional efficacy, fosters adaptive functioning, whereas negative self-definition, such as high self-criticism, leads to maladaptive functioning (Blatt, 2008). While efficacy refers to feelings of competence and inner strength, self-criticism is characterized by a preoccupation with achievement and negative appraisals of the self, including guilt and fear of losing approval in the face of failure to live up to certain standards. Strong trait efficacy is assumed to support goal pursuit as challenges are seen as tasks to be mastered (see also Bandura, 1977). In Edwin Locke and Gary Latham's (2002) goal-setting theory, efficacy is a key factor in initiating and propelling goal pursuit—a claim that is empirically well established (Maddux & Volkmann, 2010). Self-criticism, by contrast, should compromise goal striving because self-critics invest their resources in avoiding possible failure and loss of approval rather than investing these in actual goal pursuit (Powers et al., 2009).

According to the SDT (Ryan & Deci, 2000) and the more goal-specific self-concordance model (Sheldon, 2002), self-determined motivational orientations are important precursors of goal pursuit. A behavior is self-determined or self-concordant when individuals perceive themselves to be autonomous agents with a full sense of volition and choice. Such motivational orientations are thought to be aligned on a motivational continuum of increasing self-determination ranging from amotivation via external and controlled factors to internal and autonomous forms of motivation (Deci & Ryan, 2000). Amotivation represents a lack of volition toward one's behaviors; that is, amotivated individuals typically do not have strong intentions when they act. Self-determination increases as people's motivations shift toward autonomous motivation, which indicates behavior that is self-initiated and freely chosen. The more a behavior is self-determined, the more it is thought to contribute to a person's successful goal progress, such as goal investment, and lack of goal-related stress. Amotivated individuals cannot see a connection between their actions and the outcomes of their behavior (Pelletier et al., 2001). Thus, they often feel they lack control over their actions; and, consequently, they are less likely to invest time and energy in goal-directed behaviors (see Legault et al., 2006). Pursuing goals might also be an unpleasant and stressful experience for highly amotivated individuals (see Baker, 2004). In contrast, highly autonomous individuals engage in behaviors that are concordant with their interests and values (Deci & Ryan, 2000; Sheldon, 2002). They should thus be particularly able to channel resources into the pursuit of developmental goals, which should be reflected in high levels of goal investment and progress. As autonomously motivated individuals should also be better at selecting goals that are in line with their personality and inner needs, they should experience lower levels of goal-related stress (Sheldon, 2002). Finally, individuals whose behaviors are highly driven by controlled motives look for external rewards or seek to avoid guilt, shame, and anxiety (Deci & Ryan, 2000). Although this controlled motivation might contribute to goal importance, it is often inefficient for goal progress (Koestner et al., 2008).

Turning to support resources, we note that although young people are expected to become responsible for the attainment of goals through successful manipulation of the environment (Hauser & Greene, 1991), the transition to adulthood is facilitated by a supportive environment. A major task during this stage is developing personal responsibility for one's own life (Williamson & Bray, 1988). However, this personal responsibility is consolidated within a close and supportive relationship with parents in which parents give their blessing and support their offspring in becoming "separate" adults. Similarly, Shmuel Shulman and his colleagues (2005) found that *emotional autonomy*, namely the capacity to internally regulate self-esteem, is related to the shift toward a mature relationship with parents. Differentiation from parents without severing parental ties and continued parental availability in case of need are sources for young adults' improved ability to decide on personal and relationship goals and commitments. Without the attainment of some degree of independence from parents, combined with parental support, young adults have difficulties meeting the developmental tasks of this transitional stage (O'Connor et al., 1996). Of note, despite the major role of family in individual development and adaptation, the role of peer support cannot be underestimated and is important for a young person's self-esteem and adaptation (Galambos et al., 2006), whereas absence of social support might itself become a source of stress.

Considered together, we assumed that success or failure in the transition to adulthood is likely to be determined by personal resources and availability of support systems. Thus, the aim of the first stage of the project was to examine the extent to which personal resources—low self-criticism, efficacy, and inner motivation combined with availability of parental and peer support—would explain higher levels of goal investment and goal progress and lower levels of goal stress. It was planned to examine these assumptions over a 1-year follow-up and again after another 5 years. We believe that a number of assessments over a greater period of time could provide information on the change between two assessments (the 1-year follow-up design), as well as about possible developmental processes during emerging adulthood.

Success and failure in meeting developmental tasks in emerging adulthood—Outline of the initial stages of the project and their major conceptual findings

Conceptually, as summarized above, we argued that emerging adulthood does not necessarily have to be understood from a deficit perspective. Focusing on periods, or individuals, when loss of one's way can be observed cannot be indicative of emerging adulthood at large. For this purpose, in the initial stage of the project we decided to assess our participants three times, at ages 23, 24, and 26.5. Based on the initial findings described later in this chapter and our aim of understanding how settling down takes place, we decided to continue following our participants. They were approached again at the ages of 29 and 35. They were assessed five times in total—of note, in Israel young people are subject to compulsory military service of 3 years for men and 2 years for women, and our participants were approached after completing their military service.

The sample

Participants were 205 young adults (111 men and 94 women; M[age] = 23.11, Md = 23, SD = 1.83) enrolled in two preparatory academic programs, one in the center and one in the south of Israel. The preparatory academic programs are government-sponsored and aim to promote academic studies among young people from low-income families who have not completed their high school education or have not attained a high school diploma. These programs offer 1- or 2-year tracks in order to attain the level required for college entrance. Students are assigned to the 1- or 2-year track based on a nationally standardized entrance exam that assesses their proficiency in mathematics, Hebrew, and English.

At the age 23 assessment the vast majority of the sample were unmarried (95.7%), and most lived with their parents (70.9%). The remainder lived alone, with a romantic partner, or in other types of shared housing. Half the participants (52.11%) were employed at least part-time, while the remainder was unemployed and invested in their studies at the preparatory program. Participants belonged mainly to lower and lower-middle educational backgrounds. Although this sample may seem a homogenous group representing a lower-income population, these programs in fact provide the young people with the potential to progress in their lives. Some of the students do not meet the required standards at the end of the program and are later employed in blue-collar jobs. For a substantial number of young people, the program is the stepping stone for higher education. They successfully complete a college degree, and a few even pursue graduate studies. Thus, after all, our sample was quite heterogeneous. More than half of our participants ultimately pursued different forms of higher education, while the rest completed short-term studies that prepared them for the labor market or started working immediately after completing the preparatory program.

One year later we were able to recruit 175 participants (96 men, 79 women)— 85.3% of the original sample. At the second assessment 68% of the participants were employed full-time and 32% part-time. In addition, more than 60% were enrolled in different educational settings (42 in academic studies, 26 in technical studies, and 46 in other college preparatory programs), while the rest were not enrolled in any educational program. At the fourth assessment, at age 29, we were able to recruit 132 participants, 42% of whom were married. The majority was employed; 68% were employed full-time, and 17% were employed part-time. Only 15% were permanently unemployed. About a quarter of the participants were still studying. At the fifth assessment, at age 35, we were able again to recruit 132 participants, 75% of whom were married (6% of them were divorced), and the remainder, 25%, were not married. The majority was employed; 82% were employed full-time, 15% were employed part-time, and only 3% were permanently unemployed. Fifty-eight percent reported having a college degree.

The sociocultural context of the study—The Israeli society

This study was conducted on an Israeli sample. Two aspects of the Israeli society—its current economic state and its sociocultural norms—are relevant for understanding the ways employed by, and the pace of, Israeli young adults in their journey to adulthood with regard to career pursuit and romantic development.

Israel, located on the eastern Mediterranean shore, has a Western culture and a developed economy. Since its establishment, the country has struggled with security issues, and army service has become a norm and part of the socialization of the younger generation. There is compulsory military service of 3 years for men and 2 years for women, following high school graduation at the age of 18. Despite struggling with security issues, the country has a developed economy and is a member of the Organisation for Economic Co-operation and Development (OECD). The OECD is an intergovernmental economic organization aimed at enhancing economic progress and world trade and includes countries that describe themselves as committed to democracy and the market economy. The country has developed within this framework and is regarded as a "start-up nation," emphasizing individual initiative within an ongoing changing economy. Furthermore, Tel Aviv, the economic and cultural center of the country, portrays itself as a (Western) world city, nicknamed the "The State of Tel Aviv" (Azaryahu, 2020), and serves as a model for the rest of the country. As such, the city is a magnet for young people who aspire to succeed in the Tel Aviv metro area, in the high-tech sector or other developed fields.

Within this context, 49% of young adults earned a college or university degree. This percentage has increased consistently during recent years and is among the highest in the world (OECD, 2021). While this figure might be impressive, too many young people are overqualified and might face difficulties finding a job that suits their education. This fact, combined with the ongoing structural changes in the economy, results in young people perhaps being employed in areas for which they have not been prepared but simply where a job could be found. The rate of youth unemployment is 11.9%—still lower than in other developed countries, but nevertheless a significant number of young people might be unemployed or employed in seasonal work (Arlozorov, 2012). Thus, while for some young people the stronger economy is promising, for others the ongoing process of economic changes, accelerated innovation, and overqualification might make adaptation more challenging or difficult.

Another important characteristic of Israeli society, relevant to the current study, is Israel's historical and cultural values. The ideology of the founding fathers was to liberate themselves from the bonds of traditional Jewish ethics and return to the primal instincts of a natural nation (Almog, 2000). Within this process, an ethos of pioneering, self-defense, and hard labor was developed and encouraged. Phrases such as "we will build," "we will plant," and "we will establish" (Almog, 2000, p. 63) became characteristic modes of expression in the public discourse. Expecting volunteerism and hard work became one of the fundamental criteria according to which a person was judged, by themselves as well as by society. Of note, this strong emphasis on the value of contribution to the society fits traditional values of the Jewish society that place emphasis on communal values (Schwartz, 1994). However, over the years the change into a market economy and the decreasing value of collectivistic views, the ethos of hard work, and communal responsibility have led to an increasing emphasis on greater personal responsibility, success, and development (Almog, 2000). The "we will build" or "we will establish" has thus changed into "I will build" or "I will establish." Indeed, there are strong expectations for young people to settle down in a successful career and start a family (Mayseless & Scharf, 2003) and to attain this toward the end of the third decade of life (Shulman & Ben Artzi, 2003).

Considered together, Israeli young adults grow and are exposed to a culture and society that places emphasis on personal responsibility and success. This ethos is quite often enhanced by the compulsory military service in Israel. However, due to the competitive nature of the free-market society and the quick economic changes in recent years, a smooth transition to adulthood has become more difficult for an increasing number of young adults. To this end, universities and colleges have established preparatory programs to facilitate the transition to adulthood. Participants in the current sample were recruited in two such preparatory programs, one in the south and one in the center of the country. Of note, about 20% of Israeli society is Arab and about 10% Jewish ultra-orthodox, and these groups were not included in this study. Thus, participants represent the vast majority of young adults belonging to the Israeli mainstream.

Measuring personal resources and availability of support systems

Personal resources were measured using the Depressive Experiences Questionnaire (DEQ) (Blatt et al., 1976). For the initial stages of the project we referred to three scales: *self-criticism* reflecting a preoccupation with achievement, inferiority, and guilt in the face of perceived failure to meet standards (e.g., "It is not who you are but what you have accomplished that counts"; "I often find that I don't live up to my own standards or ideals"); *dependency*, reflecting a wish to be cared for, loved, and protected and fearing being abandoned (e.g., "Without the support of others who are close to me, I would be helpless"); and *efficacy*, representing personal resilience and inner strength (e.g., "I have many inner resources"; "I am a very independent person").

In addition, we assessed motivational orientations using a modified version of the Client Motivation for Therapy Scale (Pelletier et al., 1997), which was originally designed in line with the SDT approach (Ryan & Deci, 1985, 2000). In our project we employed three dimensions of motivational orientations: *autonomous*

("Because I enjoy what I do"), *controlled* ("Because everybody does it at this age"), and *amotivation* ("The truth is that I frequently ask myself what am I really doing").

Availability of support systems was measured by the Network of Relationship Inventory (Furman & Buhrmester, 1985), assessing perceived support of mother, father, and close friend. Participants were asked to rate the quality of their relationship with each respective figure on items such as support, intimacy, and provision of help.

Measuring developmental outcomes

We employed Brian Little's (1983) Personal Project Analysis to assess the pursuit and attainment of personal goals. Participants were first asked to write down three of their personal aims. Next, respondents were asked to appraise each goal along several dimensions. Conceptually the dimensions measured *goal investment/importance* ("To what extent is the project important to you"), *goal progress* ("To what extent have you made progress realizing this project"), and *goal stress* ("To what extent do you feel that you are interfered in your efforts to attain the goal"). Two indices were derived from this instrument—first, the particular goal a participant indicated and, second, the levels of goal investment, goal progress, and goal stress.

Participants completed these instruments at each wave of assessment. Of note, participants completed a variety of additional measures, such as psychological well-being.

Findings from the initial stages of the project and what we learned from these about the dynamics of emerging adulthood

In this section we review the findings from three studies based on the data collected from the first three assessments and highlight what we learned about emerging adulthood from these findings. In the Shulman, Kalnitzki, and Shahar (2009) and Dietrich et al. (2013) studies we learned that when asked to name their goals the vast majority of our participants mentioned appropriate age-related goals: to succeed in work and studies and to establish a romantic relationship or family. Furthermore, the prevalence of mentioning work versus love goals was consistent with age change. At the earlier ages emerging adults were more likely to mention studies and work more frequently as their goals and mentioned establishing a family less often. With age, the prevalence of the goal of establishing a family increased, while the prevalence of mentioning the goal of studies decreased. Thus, the majority of emerging adults, during their 20s, are aware of and aspire to age-appropriate goals. In the earlier stages of emerging adulthood they aspire to achieve their academic and career goals and only later become more invested in romantic relationships and the wish to start a family (Shulman & Connolly, 2013). Furthermore, some participants mentioned a goal category we termed *self-goal*. These participants expressed their wishes to be happy or to live a spiritual life. Some of the participants who mentioned work as a goal might have stated that they were looking for a job that would make them feel happy and less miserable. Interestingly, the prevalence of mentioning the self-goal was raised by less than 20% of the participants and remained stable across the five assessments. (Further description and detail about goals and their pursuit is presented in Chapter 2.) Conceptually, we thus suggest that these findings indicate that emerging adults are aware of, and aspire to attain, the age-appropriate goals of work and love. Only a minority can be considered confused or still exploring what they want to do with their lives and are absorbed in their self-goals.

An additional important finding clearly indicated that personal and support resources affect level of goal attainment outcomes. Self-criticism measured at age 24 predicted a lower level of goal investment and a higher level of goal stress than at the first assessment at age 23. In addition, efficacy predicted higher levels of goal investment and goal progress 1 year later. Finally, paternal support at age 23 predicted a higher level of goal investment 1 year later (see detailed description of these findings in Shulman, Kalnitzki, & Shahar, 2009).

The follow-ups further supported these findings. Efficacy predicted higher goal investment and progress 6 years later, while self-criticism accounted for individual differences in goal stress. In addition, autonomous motivation measured at age 23 predicted higher goal investment and progress 3.5 years later, while amotivation was associated with higher goal stress in the future. In addition, while on the group level there was no mean change in goal investment and progress over the years, there were considerable individual differences in people's goal appraisal trajectories over time. Thus, personal resources have the potential to affect not only the future level of goal attainment but also processes of change in levels of goal investment and goal progress across the years. (For a detailed description of findings, see Dietrich et al., 2013.)

The third study from our project, Shulman and Nurmi (2010b) suggests an additional perspective for understanding the processes that emerging adults undergo. We noticed that when asked to name their three main goals, respondents' goal descriptions were not limited to mentioning or not mentioning a particular goal. Descriptions of goals also ranged from concrete and limited descriptions, such as "finding a job," to more elaborate descriptions reflecting a comprehensive life plan, such as "First I want to complete my studies to be a kindergarten teacher, then I would like to get training in a good place and work in the system for a couple of years. I think I will also take some additional courses to learn additional skills. And then I would like to open a private kindergarten." However, the length of a description did not always present elaborateness. A number of long descriptions were confused or incoherent descriptions regarding the clarity of the goal. For example, "I would like to meet a partner so I can learn better about my abilities to be in a relationship and to find myself." Our major assumption here is that the elaborateness and clarity of a description are important indicators of its quality.

In order to capture the complexity of goal structure, goal descriptions were analyzed, and two categorical systems (on a scale of 1 to 5) were developed to assess the elaboration of work/studies goals and the romantic relationships/family goal. The scales were as follows: 1 = no goal defined (e.g., "I still do not know..."); 2 = self-centered, confused, or contradictory goal (e.g., "To work in a field where I can find myself and will be the least miserable"); 3 = normative goal (e.g., "To establish a family"); 4 = a goal showing some clear direction or the beginnings of elaboration (e.g., "To complete my preparatory studies, continue to my academic studies, and make a career"); 5 = integrated, complex goal or life plan (e.g., "After my studies, to develop my personal life and raise a family").

Assessment of the elaboration of work and love goals at age 23 and again 1 year later at age 24 allowed us to examine the level of work and love goal elaboration over time. Comparison of levels of work and love goals across the two points of time suggested, as could be expected, that both goals tend to become more elaborated over time. However, this significant trend did not represent all the participants consistently, suggesting the existence of individual differences. A cluster analysis was performed on elaboration levels of work and love goals assessed at the two points in time in order to detect possible different profiles.

The first cluster was termed the *progressive pattern*, and the members of this pattern represent the highest level of work and love goals. This cluster consisted of approximately half our respondents and represents emerging adults whose goals consistently became more elaborated during the following year. Members of the second cluster, consisting of approximately a quarter of our sample, represent a clear discrepancy between levels of the work and love goals. The work goal descriptions of these emerging adults were elaborated, whereas their love goal descriptions were within the lower range—lack of love goals or confusion. Thus, while these emerging adults described elaborate work goals, their goal level in relation to love and establishing a family was low. Of interest, this discrepancy remained stable across the two assessments. This cluster was termed the *love arrested pattern*. The third cluster was termed the *arrested pattern* and consisted of emerging adults who described low levels of work and love goals across the two assessments.

Considering these three studies together, we learned that there is not one route to adulthood leading to either success or failure to achieve aspired developmental goals. Individuals may take different routes on their journey to adulthood, and these routes might differ in the clarity of the goals that guide the pursuit, in the pace taken, and in the importance assigned to the aspired goals. In addition, changes along the way can be expected. Importance or clarity of aspired goals might increase or decrease over time. Finally, personal attributes as well as availability of support affect the direction and quality of navigation through the emerging adulthood years. Conceptually, we thus inferred that navigation toward aspired goals is likely to be a dynamic process of which we were not aware earlier.

Dynamic navigation to adulthood—Conceptualization and inception of the later stages of the project

Findings from the earlier stages of the project taught us that the link between the past and the future among emerging adults is not necessarily linear (Brannen & Nilsen, 2002). Resources can affect the nature and quality of future outcomes. Furthermore, considering the complexity of person–environment, there is not necessarily one way to the future. Young people might take different routes when pursuing their developmental goals, based on their capacities and environmental options. Therefore, we believe it is important also to learn more about the variety of paths that emerging adults might take on their journey to adulthood.

The search to understand different routes to adulthood corresponds to the concept of self-socialization outlined by Walter Heinz (2002) and earlier by Jochen Brandtstadter and Richard Lerner (1999). They suggested that individuals actively navigate their way through space and time. Within this process young people are supposed to make decisions on how to construct their way, which actions to maintain and which actions to change. Furthermore, the movement toward the future resembles a back-and-forth process. Based on the different actions and routes taken, an individual can decide the extent to which an earlier action was or was not successful in progressing toward an aim. In turn, evaluation of previous actions can help in weighing whether and how to modify one's mode of behavior in order to optimize outcomes. These changes and readjustments can be understood as a process of learning that will determine the direction to be taken and together result in a variety of ways and their changes across time.

This process of self-socialization explains the existence of unstable and fluid behavior observed among emerging adults. Discontinuities need not necessarily represent failure or an expression of idleness. Evaluation of earlier behavior can lead to a variety of conclusions and not necessarily the insistence of continued active goal pursuit. An individual might decide to take a temporary "time-out," which does not need to be seen as an interruption but might serve as a way of searching for other options and optimizing outcomes. "Time-out" periods might also be used to learn new skills and improve one's qualifications (Heinz, 2002, p. 233). Finally, Heinz argues that through these variant experiences a young person constructs their "biographical agency" (which will not necessarily be linear), leading to personal growth.

Jutta Heckhausen's motivational theory of life-span development is also of great relevance in understanding the meaning of fluctuations and change and the complexity of the routes that a young person might take (Heckhausen, 1999; Heckhausen et al., 2010). Heckhausen describes the different ways in which individuals cope or react when confronting unattainable goals. While active and purposeful pursuit of a desired goal is highly adaptive, continued pursuit or aspiration of an unattainable goal can itself become a source of stress. Under such circumstances, Heckhausen describes the mechanism of goal adjustment, namely, disengagement from an unattainable goal and pursuit of an alternative goal. This is the ability to realize that a desired goal is unattainable and a different goal needs to be formulated. While relinquishing one's aspired goal might seem a drawback, in reality this strategy reflects self-mastery and is beneficial to well-being. The ability to come to terms with loss or failure facilitates compromise and the formulation of a new and different goal. In contrast, continued pursuit of a goal that cannot be attained is likely to reflect an inability to identify alternative goals and might lead to fruitless efforts (Wrosch et al., 2003) and a decrease in well-being (Heckhausen et al., 2010).

Thus, successful navigation of one's career pursuit can be conceptualized as the balance between efforts to pursue one's wishes competently and the ability to align oneself with environmental reality and make adaptations or compromises (Heckhausen et al., 2010, p. 35). Successful career pursuit thus implies setting clear and realistic occupational goals and effectively pursuing these goals. Changes along the way are inevitable, at which point the way a person copes with disappointments or failure becomes critical. Is the person capable of changing course and moving toward a readapted realistic goal, or do they continue to aspire to an unrealistic dream?

Considered together, we learned that examining young persons' accounts and inner reflections on their career plans and their ability to manage both goal engagement and goal disengagement could provide a more accurate understanding of their career status and pathways, as well as give meaning to changes in direction that happened along the way. On the one hand, discontinuities might represent disruptions or a sense that development is blocked and lead to a decrease in aspirations relating to one's anticipated future career (Heinz, 2002). However, discontinuities might also represent actions directed toward optimizing one's chances and searching for and finding a new path, subsequently resulting in personal growth.

The insights gained from our earlier findings, combined with the conceptualization developed within the self-socialization framework, led us to "readapt" our project. We decided that to learn more thoroughly about the lives and the processes that emerging adults experience, we need to learn about their "life history" during the emerging adulthood years. How did it all start? What were their aims? Did they progress smoothly toward their goals or make changes and adaptations along the way? What did they learn during these years about their aspirations, about themselves? Do they regret some of their past actions, and how do they foresee their future? Based on these understandings, we decided to incorporate a narrative approach in order to learn more about the biographical development undergone by our participants during their emerging adulthood years.

The majority of research in psychology is guided by quantitative methodological approaches aimed mainly to see if the collected data supports or refutes the theory, to then be used to make revisions to improve the theory. Findings from our earlier studies suggested that emerging adulthood development is more complex than suggested by earlier theories (e.g., the concept of self-socialization; Heinz, 2002). Qualitative approaches, in contrast, are not aimed at uncovering a single objective truth but are rather aimed at the search of multiple different perspectives among participants, embracing their personal experiences that shaped their perspectives and their course of life and, above all, helped them to understand their lives (Pratt & Matsuba, 2018). Dan McAdams (2001) described that the study of life stories has the potential to contribute to a fuller and more successful conceptualization of human identity and development.

We thus developed two comprehensive interviews. The first interview focused on career history and the second on the romantic history (described in greater detail in Chapters 3 and 5). Capturing the developmental history of the two major tasks, work and love, has the potential to inform us about the complex ways that different individuals might take in the journey to adulthood and why some routes might be more successful while other associate with failures. As part of the interviews, we also inquired about the role parents and peers might have played over the years.

In sum, in line with these insights, we set out to interview our participants when they were 29 years old. Age 29 is close to the end of emerging adulthood (Arnett, 2007), and we wanted to learn of our participants' stories of development during the preceding years. To better understand the process of development and the ways in which emerging adults settle down, we approached our participants again at age 35. We were able to recruit 132 participants at this fifth assessment. Of note, in addition to the in-depth interviews that were administered at age 35, all the instruments that were administered at the previous four assessments were given again.

To summarize, the career and romantic history interviews conducted at age 29 and again at age 35 provided us with a better lens through which to look into the dynamics of the developmental processes experienced by our participants in their third decade of life. This provided information about the choices they made, the routes they took, the routes they left, and the new routes they took or whether they had lost their way. Our participants described their disappointments, reflections, and important turning points in their own words, which led us to understand that emerging adulthood need not be understood only in terms of success or failure, of continuity or change. We learned of the variety and complexity of the process and its dynamics. All these understandings are described in detail in the following chapters, in which we try to reach a new understanding of the processes that might take place during this period of life.

During the years of our project we came across new ideas and theories about personality development during the third decade of life (see B. W. Roberts et al., 2006). Theory and research on personality development have focused on changes in the Big Five and show a decrease in negativity during the third decade of life. We also collected personality data over time. We measured self-criticism, which is conceptually close to neuroticism (Blatt, 2008). In our longitudinal data, we found a significant decrease in self-criticism over time. As our study is embedded within a developmental framework, we were able to learn about the interconnectedness between personality development and developmental processes. Finally, we assessed psychological symptoms, such as depressive affect, over the 12-year span. This again allowed us to examine the question about continuity or changes in mental health during emerging adulthood. Through our findings and insights, we try to understand what really happens during emerging adulthood and how young people develop during the third decade of life.

2
Developmental Goals During Emerging Adulthood

Constellations of Goal Coordination and
Their Sequence Over Time

Personal goals and plans direct individual life paths by regulating their behavior (Haase et al., 2008) and leading individuals through their own development. Transitional periods should see the termination of earlier existing goals and the structuring of new life plans. For example, major adolescent goals during high school might be academic and social success, as well as success in sport. Following graduation from high school, decisions about future plans should be taken and, accordingly, new goals set. Individuals are expected to explore new possibilities and make choices suitable for the tasks of the new approaching period (Levinson, 1978). Setting new realistic goals and commitment to these goals are important markers of adaptation during a transitional period as they elicit elevated commitment (Nurmi, 2004). Young people often have a number of goals simultaneously—for example, they want to succeed in their studies and to have a romantic partner—but less is known about how a person coordinates between different goals.

Prior studies on the role of goals in emerging adults' development have typically focused on one life domain at a time, such as career (e.g., Dietrich, Jokisaari, & Nurmi, 2012) or romantic relationships (e.g., Dhariwal et al., 2009; K. Roberts et al., 2003). Therefore, more is needed to learn how different goals are coordinated (Ranta et al., 2014; Shulman & Connolly, 2013). In addition, goals might be changed or reformulated following inevitable changes such as achieving or failing to achieve a goal (Heckhausen, 1999; Heckhausen et al., 2010). For example, after a romantic breakup a person might decide to take a break from relationships and invest in a career. Further, once a young adult has attained a degree or a diploma, new goals should be set to direct future development.

In this chapter, following young people for a period of 12 years allows for closer examination of the goals that a young person describes and how these goals might change or evolve over time. The following describes the case of Nora, a 35-year-old woman whom we have followed since the age of 23. At age 23 Nora described her desire to pursue a culinary course, as well as to learn sign language.

A year later she first stated that she was looking for a romantic partner and then stated that she still wanted to pursue a culinary course but had not yet done this. Three years later she described that she wanted to study something interesting and to travel abroad. Did the different goals direct Nora's behavior, or were they rather confusing her? Was she aware that the different fields of culinary arts and sign language are not really connected? Nora's set of goals and their changes across the years suggest that assessing success or failure in the pursuit of one particular goal, as suggested by previous studies (Dietrich et al., 2012; Heckhausen et al., 2010), cannot tell us the full story. In this chapter we present a different approach. We assess and try to understand how young people set their (different) goals, coordinate between these, and prioritize one goal over another and, most importantly, how goals evolve or change across the years of emerging adulthood.

As indicated in Chapter 1, we followed our sample from the age of 23 to the age of 35, during which they were assessed five times. At each assessment—at ages 23, 24, 26.5, 29, and 35—participants were asked to describe, in writing, their three major goals. This data is relevant for the current chapter and provides us with rich information on the personal goals emerging adults described over the years. We analyzed this data in two ways. First, we show developmental trends describing the goals that are prioritized at the different ages and how change in the prioritization of one goal corresponds with change in other goals. Second, not all individuals necessarily follow the common developmental changes. Therefore, we will also look at possible distinctive trajectories in the setting and development of goals among different individuals. For this purpose, we do not compare individuals with regard to whether or not a certain goal was set at a specific age. We focus rather on each individual and the different goals they set at each assessment and their development over time. In line with the qualitative approach described in the previous chapter, we thus attempt to learn about the "stories" (McAdams, 2006) of the different patterns of goal setting over time among different individuals.

Reading the set of goals described by emerging adults at each assessment allowed us to examine the following aspects: the goals that are set and prioritized and how these evolve, change, and are adapted over time. We describe patterns of goal interdependence and patterns of change and development of goals across the years. We show the different patterns of goal constellations and their sequence that emerged by analyzing our data. This approach provides us with a more complex understanding of the aspirations emerging adults have at different ages and their development or change across time.

In addition, following individuals and learning about their respective goals over a long period of time can indicate whether aspirations are adaptive and consistent and have the potential to direct the individual toward expected age-appropriate achievements or whether aspirations are vague and change aimlessly.

This can be also indicative as to the extent to which aspirations were elaborated and refined over the years, directing individuals more effectively toward the achievement of aspired goals. Within this framework we describe adaptive and less adaptive developmental constellations of goals and the extent to which the different 12-year-long "stories" of goals are associated with adaptive outcomes or, conversely, with difficulties in coping with and attaining age-related tasks resulting in a person's loss of a clear track.

Emerging adulthood is a period of life during which individuals are faced with more transitions and life decisions than at any other stage of their lives (Caspi, 2002; Grob et al., 2001). These include the transition from education to work, starting a career, initiating an intimate relationship, starting a family, consolidating an ideological worldview, becoming part of a social group, and assuming civic and social responsibilities (Arnett, 2000; Caspi, 2002; Shanahan, 2000). Such transitions require a substantial amount of individual effort, such as goal setting, planning, decisions, explorations, and commitments, through which young people handle their current life situation and direct their future lives (Marcia, 1980; Nurmi, 2004).

Facing a multitude of tasks, and having to set and pursue different goals, is a new experience that emerging adults face during the transition to adulthood. In adolescence, for example, lives are mostly directed by parents and the school system an adolescent attends. While adolescents have expectations about their future (Nurmi, 2004), goals and expectations focus mainly on their immediate environments. For example, past research has shown that academic and social goals are the most prominent types of goals that adolescents strive to achieve (Liem, 2016; Wentzel, 2000), while some adolescents are also determined to excel in sport activities (Duncan et al., 2017). Thus, adolescents' lives and behavior revolve around their high school context, focusing on achievement of academic and socials goals that, to some extent, also reflect parental and school expectations.

Unlike adolescents, emerging adults' goals are meant to direct individual lives in the future and to set a life plan (i.e., in career or marital life; Levinson, 1978). In addition, during emerging adulthood the setting and pursuit of goals take place in a complex interplay between sociocultural norms, as well as individuals' own thoughts, feelings, and activities (Nurmi, 2004). Individuals bring personal characteristics developed during their earlier life into this interplay, on the one hand, and their preferences, on the other. In addition, cultural expectations, norms, and institutional opportunity structures that might vary across societies and across time can heavily impact personal aspirations (Nurmi, 2004). Further complicating these intertwined decisions, nowadays the lives of emerging adults are characterized by increased social and economic uncertainties and decisions made are not necessarily connected with outcomes (Leccardi, 2006).

Young people must resolve these multiple age-related tasks while simultaneously adapting to the context of a world that has become less certain.

In addition, individuals not only are impacted by their sociocultural environments but are also active agents in determining the direction of their future lives (Brandtstädter, 1998; Lerner, 1982). For example, young people have motives and values developed earlier in their lives that impact their choices, such as educational and occupational decisions. Similarly, they have preferences that impact the types of interpersonal relations they ultimately form. Their personality and temperamental characteristics, which are partly genetically based, also determine the types of situations they may like and in which they may feel comfortable and are likely to impact their choices of activities. Cognitive skills also provide a basis for plans and the development of a strategy to reach goals and aspirations (Nurmi, 2004). Relatedly, it is also important to understand the extent to which a goal is pursued to fulfill intrinsic values and a person's true wishes or rather reflect adherence to non-personal (external) values (Sheldon & Elliot, 1999). Personal characteristics and capabilities are even more crucial when a goal is not achieved, and every now and then individuals need to adjust their thoughts and behaviors to current realities.

Considered together, personal motives and expectations direct individual behavior, but people are also influenced by societal expectations, demands, challenges, opportunities, and constraints they experience or face at a particular time that also guide the construction of personal goals and concerns (Little, Salmela-Aro, & Phillips, 2007). Thus, examination of a person's goals can be informative of the way a young person expects to progress in domains such as studies, occupation, marriage, and style of living that will eventually define their place in the adult world and determine their adjustment (Levinson, 1978). Furthermore, the way different goals are coordinated and prioritized is indicative of the extent to which goals will be successful in directing a person's life plan. This chapter addresses all these issues.

Constellations of personal goals that individuals set during emerging adulthood: Interdependence, priorities, and change over time

Participants in our longitudinal study were first approached at the age of 23, during enrollment to two preparatory academic programs aimed at reaching academic acceptance standards in which they were behind. Participants were asked to write down and appraise the importance of three of their personal goals ("how important is the project to you?"). This procedure was replicated five times at the ages of 23, 24, 26.5, 29, and 35. At each wave, two assessors independently classified each project or goal into one of 14 categories reported by Katarina Salemla-Aro et al. (2001). In Table 2.1 we present the most common goal categories indicated by our participants and the percentage of participants who had endorsed the specific goal at each wave. Review of the types of goals shows that overall *Studies, Work,* and *Romantic Relationship—Establishing a Family* were the most endorsed goals. *Studies* is not a goal per se but rather a means to attain the education related to the development of a career. Conceptually, this suggests that there are in fact two main goals characterizing emerging adulthood. One is composed of studies and work and is aimed toward the development of career, while the second main goal focuses on establishing a significant romantic relationship that will lead to the formation of a family. We believe that career and romantic relationships capture the two main goals at this stage of life. This was indicated in the past and captures Freud's concepts of "work and love" (Levinson, 1978; Roisman et al., 2004; Shulman & Nurmi, 2010a).

A closer inspection of the distribution of goals at each assessment and across time (the five assessments) is informative about the interdependence among goals and the way this interdependence changes and evolves across time. At the earlier stages of emerging adulthood, individuals are mainly focused on academic goals. The emphasis on educational goals decreased gradually until the age of 29, when young adults placed less emphasis on progress and success in their career or work. Relatedly, the focus on succeeding in romantic relationships and establishing a family became gradually more important and endorsed by

Table 2.1 *Descriptive Statistics for Personal Goals—Percentages of Respondents Endorsing Different Goal Categories Across Age*

Goal content category (%)	Time 1 (age 23)	Time 2 (age 24)	Time 3 (age 26.5)	Time 4 (age 29)	Time 5 (age 35)
Studies	82.3	84.0	70.2	58.2	29.1
Work	38.7	50.6	66.2	89.1	86.0
Leisure	20.3	19.7	20.2	14.3	17.4
Self	18.2	24.2	24.3	23.9	15.5
Romantic relations/ establishing a family	58.1	78.1	91.8	91.3	89.6
Property/financial confidence	–	–	5.4	13.5	51.4
Good health for the family/ children	–	–	–	–	36.8

almost 90% of our participants at the age of 29. In addition, family goals were further adapted with age. At the latter stages they also wished for health for family members and adaptive development of their children.

These developmental changes are echoed when participants reported on the importance they assign to their goals. As can be seen in Figure 2.1, the importance assigned to academic goals decreased gradually across the years and reached its lowest level at the age of 35. This probably demonstrates that at the age of 34 most young people have completed or left their studies. The trend of change in the importance assigned to work is less clear. However, as of the age of 29 the importance of romantic–family goals increases significantly and reaches its highest level.

This developmental interdependence between career and involvement in a romantic relationship shows how strongly these two major aspects of life are interconnected. Entering the adult world and becoming an adult also means shifting the center of one's life from the family of origin to become "a novice adult with a new home base that is more truly his own home" (Levinson, 1978, p. 79). This can be achieved after adaptive initial choices about occupation and family life have been made.

Entering a relationship and becoming committed is not only about love, romance, and sexuality. Family and career are interconnected. A spouse also plays a crucial role in an individual's career life plan. Daniel Levinson describes how a true partner can be like a mentor by helping to live and shape a partner's life plan, believing in the partner's ability, giving a blessing, and whole-heartedly joining the journey. In connecting to the "dream" (life plan) of one's spouse, one

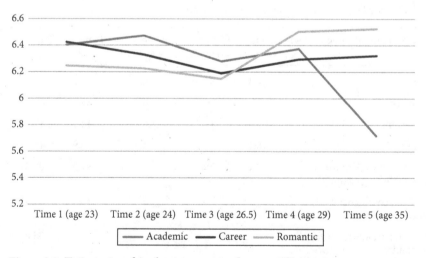

Figure 2.1 Trajectories of academic, career, and romantic importance across age

facilitates not only the pursuit of the dream but also entry into the adult world (Levinson, 1978, p. 109). The movement toward an adult role thus entails a balance between career development and romantic commitment, and within this process, educational achievement and financial achievement for oneself and a potential partner are likely to determine the likelihood of progressing into a committed relationship (Shulman & Connolly, 2013).

This changes in the hierarchy of work and romantic relationship is echoed by Manning et al. (2011). They showed that in making decisions concerning romantic relationships, young people seriously consider the educational and financial achievements of a potential partner. Young adults generally value financial security in a relationship, and the majority think it is important to be in a "financially secure" relationship. In addition, more than half of young people report caring about the financial future of a romantic partner. For example, Sneed and colleagues (2007) showed how financial success is likely to drive increasing romantic involvement.Interestingly, as can be seen in Table 2.1, as of the age of 26 an increasing number of young people started to mention the acquisition of property, or reaching financial security, as one of their three major goals. At the age of 35, more than half of our participants mentioned owning property, or financial security, as a major goal. This is probably what is necessary for starting a family, bearing children, and taking proper care of them.

While the vast majority of our young people endorsed career and family-related goals, between 15% and 25% of participants at the different waves endorsed amorphous goals such as being happy in life, finding themselves, living happily, or working in a field where they can find themselves and be least miserable. All of these examples refer to difficulties in formulating a clear role that captures age-related tasks (Nurmi, 2004) and might reflect adaptive difficulties.

Considered together, we can see that at the earlier years of emerging adulthood young people are mainly focused on completing their studies, attaining a degree or a diploma, and finding a job or developing a career. This pursuit of career is coordinated with the wish to establish a stable, intimate romantic relationship. During the years when the work goals are being realized, the role of establishing a family starts to become more prominent. At the later stages, young people appear to become more focused on ways to maintain the work and romantic goals they have achieved by aspiring for good health and the accumulation of property. In sum, goals set by young individuals are tuned toward the achievement of the major markers of an adult role: settling in a career and establishing a family, thus meeting the normative expectations typical for the society in which they live (Nurmi, 2004).

Our findings align the theoretical patterns of development described by Levinson (1978) and research conducted in different cultures (Salmela-Aro et al., 2011). The sequential coordination of career and family can probably facilitate a smoother transition to the assumption of an adult role. This ordering of the two major goals of "work and love" allows one to focus first on the goal of career and then move toward the goal of family later after significant progress has been made in the achievement of career (Shulman & Connolly, 2013). While this sequential ordering of goals is probably functional, not all emerging adults necessarily adopt this ordering of goals and their sequential pursuit. Some might describe an amorphous goal at a younger age but become more realistic a couple of years later. Alternatively, individuals may start the emerging adulthood years with a clear and appropriate goal, such as to study bookkeeping and find an appropriate job in this profession, but a couple of years later might become less focused and have difficulty naming a clear goal. They may rather describe looking for something that will make them happy: "I realized that time is passing, and it will be more important to travel now and enjoy life. I will have enough years to work."

In sum, it can be understood that not all young people set clear goals and necessarily prioritize one goal over another. Along the years there might be changes in goals, their clarity, and their order of prioritization. As described above, our participants were asked to write down their three main goals five times between the ages of 23 and 35, at each assessment. This provided us with rich information on a variety of constellations with which young people described their goals. In the next section we show the different constellations that individuals used to describe their major goals and how goals changed or were adapted across time. We assess the extent to which changes represent adaptive progression. Do goals evolve over time, become more elaborate, providing clearer direction; or are they rather unstable and inconsistent, reflecting difficulties in setting age-appropriate goals? Together, we intend to demonstrate patterns of goals that can represent movement toward settling down or difficulties moving toward a smooth transition.

Typologies of goal constellations across the years of emerging adulthood: Development and floundering

Reading the goals and their descriptions across the years spanning the ages from 23 to 35 showed that not all goal patterns described by our participants represented the penchant to progress from studies to career and then to the formation of family. While this adaptive pattern of goal ordering could be identified by a substantial number of young people, a variety of other goal constellations could be observed among others.

To understand the variety of goal development patterns, we conducted a "qualitative analysis" to explore and detect possible different goal constellations. Reading the goals that a person described across the five assessments, we focused on various components such as goal content and clarity; whether a description captured age-related relevant goals in domains of studies, career, or romantic relationships; or whether goals rather reflected general wishes such as being happy and satisfied with life. In addition, we considered the extent to which goals are adapted or change across time, representing normative expected changes due to age or circumstances (e.g., increasing importance on romantic relationships or following failure to achieve an aspired goal).

Directed by the reviewed literature on goals and development and reading the sets of goals each participant described, we employed a mixture of exploratory and confirmatory techniques (Lieblich et al., 1998) to identify distinctive goal patterns. Goal constellations that emerged from our readings refined our further reading of the material, resulting in the following manner of analysis. First, a general constellation of goal development was identified, after which the existence of the particular pattern for each participant was assessed. Refuting or negating evidence led to the rediscussion and refinement of a constellation This back-and-forth exploratory and confirmatory process led to the adaptation and reformulation of proposed constellations of goal development to ensure that all personal stories were well represented. Employing this mixture of exploratory and confirmatory techniques, two experts, developmental and clinical psychologists, identified four constellations of goal development. Subsequently, two other raters were trained to identify the four patterns of goal development, after which they coded the balance of the transcripts independently. Inter-rater reliability level was kappa = .86.

Pattern 1—Ambiguous, developmentally unrelated, and disorganized goals ($n = 17$, 13.1%)

Members of this pattern constellation described goals that do not relate clearly or directly to the expected common age-related goals of career development and establishing a significant romantic relationship. In addition, we could not detect a coherent developmental pattern of goals across the years. Goals mentioned at each assessment appeared to reflect rather momentary interests or preoccupation and were not part of a broader life plan or pursuit of common age-related goals. Goals could represent different and unrelated domains. We present the following two examples to demonstrate this pattern—the first a young woman and the second a young man.

A close inspection of Nora's goals suggests that she lacks a clear life plan (Table 2.2). She is directed by different aspirations that probably address momentary interests and do not evolve into a coherent plan. In addition, it is very important for her to feel happy—"to get up with a smile"—and this probably dictates the

36 A NEW LENS ON EMERGING ADULTHOOD

Table 2.2 *Nora: Female—Major Goals from Age 23 to Age 35*

	Goal 1	Goal 2	Goal 3
Age 23	To study a culinary course and find a job in this profession.	To learn sign language and work with deaf people.	To travel abroad.
Age 24	To find a mate, fall in love, start a family, and have children.	Study at a culinary school. I was close to doing this, but it did not work out.	To take a trip abroad with close friends.
Age 26.5	Right now, I want to get a driver's license and feel more independent.	To travel abroad. I think that in order to know my true self I have to be abroad; this can only be done when you are abroad.	To study something interesting. There are a number of fields. I think it is a matter of days till I make the decision.
Age 29	My most important goal is to find a steady job that I can get up with a smile on my face knowing that I do what I love most.	To find a boyfriend and a serious relationship. I enjoy being in a relationship. I flourish then.	To start a family. I think I am at the age that I need to settle down. It is the time for a family.
Age 35	To be happy. No matter where I am and in what status.	To find my other half, though I cannot see it coming.	To turn my hobby into a profession and see if this suits me.

types of work or relationships in which she tends to become involved. Needless to say, this set of unrelated and inconsistent goals cannot be helpful for navigating her life through the emerging adulthood years. As could be expected, the goals Nora mentioned at the age of 35 seemed to reflect some sense of giving up on a clear plan for the future. At age 35, her goals were quite amorphous, while also reflecting her sense that she has probably lost her way and given up. When asked to state her goals at age 35, Nora stated, "To be happy. No matter where I am and in what status" and "To find my other half, though I cannot see it coming."

The story of Dan (Table 2.3), another participant, is somewhat different. He defined the common and expected goals of work and family at the first assessment. However, subsequent assessments showed that he had become more preoccupied with feeling well and understanding what he really wants in life: "To feel good in life and to suffer less." While Nora kept defining different goals at each assessment, Dan lost his direction in his search for his true self and happiness. At the fifth assessment, when asked to define his goals, he stated clearly, "I wish I would have known."

Table 2.3 *Dan: Male—Major Goals from Age 23 to Age 35*

	Goal 1	Goal 2	Goal 3
Age 23	Education.	A profession and work.	Family.
Age 24	To find the correct direction in life. This is crucial.	To feel good in life and to suffer less.	That it will be good for my father.
Age 26.5	To understand who I am and my destination in life.	To make my parents happy.	To earn well and start a family.
Age 29	To understand the meaning of life.	True and not false happiness.	To live without fear.
Age 35	I wish I would have known.	I wish I would have known.	I wish I would have known.

Reading these goal "stories" demonstrates that these young adults have difficulties setting a clear and coherent life plan. They live through their 20s without the ability to navigate their lives and, in many cases, even not being aware that they are getting lost along the way. It is only toward their mid-30s that they probably realize that they have lost their way.

Pattern 2—Pursuit of career and family goals accompanied by underlying insecurities and concerns (*n* = 36, 27.7%)

Members of this pattern defined the expected goals in the domains of education, career, and establishing a family. However, it sounded as though the person was preoccupied with concerns about whether the right job or partner would be found and whether expression of one's true expectations would not be hampered. As can be seen in the case of Roni, at each stage it was important for her to emphasize how crucial it was for her to be satisfied with what she does, regardless of what she does; to feel that she is not wasting her life; and to be certain that "this is my place." Personal goals and plans are supposed to direct individual life paths and regulate their behavior. Occupational plans and goals can be helpful in reaching an adaptable balance between personal aspirations and environmental conditions, as well as finding meaning for one's life (Blustein, 2011). However, as can be seen in the case of Roni (Table 2.4), it is questionable whether the strong need to find something that would make her happy did not interfere with her capacity to cope effectively with inevitable difficulties encountered during career pursuit. Indeed, as can be seen, in the earlier years she aspired to attain

Table 2.4 *Roni: Female—Assigned Goals from Age 23 to Age 35*

	Goal 1	Goal 2	Goal 3
Age 23	Academic education.	To find a good job and succeed.	To be happy personally and professionally and do what I love.
Age 24	Education. To get a degree in social work. Will do all I can to achieve this.	To travel abroad so I can better understand myself and what I want to achieve in life.	Mostly I want to start a family but also to find a satisfying job that I will know that my years did not pass for nothing.
Age 26.5	To complete the first degree and start graduate studies.	To find a stable job that I love and to be financially secure.	To marry somebody I really love, have a family, bear children, and travel with my children.
Age 29	To find another job that I can enjoy and say this is my place for life.	To start graduate studies and gain new knowledge. To try new things.	To start a family, bear children, and balance family and work.
Age 35	To find a suitable partner and start a family.	To become more professional (in bookkeeping) and find a more stable workplace.	I want to enrich myself, my soul, have different hobbies, and activities, take trips.

an academic degree but eventually, at the age of 35, was in a low-level bookkeeping job.

Noam's "goal story" (Table 2.5) is somewhat different. On the one hand, he emphasizes his wish to find a good job and to start a family. On the other hand, his plans are not articulated; and across the years, he repeatedly mentions how important it is for him to be happy with what he does—"do what I love"; "to be happy professionally." This concern probably affected his choices and decisions. At the age of 35, he is mostly interested in job and financial security, regardless of what he does, and does not mention family-related aspirations as would be expected at this stage of life.

Pattern 3—Realistic and orderly career and family goals (n = 48, 36.9%)

Reading the stories of individuals following this pattern shows that they defined clear and age-appropriate goals. Furthermore, the order of the goals as described

Table 2.5 *Noam: Male—Assigned Goals from Age 23 to Age 35*

	Goal 1	Goal 2	Goal 3
Age 23	To work in something I love.	To be surrounded by people I love.	To be financially secure.
Age 24	To work in a field where I can express myself or suffer least.	To be financially secure and not dependent upon others.	To find a respectable job.
Age 26.5	To be financially independent so I can start a relationship.	To establish a relationship and have a warm and loving family.	To continue developing personally and spiritually.
Age 29	To earn more money.	To start graduate studies.	To progress in combat arts, something I have been practicing for years.
Age 35	To obtain tenure at my workplace.	To own a house.	To be financially secure and not burdened by issues of money, no matter what I do.

Table 2.6 *David: Male—Assigned Goals from Age 23 to Age 35*

	Goal 1	Goal 2	Goal 3
Age 23	To start academic studies.	To establish a family.	To have money.
Age 24	Love and starting a family.	To graduate.	To buy an apartment.
Age 26.5	To complete my studies successfully.	Marriage.	To buy an apartment.
Age 29	To attain a degree in electrical engineering.	To find a good and challenging job.	Getting married.
Age 35	Starting a family.	To start studying for a master's in my field.	Promotion at my workplace.

by David (Table 2.6) recalls the normative development of goals expected among emerging adults: starting with educational goals, moving toward career, and then establishing a family (Ranta et al., 2014). Conceptually, this type and ordering of goals are in accordance with the demands of the life situation; and, as such, they are expected to associate with future favorable outcomes (Salmela-Aro et al., 2001).

Though setting normative goals is likely to be adaptive (Nurmi, 2004), it is questionable whether an individual is flexible enough to make changes when required. Even an adaptive goal might turn into a source of disappointment when it becomes difficult to attain. In this case, individuals are torn between giving up the unattained goal and continuous efforts to attain this, which might exceed personal capabilities (Wrosch & Heckhausen, 1999). Better adaptation can be expected (Heckhausen et al., 2010; Shulman & Nurmi, 2010b) when goals are more flexible. Thus, we may think that some measure of flexibility might be beneficial, namely that a goal is not too narrowly described. A more elaborate and flexible goal could be an advantage under circumstances requiring reconsideration of the aspired goal. This can be helpful in finding a new direction and for the purpose of moving forward.

Pattern 4—Elaborated and progressing life goals (n = 29, 22.3%)

Members following Pattern 4 also defined clear and age-appropriate goals that were adapted with age, similar to the descriptions in Pattern 3. However, as can be seen in Table 2.7, goals of affiliates of this pattern were more elaborated and interconnected with one another. It can be seen that from one stage to the next, goals developed and became more elaborated—to succeed in law studies, to obtain a job, to succeed in this career and create an avenue for self-expression.

Parallel to this progression, Limor found a partner and established a family (Table 2.7). As time progressed she hoped for good health, so success could be maintained and continue. Reading Limor's goals at age 35 shows a well-integrated young woman who has successfully settled down.

Members of Pattern 3 also described age-appropriate goals. However, setting realistic and age-appropriate goals might not be enough. Due to unexpected personal or contextual difficulties, individuals might question their ability to attain an expected goal. According to Brandtstädter and Rothermund (2002), when goal structures are diversified and multifaceted they leave room for different interpretations, enhance flexible accommodation, and lead to more favorable outcomes (Pinquart et al., 2004). Members classified into this pattern of elaborated and progressing life goals consistently described indeed complex, flexible, and interconnected goals, which could be of help if difficulties emerge.

Limor described the importance she assigned to being challenged at work and to expressing herself. Recent developments in vocational psychology about career adaptability have transitioned from addressing the question "What and how do people do what they do?" to "Why do they do it?" (Blustein, 2011; Savickas, 2005). In particular, ongoing efforts to define career adaptability called for further attention to the need to incorporate one's inner interests, curiosity, and values (Lent & Brown, 2006; Savickas, 2005). For example, curiosity enables a person to remain open to new experiences and to increase the awareness of the

Table 2.7 *Limor: Female—Assigned Goals from Age 23 to Age 35*

	Goal 1	Goal 2	Goal 3
Age 23	To complete law and government studies, find a job in public service; hoping to go on to graduate studies.	To start a family combined with succeeding in my work and earning enough to support children.	To be happy, to travel and enjoy life.
Age 24	Complete my studies and find a job that combines the two fields (and grad studies).	I hope to strengthen my relationship so that it evolves to marriage, happiness, and mutuality.	Maybe this should be my first goal—that all those close to me will be healthy and happy.
Age 26.5	To be happy! This is the most important—it is success, love, and being healthy.	To start a family with my current partner, bear children, and raise them together happily.	That all the persons I love, in particular my parents, will be healthy and only good things happen to them.
Age 29	To be healthy and happy and also my partner and my family.	To start my family, have a happy marriage, and bear a child in the next year.	To continue building my career. To be satisfied and challenged, and go happily to work.
Age 35	That all my beloved and myself will be healthy and happy.	To express myself at work; challenges, recognition, and succeeding in management.	To continue having my happy couplehood and family and good health.

fit between oneself and the work world. Through introspection, individuals become aware of their "personal story." Importantly, they learn to recognize their inner motivations—an awareness that serves as a guide to successful negotiations in their occupations (Del Corso & Rehfuss, 2011).

The capacity to find meaning in what one does becomes more crucial when a person has not developed an impressive career such as Limor did. For example, Ariel (Table 2.8) completed the preparatory program but did not pursue academic studies. Indeed, at the first assessment he did not mention any academic or career goal. After completing the preparatory program, Ariel's goals were to find a job where he could earn money and start a family. He started working as a plumber, where he succeeded and became financially secure. This allowed him to invest in the two domains that he perceived as more central in his life—enjoying his family and developing and enjoying his hobby. Thus, despite the fact that Ariel did not have a particular professional goal, he was able to navigate his life successfully, to succeed in establishing a family he loved, and to become

Table 2.8 *Ariel: Male—Assigned Goals from Age 23 to Age 35*

	Goal 1	Goal 2	Goal 3
Age 23	To have positive experiences.	To find love.	Good health.
Age 24	Happiness.	To find a good job.	Good health.
Age 26.5	To be satisfied with what I do.	To continue and develop my romantic relationship.	To earn more money at work.
Age 29	Start a family; have children.	To continue developing in my job and earn more money.	Good health.
Age 35	Earn enough money to live in comfort.	To spend more time with my family (wife and children).	To continue my hobby of motorcycling.

financially secure. Yet, his life plan was more elaborated than the achievement of work and family goals, it was important for him to enrich his life by developing his hobby of motorcycling.

Typology of goal constellations across the years of emerging adulthood: Conceptual meanings and future outcomes

Past research has mostly focused on individual goals and showed that factors such as importance or controllability assigned to a goal are important markers for understanding future outcomes (Nurmi, 2004). Examining goals over five different periods of time showed that a more comprehensive assessment of goals could provide us a richer understanding of the ways that young people approach, develop, and handle their transition to adulthood. The four patterns of goal constellations we found among the young adults showed differences in the quality and complexity of goal setting among emerging adults. These ranged from difficulties defining clear and coherent goals, through assignment of realistic and age-appropriate goals with some reservations about the goals defined, to a higher capacity to define elaborated goals, coordinating between the different goals and temporal adjustment of goals in accordance with personal and environmental changes.

Following our participants for a period of 12 years allowed us to examine whether and the extent to which our proposed typology of the patterns of goal "stories"-constellations associates with different future outcomes. First, we assessed the level of salary that our participants reported earning at the age of

35. Participants were told that the average monthly income in Israel at the time of assessment was 7400 NIS (approximately US $2215). They were asked to indicate whether their monthly income is about average (2), below the average (1), or above the average (3). Comparison among the four patterns showed that members of the *ambiguous, developmentally unrelated, and disorganized goals* pattern reported an income below the national average, whereas members of the *elaborated and progressing life goals* pattern reported an income above the national average. The two additional patterns reported an approximately average income (see Table 2.6).

Significant differences also emerged regarding the marital status of pattern followers at the age of 35. Members of the *ambiguous, developmentally unrelated, and disorganized goals* pattern were less likely to be married; 12 of 17 members of this pattern were not married ($p = .000$). In contrast, members of all three other patterns were more likely to be married. In particular, this trend was the strongest among members of the *elaborated and progressing life goals* pattern, where 28 of 29 participants were married ($p = .000$).

Additional comparisons between the four goal patterns on levels of career commitment, career reconsideration, self-acceptance, and depressive affect at the age 35 assessment also revealed significant differences. As shown in Table 2.9, members of the *ambiguous, developmentally unrelated, and disorganized goals* pattern reported the lowest level of career commitment and self-acceptance and the highest level of career consideration and depressive affect. In contrast, members of the *elaborated and progressing life goals* pattern reported the highest levels of career commitment and self-acceptance and the lowest levels of career consideration and depressive affect. While members of the two additional patterns did not consistently differ from the members of the adaptive goal pattern, closer inspection of the comparison between the four types revealed some further distinctions. For example, members of the second type, characterized by increased concerns about the possibility of pursuing their goals successfully, reported a higher level of depressive affect, while members of the *realistic and orderly career and family goals* pattern reported a significantly higher level of career reconsideration. Of note, no differences between the four patterns of goal constellation on the future level of anxiety were found.

Conceptually, our findings emphasize two aspects that should be considered. First, while emerging adults might describe a variety of important goals at this stage of life, there are in fact two main goals—career/studies and family development. Though the balance between these two main goals changes during the 20s (Shulman & Connolly, 2013), work and family continue to be the main goals that young people aspire to achieve. The centrality of the "work" and "love" goals recalls the seminal writings of Freud, as well as aligning with recent writings (Levinson, 1978; Shulman & Nurmi, 2010a).

Table 2.9 *Patterns of Goal Constellation Across Emerging Adulthood and Outcomes at Age 35: Means, Standard Deviations, and Significance of Differences*

Goal constellation	Ambiguous	Realistic but unsecure	Realistic	Elaborated	F
Salary level	1.25 (.85)	1.80 (.88)	1.79 (1.08)	2.18 (.0.82)	3.28*
Career commitment	2.72 (1.15)	3.13 (1.1)	3.11 (1.1)	3.77 (0.81)	4.30
Career consideration	2.91 (.98)	2.23 (.95)	2.30 (1.04)	1.76 (0.79)	5.07**
Self-acceptance	4.10 (1.71)	4.70 (1.11)	4.78 (1.17)	5.55 (.83)	5.92**
Depressive affect	1.61 (1.2)	.83 (.79)	.75 (.7)	.41 (.48)	8.63***
Anxiety Symptoms	1.27 (1.03)	.84 (.64)	.97 (.64)	.83 (.48)	1.76

*$p < .05$. **$p < .01$. ***$p < .001$.

Second, our findings suggest that successful progression toward transition to adulthood is facilitated by setting realistic goals and the ability to elaborate or readapt goals along the process and to find meaning in one's selected goals. The elaboration and readaptation of goals along the process are likely to lead to the most optimal outcomes (Heckhausen et al., 2010). In contrast, ambiguous and inconsistent goals cannot lead to adaptive progression as the individual will flounder between different goals and tasks across time. Setting realistic goals while simultaneously having some inner reservations or concerns about one's choice might not necessarily hamper progression. However, progression might be accompanied with self-questioning about one's path and increasing depressive affect.

A closer inspection and comparison of Nora's and Ariel's goals can shed further light on the adaptive and less adaptive patterns of goal pursuit that different individuals employ during emerging adulthood. Nora's goals were ambiguous and changed from one assessment to the next. No clear realistic and developmental sequence could be identified in her goal story. This explains well why, at age 35, it seemed that she had lost confidence in her ability to achieve major goals in career and relationships. Ariel was classified as the fourth type, representing elaborated goal pursuit. However, reading the goals he defined showed that this was not simple for him. At the end of the preparatory program he realized that he was not interested in (and maybe not suitable for) academic studies and started learning to become a plumber. Once he settled down as a plumber it was important for him to learn to love what he did and to earn money. He was able to find additional meaning in his life by investing in the building of his family and in his hobby. Thus, looking at Ariel's life as a whole, despite the need to make compromises, he was able to develop his vocational skills and become a plumber and to have a reasonable income. To add meaning in his life—he was invested in his family, he loved cooking together with his wife—he developed a hobby that he cherished. Considered together, emerging adults employed different ways to pursue their goals and to coordinate between the various goals along the process of pursuit. In addition, it is evident that emerging adults focused on two major goal domains: studies/career and the establishment of a family. In the next two chapters we focus on the two major tasks of emerging adults: career development and family formation. Based on the rich data we have collected through extensive in-depth interviews, we examine how individuals coped during their years of career pursuit and their progression toward romantic commitment and establishing a family. We analyze these interviews and discuss the life stories that individuals present of their experiences along the years while navigating the domains of career and love within their lives. We intend to show again the variety of pathways that young people take during the journey to settling down. The distinctive ways that young people pursue and readapt career aspirations, as well as the ways that young people engage in romantic relationships and develop (or do not develop) toward intimacy and commitment, can reveal the inner lives and aspirations that young people have and the ways that lead them to success or failure.

3
Pathways of Career Pursuit—Consistency, Detours, Disappointments
Finding One's Way or Getting Lost

As seen in the previous chapter, clear and consistent goals are very helpful in directing individual life paths by staying focused on one's aspirations and regulating behavior toward achievement of the desired goal (Haase et al., 2008). In his seminal work, Levinson (1978) described the importance of having a dream that serves as a continuous guide in navigating personal aspirations, decisions, and behavior. The existence of a realistic dream that suits a person's capacities and considers environmental circumstances (Nurmi, 2004) can thus become a source of strength in the progress toward, and successful transition to, adulthood. Notwithstanding the crucial role of a goal or a dream and how clear it is, this needs to be implemented into actual decisions and behavior. Not all individuals necessarily pursue their dream in a similar way. Although it may appear that for those who have an articulated goal, their goal is likely to define their track and guide them. However, along the way a goal might become too difficult to attain, or interest might be lost in an aspired goal. In addition, it has become more common to find young people who have less clearly articulated occupational goals and unfocused strategies for negotiating the transition (K. Evans & Heinz, 1994; Settersten & Ray, 2010), and observation of the lives of many young people shows that they may move between transitory and inconsistent states (Cohen et al., 2003). How can we explain all the instabilities and fluctuations of young people in their occupational lives? By reading and analyzing the in-depth interviews in which our participants were asked to describe their career history, we describe the different pathways that young people take on the journey of developing a career. We describe those who are successful in following their plans, those who have to give up an earlier plan, and those who lose their way. Listening to their stories helps us to understand the lives of young people better and the roads they follow in the pursuit of their dream.

As described in the first chapter, our participants were followed from the age of 23 until the age of 35 and were assessed five times during these years. At each wave participants were given different questionnaires as outlined previously. For example, at each assessment participants were asked to describe their three major goals. At the fourth assessment, when participants were about 28–29 years old, 100 (who were selected randomly from the 130 participants who participated in the fourth wave) were given an in-depth interview in which they were asked to describe the story of their career pursuit. This was done in order to learn, in greater detail, about the ways these young people employed to pursue the goals to which they aspired. In this chapter we describe how we analyzed these interviews and what we have learned about the possible different pathways they took in their career pursuit.

The career history interview was comprised of two stages: first, a spontaneous story was told, after which the questions were presented (Rosenthal, 1993). In the opening question, participants were asked to tell the story of their career pursuit and development over the last years in their own words and from their own point of view. The second stage was comprised of questions that attempted to reference specific topics that they had raised themselves more accurately. In line with the study questions, participants were probed about their current work status, work/study experiences, difficulties they might have had in the past and how they coped with these, and feelings and expectations about work/study and its meaning. In particular they were asked to elaborate on their personal, social, and professional dreams, as well as to reflect on changes and turning points in their recent work and career histories. To capture and address inner processes, participants were encouraged to talk about, and elaborate on, their various experiences and to reflect on the extent to which they felt that they had progressed on their aspired track or the extent to which they were still uncertain about what they really wanted to do in life. Interviews were recorded and transcribed.

As could be expected, individuals have their unique stories of career development, their efforts, their successes and failures, as well as their recoveries or downfalls. In their stories, goals played an important role in guiding them, at least at the beginning of their adult life. Reading the interviews showed that individuals employed distinctive ways of pursuing their careers. Often, individuals start their pursuit by setting a goal that evolves and becomes more complex or is transformed to meet personal capacities and environmental realities. Within this dynamic development individuals employ a variety of mechanisms to succeed in attaining a career that supports them financially and is intellectually interesting.

In the following section we describe four distinctive pathways that emerged from reading and analyzing the interviews. First, we describe the method of narrative analysis we employed to identify different pathways. Second, we describe the four pathways that emerged and provide examples for each pathway in the words of our participants. Finally, we discuss the conceptual meaning and implications of the identification of different pathways.

Identification of pathways of career pursuit

We employed a mixture of exploratory and confirmatory techniques (Lieblich et al., 1998) to identify possible career development pathways. The following describes our approach: Guided by the theory on goals (Nurmi, 2004) and principles of developmental regulation (Heckhausen et al., 2010), we considered various components such as describing goals, decisions, events, difficulties, and coping as highlighted by these theoretical approaches. In addition, we considered the extent to which occupational whereabouts and outcomes were associated with inner personal preferences and inclinations. Themes that emerged from interviews refined our further reading of the material, resulting in analysis being conducted in the following manner. First, a general pattern of career pursuit and development was identified, after which the existence of the particular pathway in each interview was assessed. Refuting or negative evidence led to the re-discussion and refinement of a pathway. This back-and-forth exploratory and confirmatory process led to the adaptation and reformulation of proposed pathways of career pursuit, to ensure that all personal stories were well represented. Employing this mixture of exploratory and confirmatory techniques (Lieblich et al., 1998), we identified four pathways. (Two raters coded transcripts independently across the entire sample. Inter-rater reliability was at the level of kappa = .87.)

Pathway 1—Consistent pursuit

Individuals affiliated with this pathway described having a clear and articulated life plan that was complex, diversified, and connected to inner aspirations. While consistently pursuing their plans and being persistent, individuals described that they were sufficiently open and flexible to consider circumstances and make adaptations that were required from time to time. It is noteworthy, however, that changes made along the way were not major and substantial. For example, one participant studied chemistry and over the course of time made some change—within chemistry they shifted to physical chemistry. Overall, individuals affiliated with this pathway knew what they wanted, pursued their goals actively, were not discouraged by setback, and continued to pursue their dream. Twenty-four percent of our sample was affiliated with this pathway.

Alex, aged 29, is a good example of a person who pursued his career consistently and persistently. Alex participated in our study from the start and was first assessed when he was 23 years old. Alex is the oldest in a family of three children. Both his parents have only a high school education and have constantly been employed. Alex's father has a technical job in a company that sells electrical appliances. Over the years he was promoted in the company and is now responsible for a number of shops. His mother used to be a salesperson in a clothing store. Due to medical problems, it is difficult for her to stand for long hours, and she is now employed only part-time. The rest of her time is devoted to her hobby of gardening. She has a big garden in which she grows vegetables and enjoys every moment. As can be seen, both of Alex's parents are hardworking people who value working. As is described below, Alex combined work with his high school studies and started to work at the age of 14.

At the age of 29, Alex was given an in-depth interview where he was asked to describe the history of his career development. Alex is an example of a young man who had a clear and definite goal. Since adolescence Alex was sure that "he is meant to work in computers," and this directed decisions with regard to higher education, workplace, and even type of work he looked for as an adolescent. Even during high school, when possible, he looked for work associated with computers.

In the interview, Alex described that he is employed as an intern in a small computer company. Alex explained that since his early teens he has worked in different jobs in the afternoons. However, due to his interest in and love for computers, as early as the age of 14 he was helping in a computer shop. He did not have good grades in high school, which prevented him from applying to university. Then he added,

> I always knew that I wanted to do something with computers, but I learned along the way that having an interest in, and loving computers is not enough. Then I decided to study for a degree in engineering, but as I did not have a full matriculation, I could not apply to university. Therefore, I had to take the preparatory program in order to be accepted to university. This was a long process considering that I had to work to support myself.

Reading Alex's story demonstrates that from adolescence he was attracted to computers and felt that this was what he wanted to do in his life. He did not settle for a lower-level job in computers and did not give up when he realized that he could not apply for academic studies, and he enrolled in the college preparatory program. Furthermore, along the way, again he was not discouraged when he did not get the job he was looking for. He learned that he needed a degree to get a higher-level job and worked hard to earn the degree. Thus, Alex had a clear goal of working in a field associated with computers. He continuously coped with setbacks along the way and further elaborated his goals, directing him to pursue a degree in engineering. It was not easy to combine work and studies, but he was persistent; and this persistence led him to complete his studies. Of note, he was not distracted from his persistent pursuit of his goal by his romantic involvement and proposal to his girlfriend.

Alex's career development story is impressive and represents a young man who, from adolescence, wanted to have a career associated with computers; and, as can be seen, he achieved his dream. At age 29, when interviewed, he was a few weeks shy of receiving his degree in electrical engineering. The degree will afford him the opportunity to get a higher-level, full-time job at the company in which he is employed and that he loves. Alex's career story might sound like a demonstration of Nurmi's (2004) contentions that setting clear and realistic goals and commitment to these goals are particularly important markers of adaptation during a transitional period as they elicit elevated commitment. Indeed, Alex was very consistent in the goal he was pursuing and committed to his career at the different workplaces where he was employed.

However, a closer inspection of his career story showed that he faced a number of successive setbacks over the years. He failed to attain matriculation, which is required for applying to university. He started a low-level job in a company and then realized that in order to be promoted he would need a degree. He took the college preparatory program while he was working as he had to support himself. Later, he compromised and studied at a college in the area where he had his job and not at the university he would have chosen in the first place.

Despite facing a number of obstacles along the way, Alex was able to "adapt" his master plan considering the circumstances. Alex did not have to withdraw from his primary goal to work in the area of computers and set a new goal (Heckhausen et al., 2010). However, over the years Alex had to make adaptations that could, to some extent, be seen as a process of developmental regulation as described by Heckhausen and colleagues. Within this process, Alex's goals were adapted and elaborated, which helped him to navigate over the years toward becoming an electrical engineer who specializes in networking.

Sometimes you need to change course

Unlike Alex, others were not necessarily as consistent and successful in achieving their earlier goals. Even appropriate age–related goals and aspirations were not always attained, and individuals periodically needed to adjust their aspirations and behavior to changing realities. For example, failure to attain an expected goal (due to changes in the job market, personal failure, or realizing that this career might not suit the person) requires young people to reconsider whether to continue aspiring to the specific goal or to adjust their goals (Brandtstädter & Rothermund, 2002; Salmela-Aro et al., 2001; Seiffge-Krenke, 1995). The career stories that the young people told us were helpful in understanding their behavior, cognitions, and feelings under different circumstances and provide further understanding of the variety of ways young people use to navigate through these years.

Heckhausen's motivational theory of life-span development is of great relevance in understanding the meaning of fluctuations and change described by our participants (Heckhausen, 1999; Heckhausen et al., 2010). Heckhausen describes the different ways in which individuals cope with, or react to, facing failure or confronting unattainable goals. While active and purposeful pursuit of a desired goal is highly adaptive, continued pursuit of, or aspiration for, an unattainable goal can become a source of stress. Under such circumstances, Heckhausen describes the mechanism of goal readjustment, namely, disengagement from an unattainable goal and pursuit of an alternative goal. This involves the ability to realize that a desired goal is unattainable and the necessity to formulate a different goal. While relinquishing one's aspired goal might seem a drawback, in reality this strategy reflects self-mastery and is beneficial to well-being. The ability to come to terms with loss or failure facilitates compromise and the formulation of a new and different goal. In contrast, continued pursuit of a goal that cannot be attained is likely to reflect an inability to identify alternative goals and may lead to fruitless efforts (Wrosch et al., 2003) and a decrease in well-being (Heckhausen et al., 2010).

Pathway 2—Adapted pursuit

Individual accounts in this pathway were characterized by disappointments or failures that led to a change in the area of studies and/or a shift to a different field of work. Despite experiencing disappointments and, in some cases, quite substantial difficulties, individuals made impressive adaptations. Individuals described their new field of studies or workplace as interesting, fulfilling, and on a par with inner aspirations. This pathway includes cases where individuals started a job incidentally, found it to be interesting and meaningful, and now considered it a career for life. These individuals were able to surrender an earlier aspiration, cope with failure or disappointment along the way, and then find a new goal that gives meaning to their lives. Thirty-four percent of the sample was affiliated with this pathway.

The case of Becky demonstrates this pathway well. Becky was 22 years old when she was recruited to the study. She comes from a family of four children in a small town in the north of Israel. Both her parents have a high school education. Her father is employed as a taxi driver in a large taxi company. Her mother is a part-time receptionist at a school, and Becky added that her mother perceives her main work to be at home, taking care of the household issues. Though both her parents work in not high-ranking jobs, they never missed a day at work: "even when they are sick, they go to work." Becky did not work during her high school years, besides babysitting here and there.

Following the completion of the college preparatory program, Becky started studying behavioral sciences with the aim of continuing to a second degree in clinical psychology. Becky described that she liked her studies, enjoyed the campus atmosphere, and was able to work part-time as a waitress to pay her tuition. Furthermore, she said that since childhood she had dreamed of being a psychologist and working with younger children. However, in her third year of studies some questions started to arise, and she found herself asking whether this is really what she wants to do in life and whether she will be successful in being accepted to graduate studies in clinical psychology. "I decided that I need to switch a number of courses and focus more on human resources, which is also sort of psychology. I believed that the studies would provide me with knowledge and sort of expertise to find a job." Upon completion of her studies Becky started to look for a job in human resources, for which her degree in behavioral sciences prepared her.

She was interviewed and accepted for a number of jobs she describes as a "good job." However, to her surprise, she adds,

> The salary offered was low, the companies were small, and I was not sure for how long these companies will survive. There were good offers in the market, but the other companies were looking for people with experience and not somebody who just had graduated. I felt this is not for me. This will be something temporary with no future.

Becky added, "I am not the person not to work for even one day," so she found a job that was less interesting to her, working as a secretary, and continued to look for a different job that aligned more with her interests. After a year and half, she received an offer to work in a bank. Although she was not trained to work in a bank, she explained that her degree helped her to be open and look for a job in a different field. "I think that life sometimes takes us to places we had not thought about, and I am open to new experiences. If I see something and think it has the potential for success, I will not hesitate and will take the chance." Currently, she works in a bank and sees this as her future career. "I find the work in the bank interesting; it is a position where I can develop and work for years. I am ready to give whatever is needed of myself to succeed, to advance there. I will do whatever I can to get into this world [of banking], I believe it will go well."

Similar to Alex, Becky also had a dream for many years. She hoped to become a psychologist. During her first years at college, she realized that psychology was not what she really wanted to do. She "disengaged" from her dream goal (Heckhausen et al., 2010) and compromised on another goal that was still associated with the topic of her studies—human resources. When looking for her first job she realized that she would not be able to make a living starting from the bottom in human resources. For almost a year and a half she worked as a secretary—a job that she hated and that had nothing to do with her qualifications. Yet, in retrospect, as suggested by te Riele (2004), that unexpected switch was not necessarily negative.

During this period, which she described as miserable, she remained open enough to search for different options. Finally, she found a position in banking, which she came to see as her future. It was probably Becky's openness to new experiences as described in her own words that facilitated the finding of a new goal, directing a new path in her career development. Unlike Alex, Becky did not follow her earlier goal but was able to find a new goal (banking) and to engage wholeheartedly in the new goal.

Pathway 3—Survivors

Young people affiliated with this pathway worked permanently or were studying for a degree. On the surface their daily lives seemed settled, but when asked to reflect on their feelings about their occupation, they reported that their work (and even their field of study) was not satisfying and did not address their inner aspirations. Some described their lives as colored by a sense of instability and failure. If they had goals, these were quite amorphous or unrealistic. As a result, they continued to aspire to a goal that they hoped, but were unable, to reach and felt that their current work did not suit their capabilities or interests. Moreover, despite describing a dream, it was, in fact, common that no steps were taken in pursuit of their dream. Twenty-eight percent of the sample was affiliated with this pattern.

Being invested in your job but having dreams of doing something else

Roni is an example of a young woman who has a full-time and stable job but simultaneously has a dream to do something else. Roni was 25 years old when she started the college preparatory program and was recruited into the study. Roni originates from a large family of six children, and neither of her parents had completed their high school education. Roni's father had worked in a company for years, delivering goods to shops. At some point he wanted to be self-employed and started his own little enterprise, but he went bankrupt after a couple of years. Since he is at the age of retirement, he did not look for a new job. Her mother works as a custodian in a school. Roni added that as her parents saw work as a means to support the family, they never missed a day of work. "Even during school recess my mother looks to do something. She never goes idle."

At the time of the interview Roni, at age 30, was working for a weekly magazine covering municipal issues. Only she and the manager work there. She is responsible for almost every aspect of the work there: contact with subscribers, obtaining advertisements, bookkeeping, printing, and answering the phone. On Tuesdays, when the magazine is published, she might stay at work until the late hours of the night.

Roni used to work in temporary jobs, and then she was introduced to the manager of the magazine and started working at the editorial office. Roni likes this workplace. "This is not a job I chose; it came up. I like the work here. I like the responsibility. The atmosphere is also great." Despite loving this workplace, she is not sure whether this is the work she truly wants.

Roni further elaborated, "I studied a topic in which I was not interested, like my current job." When asked whether she can describe what she really wants to do in her life, she responded, "I think the fact is that I do not know exactly what I want to do. I have a general direction but am not sure that there is a specific field toward which I can direct myself." She hopes that when she matures (she was 29 years old during this interview) she will know better what she wants for the future. Of note, though Roni does not have a clear goal and it is difficult for her to define exactly what she would like to do, she holds a stable job.

Reuben, age 26.5, who was also classified in the *Survivors* pathway, is employed in an insurance company. Reuben is among our youngest participants and joined the study (and the college preparatory program) when he was somewhat younger than 21 years. Reuben also originates from a lower-middle-class working family, where he is the second of three children. His father has a high school education and is self-employed as a construction contractor. His mother has only 11 years of schooling and works as an elementary school secretary. Reuben describes that his family is doing very well and love their work. In fact, he added "My mother does not have to work. She could stay home, but she is not this type of person."

Like Roni, he hates his workplace, the insurance company. Describing his current job, he says, "I hate this job. It is not satisfying. I feel I can do more but am limited, not allowed, this is the job, and this is what you have to do. So, I feel I am stuck."

Contrary to Roni, Reuben seems to have a clear goal. He is in the second year of a degree in business administration. Yet, while on the surface it seems that in the meantime he is pursuing his educational goal, he told us that he applied at the last moment for studies at a low-rated college. He regrets attending this college but will not change now. He does not feel confident to make a change at this time.

When asked to elaborate about his future plan, Reuben commented, "I do not have a definite plan. I want to do something in export–import, to open a store with a friend of mine." Unfortunately, Reuben was not able to describe his new plan. "It is a general idea, more like a dream than a plan."

Both Roni and Reuben are steadily employed, on the one hand, while, on the other hand, they aspire for a different career that is not well defined or clearly articulated and that cannot guide them toward taking action to achieve their dream. Their amorphous dreams and their inability to disengage from these dreams (Heckhausen, 1999) interfere with their capacity to search for different dreams that might be fulfilling. In the meantime, due to their need to earn money and support themselves, they are stuck in jobs they do not like.

Pathway 4—Confused/vague

Those affiliated with the *Confused/Vague* pathway were unable to provide a clear and coherent idea of what they would like to do with their lives throughout the interview and appeared to feel miserable. Some of these young people work but are unable to stay at one job for a long period and seem to be continuously moving between periods of employment and unemployment. Others are likely not to work for extended periods of time, and their lives are unstable. Fourteen percent of the sample was affiliated with this pathway.

Nora, who was not able to articulate any clear goals (see Chapter 2), represents the young people who were classified into this career pursuit type well. Nora was 21 years old when she started the college preparatory program and was recruited into the study.

Nora provided a very gloomy description when asked what she does at this stage of her life (age 27): "I am in a very bad place. I work in something I do not like. Awfully dislikes. I worked for a long time as a waitress and I felt I have done too much of this type of work, it is time to do something different. But actually now, because I have to pay my rent, I cannot go idle. And when I go to work it is awful, I feel very bad, and I hate myself." Asking her whether she any plans to study, she responded, "This is even worse. I wish I had a plan. I am afraid of studying; I hardly completed my matriculation." Nora was then asked whether thoughts about the future cross her mind, and her answer was distressing.

> I always think about the future. I see what my friends have achieved. And I nothing. I think it is because I was always indifferent. What was important for me was to have money to go out. To meet. I did not think more than this. But I still hope that in the future I will find a place that will make me happy, a job

that I like and is also secure that they cannot tell me from one day to the other goodbye.

At the end of the interview, it becomes clear that Nora is unable to set a clear goal that will direct her future search for a job she will like. Her work at different places also did not help her find her direction. The responsibility for the future is transferred to the job in which she might be employed, a job that "will make me happy."

Pathways of career pursuit: Exploring and floundering

Analysis of the in-depth interview data was guided by Nurmi's (2004) accounts of the centrality of goal construction and Heckhausen's motivational theory of life-span development (Heckhausen, 1999; Heckhausen et al., 2010). Bynner (2005) described that individuals take different pathways in the transition to adulthood. Reading the career histories of our participants demonstrated that distinctive pathways are characterized by different constellations of balancing goal engagement and goal disengagement. In addition, the extent to which a career was described as suiting one's values and dreams and addressing one's curiosity emerged as a central theme in typifying a pathway (Levinson, 1978; Savickas, 2005).

As can be seen, only about one quarter of our participants who described having a clear goal were able to pursue their goal persistently. Alex's career, which clearly represents a consistent pathway, showed that, despite being on track, he experienced setbacks along the way. He did not graduate high school with the necessary qualification for starting college. Yet, over the years he was able to find the resources to progress toward his initial goal. Indeed, at the fourth assessment he was about to attain a degree in electrical engineering that would open doors for him to find a respectable job in the field of computers. Alex may appear to belong to a previous generation when young people were more successful in finding jobs that meet their dreams. Reading Alex's story of development, however, showed that he too had to struggle and to put much effort into staying in line with and achieving his goal.

While members of the *Consistent Pursuit* pathway successfully progressed quite consistently toward their initial goal, members of the *Adapted Pursuit* pathway, which accounted for almost a third of our sample, described that along the process they had to disengage from a goal due to failure or disappointment and set a new goal. They were, however, capable of competently pursuing the new goal that was meaningful for them. This is not an easy task. Becky floundered (Arnett, 2004; Krahn et al., 2013) for a couple of years until she was able to change direction, finding a job in banking, a totally different field from the degree she had studied, and feeling that she had found her new dream. In describing her shift, Becky was optimistic; and from the time she moved to the new field she described feeling that this would be an interesting job, that she would meet interesting people, and, above all, that this was her future.

Reading the qualitative data carefully suggests that it is the capacity to remain open to new experiences that facilitates finding a new direction and setting a new goal. Under such circumstances, these changes can become beneficial in helping the young person find a different career or job with which they identify or a niche that suits them better (Arnett, 2006; Krahn et al., 2013; te Riele, 2004). Within this process, an earlier dream is given up; and through a prolonged process of searching that might consist of switching between different options along the way and exploring different alternatives, a new goal is set. The qualitative data additionally sheds light on the internal questions, fears, hopes, and adaptations that young people might make along the way when pursuing a goal and when they have to change course and define a new path (Heckhausen, 1999; Heckhausen et al., 2010; Savickas, 2005). Considered together, the capacity to disengage from a dream that became irrelevant and to find and set a different and new goal is what determines the extent to which the young person has rediscovered direction in life. Krahn and colleagues (2013) found that educational changes are likely to have positive effects, representing engagement to a new goal, which is in line with the principles of developmental regulation (Heckhausen et al., 2010). In contrast, changes in employment were found to associate with lower future outcomes because these might decrease personal capital—one's competence in finding a suitable job as well as decrease in social capital—due to a decrease in support from a workplace (Krahn et al., 2013). Our findings suggest that for some individuals change of employment might open new options and thus help embark on a more adaptive pathway (te Riele, 2006).

Counting the members of the *Consistent Pursuit* and the *Adapted Pursuit* together suggests that almost 60% of our participants reported an adaptive career pursuit history. They were able either to progress consistently toward their initial goal or to disengage from a goal in case of failure or disappointment and to set and successfully pursue a new goal that was meaningful for them. These findings suggest that periods of instability, fluctuation, and feeling stuck "nowhere" (Arnett, 2004; Bynner et al., 1997; European Group for Integrated Social Research [EGRIS], 2001) may, after all, be functional as a ground for finding one's niche in a changing world. Conceptually, we might suggest that what could have been seen as floundering at an earlier point in time was actually a process of functional exploration, but this could be evaluated only in retrospect.

Another third of our sample, the *Survivors*, appeared to have settled down and managed their daily lives properly. However, despite their daily functioning, they reported an inner feeling of dissatisfaction with their current occupations and little emotional connection with their jobs. These young people described still aspiring to a goal that was difficult for them to actually pursue. Among affiliates of this pathway, it was common to find that the aspired goal was not clear enough or well defined and, therefore, could not be realized. Furthermore, aspiring to an unattainable, and sometimes unrealistic, dream has the potential to become a source of disappointment and frustration to these young people (Heckhausen et al., 2010). *Survivors* probably experience a sense of inner contradiction—on the one hand, their stable employment and ability to provide for themselves contributes to their sense of progress. On the other hand, they feel that they have failed to pursue a goal to which they aspired. This inner sense of failure is likely to give rise to negative effects (Sheldon & Elliot, 1999; Shulman et al., 2005).

The steady employment of these young people together with the feeling of disconnection from what they do raises the question as to whether these young people could ultimately find meaning in what they do in the future (Blustein, 2011), become more satisfied, and give up their unarticulated and unrealistic dream. It is important to examine this in following our participants and learning what direction the *Survivors* take in their lives. Have they settled down, or are they still preoccupied by a dream or, as better defined by Levinson (1978), an "illusionary dream"?

The fourth pathway, the *Confused/Vague* pathway, recalls the typical descriptions of emerging adults (Arnett, 2004; EGRIS, 2001). These young people either do not have any clear plans or might even be afraid of aspiring at all. They are employed only periodically and have a sense of being marginalized. Some are young people demonstrating a variety of adjustment problems that prevent them from coping with age-related tasks. However, this pathway comprised only about 14% of our sample, suggesting that being lost and confused is not the norm.

In sum, the in-depth accounts provided a better understanding of setbacks, fluctuations, and changes that young people make during the process of pursuing a career. These allowed us to learn how young people define and articulate their plans, move to implementation, cope with the inevitable difficulties that arise along the way, and find new avenues that might better suit their capacities and raise new interests in these. Conceptually, this can help us further understand when and why a change can be adaptive and when it reflects a difficulty or indicates inability (Krahn et al., 2013; te Riele, 2004).

The majority of existing conceptualizations, as well as research on emerging adults, describe the postponement in career and romantic commitment and emphasize the instabilities and fluctuations that characterize the vocational lives of young people in our times (Arnett, 2004, Settersten & Ray, 2010). We believe that these understandings correctly describe the way young people live today. However, following young people across their 20s and learning from them, in their own words, about their career pursuit demonstrates a more complex narrative. Indeed, a substantial number of young people were observed to flounder across this period of development, yet we also noticed that these instabilities, coupled with openness to one's environment, could serve as the ground for development and progress toward finding one's niche.

Career pursuit pathways and attainment of career goals

We were interested in examining the extent to which different career pursuit pathways are associated with level of goal striving and goal stress in the domain of career, as well as the level of satisfaction and number of depressive symptoms among the participants at age 29. For this purpose, a modified version of Little's (1983) Personal Project Analysis was used. Participants were asked to write down three of their most important goals. In this chapter we refer to their career goals. Participants were then asked to appraise their career goal along three dimensions: goal importance ("to what extent is the project important to you"), goal progress ("to what extent have you made progress realizing this project"), and stress ("to what extent is it stressful to attain the goal").

We expected members of the *Consistent Pursuit* pathway, compared to *Survivors* and those of the *Confused/Vague* pathway, to report higher goal importance and goal achievement but lower levels of goal stress. Considering the major changes the members of the *Adapted Pursuit* pathway underwent with regard to their goals, we were not sure how they would rate themselves on these indices. In addition, we assessed change in level of depressive affect between the first assessment at age 23 and the fourth assessment at age 29. Again, we expected to find greater decreases in depressive affect among the two more adaptive patterns in contrast to increases in depressive affect in the two less optimal pathways. Finally, we expected members of the *Consistent* and *Adapted Pursuit* pathways to report the highest level of life satisfaction.

As can be seen in Table 3.1, the first three career pursuit pathways reported similar levels of goal importance compared to members of the *Confused/Vague* pathway, who reported the lowest level of goal importance. As could be expected, members of the *Consistent Pursuit* and *Adapted Pursuit* pathways reported the highest level of goal achievement, *Survivors* reported an intermediate level, while members of the *Confused/Vague* pathway reported the lowest level of goal achievement. Concerning goal stress, members of the *Consistent Pursuit* pathway reported the lowest level of goal stress compared to the other three pathways. These findings support and further illuminate the distinctiveness of the four pathways as described by participants in their own words. The *Consistent Pursuit* pathway and the *Confused/Vague* pathway represent the two

Table 3.1 *Levels of Work Goal Projects, Satisfaction, and Depressive Symptoms Across the four career pursuit pathways: Means, SDs, and F values*

	Confused/vague	Survivors	Adapted pathway	Consistent pathway	F
Goal importance	5.18 (1.27)	6.3 (.82)	6.59 (.55)	6.47 (.6)	9.16***
Goal achievement	3.82 (1.47)	4.89 (.86)	5.86 (.91)	5.51 (.83)	12.91***
Goal stress	3.0 (1.12)	4.26 (.92)	4.21 (1.33)	3.69 (1.86)	2.79*
Satisfaction	3.18 (.84)	3.39[a] (.62)	3.96 (.59)	3.7 (.98)	4.72**
Depressive symptoms (Age 23)	1.34 (1.21)	1.13 (.59)	1.19 (1)	.62 (.6)	2.84*
Depressive symptoms (Age 29)	1.77 (1.15)	1.14 (.86)	.71 (.78)	.37 (.46)	10.31***

[a]Satisfaction with life.
*$p < .05$. **$p < .01$. ***$p < .001$.

edges of adaptation: those who pursue and guide their career lives competently and those who have lost their way and are confused. While members of the *Adapted Pursuit* pathway have the sense that they have achieved their goals and that these goals are important to them, they still reported higher levels of stress, which probably reflect the difficulties they experienced over the years. *Survivors* reported elevated stress as well as lower achievement of their goals, as could be expected. In contrast, they reported a similar level of goal importance to that of the more adaptive pathways. This probably reflects their daily investment in jobs that they did not necessarily choose or enjoy. Level of satisfaction differed across the four pathways, as could be expected. Members of the *Consistent Pursuit* and *Adapted Pursuit* pathways reported the highest levels of satisfaction, while *Survivors* and members of the *Confused/Vague* pathway reported the lowest level of satisfaction.

Comparison of the four pathways on changes in level of depressive affect over the years further contributed to our understanding of the four pathways. Means and standard deviations of depressive affect at the first and fourth assessments are also presented in Table 3.1. Considering the longitudinal nature of our data, additional analyses of variance with repeated measures were conducted to compare trajectories of the three patterns on the different indices of psychosocial functioning. Only one significant interaction between pattern of career pursuit and change over time on number of depressive symptoms was found, $F = 5.89$, $p < .001$. Among members of the *Consistent Pursuit* and *Adapted Pursuit* pathways level of depressive symptoms decreased over time, while among the members of the *Confused/Vague* pathway this increased significantly over time. Interestingly, number of depressive symptoms among *Survivors* did not change over time, suggesting that their pattern of career pursuit was not associated with increase or decrease in depressive affect. Of note, differences between the three patterns of career adaptability on the number of depressive symptoms at the first assessment were not significant.

Summary

Reading the stories of our participants showed that the majority of young people struggle to find their way in this changing world—to have a career that expresses their personal aspirations as well as to be able to make a living. A substantial number of young people did find their direction and achieved this despite difficulties finding their direction over the years. Even those who had difficulties pursuing and achieving their dream, such as the *Survivors*, were still struggling to keep the job they did not necessarily like but understood that this was the way they could adapt in the current world. Thus, the majority of our participants were active and employed a variety of ways to navigate their lives. Only a small proportion, less than 20%, could be defined as losing their way and characterize the stereotypical descriptions of emerging adults (Arnett, 2004; Côté, 2000).

We believe that additional information about the lives of our participants after the completion of their emerging adulthood years (age 29) could further highlight the ways that career pathways continue to develop toward settling down during the mid-30s. Considering the existence of individual differences, we followed our participants at the age of 35. They were again given an in-depth interview about their careers. We will present this in the following chapter and learn, in the participants' own words, how they moved toward settling down. We will describe the unfolding career stories of our participants and in particular the cases described in this chapter. Do they stay stable, or do they change and in what direction? In addition, based on the stories of career settling down, we will explore the possible different pattern constellations to characterize the modes of "settling down" among young people.

4
Aspirations, Flourishing, and Compromises
Career Pursuit Pathways and Settling Down

In the previous chapter we described the different pathways that emerging adults take in pursuing their careers. Affiliates of the four pathways—*Consistent Pursuit, Adapted Pursuit, Survivors,* and *Confused/Vague*—raised the different life stories in the process of career development. Our proposed typology gave serious consideration to the extent to which one's life is directed or not directed by previously set clear goals (Nurmi, 2004) and the ability to disengage from goals that have become unattainable, to set new and different goals, and to pursue them competently (Heckhausen et al., 2010). Conceptually, these notions are guided by, and emphasize, the centrality of inner motivation in directing one's life and determining its path of development (Ryan & Deci, 2000a).

Notwithstanding the importance of inner motivation in guiding a person's career development, social and economic developments in the last decades have drastically changed the lives of young people. Job uncertainty has increased, and young people might find it increasingly difficult to achieve even modest goals of affluence and job security (Furlong & Cartmel, 2007). Considering the obscure and ever-changing career climate, young people might need to compromise by taking a job that is available, which they had not considered in the first place (Briscoe et al., 2006). Under these circumstances, it is reasonable to question the extent to which earlier dreams are relevant under the current social and economic conditions. We show that young people had to settle for the job that was available, though this did not meet earlier expectations. Should compromises like these be considered an *adaptive career outcome* nowadays? In this chapter we will try to answer these questions.

Career adaptability has been widely discussed within the framework of vocational psychology. Career adaptability has been conceptualized and developed to assess a person's capacity to prepare for and participate in a work role and was rooted in the assumption of stability and security of the job market (Savickas et al., 2009). Within this framework, aspects such as career decision self-efficacy, career choice commitment, career planning, and identification with a school or a workplace were emphasized (Duffy & Blustein, 2005). Mark Savickas (1997) suggested that career adaptability could be understood by using developmental dimension of the self. In this way, career adaptability includes not only looking ahead to the future (planning) but also making suitable and viable choices (deciding) and looking around at the opportunities available (exploring)—in sum, self-regulating. Thus, self-regulatory mechanisms probably also become relevant to career adaptability as they are likely to play an important role in times of stress and change or when confronted with novel and unexpected challenges (Creed et al., 2009). Furthermore, these mechanisms become even more crucial as the time to settle down approaches, pressure to assume an adult role probably increases, and a person might have to make certain compromises.

To better understand how young people complete the transition to adulthood and settle down in a career, we approached our participants again when they were at about 35 years old. They were again given an in-depth interview in which they were asked to describe the story of their career development over the last 6 years. Participants were probed about their current work status and work experiences, difficulties they might have had in their workplaces, and feelings about their work and its meaning for them. In addition, they were asked to reflect on changes and turning points in their recent work histories. To capture and address inner processes, participants were encouraged to talk about, and elaborate on, their various experiences and to reflect on how they understand their current career status and its meaning for them.

This rich data provided us with a lens into the lives of our participants into their earlier 30s. In this chapter we follow the young people belonging to the four pathways of career pursuit we described in the previous chapter. By doing this, we aim to learn how earlier plans and dreams, as well as actual work experiences, unfolded over the years and how these young people moved into a new stage of their life of settling down and having a stable job. Through the unfolding of the different career stories, we try to understand additional mechanisms that are likely to play a role in the process of settling down. Finally, we conceptually explore the existence of possible patterns of settling down that might characterize young people and discuss their relevance to career success and well-being.

Dreams, planning, refinding one's way, and flourishing

The story of Alex, described in the previous chapter, is a good example of a young person following the *Consistent Pursuit* pathway. Alex had an articulated plan to become an engineer and work in the field of computers. Along the way he coped competently with setbacks at the place where he was employed as an intern and progressed toward his goal. At age 35 we found that Alex had relocated and was working at an advanced level in a large computer company in Calgary.

In the interview, conducted via Skype, we first asked Alex to describe, in a few words, what his current job meant to him.

> Enjoyment, I really love what I do. Each day I am waiting to get to work. It is fun. I enjoy the work I have to do and enjoy working with the people at work. I feel that this job is *Self-Actualization*. I believe that I have reached the point I was tuned to along the years. My knowledge contributes to what we do here, and it makes me happy.

Alex told us that he is a representative for an Israeli company—Comsolutions—and that his job is to integrate the new techniques and procedures offered by the company. After graduating in electrical engineering, he was still working in the former company he described at age 29. He was waiting for an opportunity to arise. He found the job in Comsolutions, where he felt he could develop further. Moreover, in the new company they encouraged him and helped him when he studied for his master's degree.

To better understand his feelings about the route he took in his life across the years, we asked him whether he has any regrets. Alex answered, "No, and I do not have any regrets. I would repeat it. It was right to move from technical assistance where I was a real expert and start from the bottom in a more promising field."

It was impressive to hear about his sense of competence in leading his life and making changes even when he was employed at a good workplace. In addition, Alex told us that the new job and the relocation were good for his family life.

> We have two little boys. Back home, technical assistance is a 24/7 job. They could call me at 4 am—with just silly problems. So, I was also looking for a job with a better work–life balance. I work now from 9 am till 6 pm. I am invested in my job, but as long as it does not hurt my family.

Over the years Alex was not only focused and consistent in pursuing his goal but also active in searching for the work environment that would allow him to best achieve his goals and to develop further. Alex's inner motivation guided him to cope well with inevitable obstacles and what he described as "political issues" at the first workplace. He was confident enough to leave a workplace that could not provide what he was looking for and offer an opportunity to develop.

Two additional noteworthy aspects arose in Alex's interview. First, Alex described that he feels that he has accomplished his dreams. He greatly enjoys what he does and feels that he has achieved self-actualization. We will discuss this aspect later in this chapter. Second, despite his investment in his career over the years, the family that he has established also plays a central role in his life; and it is important for him to find a good balance between his work and his family. Balancing work and family will be discussed later, in Chapter 7.

Unlike Alex, Becky, classified as belonging to the *Adapted Pursuit* pathway, made a number of changes in her career development. She studied psychology but during her studies felt that psychology was not the field in which she saw herself working in the future. She switched to human resources but did not find a job in this field in which she was interested and that paid well. She worked as a secretary in a firm—a job she disliked. Then, by chance, as better described at the age 35 interview, while working in the firm, a friend introduced her to her husband-to-be. Her husband-to-be lived in a different city, and after 2 months, they decided to live together. This young man was working in a bank at the time, and with his advice and help, Becky found an opening in a bank. At first, she considered this a workplace of convenience. Yet, little by little she found her work more interesting. "I think my studies helped me to adapt well and cope with the requirements of the job in the bank. They like me and I like them. They learned that I am a hardworking person who is willing to learn and to contribute, and after two years I got tenure."

Over time, Becky found meaning in her work at the bank. She explained in detail why she enjoys her work.

> It is really fun and satisfying. It might sound boring to work in a bank. Paperwork and all nonsense formalities. But there are many challenges. Today, banking is marketing. It is a lot of work, sort of psychology with the customers. And I really enjoy it when I see that there are outcomes. It is very demanding in particular when you care about your customers. It requires creativity, people are satisfied. It is fun for me to go to work.

In addition, Becky did acknowledge that she was partly convinced by her future husband to take the job in the bank.

"To be honest, I was looking for this (job) because of convenience. I knew that as a mother I will not be able to take a job where I have to stay for long hours." However, Becky does not see her current job as a compromise, and when asked whether she has any regrets she answered, "No, I am at peace with myself." She added that had she not found the job in the bank, she might do something else. "But in the long run, it was not a mistake. This is part of my development." She again added that she enjoys being able to help the customers and feels that they respect her help and advice.

Becky summarized that she found the job she likes. She added that she might have earned more in a different job but would not have the flexible hours with raising her children. "It is even more than this. I feel that I have an impact at my work. Quite a major impact. People know that if they have a problem, I will do the best to solve their problem. They will be satisfied. And I feel they respect what I say or suggest."

Becky was classified as belonging to the *Adapted Pursuit* pathway. She made a number of changes in her studies and in temporary jobs until she found the position at the bank and settled down. Becky is realistic about the changes she made but perceives the different experiences, even those such as the temporary jobs, as opportunities to learn and that led her to the career in banking she loves (te Riele, 2004). Repeatedly she demonstrated her self-regulatory skills. She was open to advice; capable of learning new skills, coping with challenges, and becoming more established in her position in the bank (Creed et al., 2006); and finding self-expression in her career (Savickas, 1997).

In addition to these achievements, Becky was able to find meaning in her current banking career (Blustein, 2011). Recent developments in the understanding of career adaptability have moved from the question "What and how do people do what they do?" to "Why do they do it?" (Blustein, 2011; Savickas, 2005). These ideas call for paying attention to the importance of one's inner interests, curiosity, and values (Lent & Brown, 2006; Savickas, 2005). Through introspection, individuals become aware of their "personal story" and learn to recognize their inner motivations, which serve as a guide to successful negotiations when considering their occupational realities (Del Corso & Rehfuss, 2011; Savickas, 1997).

Both Alex and Becky were able to achieve what has recently been considered an additional hallmark of career adaptability—the ability not only to cope with inevitable challenges and developments that are common in every career but also to find personal meaning in their careers (Blustein, 2011). This progress is particularly impressive for Becky, considering the major changes and readaptations she made along the way in the area of her career. Yet, despite all the changes, she found her niche. She is flourishing and looking forward to more success in the future.

Searching for your way, adaptations, and compromises

Reading the interviews of the *Survivors* at age 29 and age 35 shows that they were fully employed but that their work was not the career of which they had dreamed, if they had an articulate dream at all. Their stories at the age of 35 demonstrate that many *Survivors* had not made any significant changes in their career. They were still not satisfied with what they did and would prefer to do something else (in some cases, something not clearly defined). They employed a variety of mechanisms and rationalizations to help them remain in their current jobs.

At the second interview, when Reuben was 32 years old, he was still working at the same insurance company. When asked to describe his current work in a few words, he replied, "Compromise and convenience. It is a compromise to be employed in a job I am not interested in. I do not feel that this work is what I am or want to be. Yet, it is stable, and I know that I have the salary I need to support my family." To his credit, Reuben added that although he works to bring a salary home and survive, it is also socially important for him to be employed: "Even if we had enough money, I would not stay home and watch TV all day."

Interviewing Roni 6 years later, she also told us that she was still at the same workplace, the management of a local weekly where she had been working for 8 years. We met her at a delicate time. Due to financial problems, the weekly was to close shortly, and Roni was part of the team in charge of handling the financial aspects of the closure. Though Roni did not enjoy the type of work she was doing, she learned to become part of the place. She was not married, and her workplace was like her family. Due to the emergence of electronic media, the weekly was losing money, and many workers were fired. Roni was liked at the place, and since she was considered broad-minded, she was offered a position in bookkeeping. She learned this work and for 3 years had been working in bookkeeping and customer service.

In retrospect, Roni described that although she did not enjoy her work, she learned how to get along at a workplace and gained confidence. She hopes that her bookkeeping job will offer stability and added that she would like to become more professional in her new job. However, despite looking for her future in bookkeeping, she still has some doubts as to whether she is in the right place. "I feel that I do not make decisions, but find myself being led by the circumstances. I find myself in some place I did not plan earlier." Her doubts surface even when she feels that she enjoys the bookkeeping job. "I like bookkeeping. I am probably a numbers person. Others say this is boring, but I don't agree with this. It is not boring to me." However, her doubts resurfaced in the next sentence: "I am afraid I will become more professional, and then after a couple of years I will realize that this is not for me."

Considered together, Reuben perceives his current work as a compromise he has to make to survive, despite the fact that he has reached a managerial level at his job. Although Roni liked bookkeeping, she felt that she did not make the right decisions that led her into this field of work. On the one hand, both are invested in their current work; but there is something that prevents them from finding, or pursuing, meaning in this. Reading the interviews more carefully suggests that Reuben still dreams about doing something else (that is not clearly defined) and that this prevents him from being more at peace with himself. Similarly, Roni is not too sure that in a few years from now she will not regret continuing working in bookkeeping. Levinson (1978) described a similar phenomenon where people who are successful at their workplace, earn a reasonable salary that provides them financial security, and even enjoy their workmates are still not satisfied. Despite all the rewards that their work carries, it still falls short of gaining personal meaning and does not have true value for them. Furthermore, these "external" achievements come with great internal costs of not finding one's aspired way.

Unlike Becky and Reuben, who are bothered by not finding meaning in their work, Aron's story is not that he does not and did not have a dream that he gave up. In his career story he describes that he worked even while studying in the preparatory program and was always employed in some kind of work he found: head of security in a retailing firm and for the last 5 years in charge of a warehouse in a large company. After completing the college preparatory program, he studied in a technical college, realized that this was not for him, changed to history, and was currently a third-year history student at a university while working a full-time job in customer service. Aron describes himself as a very practical person. "Work is the means for getting money and status," and this has directed his changes in workplaces during the years. When looking for a job, he found a junior job in the warehouse where he works now. The manager of the warehouse came to like him and appreciate his capabilities. The manager also was very considerate when Aron had assignments at the university. When the manager was promoted to a higher-ranking job in the company, he recommended Aron for his job as head of security. This was an unexpected promotion for him.

Despite his current high-level job, nice salary, and car that is provided, Aron is somewhat ambivalent about his job:

> I have to do the dirty work, to be tough with other employees. I see that a person is fired after realizing that he does not really care about the work, but I feel bad. I know it was a just decision, but it is difficult for me.

(How do you explain to yourself having these difficult feelings?)

> I think that this is inside me. It is since childhood and was never resolved. I am afraid of making difficult decisions. And I have to admit to myself, would it not be the former manager I would never pass for this type of job and become a manager, though after all I am not so bad and I bring my voice to this position.

Though Aron is in a good position, he feels that this is a "dirty" job because he has to be tough and strict with others, which he says does suit his character. However, he stays in this position and turned down an offer in a job related to his field of studies because stability is most important for him.

> Stability is most important for me. Making a living, having money for the family. Self-actualization is not my field. It is also important for me to have the flexibility to decide when to come to work and when to go.

Summing up the interview, Aron told us that he does not think of the future.

I live [in] the moment. I know this is not healthy, the market is cruel and might change, I am afraid. And instead of continuing to develop, becoming more professional in my field [the current job], I focus on coming to work, doing my job, and going back home. I am afraid I'll pay for this. And whenever I try to think about the future, I push these thoughts away quickly.

On the surface, Aron has a respectable and well-paying job. He was continuously employed and never out of work. Due to a lack of a dream or a goal, he was always practical, and this worked for him. However, despite this seeming success, Aron was worried about the future and changes that might impact his routine and stability. His only way to cope with these anxieties about the future was to suppress them. Considering together these three career histories suggests that these young people feel that financial security directs their career behavior and leads them to make compromises they necessarily do not like.

Rivka and Ariel were also not guided by a clear plan and switched between domains of studies and jobs in order to be financially secure. They held stable jobs, which they were able to find at that time. Yet, reading their stories at the age of 35 suggested that over time they had developed a number of mechanisms that helped them to feel more satisfied with their lives. First, they started to find some meaning in their work. In addition, they were invested in other aspects of their lives, which led them to experience increasing confidence and greater overall satisfaction with their lives.

After completion of the college preparatory program Rivka started her studies toward a degree in technical management. At the end of the first year, she realized it was too difficult for her and found a job as a secretary. She started computer sciences, which was too difficult and which she did not like. Probing her description of her career story 6 years earlier at age 28 yielded a somewhat different story. She started studying technical management, and to support herself, she worked as a secretary. At some point it was too difficult for her to combine both studies and work. It became too much for her. She told us she physically collapsed. "I did not know where to invest more, where to be more focused. This led to my losing my strength. I became quite desperate and could not carry on. I quit my studies. I wanted freedom and nothing interested me." It took Rivka some time to get back to herself. "I found a job in an advertising agency, got married, and had a child." She completed the interview with "and now I am stuck at home."

Six years later, at the age of 34, Rivka told us that she reached the conclusion that combining a career and raising children is too difficult. It is more important for her to be with her children than to develop her career. However, she added that she realized that working in a nursery school would allow her to be with her children. At age 33 she started to work as an assistant caregiver in a nursery school and enjoys her work: "I am happy to work with children—it is listening to them, it is happiness." Furthermore, she sees herself developing in this field of work and starting her own nursery school.

Rivka moved between studies and different jobs, and her plans changed from time to time. At this stage of her life, age 34, after becoming a mother, the work at a nursery school seemed to fit well with being a mother of a young baby. (Gendered career pathways and women's compromises will be discussed in more detail in Chapter 9.) She appears to be satisfied with the compromise that she made. This could be related to the importance she gives to her being a mother, but it could also be attributed to the fact that she was in the process of developing a new goal to own a private nursery school and perceives that her current position could prepare her for her aspired goal.

Over the years, Ariel, aged 34, could not describe a goal or a dream that he would strive to achieve. For Ariel work meant earning money and achieving greater comfort—to work close to home, and "I cannot see any other meaning." During the year that he was in the preparatory program, a small firm that does carpentry work was looking for a worker. Ariel had no previous experience in this field but was accepted, and he started working there. He has been working there for 12 years. He feels comfortable in this workplace and adds that he is well appreciated there. Furthermore, Ariel described, "it is not that boring, there is room for creativity, and I can sit down and make my time schedule, what sketches to draw. So, it is fun after all."

When asked whether he regrets the choice he made, he answered,

> Sometimes thoughts cross my mind that I could have done something different, more interesting and earn more money, but overall after all these years, it has become easier and you know it is quite good here. But not the materialization of a dream. [For emphasis]

Though Ariel feels that he did not materialize a dream, he started learning to enjoy other aspects of life. He enjoys cooking, and more recently he developed a hobby: "And in last years I am busy with motorcycling, which I really enjoy doing every weekend."

Ariel is also an example of a young man who did not and does not have any clear goal. He found a job in a small carpentry firm, where he has been employed for 12 years. Though disappointed that he had not done more with his life, he continues with his routine and enjoys the stability. Interestingly, despite the fact that he has started to see additional aspects of his current work—that it allows creative expression—he still does not find meaning in what he does. However, as he added at the end of the interview, he became invested in a hobby—motorcycling—and we asked ourselves whether this is a different avenue in which to find and add meaning to one's life, if that meaning is not found in one's work.

Conceptually we might suggest that the career achievements and current status of these *Survivors* suit the earlier definition of career adaptability (Savickas, 1997)—being steadily employed, making a living, and supporting one's family. Of note, many described that they are competent in their current (not aspired) job. Their stories include examples of successful mastery of tasks and the ability to work with others and to enjoy being with work colleagues. Despite being invested in their work and considered good workers, *Survivors* do not seem to psychologically attach to what they do at their jobs and feel that they are missing something. This negative attitude probably interferes with finding some meaning in what they do.

We asked ourselves what could help these young people in their psychological lives. Reading the interviews, it seems that among a number of *Survivors* we could identify the emergence of several mechanisms that could become helpful over the years in changing their attitudes toward their jobs. Rivka, for example, has started to articulate a dream—to become the owner of a nursery school. This might guide her to start perceiving her work as a basis for a future career still to be developed and that would suit her motherhood. Ariel appeared to employ a different mechanism. He became interested and invested in a hobby that might give him the experience of doing something for his soul. Conceptually we suggest that a number of *Survivors* might start looking for different ways to find more meaning in their lives, by either planning for the future or looking for a hobby. Aron, in contrast, was not able to think ahead and prepare for the future. He continued to be invested in his current obligations and consistently removed any thoughts about the future.

Living from one day to the next

Another group of our participants did not develop a career and quite often had not worked in the same workplace for a long period of time. Nora was classified as belonging to the *Confused/Vague* type at our fourth assessment. Interviewing her again 6 years later at the age of 32, Nora had been working for almost 2 years at a small company that provides internet services. When asked to tell us about her current work, she said, "I enjoy it. The people here became my friends and I get up in the morning with a somewhat better feeling." But despite loving her colleagues, she feels that she is not progressing. "It is routine, routine, routine, I am fed up. I was looking for something else but there is nothing on the horizon [for emphasis]."

Nora had recently started studying for a degree in education (which in her words has nothing in common with what she does) but left after a couple of weeks. "I almost broke realizing that this is not for me." Nora further described that she is stuck with a dream of getting a degree that will probably not materialize and decided to live in the moment and move between simple jobs but never miss a day.

Despite being employed for a significant period of time, Nora was not able to find any special meaning in her work. Once she felt bored, she was ready to leave for something that she still did not articulate. She is also confused about studies. At the end of the interview, we got the impression that for Nora being able to have free time was the most important issue in her life. Her daily life was handled from one day to the next.

In their fifth assessment other members of the *Confused/Vague* type described similar experiences of working in temporary jobs, trying to make a living. They might move between different types of work and did not develop expertise in a clear and defined field. One interesting exception was the story of Ronen, aged 34. Over the years Ronen was what he termed a "zigzag worker." He moved between different jobs. Four years previously he found a job in delivery at DHL, which suited him. One day he had a minor accident and was moved to the office. This developed into a steady placement. They liked his commitment, and he stayed in the office. He had recently been promoted and was likely to become assistant manager of a major branch. Ronen was very satisfied with his current position and said that the money was not important to him—he simply enjoys what he does and finds it interesting. Ronen appears to be satisfied with his current job: "it is interesting to work with the different airlines." Ronen was flexible and open enough to develop a positive and committed feeling toward his work, following the change made by his superiors. In contrast, the majority of the *Confused/Vague* type were not able to make any significant progress and continued to live in the moment, moving between jobs.

Conceptualization of the patterns of settling down

Following up on our participants showed that earlier career pursuit pathways played a significant role in the way the young people had progressed toward settling down. Emerging adults who persistently pursued their goals, as well as those who had to give up their earlier goals but were able to identify and consistently pursue a new goal (Heckhausen et al., 2010), described being invested in the career they chose, progressing and seeing their future in that field. *Survivors* employed a variety of mechanisms and adjustments to keep and remain in their jobs. *Survivors* commonly explained that they regarded their work as providing financial security, which became even more important once they established a family. Those who were earlier identified as *Confused/Vague* were generally unable to provide a clear and coherent idea of their occupational lives, and many tended to be unemployed for extended periods of time.

A conceptual reading of the interviews led us to identify three processes that could characterize the patterns of settling down and differentiate between distinctive patterns. Those who belonged earlier to the *Consistent Pursuit* and *Adapted Pursuit* pathways were directed by their goals (either earlier goals or new goals that they had adopted). This ability to pursue goals and readapt to new goals captures the capacity for regulation across development (Heckhausen et al., 2010). This developmental approach, recalling notions in vocational psychology, emphasizes the centrality of self-regulatory processes in career adaptability (Dietrich, Parker, & Salmela-Aro, 2012). This approach emphasizes the importance of planning and the ability to cope with difficulties when facing stress and challenges, to make adaptations, and to be committed to one's new goal. This capacity is crucial, in particular under the current unstable economic and societal conditions (Furlong & Cartmel, 2007). Under these circumstances, the ability to be open and flexible and to accept unexpected and less desired job opportunities has become even more crucial for young people nowadays (Fadjukoff et al., 2010).

Thus, in addition to the importance of goal engagement (or re-engagement) for future flourishing, it is also important to be able to cope with the inevitable challenges at a workplace. Overall, the majority of *Survivors* also described the ways they had to cope, or even struggle, to secure their workplace and achieve financial security; but they focused on "surviving" and lacked any clear plans for the future or how to progress. Furthermore, among those who earlier belonged to the *Consistent Pursuit* and *Adapted Pursuit* pathways described that their progress in their careers also led to finding meaning in what they do (Blustein, 2011; Savickas, 2005). As described in Becky's story, over time she found that the job at the bank connected well with her inner interests, curiosity, and values (Lent & Brown, 2006; Savickas, 2005). Those belonging to the *Consistent Pursuit* and *Adapted Pursuit* pathways were capable of developing and elaborating their "personal stories" within their careers, which further served them for continued progress and learning to recognize their inner motivations. These serve as a guide to successful progress, unlike *Survivors* who were mostly able to just keep their jobs.

Needless to say, those identified earlier as *Confused/Vague* did not describe any of the above skills. They were more likely to be employed in temporary jobs and tended to switch jobs once they had to face a difficulty. Finding meaning in their work was irrelevant or illusory for them. Conceptually we might suggest that the optimal group was guided by their goals, coped competently with work-related demands and stressors, and finally was able to find meaning in their careers. *Survivors* exhibited reasonable capacities to handle work-related demands, which helped them remain stable in the same job for a long period of time. This stability contributed to their financial security and sense of confidence in a job that was not their dream. Of note, a few of the *Survivors* employed additional mechanisms to stabilize their lives. They either started to explore new options that might develop into a dream or became invested in a hobby that they enjoyed and that probably helped them remain stable at work. Members of the *Confused/Vague* pathway often had no clear goals, had difficulties coping with workplace stressors, and, of course, did not find any meaning in their work or any avenue to alleviate their dissatisfaction with their life.

The prevalence of patterns of career adaptability in our sample

In order to identify and find prevalent career adaptability patterns at age 35, during the period of settling down, we employed a mixture of exploratory and confirmatory techniques (Lieblich et al., 1998) to identify the career pursuit pathways at age 29. Through this process of qualitative analysis, three patterns of career adaptability, described below, were found. Subsequently two raters were asked to assign each interview to one of the three patterns. Inter-rater reliability was at the level of kappa = .89. The three patterns of career adaptability, as well as their representative cases, are described below.

Pattern 1—Integrated pattern of career adaptability: 43%

Individuals in the *Integrated* group described being currently employed and enjoying their current occupational status. As exemplified by Alex's case, among affiliates of this pattern, career is associated with an articulated life plan that is complex, diversified, and connected to inner aspirations. While talking about their work and study for both past and current status, these individuals described that they were open and flexible enough to take into account circumstances and to make adaptations required from time to time. Some, such as Becky, had made major changes in their area of interest and work along the way and had found a different career that they felt suited them and was meaningful for them. Overall, individuals belonging to the *Integrated* pattern know what they want, are committed to their career, talk warmly about it, and see their work accomplishments as epitomizing their interests and their future.

Pattern 2—Compromised pattern of career adaptability: 38%

Individuals belonging to the *Compromised* group were permanently employed, and their lives appeared settled. Exemplified by the stories told by Reuben and Roni, when these young people were asked to reflect on their feelings about their careers, their affect conveyed some sense of dissatisfaction and possibly even negativity. They reported that they were not really connected to their occupation and had a sense that they would have preferred to do something else. However, their aspirations were quite amorphous and not focused. Moreover, in the background they had some sort of dream to do something else, but the dream appeared and felt quite remote. In other cases, as exemplified by Aron's story, there were young people who are very "practical," were dedicated to their current work (which could be a good job), and did not think about the future. Yet, when further probed about their careers, they were clearly worried about the future and not confident that the current job would last forever.

Pattern 3—Vague pattern of career adaptability: 19%

Throughout the interview, individuals belonging to the *Vague* pattern were unable to provide a clear and coherent idea of what they would like to do with their lives. They were unable to hold a job for a prolonged period and seemed to be continuously moving between periods of employment and unemployment. They had difficult feelings about work in general—"it would be better if I did not need to work." They lacked any articulate plans to which they could stay committed. Their life was characterized by constant daily struggles that hardly left any room for self-expression or reflection. Even Nora, who had been in her current job for almost 2 years, was not attached to her job and was ready to leave when another opportunity presented itself.

Taken together, more than 40% of our participants described their careers as being associated with an articulated life plan that was complex and diversified (Heckhausen et al., 2010), and they were able to cope with challenges and stressors (Dietrich, Jokisaari, & Nurmi, 2012). In addition, their careers were connected to inner aspirations and were meaningful to them (Blustein, 2011; Savickas, 2005, 2011). In contrast, about 20% were not able to provide a clear and coherent idea of their occupational lives, and they tended to be unemployed for extended periods of time.

The identification of the *Compromised* pattern, which represented almost 40% of our sample, was new to us. This group of young people appeared to have settled down, managed their daily lives, and made the transition quite successfully.

However, despite their daily functioning, they reported an inner feeling that their current occupation was not exactly what they would have wished to do, and they did not feel fully emotionally connected to their jobs. These young people appeared to have compromised on a job that did not truly fit their inclinations and interests (Lent & Brown, 2006; Savickas, 2005) and still did not find meaning in this (Blustein, 2011).

However, as arose in the interviews of members of the *Compromised* pattern, the act of settling down was to some extent the result of examining the circumstances and honestly weighing one's capabilities (Dietrich, Jokisaari, & Nurmi, 2012). Under certain circumstances (and probably considering the current economic instabilities), some young people probably decided to settle down and assume an adult role, although some dreams or hopes to do something else might still exist. In her model of developmental regulation, Heckhausen (1999) described the mechanism of goal adjustment, namely, disengagement from an unattainable goal and the pursuit of an alternative goal. The ability to realize that a desired goal is unattainable and that a different goal needs to be formulated enhances one's self-mastery and is beneficial to well-being. We would like to extend Heckhausen's model and suggest that being able to go on with one's life despite the existence of a dormant dream might also be considered a form of adaptation. The *Compromised* pattern of career adaptability may also recall an identity status that is short of identity achievement but more advanced than foreclosure, as described by Luyckx and colleagues' (2006) integrative model of identity formation. Furthermore, the stories of the members of this pattern suggested that there was an initial penchant to search for meaning in what they do. Ariel's story was particularly interesting. He settled for his carpentry job, and at some point it appeared more than routine work for him. In addition, he started to find other avenues for meaning in his life. He learned to enjoy cooking and, above all, developed a hobby for motorcycling, which became very meaningful to him.

In sum, we may suggest that considering the current conditions of increasing unemployment and economic uncertainty (Furlong & Cartmel, 2007), some young people have to make compromises so that they can carry on with their lives and hold a job, even if it is not the job they dreamed of doing.

Patterns of career adaptability and well-being

In order to further understand the future outcomes of the three career adaptability patterns, we compared members of the three patterns in terms of settling on their level of salary, satisfaction at work, and satisfaction in general at age 35. (To rate level of salary, we told participants the level of average income in Israel. They were told to indicate whether their income is below the average [1],

Table 4.1 *Outcomes at Age 35 Across the Three Career Adaptability Patterns: Means, SDs, and F values*

	Integrated	Compromised	Vague	F
Level of salary	2.11 (.88)	1.78 (1.01)	1.28 (.83)	4.92**
Life satisfaction	4.05 (.71)	3.55 (.59)	3.43 (.85)	6.37**
Work satisfaction	4.04 (.86)	3.59 (1.01)	3.08 (1.07)	5.94**

**$p < .01$.

about the average [2], or above the average [3]; satisfaction was rated on a level from 1 to 5.) Findings are presented in Table 4.1. As can be seen, members of the *Integrated* pattern reported the highest level of income and were most satisfied with their work, compared to members of the *Vague* pattern. Compromisers were in between and did not differ significantly from the two other patterns of settling. However, when level of general satisfaction was assessed, compromisers reported a lower level of satisfaction, were more similar to the members of the *Vague* pattern, and differed significantly from members of the *Integrated* pattern. This suggests that compromising at the stage of settling down might bear a cost.

In sum, reading the in-depth interviews collected at about age 35 and subjecting these to a qualitative analysis yielded three different career adaptability patterns that characterized the patterns of settling down in the mid-30s. A substantial number of young people successfully attained *Integrated* career adaptability—they followed or adapted their dreams and found meaning in what they did. In contrast, a small number of young people were found to be vague or confused about their occupational plans and were not satisfied with their lives. A third group, comprising almost 40% of our sample, functioned well on a daily basis but continued to mention an unfulfilled dream or that they were still looking for a dream. It appeared that once these young people were supposed to start settling down, they made compromises considering their life circumstances or employment options. However, despite making a compromise, they could not give up on a dream that was in many cases unattainable, unrealistic, or even not yet well defined.

Considered together, our findings describing development from the age of 23 until the age of 35 suggested that while periods of instability, such as changes in workplaces or careers, were found, these changes resulted in finding anew one's goal or making comprises and moving forward toward settling down. We observed that young people made adaptations at two stages. First, during the earlier years of emerging adulthood, among those who lost their way, a substantial number were able to find, become invested in, and achieve a new goal (career). Among those who were not successful in setting a clear goal or achieving a goal to which they had aspired for a substantial number of years, some found a stable job, made compromises, and settled down. Previous studies used *floundering* to characterize the lives of emerging adults (Krahn et al., 2013; Nelson & Padilla-Walker, 2013). Our findings, collected over a period of 12 years, indeed also found that floundering was quite common. Yet, more important was to observe the processes of exploration in which individuals sought the work or career that would best meet their career expectations or were ready to make compromises in order to settle down. Conceptually we thus suggest that it is important to uncover the processes of adaptation and growth that characterize the lives of emerging adults. In the following two chapters we present and discuss the development of and changes in romantic experiences and relationships that take place in the lives of emerging adults.

5
Romantic Pathways Among Emerging Adults

Between Fluidity and Progression

The achievement of intimacy and commitment in a romantic relationship is considered one of the critical developmental tasks marking the entry into adulthood (Conger et al., 2000). However, nowadays fewer young people are involved in long-lasting and committed relationships, and the age of marriage has been postponed to the later 20s (Shulman & Connolly, 2013). Many young people are in and out of relationships, while an increasing number tends to engage in short-term relationships or casual sexual encounters. In this chapter we try to describe and understand the meaning of the different romantic experiences. Do short and casual encounters simply represent instabilities and floundering during the emerging adulthood years, or can the different experiences also serve as an arena in which to learn how to handle and master romantic relationships and progress toward commitment?

As described in Chapter 1, our participants were given two in-depth interviews at the fourth assessment when they were about 28–29 years old. In the first interview they were asked to describe their career history, described in Chapter 3. In the second interview, relevant to the current chapter, they were asked to tell the story of their romantic life. This rich data provides us with insights into the different ways that emerging adults handle and progress in their romantic lives. Employing a multi-method approach, we explore the diverse pathways of romantic experiences and the extent to which different experiences led to progress into stable, intimate, and committed romantic relationships. Our analysis of the interviews is supported by the stories told by our participants, and in their words, to demonstrate the different romantic pathways.

Statistics and demographic studies from industrialized countries have shown that the period during which young people assume adult responsibilities, gain economic independence, and marry has moved to the end of the third decade of life (Arnett, 2004; Settersten & Ray, 2010). The earlier entry into romantic relationships in adolescence, combined with the postponement of age of marriage, means that it is quite common to find individuals who engage in premarital relationships over a decade (Carver et al., 2003). Observation of the romantic lives of the majority of young people during these years shows that they might move between transitory and inconsistent states, being in and out of relationships (Cohen et al., 2003; European Group for Integrated Social Research, 2001). In a study following adolescents until the age of 25, Rauer and colleagues (2013) found that about 60% were involved in short-lived and non-stable relationships across the years. Even among those observed to be in steady relationships at one point in time, there was only a 56% likelihood of them being in a steady relationship at the later assessment, and not necessarily the same relationship (Meier & Allen, 2009). Furthermore, even cohabitation, which in the past often led to commitment and marriage, has become just another form of a non-stable relational pattern for many young people (Manning & Smock, 2005).

This delay in marriage, and the lesser importance placed on being married, has been associated with sexual permissiveness among emerging adults (Carroll et al., 2007). Within this context, an increasing focus on the study of casual sexual relationships among young adults, and among college students in particular, can be observed. A number of studies conducted on college students suggest that more than half have been involved in casual sexual encounters (Claxton & van Dulmen, 2013). These encounters take place either with a familiar person (friends with benefits) or with a stranger (Halpern-Meekin et al., 2013). While in some cases these encounters might be motivated by the hope of starting a relationship (Owen & Fincham, 2011), in most cases there was no expectation of a continued romantic relationship (Bogle, 2008).

Considered together, the romantic lives of emerging adults were found to reflect a general pattern of fluidity in life task commitments. The delay in commitment and frequent involvement in non-stable romantic and sexual relationships have been attributed to the abundance of demands that emerging adults face. Emerging adults must navigate their own life tasks (such as work/education and the development of financial resources), as well as coordinate these decisions with their partners. Due to the highly unstable social and economic circumstances in today's world, working through these tasks has become difficult, leading emerging adults to postpone long-term commitments in favor of less restricting short-term involvements (Shulman & Connolly, 2013). A young person might deliberately decide not to become romantically committed or even opt out of a lasting relationship that is stressful or does not support their career or educational aspirations (Shulman & Connolly, 2013; te Riele, 2004). In contrast, involvement in a long-term, committed relationship might not necessarily indicate greater romantic competence. A person might "slide" into a relationship that is not necessarily optimal yet provides some sense of security and economic stability (Rhoades et al., 2006). Thus, it is very possible that fluctuations and changes might be functional when they are aimed at finding the most suitable romantic affiliation considering one's circumstances.

Thelen and Smith's (1996) developmental systems theory contends that development is not necessarily always linear. Progressions are preceded by regressions but can also be followed by regressions. New structures or forms of behavior can become stable only after a period of exploration and mastering of new skills. The completion of change can be expected only after different skills have been successfully reorganized into a new integrated function or ability (Mayes, 2001).

Thus, individual fluctuations, as well as a variety of paths taken by different individuals, can be expected in the process of learning a new form of behavior. In a similar vein, romantic and sexual fluctuations among emerging adults can be understood as part of a process of exploring relationships and searching for one's niche. Different paths, including back-and-forth fluctuations, can thus be expected. Individuals might alternate between casual sexual encounters and short-lived or long-lasting romantic relationships, until the time they learn to handle a long-term relationship and are ready for commitment. The ability to become intimately involved in a stable relationship signifies if and when a "new and stable form of behavior" has been achieved (Lewis, 2011; Thelen & Smith, 1996).

Thus, it is important to understand the dynamic of a romantic or sexual encounter and not assess it only with regard to its stability or linear progression. Fluctuations might be functional when they are aimed at finding the most suitable romantic affiliation considering one's current circumstances such as career-related responsibilities, while remaining in a difficult relationship is not necessarily adaptive. This calls for a more extensive understanding of the patterns that romantic fluctuations might take during emerging adulthood and their meaning within a broader process of development over a period of time. In the next section we describe the romantic history interview that participants were given and how the interview was analyzed.

The romantic history interview and its qualitative analysis

The interview was comprised of two stages: first, a spontaneous story was told, after which the questions were presented (Rosenthal, 1993). Participants were asked and encouraged to tell the story of their romantic life over the last years, from their own point of view. They were subsequently asked to elaborate and further explain topics and issues that were raised in their stories. In particular, they were asked to elaborate on their personal, social, and romantic/family dreams, as well as to reflect on changes and turning points in their romantic histories. To capture and address inner processes, participants were encouraged to talk about, and elaborate on, their various experiences and to reflect on the extent to which they felt that they had progressed on their aspired track or the extent to which they were still uncertain about what they really wanted in their romantic lives.

Employing this technique of interviewing, we were able to obtain detailed information about their current and recent romantic experiences, as well as about difficulties they might have had in the past and how they addressed these feelings and expectations about their romantic involvements and experiences and the meaning of these to them. Interviews were recorded, transcribed, and analyzed as follows.

We employed a mixture of exploratory and confirmatory techniques (Lieblich et al., 1998) to identify pathways of romantic development. To this end we considered various components such as describing decisions, events, difficulties, and coping, as highlighted by the different theoretical approaches and research findings cited above. In addition, we considered the extent to which romantic fluctuations (sporadic involvements, on/off relationships, sexual encounters) were associated with, or led to, later involvement in a lasting relationship and achievement of intimacy. Themes that emerged from interviews refined our further reading of the material, resulting in analysis in the following manner. First, a general pathway of romantic development was identified, after which the existence of the particular pathway in each interview was assessed. Refuting or negating evidence led to the rediscussion and refinement of a pathway. This back-and-forth exploratory and confirmatory process led to the adaptation and reformulation of proposed pathways of romantic development to ensure that all personal stories were well represented. Of note, the majority of respondents tended to describe their romantic history from the time of their graduation from high school. Fewer described their history from the early stages of adolescence.

Identification of romantic pathways

Employing a mixture of exploratory and confirmatory techniques (Lieblich et al., 1998), two expert developmental and clinical psychologists identified four different pathways. Of note, three women and two men identified themselves as homosexuals. One of the women described that though she would like to get married, she had also considered a relationship with a woman. The stories of these young men and women were not included in the current analysis, which is a limitation of this study. However, later in the chapter, we will refer briefly to this topic. In addition, we did not reach agreement on the classification of three cases. As a result, the current findings relate to only 92 participants. Two raters were trained to identify and differentiate between the four pathways on 10 transcripts. Subsequently, they coded the rest of the transcripts independently. Inter-rater reliability was at the level of kappa = .86.

In the next sections we describe the four romantic pathways that were identified. For each pathway we present the stories of different individuals to better capture the nature and the developmental history of young people belonging to each pathway.

Pathway 1—Sporadic short involvements and casual romantic encounters

This pathway is characterized by romantic fluctuations that never moved toward or developed into steady and long-lasting relationships. Members of this pattern group might quite often be involved in casual encounters or short-duration involvements. However, there might be long periods of time between one romantic involvement and the next. Some of these individuals described difficulties in being close to another person to become intimately involved. Others described negative experiences with a past partner involving harm or betrayal. This type of event was described as a sudden moment of acknowledgment or painful insight, which led to the termination of the relationship at the time, as well as to suspicion, reservations, and difficulty trusting partners and establishing future relationships. This pathway included 35.9% of the sample.

Daria, a 29-year-old woman who works with her parents in a small business they have, is a good example for this pathway. When asked to describe her current romantic status, she responded, "On the edge. Yeah on the edge as you hear. I date from time to time, but I hardly had a serious relationship." Daria was once involved in a relationship that lasted for 4 months. She attributed the reason for hardly having been in a romantic relationship to her attitude and behavior: "I am very closed, keep distance. This was the reason that my first boyfriend left. This is what I am, it is difficult to change." For this reason, she only dates once in a while.

In the interview, in quite a flat tone, Daria described that this pattern of life suits her. Of course, she hopes to establish a family; but now work keeps her busy, and she claims to have less time to invest in her romantic life.

Joseph, also aged 29, described a similar romantic history and is an additional example who demonstrates the romantic attitudes and behavior of affiliates of the *Sporadic* pathway. He hardly dates and during the years had only two relationships that did not last longer than 4 months. "This is a problematic issue for me. But to be honest I do not have time to be in a relationship. [He is studying for a degree in [c]omputers.] I don't say it based on my experience but my friends told me that a girl wants to talk with you for 2 hours on the phone, I hate talking on the phone and have not time." Additionally, Joseph told us that he was discouraged on one of his dates and decided to take a break. "We went out, it was fun, but then the girl told me that I am selfish and not a nice person." In his opinion, this was very insulting because he considers himself to be kind and willing to help.

Both Daria and Joseph date from time to time, but overall they are, as they said, "not [invested] in this business." Reading their interviews suggests that they probably have difficulties establishing relationships and use different explanations such as that it demands too much investment, which does not suit them at this stage of their lives.

Yossi, also aged 29, described a different romantic experience that led him to refrain from dating. When he was 25, he dated a girl for a couple of months and fell in love with her. To his surprise, he found out that she was married and was cheating on her husband. Since then, he replied, "I simply stopped trusting women."

Close examination of the participants belonging to the *Sporadic* pathway suggests that this type of romantic behavior (or non-behavior) can be attributed to personal difficulties, such as feeling uncomfortable getting close to another person. It might also be a response to a traumatic event in a previous romantic relationship. At this stage it was difficult to assess whether these young people would have the skills to "grow out" of this condition. It sounded as though Yossi was hinting that he had started considering moving forward, but this was not the case with Daria and Joseph.

Pathway 2—Lengthy relationships but absence of experiential learning

This pathway includes individuals who reported involvement in lasting relationships that were not necessarily intimate and mutually respectful. Relationships were described as part of a routine. For better or for worse, partners did not wish to make any significant changes. Some individuals described efforts to appease a partner in order to maintain a relationship intact. Members of this pathway could not reflect on what was happening in their relationships. For example, when asked why a former relationship ended, they were not able to offer an explanation or offered insufficient, or even unreasonable, explanations for a significant change in their romantic history. They were also not able to point to any significant turning points in their lengthy relationships. Of the sample, 10.9% was affiliated with this pathway.

The story of Nora, aged 27, whom we have described in the previous chapters, exemplifies this pathway well. Nora started telling us that she is "recovering" from a separation 4 months earlier. She was in a relationship for about 2 years that they defined more as friends of a sort. About 8 months before the separation, the relationship evolved into a boyfriend/girlfriend relationship. Nora described that they had enjoyed being together, and she was very much in love. However, at some point Nora felt that he "evaporated" and was not available. She asked him to be clearer, and he sent her an e-mail that he was not interested in her.

Nora was very hurt and could not understand how this happened. Listening to Nora's story suggests that she did not describe the relationship she had. She mostly described how much she had enjoyed it, going out with him, but not much more. The young man probably did not consider their time together as a relationship, but she was not aware of this. Nora has no idea why he broke off the relationship or what went wrong and hopes that he will return to her.

Nora is still in pain in reaction to the last separation, but her story of the relationship is not very coherent. This incoherence and lack of any reflection also appeared in her former romantic relationships. When she was 19 years old, she was in a relationship for almost 3 years with a man 8 years older than herself. Later she was in a relationship for 4 years with a divorced man 15 years older, which also ended. Nora described that "All my boyfriends wanted to marry, to settle down but I did not feel I am ready." Nora was unable to clearly explain what exactly happened in her previous relationships.

Racheli, aged 28, is a young woman in a 6-year-long relationship. She describes the relationship as on and off due to quarrels that break out from to time. When asked to explain how they manage the fights, Racheli commented, "We learned how to get along with the fights—a status quo."

Describing the history of her relationship, Racheli told us that she met the boy at the preparatory program, but he was not interested in her. She decided to persevere with him until he gave in:

> I would come to his place, stay till after midnight, and next day again. I was fighting and I was successful. He understood that I am serious. But then problems started. He dated at the same time another girl. But insistence is paying off.

They are still together, though it is not clear how much the boy is really interested in her.

Considered together, both Nora's and Racheli's romantic histories represent a pattern of involvement in long-lasting relationships, contrary to the impression that emerging adults fluctuate between relationships and casual encounters. However, for each of them in their unique ways, the relationships did not develop over time. Nora was mainly invested in her daily whereabouts in each relationship, having fun and enjoying being with a partner. Her stories did not include events in which they had to address problems. The only problem she described was when her boyfriend decided to separate.

In her relationship, Racheli tried to avoid conflicts and "solve" them in 5 minutes. Racheli's description of her behavior in the relationship, as well as the behavior of her boyfriend, clearly demonstrates that they did not "see" one another's perspective (Shulman et al., 2011). Racheli did not want to accept that the person she had a crush on was not truly interested in her. She was not able to see the difficulties in the relationship and to learn how to handle them competently. Tuval-Mashiach and Shulman (2006) described that the capacity to address disagreements facilitates the deepening of a relationship and the development of intimacy. Thus, though being involved for long periods of time with a romantic partner, in the two cases of Nora and Racheli, their long-lasting romantic involvement did not and could not serve as a learning experience for progression toward intimacy. Moreover, it seemed that Nora tended to replicate this non-adaptive relational pattern in her relationships.

Pathway 3—Moving from casual to steady involvements

The romantic course of members of this pathway took different forms and could mostly be described by instabilities and fluctuations across the years. However, a closer inspection of this pathway suggested that overall these emerging adults were moving toward a steady involvement after a period of exploration. Most importantly, they were able to reflect on their romantic involvements and described a process of learning from experiences (similar to that described in Pathway 1), which led them to be able to express and accept intimacy and develop toward commitment. Past experiences could also be difficult; for example, a young man described that he had learned in a former difficult relationship that he had to keep his voice, and this helped him develop an intimate and committed relationship with a new partner. Of the sample, 32.6% was affiliated with this pathway.

Rafi's romantic experiences are a good example of this romantic pathway. At the age of 28 (the fourth assessment), Rafi was still studying for a degree in engineering and was employed part-time in a high-tech company. He started dating quite late, when he was 22 years old. He fell very much in love with a girl. Then Rafi added that

> I loved her more than I loved myself. At times, I was her dog, really for her I was a dog. I learned OK you have a girlfriend, you love her. But you are a person, not a puppy to play with. If she steps on you and you say ouch she has to understand, to hear it, to listen.

Rafi decided to end the relationship. Since then he has not been in a long relationship but explains that this relationship was a learning experience for him. He learned that he should not silence his voice in a relationship and expect to be respected. He understands that there might be disagreements and conflicts, but these need to be discussed, not suppressed, in order to keep the relationship intact.

At the time of the interview, Rafi had been in a new relationship for a short time. He described that he was very cautious at the beginning and was constantly checking if the girl respected him and his point of view. He realized that she was kind and his wishes were respected. Rafi added, "Look, we are both stubborn but we have learned to work together and I appreciate the way she [treats me]. We both learned to make compromises." Rafi ended the interview by telling us that he feels that this is a relationship in which they respect one another.

Reading Rafi's story shows that he was not steadily dating, but one relationship in which he was involved shaped his understanding of how to handle a relationship and negotiate between his own and his partner's wishes. It was a difficult and, to some extent, an abusive experience that significantly affected his behavior. Most importantly, he learned to listen to his own voice, not to silence himself (Jack, 1991), and this realization was carried forward into his current relationship, with which he is satisfied.

Gideon (aged 30 at the fourth assessment) described a romantic history that recalled Rafi's. After completing his army service (at the age of 21) he had been in and out of romantic experiences that never developed into relationships that lasted more than 2 months. At the age of 24 he met a girl: "It was a long relationship, exhausting and in some way painful. It was awful, only demanding, demanding, demanding and giving nothing, nothing." They separated but met again by coincidence and moved in together. However, fights became a common scene, and they separated again. Gideon told himself that she is not the only girl in the world and that there are better girls out there, but since then he has not been in a serious relationship for more than a year.

In retrospect, Gideon commented that this was an important experience for him. He realized that he was attracted to her physically. It raised his self-esteem dating such a beautiful girl. "My friends were very impressed. But I think this was childish." Gideon added that this relationship was a turning point for him.

> After I left I realized that there were many issues where I closed my eyes. You should not close your eyes. You should not give in. Sometimes you have to ask, to insist and if it does not change to leave, to let it go. I learned that the physical aspect is not the most important part. Your partner has to be first your close friend, like a buddy. A healthy relationship is built on something beyond sex. After all, it was a special period and it made [me] ready for a real relationship.

Like Rafi, Gideon learned from a difficult relationship how not to behave in a relationship—"don't give in, say what you think." Both men were able to draw lessons from their former relationships, which helped them handle their future relationships more competently. Interestingly, Gideon indicated that his casual encounters also helped him to learn more about himself and how to behave with a partner. In sum, these young people were capable of growing out of, and reflecting on, a difficult romantic experience, even casual encounters, and moving on successfully toward a stable and fulfilling relationship.

Pathway 4—Steady relationships

Individuals affiliated with this pathway described a tendency to form and maintain long-lasting relationships. It was quite common for our participants to form their first significant romantic relationship during their military service, and many of the members affiliated with this pathway were still involved in this relationship and had married, or had plans to marry, this partner. These young people consistently described a process of learning that took two forms. Individuals described learning lessons from past less successful romantic involvements about how to interact efficiently with a partner and develop true intimacy, recalling the *Moving from Casual to Steady Involvements* pathway. Others described a process of learning that took place, or still takes place, within the relationship, such as learning to trust and rely on a partner. In contrast to emerging adults following Pathways 2 and 3, these individuals show a short exploration period, after which they develop and learn within a long-lasting relationship. Alternatively, their "exploration"—process of learning—takes place within a long relationship that is not necessarily as they would have wished. A little over 20% of the sample was affiliated with this pathway.

Alex, whose career development we described in Chapters 3 and 4, also described an early learning experience. When he was much younger he had a girlfriend he describes as "very provocative," with which he did not feel comfortable; but that taught him the type of girl he wanted. At the fourth assessment, at age 29, he had been in a relationship with the same girl for 6 years, and they were about to get married. Alex is very determined in his attitude toward relationships. Asking him if they had experienced any separation, he answered, "No, I do not believe in on–off relationships. If there is a major problem that you need to separate probably it is better that you don't return to each other." They might have disagreements from time to time but have learned how to cope with these. "We had to learn that we do not agree on everything," but they also learned "not to stay angry." We got the impression that this is a relationship that emphasizes "practical good management," though Alex also emphasized the importance of investing in your relationship.

Natalie is in a relationship that has lasted for almost 3 years. She met D. while backpacking abroad, and they enjoyed one another's company during the trip. However, things started to change after they returned. Natalie learned that D. is hardworking and very calculated. They hardly found time to meet. Natalie told us that she loves D. and sees her future with him, but she does not want to sit the whole week waiting for him. She started to hint that she might leave this relationship. D. was very hurt and said that he is ready to make compromises. Natalie loves the boy; she thinks he is kind and affectionate, but they still need to learn to find more quality time to be together.

Unlike Alex whose relationship was developing toward greater intimacy and commitment, Natalie's relationship is more complex. She is still considering if the relationship with D. meets her expectations. It is quite clear that a process of learning took place in this 3-year-long relationship, yet Natalie is not still sure in which direction this relationship will develop. It appears that even if she and her boyfriend are not able to resolve their differing attitudes successfully, they will be able to learn a lesson from this long joint experience that would contribute to a future relationship.

Romantic pathways among non-heterosexual young adults

As indicated above, the sample included only a few non-heterosexual participants, and our data cannot provide clear information about possible romantic pathways among non-heterosexual young adults. However, the stories of two participants might be indicative. Yair describes himself as homosexual and not looking for a relationship. He is active on Tinder and looks for a sexual partner once a week. They are casual encounters that are not aimed at finding a relationship. Yair told us that this is the life that suits him and will continue for the foreseeable future. Yair did not wish to comment further, and our impression was that he feels that this "sporadic" pattern suits him best.

In contrast, Elchanan's romantic life story is completely different. Elchanan grew up in a religious family, and it was very difficult for him to realize and accept that he is gay. There were years when he was quite depressed and refrained from dating and going out. Slowly he entered the gay community and was introduced to casual encounters, but he realized that this was not the lifestyle he wishes to pursue. During these difficult years he was more invested in his studies and recently completed a master's degree in economics. Elchanan was looking for what he termed a "serious relationship." Two years ago he met a guy of whom he is fond, and they have developed a close and intimate relationship. Elchanan plans and hopes that they will get married and have children. Elchanan's romantic history recalls the *Casual to Steady* pathway. However, unlike among heterosexual partners who have to learn how to develop and substantiate their relationship, Elchanan had to come to terms with his sexual identity before he was ready to pursue a relationship in a serious manner. A separate study on non-heterosexual young adults is necessary to better understand the road that these young people need to take in their romantic exploration and development (Macapagal et al., 2015).

Pathways of romantic involvement: Between fluidity and progression

By analyzing in-depth interview data, and guided by the developmental systems theory (Mayes, 2001; Thelen & Smith, 1998), we found that emerging adults' romantic involvements across the years could be characterized by four different pathways of integrating fluidity and stability. The majority of our participants—68.5%—comprising the *Sporadic* and *Casual to Steady* involvement pathways, could be characterized by pathways indicating a variety of fluctuations between casual sexual and romantic experiences, short-lived relationships, or periods of having no romantic interaction and sometimes interest. This recalls the classical descriptions of emerging adulthood instabilities (Arnett, 2004; Cohen et al., 2003) and more recent findings that the majority—almost 60% of emerging adults—were involved in non-stable relationships most of the time (Rauer et al., 2013).

However, members of the *Casual to Steady* involvements pathway, which accounted for half of the fluid cases in our sample, were able to learn from their previous romantic experiences, whether these were short and non-stable or lasted for some time. They were able to overcome failures and disappointments and move toward the establishment of stable and intimate relationships. While previous studies perceived such fluctuations as less adaptive (Arnett, 2004; Cohen et al., 2003; Meier & Allen, 2009), our findings suggest that experiencing fluctuations might, after all, be beneficial. The stories told by these young people indicate that involvements in sporadic relationships, and even abstinence for an extended period of time, can potentially serve as an arena for learning how to interact within, and solidify, a close romantic relationship (te Riele, 2004). In contrast, members of the *Sporadic* pathway did not gain anything from their variety of romantic experiences. Their stories focused mostly on their mundane experiences and were void of any reflection. Alternatively, some of the stories revealed that these young people were still preoccupied with a previous, difficult romantic experience that they were not able to overcome. Their dwelling on a past difficult experience prevented them from moving toward a different and more flexible romantic attitude. They appeared to focus too much on their wounds and lacked the capacity to integrate the perspective of their partners for the benefits of a more mature relationship.

Members of the *Steady Relationships* pathway, like members of the *Casual to Steady* involvements pathway, also described a process of learning and evolving within their relationships. Their stories included examples of learning from past successful and less successful romantic experiences, which together enabled them to learn how to interact competently with a partner and develop true intimacy. Past findings described that positive life events can lead to new opportunities, enhance self-esteem, and facilitate adaptation to new situations, while negative events set in motion negative chain reactions that are highly likely to worsen one's opportunities (Rönkä et al., 2001; Stanley et al., 2006). Our findings suggest that the process is even more complex and that not only positive experiences led to change and growth. A significant number of our participants described difficult experiences such as betrayal. Yet, these difficult experiences led them to new realizations about themselves in a relationship and facilitated the building of a new significant intimate relationship. Thus, it is the ability to face an event, even when it is painful, that has the potential to lead to favorable change.

The *Lengthy Relationships but Absence of Experiential Learning* pathway might appear an adaptive pattern (Meier & Allen, 2009; Rauer et al., 2013). However, in-depth interviews with these young people showed that while they tended to be involved mainly in long and lasting romantic relationships, they were not able to develop within these relationships and move toward real commitment. Furthermore, in the interviews they were not able to explain events in their relationships and the reasons a relationship took a certain direction. Their behavior resembled that of individuals who "slide" into relationships that are beneficial and secure at a certain point in time but do not necessarily develop and deepen over time (Stanley et al., 2006).

Considered together, the romantic pathways that emerged in the current study recall, to some extent, romantic patterns described by Meier and Allen (2009) and Rauer and colleagues (2013) that range between "chaos and order" (Mayes, 2001). Conceptually, the different romantic pathways we identified, and in particular the ways participants described their progression, can be embedded within the developmental systems theory (Thelen & Smith, 1998). Development is intuitively perceived as one growing, learning, maturing, and becoming bigger in size and better. As such, it is expected that romantic relationships will develop linearly, from sporadic and non-stable encounters to committed relationships (Shulman & Connolly, 2013). However, development is not necessarily always linear, and fluidity also characterizes children's course of development (Knight, 2011). As children grow, they have to adjust to changing circumstances, new information, and changing capabilities that need to be slowly transformed into new structures. Until new forms of organization are consolidated, behavior might seem unstable and even chaotic. New structures or forms of behavior only become stable following the completion of change in an old function and reorganization of different functions into a new integrated function or ability (Mayes, 2001). Embedded within the developmental systems theory, Linda Mayes (2001) emphasizes that what might seem chaos or disorder to the outside observer might encapsulate normative processes of variability and instability where new structures are learned and aimed toward integration. This is the way we suggest understanding romantic fluidity among emerging adults.

In their outline of the developmental systems theory, Thelen and Smith (1998) described how different and sometimes contradictory "pieces" of behavior are organized into a new structure. However, they did not describe how organization is achieved. In addition, the studies conducted within the framework of the developmental systems theory focused on motor development among young children. Interviewing individuals about their romantic history, as was done in our project, helped us capture the variety of romantic processes characterizing emerging adulthood. Our qualitative data indicated that individuals' ability to reflect on, and learn from, their romantic experiences is conducive to understanding the meaning of the various changes that occur within a relationship and benefiting from these. Thus, the ability to reflect on, and learn from, one's experiences is probably the mechanism that paves the way for a "new structure" of relationship (Fonagy & Target, 2005). Fluctuations can thus become an impetus for learning new experiences, while staying in a long-lasting relationship is not always beneficial.

Romantic pathways and attainment of romantic goals

We were interested in examining the extent to which different romantic pathways are associated with the level of goal striving and goal stress in the domain of romantic relationships, as well as the level of satisfaction and the change in number of depressive symptoms in participants at age 29. To this end, participants were given a modified version of Little's (1983) Personal Project Analysis. Participants were asked to write down three of their most important goals. In this chapter we focus on their romantic goal. Participants were then asked to appraise their romantic goal along three dimensions: the importance they assign to striving for this goal ("to what extent is the project important to you"), goal progress ("to what extent have you made progress realizing this goal"), and stress ("to what extent is it stressful to attain the goal").In addition, participants were asked to complete a seven-item measure that assessed their life satisfaction in regard to different domains such as social relationships and leisure activities (Zullig et al., 2009). Items were rated on a scale from 1 (*not satisfied*) to 5 (*very satisfied*). Cronbach's alpha was .88. Finally, we compared changes in levels of depressive symptoms across the four romantic pathways between the first assessment at age 23 and the last assessment at age 35. For this we used participants' report on the level of depressive symptoms at these two assessments. Depressive symptoms were assessed via the six-item Depression subscale (e.g., "How often did you feel lonely during the last month?"). Items were rated on a five-point scale from 1 (*little or no symptoms*) to 5 (*many symptoms*) from the Brief Symptom Inventory (Derogatis & Melisaratos, 1983). Cronbach's alphas for the two assessments were .92 and .94, respectively.

We expected that members of the *Steady Relationships* pathway and those progressing from *Casual to Steady* would report the highest level of goal persistence and goal attainment as compared to members of the *Sporadic* pathway. Indeed, as shown in Table 5.1, this assumption was supported. As expected, members of the two *Steady* pathways reported higher levels of persistence and attainment of their dating goals compared to those who belonged to the *Sporadic* pathway. Those involved in *Lengthy Relationships but Absence of Experiential Learning* reported a low level of goal importance, similar to that of the members of the *Sporadic* pathway. This probably reflects that the members of the *Lengthy Relationships but Absence of Experiential Learning* pathway were drawn into their long relationships and were afraid to make changes in their relationships and reconsider the extent to which the relationship is or is not important for them. Relatedly, this also explains why, despite being in a relationship for a long period of time, they reported a lower level of dating goal achievement. As described above, Racheli was well aware that her boyfriend was not interested in the relationship, but they were probably maintaining the relationship for the sake of mutual convenience.

Table 5.1 *Romantic Pathways, Romantic Goal Levels, and Life Satisfaction*

	Sporadic	Long no progress	Casual to steady	Steady	F
Romantic goal importance	6.07 (0.83)	6.14 (0.82)	6.69 (0.60)	6.81 (0.40)	5.53**
Romantic goal progress	4.48 (0.10)	5.32 (0.89)	5.81 (0.68)	6.16 (0.77)	15.80***
Romantic goal stress	4.06 (1.58)	4.47 (1.58)	4.13 (1.26)	3.1 (1.45)	2.27
Life satisfaction	3.54 (0.73)	3.4 (0.59)	3.76 (0.6)	3.46 (1.1)	0.80
Depressive symptoms	1.03 (1.14)	1.4 (0.79)	0.83 (0.8)	0.46 (0.46)	2.89*

*$p < .05$. **$p < .01$. ***$p < .001$.

Comparison of the four pathways on level of dating stress was only marginally significant ($p = .08$). Closer examination showed that only the *Steady Relationships* pathway reported a lower level of dating stress. Probably involvement in a steady relationship over a longer period of time provides confidence and decreases the sense of stress. All the other pathways, including the *Lengthy Relationships but Absence of Experiential Learning*, are probably still stressful. Contrary to our expectations, no differences were found between the four pathways on level of satisfaction. (We will try to understand this fact when we compare career and dating pathways in Chapter 7.)

Comparison of the level of change in depressive symptoms across pathways yielded a significant interaction, $F = 2.89$, $p = .04$. As can be seen in Figure 5.1, levels of depressive symptoms at age 23 did not differ across the four pathways. However, two significant changes were found when comparing the level of depressive symptoms at age 23 and age 29. Members of both the *Sporadic* and the *Casual to Steady* pathways reported a similar number of depressive symptoms at the first assessment and 4 years later. In contrast, members of the *Lengthy Relationships but Absence of Experiential Learning* pathway reported an increase in level of depressive affect, while members of the *Steady Relationship* pathway reported a decrease in depressive affect. Probably the capacity to become more intimate and committed associates with a greater sense of well-being. In contrast, being in a relationship that does progress toward intimacy for an extended period of time is likely to have an adverse impact on well-being. It is possible that the *Sporadic* pathway is perceived as transitional and, therefore, was not associated with change in levels of depressive symptoms.

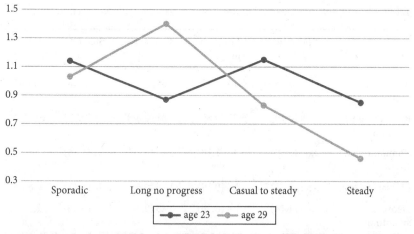

Figure 5.1 Changes in depressive affect between age 23 and age 29 across the four romantic pathways

Summary

Reading the in-depth interviews and subjecting them to qualitative analysis allowed us to learn about the diverse pathways that emerging adults take while pursuing their romantic lives. While emerging adults' romantic lives have been described as fluid and unstable (Claxton & van Dulmen, 2013), our findings suggest that fluctuations in romantic and sexual experiences of emerging adults do not necessarily represent confusion but might also serve as an arena for learning about relationships. Adopting a developmental systems perspective (Thelen & Smith, 1998), we suggest that periods of instability, and even regressions, can be part of the developmental reorganization and are aimed at finding and developing new forms of behavior that address the need and potential for change and growth (Knight, 2011; Mayes, 2001). In general, and as shown by our findings, emerging adults progress toward settling down in the romantic domain (Cohen et al., 2003; Connolly & Goldberg, 1999; Levinson, 1978). Yet, while fluctuations can be beneficial and serve as a platform for change and growth, our findings show that not every individual necessarily gains from different romantic experiences. There are individuals for whom romantic instabilities might become a pattern of life (Shulman et al., 2017).

In this chapter we have described the different romantic pathways that individuals took across their emerging adulthood years. Approaching the age of 30, young people progress toward settling down. It will be interesting to examine which of the pathways are associated with settling down and marrying. From a psychological perspective it is also important to better understand the romantic status the young adults reached. If they are married, we may ask whether the relationship they established is intimate. Do they feel committed? Relatedly, we will also examine those who have not progressed toward commitment and learn how they understand their romantic status. Is their non-commitment associated with an emotional deficiency or rather a calculated decision to postpone settling down? We will learn from their own words how these emerging adults understand their progression or delay in commitment.

6
Romantic Intimacy Statuses and Progress Toward the Future
There Is Hope for Change

In Chapter 5 we described the different romantic pathways that characterized the romantic lives of our participants across their 20s. While a substantial number of young people described being in and out of relationships along the years, analysis of their stories showed that fluidity could also serve as an arena for learning how to handle a relationship. Approaching the age of 30 the vast majority of young people get married. For example, the mean age of first marriage in the United States in 2017 was 27.4 for women and 29.5 for men. In Israel, the mean age of first marriage in 2015 was 26.1 for women and 28.0 for men. These figures are similar to those in other Western societies. Thus, while the age of first marriage was postponed until the end of the 20s, we should also note that a vast majority of young people are in fact married when approaching the age of 30 (Cohen et al., 2003).

Chapter 5 indicated the importance of understanding the meaning of the different expressions of romantic behavior. Fluidity is not necessarily negative, and stability does not necessarily represent involvement in an optimal romantic process. The purpose of this chapter is to understand the meaning and quality of the romantic intimacy status that a person has reached when approaching the age of 30. At the fourth assessment, when our participants were at about 28–29 years old, an additional interview was conducted to examine their ability to become intimately involved and committed. Analysis of these interviews provides us with additional insights into the quality of the romantic lives of young people during the progress toward settling down. We were also able to interview a substantial number of our participants again at the age of 35 when they were again asked to relate the story of their romantic status development and describe how they reached this status. The information from the two interviews provides us with a broader perspective of the processes that young people experience while progressing toward settling down.

Observation of the romantic lives of young people approaching the age of 30 suggests clear progress toward stabilization. As we have indicated above, demographics suggest that by the age of 30 a substantial number of young people have married (US Census Bureau, 2017). In addition, cohabitation has become a normative and acceptable union for young adults, partly due to the postponement of age of first marriage and the prolongation of young adulthood (Manning, 2013; Settersten & Ray, 2010). However, while in the past cohabitation was a step toward marriage, in recent years fewer cohabitations progress to marriage (Bumpass & Lu, 2000; Guzzo, 2014). An increasing number of young people report experiences of multiple cohabitations (Lichter et al., 2010), suggesting that, in contrast to the past, cohabitation is becoming disconnected from marriage. Nowadays fewer cohabitations might begin with marital intentions (Vespa, 2014). In the past it was highly likely that living together was the result of a deliberate decision. In recent years a young person may "slide" into a relationship that is not necessarily optimal yet provides some sense of security and economic stability (Rhoades et al., 2006). This calls for a more extensive understanding also of romantic involvement in the latter stages of emerging adulthood. For example, does living together represent a mature relationship or rather a condition the partners did not plan in the first place and just found themselves in? Relatedly, not being in a relationship might also result from a deliberate decision to invest currently in issues related to career, studies, or work (Shulman & Connolly, 2013; te Riele, 2004). Thus, a more extensive understanding of the meanings of romantic involvements as well as the extent to which commitment has or has not been reached is needed.

Two theoretical approaches direct our conceptualization of the nature and quality of romantic involvements among young people. The first follows Orlofsky's (1993) conceptualization that originates from the Eriksonian theory (Erikson, 1968), while the second follows the recent developments in romantic stage theories (Brown, 1999; Connolly & McIsaac, 2009; Seiffge-Krenke, 2003). Erikson (1968) described the crisis of intimacy versus isolation in which, as a central task of young adults, individuals are expected to develop intimate relationships with others without fear of losing their identity. Positive outcomes of this stage are the development of close, intimate, loving, and sexual relationships. Fear of losing one's autonomy might lead to repeated disappointment in relationships, resulting in involvement in superficial relationships or remaining alone.

According to Erikson, intimacy is the establishment of a healthy balance of closeness and individuality, as well as reference to the ability to commit oneself to a relationship (Marcia, 2002), and is therefore especially relevant to our understanding of romantic involvement toward the end of the 20s. In a similar vein, the romantic stage theories also suggest that establishing intimacy precedes commitment to a relationship (Brown, 1999; Connolly & McIsaac, 2009; Seiffge-Krenke, 2003). Following the establishment of both intimacy and commitment, a relationship can become the most important source of support, as is expected among adults (Connolly & McIsaac, 2009).

Elaborating on Erikson's conceptualization, Orlofsky (1993) suggested that in assessing a person's romantic relationships it is important to consider whether one is involved in a superficial or a deep and intimate relationship, as well as a person's ability to be involved in an enduring and committed relationship. In healthy relationship development, as in other domains of development such as career, individuals tend to explore and experience a number of possible involvements prior to reaching a more nuanced conception of what suits them best (Marcia, 2002). Subsequently, they are expected to gradually make personal commitments to deep and intimate relationships. Thus, the capability of integrating intimacy and commitment is a better indication of the quality of young people's romantic involvements than whether they are romantically involved at a given point in time. Furthermore, it is only after achieving the capacity to become intimately involved that true commitment can be pursued and established. In the next section we describe the romantic status interview (Orlofsky, 1993) conducted with participants, how the interview was analyzed, and how it helped us understand how young adults balance autonomy, intimacy and commitment.

The Intimacy Status Interview, its qualitative analysis, and its classification

At the fourth assessment the Intimacy Status Interview (Orlofsky, 1993; Orlofsky & Roades, 1993) was conducted with 100 participants who were randomly selected from the broader sample. This is a semi-structured, about 60-minute interview designed to examine individuals' interpersonal attitudes and behavior and their capacity for intimacy in romantic relationships. Participants were asked about emotional closeness, conflict resolution, involvement and autonomy, satisfaction, and commitment in their relationships with past and/or present romantic partners. The interview assesses the capacity for intimacy based on past and present relationships, even if the respondent is not in a romantic relationship at the time of the interview, and captures optimal ability, not necessarily current characteristics. For example, with regard to self-disclosure the rater assesses the extent to which such disclosure was apparent based on the quality of past and present relationships.

The interviews were audiotaped and rated, according to the manual (Orlofsky & Roades, 1993), on a 9-point scale (ranging from 1, the low end of the scale, to 5, the high end): commitment (duration and quality), communication (intra- and interpersonal), caring/affection, knowledge of partner's traits, perspective-taking, power/decision-making, maintaining own interest, acceptance of partner's separateness, and dependency/detachment. To establish reliability,

25 interviews were coded by both raters. Inter-rater reliabilities ranged from .84 to .91.

Based on scale scores, two raters classified participants into one of the following intimacy statuses (Orlofsky & Roades, 1993): *Isolates*, who had not had any romantic relationship with a partner; *Stereotypes*, who lacked open communication and emotional closeness in their relationships and had not established any long-term commitment; *Pseudo-intimate* participants, who lacked closeness in their relationships yet had established a long-term commitment; *Mergers/Committed*, who had established long-term relationships but were highly dependent on their partners to the extent of waiving their own interests and sense of separateness; *Mergers/Uncommitted*, also characterized by high enmeshment but in a non-committed relationship; *Pre-intimates*, who were, or had been, involved in an affectionate, deep, and mutually respecting relationship yet were not, or had not been, committed to this relationship; and *Intimates*, whose relationships are optimal, like those of the *Pre-intimates*, but they are highly committed to their relationships. The Orlofsky Intimacy Status Interview was used in the past with late adolescents and college students. The current study, conducted on older emerging adults, yielded an additional relationship status: participants who were involved in a long-lasting and committed relationship, though of very low quality. We termed this status *Conflictual but Committed*. There was 96% agreement between two different raters on 25 interviews.

In line with the literature reviewed above on romantic intimacy (Erikson, 1968) and the romantic stage theories (Brown, 1999; Connolly & McIsaac, 2009), we collapsed the eight Orlofsky (Orlofsky & Roades, 1993) statuses into four patterns capturing the extent that intimacy and/or commitment was attained in a relationship:

Non-stable (low on intimacy and commitment)—includes the statuses *Isolates*, *Stereotypes*, and *Mergers/Uncommitted* and refers to individuals who have difficulties establishing relationships or maintaining these for longer than 2 months.

Non-intimate Commitment—includes individuals who reported involvement in lasting relationships; however, these relationships were not intimate and mutually respecting. This pattern included the *Pseudo-intimate*, *Mergers/Committed*, and *Conflictual but Committed* statuses.

Intimate but not Committed—includes individuals who are, or were, involved in an intimate relationship but could not indicate commitment and future plans. This pattern included the *Pre-intimate* status.

Intimately Committed—refers to involvement in an intimate and mutually satisfying relationship with high commitment to the relationship and includes the *Intimate* status.

Intimacy statuses: Personal accounts

Participants who were classified as *Non-stable* described similar stories to those with a *Sporadic* romantic history (these two categories are highly associated, as will be shown below). Due either to personal difficulties in becoming close to others or to a difficult experience of rejection, these young people developed a fear of becoming romantically involved. Similar to the stories of Daria and Joseph, who were classified as belonging to the *Sporadic* pathway, Sasha, a 30-year-old young man, described his experience:

> I cannot be open with someone else. I must protect myself. I was in love, I was madly in love and shared everything with her. She used this against me. I was deeply hurt. I could not look her friends in the face for two and a half years on campus. I was so stupid to get close to her and trust her. I will not let myself be stupid again.

This feeling was strongly expressed in his intimacy interview and prevents him from becoming romantically involved.

In contrast, 30-year-old Katy was classified as *Intimately Committed*, with a mature understanding of relationships and how to support intimacy development; and she told a different story. Katy was interviewed 3 weeks after she got married:

> I have been with J for 4 years now. Over time you get into sort of a routine, so you have to search for the love to find it. If there is no true friendship love will end. I mean feeling comfortable, telling everything, not being ashamed of what you do or think or feel. Simply to feel free, not to worry who and what you are. You will always be accepted.

Katy described that during the time she and her boyfriend were living together, both were between jobs. "It was not financially easy. The stress could have ruined us, but we were able to enjoy this period together till we found work again." During a stressful period, Katy and her boyfriend were able to gain support from one another, which deepened their relationship and intimacy. Katy's romantic story represents the *Intimately Committed* status well, where partners are involved in a long-lasting relationship in which they learned how to cope with difficulties and enhance their intimacy. The experiences told by Katy also resemble progression made by affiliates of the romantic *Casual to Steady* pathway. Participants belonging to the *Casual to Steady* and *Steady Relationship* pathways described close and intimate relationships that developed during the years and led to greater investment in the relationship and to commitment.

In addition to the *Non-stable* and the *Intimately Committed* intimacy statuses, two further statuses were identified, capturing Orlofsky's conceptualization of intimacy. One was *Intimate but not Committed* and the other was *Non-intimate Commitment*. Yuri, aged 28, classified as *Intimate but not Committed*, has been in a relationship for almost 3.5 years, keeping his separate residence.

> This relationship is different from the previous one. In past relationships I felt I was in the clouds, euphoria. This relationship is very important for me. I have changed a lot. I am more open, learned about myself, more confident, and I share.

However, despite the sense of intimacy, they did not live together and had no plans to marry. Yuri described that he did not want to get married at this stage of life. His girlfriend suggests that he stay over from time to time, but she too does not want to make this permanent. Probing the reasons that the relationship does not evolve, Yuri attributed this to his heavy load in work and studies. In sum, Yuri described a close relationship in which he has developed emotionally and overall is happy. However, due to his obligations at work and with his studies, Yuri cannot commit himself at this stage of his life, though he does not dismiss the possibility that he and his girlfriend might get married later.

While Yuri attributed the postponement of commitment to current investment, Dan attributed his difficulty with commitment to his desire to keep his options open. He explains that he is not confident in his ability to stay in a relationship for a long time. He might become cold and indifferent and might want to hurt the girl or be hurt. He further elaborates that while a relationship goes well and both are in love, things might change. In this case, he wants to be able to leave and say: "Bye bye. This is the way I learned to be with girls; some I can trust and others not."

Yehoshua, almost 30 years old, is completing a degree in engineering and has been in a relationship with M. for almost 3 years. When asked to tell us about his relationship with M., Yehoshua started to describe that he loves his girlfriend and that she is very special. However, "We have ups and downs, despite loving one another, and we are very close, we are not sure that we suit each other." Yehoshua added that he is afraid that if they decide to get married, they will realize that they should separate but that they do not want to separate. At this point in time, they are unable to develop their relationship further, and he concluded, "I have no idea where we go from here, but we love and cherish our relationship."

Yuri, Dan, and Yehoshua described difficulty making a commitment, although their relationships were close. Yet, it appears that different reasons led to the difficulty to make the commitment. Yuri is preoccupied with his career and decided to postpone commitment, although he felt close to and appreciated his partner (Shulman & Connolly, 2013). Dan, in contrast, described a personal difficulty in making commitment, although he was able to be romantically involved until the issue of further commitment arose. In quite a similar vein, Yehoshua is afraid that, despite the love and closeness, he and his girlfriend might not be suitable; but they are unable to make a decision. Considered together, there are young adults who developed a close and intimate relationship with a partner, but for a variety of reasons they had not progressed toward commitment.

The analysis of the interviews yields an additional pattern—*Non-intimate Commitment*. Members of this intimacy status were involved in romantic relationships for extended periods of time; however, when asking them to describe their relationship, their stories lacked closeness, warmth, and intimacy. We also observed this pattern among a number of participants who had married during their 20s, but their relationship represented more a marriage of convenience.

Racheli, age 29, mentioned earlier, has been involved in a relationship for almost 6 years. She is in this relationship despite the fact that her partner told her from the very beginning that he was not interested in a serious relationship. Despite his attitude, she insisted and did not give up until (in her words) "he realized that I am a caring person and persistent." Racheli believes that her persistence has kept the relationship intact for years. Over the years, they have fought, and even separated for short periods, but learned to resolve the conflicts quickly and move on. Despite staying together for a period of 6 years, Racheli describes that once she mentioned "marriage," he started to scream. This has changed because she, in her words, took a step back. Despite this situation, they plan to buy an apartment together, and she believes that they might have a "wedding party" but will not get married.

Reading the interview showed that Racheli and her boyfriend struggled over the years but learned to solve the problems. It was not clear, however, how close their relationship truly is and whether they had been able to develop true intimacy. To better understand their relationship, we asked Racheli whether she feels committed to this relationship. In our opinion, Racheli's answer clarified the nature of this relationship:

> I am very committed to him. To the relationship. But sometimes I look to the outside. Wow, I would like to go out with somebody else, to feel the excitement, a new beginning. But I am committed. And I love being with him. But I have two persons within myself. At this point the commitment overcomes.

Sarah, aged 27, had been married for 2 years and was in the last months of her pregnancy at the time of the interview. She told us that there are many couples who live together but are not sure whether they love one another. It is part of their routine. She then disclosed, "With me it [living together before marriage] was part of my routine. I lived with my partner [husband] for 5 years, not in the same house, but we met every weekend because he was serving in the army." This and talking on the phone were enough to keep "a small flame."

Sarah's story is similar to the stories of a number of young women who had married earlier. In some cases, they fell in love and got married quickly, not finding out how much they and their future husband have in common. In other cases, women who married early "slid" into a relationship that was not necessarily optimal yet provided them with a sense of security, economic stability, and, above all, the sense that they had reached the milestone of getting married (Rhoades et al., 2006). Racheli exemplifies a different pattern of young women who are involved in relationships that last for long periods of time but do not develop into true intimacy. In both cases our impression was that these young women were involved in relationships that were not optimal. They stayed in the relationship in the hope that it would become more intimate, as in Racheli's case. Among the married women, the marriage appeared to be something of a compromise in order to marry, have a stable relationship, and bear children.

What can the patterns of intimacy status teach us about romantic relationships among emerging adults?

Frequencies of the four intimacy statuses showed that 27% of our 100 participants were intimately committed and that an additional 14% were involved, or had the capacity to be involved, in an intimate relationship but were not committed (*Intimate but not Committed*) and that 27% were involved in long-lasting relationships that were not truly balanced or intimate (*Non-intimate Commitment*). The remainder, 32%, either had not been romantically involved for extended periods of time in relationships that were intimate or committed (resembling friends with benefits) or were more likely to be in and out of relationships (*Non-stable*).

Close examination of our findings suggests that the majority of our participants are characterized by patterns indicating a variety of difficulties in successfully integrating intimacy and commitment. A substantial part of our sample had difficulties either developing intimacy or becoming committed. Almost a third of the sample had difficulties both developing intimacy and making a commitment and either had not been romantically involved for an extended period of time or were more likely to be in and out of relationships. The rest revealed two different constellations of the intimacy and commitment dialectics. One group was involved in intimate relationships lacking commitment, while the other group was committed to their relationships, although these were not necessarily intimate or adaptive. Only 28% of our participants had reached the optimal integration of intimacy and commitment and were intimately committed toward the end of the 20s. Our findings are in line with the documented recent tendency of postponing romantic commitment and of relational fluctuations (Manning, 2013; Meier & Allen, 2009; Settersten & Ray, 2010). Yet, our findings provide further understanding of the quality of relationships of those who were romantically involved, and the ability to develop intimacy and commitment among those who might not have been romantically involved, at the time of the assessment.

According to Erikson's theory (1968) as well as to the recent developmental theories (Brown, 1999; Connolly & Goldberg, 1999; Connolly & McIsaac, 2009; Seiffge-Krenke, 2003), commitment optimally follows the establishment of deep and intimate relationships. The *Intimately Committed* pattern represents progression on both dimensions, whereas the *Intimate but not Committed* pattern represents those young people who have not yet reached the stage of commitment (Brown, 1999; Connolly & Goldberg, 1999). The question is why some young people are unable to become committed despite having established a close and supportive relationship. What prevents them from taking the next step? In addition, what led some young people to become committed despite the lack of intimacy is also questionable, and this pattern represents a quarter of our sample.

Reading the stories of our participants suggested that for some individuals, such as Yuri, settling down means completing education and having a stable career. These young people will be ready to commit to a relationship and to get married (Shulman & Connolly, 2013) only after achieving their career goals. In contrast, career did not prevent Dan from progressing toward commitment— his inner doubts prevented him from taking the next step. Embedding these dynamics within an emerging adulthood perspective can further explain the developmental function of this intimacy status. Existing research describes the instabilities and romantic fluctuations that characterize the romantic behavior of young people (Arnett, 2004; Cohen et al., 2003). Our findings show that there might be an additional way of postponing commitment and settling down. A substantial number of emerging adults are involved in a romantic relationship for an extended period of time. However, difficulties either in establishing intimacy or in committing due to prioritization of career might interfere with the progress toward an intimately committed relationship that epitomizes the higher stage of romantic development (Brown, 1999; Connolly & Goldberg, 1999).

Postponement of commitment is probably one of the ways emerging adults employ to postpone marriage. This behavior represents emerging adulthood and the preference to prioritize career over romantic relationships (Shulman & Connolly, 2013). Being committed to a relationship that lacks intimacy, in contrast, recalls a dynamic described in the family systems and family therapy literature. Wynne (1984) showed that there are individuals who might compromise for the sake of security and remain in relationships that are not optimal. According to Wynne, there are two patterns of committed relationships. The *Intimately Committed* have successfully negotiated issues of closeness and individuality that lead to the establishment of intimacy and true mutuality (Wynne, 1984), and on this basis, commitment was consolidated. The *Non-intimately Committed* are involved in relationships that are not very close and supportive or where one of the partners is highly controlling or dependent upon the other. Nevertheless, they were committed to the relationship. This process of consolidating a relationship that has not progressed through true exploration or negotiation with a partner recalls the "foreclosure" construct described in the Eriksonian theory. Among those who are unable to achieve true intimacy with a partner, a substantial number might settle down for the sake of stability and security (Marcia, 2002).

Considering the possible developmental changes that take place during this period of life, it is interesting to further examine the extent that the romantic patterns we have found—both the romantic pathways and the intimacy status patterns—remain stable or change over time. In order to understand the possible processes of both continuity and change, we followed the evolvement of the romantic lives of our participants until the age of 35. Based on the in-depth interviews conducted at the age of 35, we will explore the different possible trajectories of either continuity or change as told by our participants in their own words.

Romantic pathways and intimacy statuses: Continuity, change, and future outcomes at age 35

Cross-tabulation of the pathway affiliation and intimacy status patterns is presented in Table 6.1. Overall, affiliation with a romantic pathway significantly associated with one intimacy status, $\chi^2(df, 9) = 68.97, p < .001$. As we expected, most emerging adults classified as belonging to the *Sporadic* pathway were also categorized as belonging to the *Non-stable* romantic status. Similarly, a significant proportion of members of the *Casual to Steady* and the *Steady Relationships* pathways were categorized as *Intimately Committed* at age 29 on the Orlofsky classification scale. However, only about half of those classified as belonging to the *Steady Relationships* pathway were categorized as *Intimately Committed*, while the other half were categorized as *Non-intimately Committed*. This unexpected disparity suggests that the roads taken by young people toward settling down are more complex. Being mostly involved in steady relationships does not guarantee that intimacy will be reached.

Reading the age 35 interviews can further contribute to our understanding of the dynamic, the hopes and the worries that young people experience with

Table 6.1 *Cross-Tabulation of Romantic Pathways and Intimacy Statuses*

Intimacy status	Romantic pathways			
	Sporadic	Long no progress	Casual to steady	Steady
Non-stable	25	3	0	0
Non-intimately Committed	2	3	10	10
Intimate not Committed	6	2	5	0
Intimately Committed	0	1	15	9

regard to becoming romantically intimate and committed. More importantly, following our participants for an additional 6 years (overall, they were followed for about 12 years) allows us to better understand their progress (or lack of progress) in their romantic relationships. In particular, it helps us to understand the unexpected outcomes—for example, how young people who were not intimately involved or committed were able to develop an intimate and committed relationship 6 years later—and to learn what led to the significant changes. In the following sections we present additional excerpts from the romantic status interviews, as well as the interviews conducted at age 35, to further understand the process of settling down and its evolvement over the years. By focusing on the interviews of three of our participants, we will describe the evolution of romantic patterns from a particular romantic pathway through the construction of an intimacy status and to the stage of settling down at the age of 35. In this manner we will point to the complexity of development over time and show that while there is significant continuity from one stage to the other, change is also possible at all stages of development.

The *Sporadic* pathway, the *Non-stable* romantic intimacy pattern, and future developments

As indicated above, the majority of those who described a *Sporadic* romantic history were assigned to the *Non-stable* intimacy status, suggesting that they have not achieved intimacy or commitment. For example, Daria described her difficulty of many years to establish and become involved in a romantic relationship. Her attitude and concerns were also evident in her intimacy interview and characterized her romantic life at age 35. Daria had hardly dated in recent years. When asked to describe what she would wish to have in a relationship, she answered, "I think we should fit, in our way of life, way of thinking. We have to have a 'good fit.'" Daria added that she has to have patience: "It is a mistake to rush and look for somebody. I know that I'll be 35 this spring, but to rush and do what others expect from me will not make me happy later." She then added, "I know many couples who got involved quickly in order to satisfy others, and it was not always good."

Mayer was 31 years old at the fourth assessment. When asked to tell us about his romantic status, he said, "I am ALONE. I have a female friend and we go to the cinema or a restaurant from time to time. But we are childhood friends and nothing serious." And Mayer then added that being in a romantic relationship frightens him. He is always careful not to become too close to others and then is disappointed. Meeting Mayer 6 years later and asking him about his current romantic status, he responded with humor, "I have been 'dating' my psychologist for almost 3 years." But he is still afraid of dating. Mayer then disclosed that watching the fights between his parents resulted in the fear that he would replicate his parents' relationship model.

These stories of Daria and Mayer represent the stability and consistency of relational patterns described in the research literature. For example, Furman and Winkles (2012) contended that patterns of interactions such as negotiating disagreements experienced in one romantic relationship are likely to be carried forward and enacted in a future relationship. In a similar vein, the attachment theoretical framework demonstrated how earlier experiences within the family are enacted in future significant relationships. Models of self and other that develop from early relationship experiences influence the nature of interaction with the environment, expectations concerning availability, responsiveness and attitudes of others, as well as expectations about the self in relationships (Sroufe & Fleeson, 1986). The clinical literature contends that experiences can become internal scripts guiding future romantic behavior (Byng-Hall, 1995b). Mayer's inability to cope with, and change, past family scripts echoes Crittenden's (2006; Crittenden et al., 2000) model of dispositional representations that further elucidates the ways that one's own present parental behavior. In Crittenden's view, representations are not mere retained static memories of past experiences but also "disposing to action." Dispositional representations shape an individual's perception of the world and their relation thereto and dispose a person to act in a particular way (Crittenden, 2006). This is exactly what Mayer was describing.

Reading additional age 35 interviews, however, showed that there is also room to change either practically (getting married) or emotionally and develop an intimate relationship. Maya's romantic history during her 20s clearly showed that she was very often in and out of romantic relationships. In the romantic status interview at age 29, when asked about her current romantic status, she stated, "I do not want to be in a relationship now. I am out of this. But this can change within 2 weeks. I left a relationship that was intensive, in which I felt I was *suffocating*."

Then she added, "But this can change within days once loneliness floats to the surface again."

At the age of 36 when we interviewed Maya again, she had been married for 4 years and had two young children. "He [her husband B.] showed up at the exact time. He was ripe for marriage, and I told myself he is a nice guy and he will accept me as I am, so why not? This can work." However, Maya is still on guard in her relationship. She criticizes her behavior toward her husband and wishes she could be more involved with and committed to him. She attributes the pattern of her behavior to her relationship within her family of origin. She explained that it would have been better if her parents had divorced. Yet, she replicates this pattern in her own family: "I do not share my feelings, my secrets with him, and he gave up."

It appears that earlier personal or family difficulties led Daria and Mayer to retreat from being actively involved in romantic relationships. Yet, Maya took a different approach. She made a deliberate decision to get married and to keep an emotional distance between herself and her husband. While this situation is not optimal for her husband (whose motivation we do not know), for Maya this marriage was a compromise toward establishing a family and having children; and at age 36 we could consider her to be *Non-intimately Committed*. Due to earlier difficulties, neither Maya nor Mayer were able to progress and develop an intimate relationship, although each expressed this difficulty differently.

In contrast, there are cases where individuals successfully develop intimacy despite earlier difficulties in remaining involved in lasting relationships and progress toward intimacy. The next two stories demonstrate the progress that two young men made from being *Isolates* toward the establishment of an *Intimately Committed* marriage. At the age 29 interview Joseph still described difficulties trusting a partner, echoing his deep insult and betrayal by a girl a few years earlier. When meeting Joseph again at age 35, he was married. He told us that at the age of 29, shortly after he was interviewed by us, he met a girl. He fell in love, all seemed bright to him, and they got married. "I loved her and did not think too much. I was hungry for love. She was pushing to get married." So, he decided to get married. However, a few months after the marriage, he realized that this relationship was bad for him: "She was controlling. I could not believe how a person could become so different. Before the marriage everything was fine." They divorced after 8 months.

This short marriage appears to have served as an important learning experience for Joseph—to respect your partner is important, but it is also important to be respected by your partner and not to stay in a relationship because you are hungry for love. Nine months after the divorce he met G. Joseph went into detail to demonstrate how she was understanding (his trauma), respecting, and did not push toward marrying. They dated for 3 years and got married and now have a son. Joseph is very happy with this relationship and added, "I do not regret anything. I am very happy and would repeat it."

It appears that while a large number of young people undergo significant experiences in their different romantic relationships and encounters, as described in Chapter 5, the different experiences help some of them to learn about relationships and, most importantly, prepare them to progress toward intimacy. Joseph's learning process was more complex and painful, but ultimately, he was able to accomplish this process. That being said, we cannot dismiss the role of Joseph's wife in this corrective process. She was accepting, understood the trauma he had experienced, and was willing to wait. At some point D. probably started to feel the need to ask herself where the relationship was going. Joseph felt he was again losing his personal space and initiated a separation. Yet, the 3-year supportive experience with D. probably allowed him to better evaluate this relationship and to feel confident in resuming the relationship with D.

Joel was also classified as belonging to the *Sporadic* pathway and as nonintimate and non-committed regarding his intimacy status at age 29. He explained that he does not feel that he can get close to another person and is more afraid that this will lead to marriage and children.

We were surprised meeting Joel at the age of 35 and finding that he was married with two young children. He cherishes his wife because she is very committed to and caring toward the children. He attributed the change to the fact that they met when he was her tutor, which did not frighten him. He further emphasized her supportive attitude, which helped him "to see life and people differently." Interestingly, despite this positive experience, Joel still describes that he feels that he carries "some remnants of his earlier fear of closeness."

In sum, as could be expected, earlier difficulties in establishing a relationship and becoming emotionally close are likely to stay stable over time and affect future romantic encounters. However, at the same time, it was also important to see that there were changes over time. There are individuals, such as Maya, who made a deliberate decision to settle for a relationship that was less than they expected but saw this as a way to establish a family. The marriage they established might recall the *Non-intimately Committed* category, to be further described below. Conceptually, we argue that Maya carried her earlier difficulties forward into the marriage she established. In contrast to Maya, Joseph and Joel were capable of progressing toward developing an intimate marriage in their mid-30s. It was meeting a supportive and understanding partner that helped facilitate a process of learning how to become close to a partner, to develop intimacy, and ultimately to become committed. Meeting a supportive and understanding partner can probably serve as a turning point and change an earlier, less adaptive pattern (Rönkä et al., 2002).

The *Lengthy Relationships* pathway, *Non-intimate Commitment* status, and future development

The *Lengthy Relationships* pathway and the *Non-intimate Commitment* status seem conceptually close. In both categories young adults are involved in long relationships that do not have the potential to lead to the development of intimacy. Indeed, following these cases into their mid-30s showed that nine out of 10 were not capable of developing into an intimate relationship.

Nora, who was described above, was alternating between involvement in a long relationship that led nowhere and short encounters. Prior to the second interview, Nora was involved in long relationships in which she gave up her wishes in order to maintain the relationship and prolong its existence. She was in a relationship that she idealized but in fact lacked any aspect of reciprocity and chance of learning. All she had experienced was how to please a partner, which did not lead to the development of romantic competencies to help her handle another relationship. Nora was in a relationship for an extended period of time; but she silenced her voice (Jack, 1991), and her behavior was mostly aimed at pleasing her partner. When her partner broke off the relationship, she was broken and in mourning for quite a long time. She did not understand what went wrong. When we met her at the age of 34, she was alone. When asked about her romantic status and expectations, she answered, "God knows."

It was surprising to hear from Racheli, who over the years worked hard to maintain her relationship intact, that she was also looking for some "extra relationship" affair. Despite her "success" in maintaining the relationship intact, Racheli and her partner probably learned to cope with daily issues that arose by downplaying difficulties or misunderstandings. They did not truly and constructively deal with their difficulties and preferred to refrain from addressing these directly (Tuval-Mashiach & Shulman, 2006). Racheli and her partner probably did not achieve a sense of "we-ness," which led to ideas of breaking out of the relationship. Interviewing Racheli 6 years later at the age of 35, she was married to a different man and had a daughter. "It went quickly. We met and after 2 weeks we moved in together. He proposed after 4 months, and we got married within less than a year. One year later we had our first daughter." It appears that both Racheli and R. moved quickly from their previous relationships into this relationship. Racheli describes that both she and R. invest in the family and in the children, but otherwise their marriage is mostly routine and nothing special. When asked to describe their relationship, she responded,

> We are totally in this relationship. We are not . . . I am quite sure that he will never be less committed in this relationship. I . . . don't know . . . I am invested

but I will lie if I tell you that I do not have thoughts about the future. I do not do anything. But thoughts.

[Can you elaborate?]

Thoughts that when the children grow up we will separate. He will find somebody better for him and I'll look for somebody with more passion for life.

Taken together, we might suggest that neither Nora nor Racheli gained any insights in the long relationships in which they were involved. Nora was pleasing her partners, which cannot be considered a relationship. Though she appeared to be in a relationship, in fact she was alone and later remained single at the age of 35. Racheli was struggling in her relationships. In her words, she was expecting to become committed and blamed her partner for not becoming committed. Observing her behavior more closely over the 13 years, we asked whether the difficulty in becoming committed she described at age 29 was not replicated in her marriage. Conceptually, we may argue that although relationships can serve as an arena for growth and change (Shulman et al., 2013, 2018), there are relationships in which individuals do not "grow" or gain any insights. There are relationships that lack the capacity to develop over time. Furthermore, the pattern of not being intimate or committed was replicated and expressed in future relationships (Byng-Hall, 1995b; Crittenden, 2006).

The *Intimate but not Committed* status and its future outcomes

We argued above that achieving intimacy and commitment probably characterizes the latter stages of emerging adulthood (Brown, 1999). At the earlier stages, individuals are in and out of relationships, and their romantic lives might be fluid. In contrast, in the later stages, though an increasing number of emerging adults can be found in lasting and intimate relationships, some remain short of becoming committed. Different reasons for the postponement to commitment and possible marriage were raised by our participants. Meeting them 6 years later helped us to examine whether or not they were able to progress toward commitment and to try to understand the mechanisms that might have facilitated or hindered the transition to commitment.

At the age of 29, Yuri was involved in a close and intimate relationship and told us that they did not commit as they are invested in their studies. Meeting Yuri 6 years later, he had been married for 2.5 years to the girl he was dating when interviewed at age 29. He explained that after graduation they decided to get married. Yuri added that there are still pressures with regard to work and the question of where to live, next to his workplace or hers. However, he added, "She helps a lot. She guides me, gives me tips, and we build the future together."

Contrary to Yuri's smooth transition, Dan traveled a different road. Dan was also married when interviewed at 35, and they were expecting their third child. At the age 29 interview Dan had been in a relationship for a year and half. Though he described the relationship as close, he was not truly committed to his girlfriend. Six years later he was not married to this girl, and we do not know what happened in that relationship. A couple of months after breaking off with his former girlfriend, he started dating his current wife. Three months after they started dating, Dan was involved in a car accident and broke a leg and an arm. She stayed with him in the hospital.

> This was special. Though we had been going out only for 2 months, I felt her motherly care. She came all the time and cared for me. And then I told myself she could be my wife. She is the girl I want for a wife. After about 8 months I proposed.

It was R.'s motherly care during his hospitalization that helped Dan make the transition. Later in the interview he disclosed that it was not easy for him to commit because he used to go out with many girls, but he realized that he wanted something else in life and was ready to give up his bachelor's way of life. It was the warmth and support that Dan's girlfriend provided during his injury that probably triggered the process of change (Rönkä et al., 2002).

Yehoshua was 36 years old when he was interviewed again. He was in a relationship with a woman, D., nine years his junior. On the one hand, he described a very close and loving relationship. This is not a "relationship of convenience," and he misses her a lot when they are not together. Despite this great love, they do not live together; he explained, "We can't be close too much, we only meet about twice a week in the evenings." Though Yehoshua mentioned that he might marry D. in the future, it sounded more like a remote idea. The status of his current relationship at the age of 36 still represented the *Intimate but not Committed* status that he replicated in his current 2-year relationship.

Meeting our participants at the age of 35 showed that the substantial majority had made the transition to commitment, and seven of the 10 members of the *Intimate but not Committed* status were married. As exemplified by the story of Yuri, the transition went smoothly and naturally once he gained greater career security. For Dan, a significant event highlighting his wish for close and motherly support initiated the change and his becoming committed. In contrast, Yehoshua still had difficulties becoming truly involved in his relationship with D. Despite the high appreciation and love that he claimed to feel and to receive in the relationship, Yehoshua and D. were still not able to become closer and to commit. It will be interesting to understand what might lead to a better understanding of the reasons leading to Yehoshua's difficulty in becoming committed and genuinely settling down.

Summary

Employing in-depth interviews and their analysis yielded a more comprehensive understanding of romantic involvements and their development across emerging adulthood. The Intimacy Status Interview showed that toward the end of their 20s, almost half of the emerging adults were involved in a committed relationship. These findings echo Cohen and colleagues' (2003) findings indicating the increasing penchant toward settling down. Yet our qualitative data showed that this progression is more complex. While an increasing number described themselves as being involved in a committed relationship, for a significant number of them this commitment was not necessarily accompanied by intimacy. For some young adults the urge (and sometimes the pressure) to settle down might lead to a compromise and becoming committed in a relationship that was not the relationship of which they dreamed. Despite some reservations, a decision to settle down was made. For a number of young women, it was the wish to have children that led to the compromise—"he will be a good father." This gender aspect will be discussed in Chapter 9.

At the same time, we found young adults who, despite their capacity to establish intimacy, had not completed the transition and whose close relations did not evolve into commitment. Postponement of commitment was associated either with developmental aspects, such as the wish to establish economic security, or with personal tendencies such as fear of intimacy or a strong need to continue romantic exploration.

Following our participants until the age of 35 showed us that the urge to commit is strong, and a number of our participants were married at this age. Reading their interviews shed light on the mechanisms that led to these changes. First, commitment took place after partners completed their education and found stable jobs. This process aligns with existing research suggesting that young people believe that marriage should occur after attaining financial security (Smock et al., 2005). In addition to normative processes such as attaining financial security, it was impressive to learn that significant events served as turning points and led individuals to change course and to commit (Rönkä et al., 2002: Tuval-Mashiach et al., 2014).

Interestingly, though we found an increased tendency to become committed, there were individuals who were involved in a close and loving relationship (even at the age of 36, such as Yehoshua) but were unable to commit. We asked ourselves whether this intimacy was a form of postponing commitment among those who might be scared of making the commitment. Reading the stories of the interviewees did not provide us with an explanation as to why an individual could not become committed or why they committed to a relationship that was not satisfactory. We collected personality data and the nature of support systems when our participants were 23 years old. In Chapter 10 we will examine the possible antecedents of the various intimacy statuses at age 29 as well as the romantic status at age 35.

7
Career Pursuit and Romantic Investment
How Do They Go Together?

Yochanan was 31 years old at the fourth assessment when our first in-depth interview was conducted. At this stage he was married, had recently fathered a child, and was employed in a high-tech company. In the interview he described that it took him some time until he felt confident that committing himself to a relationship would not interfere with his life plans. After getting married, to his surprise and contrary to his earlier anxieties, he found marital life was very satisfying and did not interfere with his professional aspirations. Moreover, he felt that he was supported in pursuing his professional plans, commenting: "Had I known that it works so well]family and work[, I would have married earlier." We were somewhat surprised to hear Yochanan's reflection. Is it really so easy to handle career and family demands? Do partners complement one another or rather interfere with one another, recalling Yochanan's earlier reluctance to become romantically committed before accomplishing career success?

In Chapters 3–6 we described the variety of ways that emerging adults take in their career pursuit and progress toward romantic commitment and marriage. We focused on the two domains, career and relationships, separately. In reality, both career and family domains are interconnected parts of our lives, and it is questionable whether they can be kept separate. In Chapter 2 we discussed the ways that emerging adults coordinate their different goals during their 20s. Career and family are a person's two main goals, and we showed the interplay between the two across the years. In the earlier 20s career goals have priority over relationship goals, while toward the end of the 20s family goals take first place. In reality, however, over time young people have to coordinate between their investment in career pursuit and relationship progress. In this chapter we examine how young people address these two main developmental tasks simultaneously. What priorities do they set? Is one domain—work or family—prioritized over the other? Finally, the modes of coordinating work and relationships will be discussed within the life-history and evolutionary frameworks.

Work–family spillover has been studied extensively among married couples within the framework of occupational psychology. Theory and research suggest that responsibilities in each domain compete for finite amounts of time, physical energy, and psychological resources. Demands or strains in one domain might result in a variety of negative consequences for both work and family (for a review, see Grzywacz & Marks, 2000). For example, difficulties at work weaken an individual's ability and enthusiasm to meet demands within the family domain. Once resources are drained at work, little energy is left to deal with family issues. In a similar vein, difficulties in family life hinder the performance of work duties and obligations because emotional resources are invested in the family (Frone et al., 1997).

This body of research among married couples could serve as a model for understanding the work–relationship interplay among emerging adult couples as well. However, young people face more complex dilemmas. Emerging adults are in a process of transition toward the assumption of adult roles, during which they are required to balance between different "personal" dreams, potential partners, and "couple dreams" (Levinson, 1978). Furthermore, a balance reached during transition may determine the nature and quality of the work–family balance in subsequent years (Seiffge-Krenke et al., 2014).

Considered together, we suggest understanding the balance between work and family among emerging adults from three perspectives—individuals' coordination between the *personal aspired goals* of work and relationship that we discussed in Chapter 2, coordination of level of *investment* in both work and relationship tasks among dating partners and the way they expect to balance career and family in their future married lives, and finally the *balance between work and family* among young couples that resembles the issue of spillover of work and family that was examined among married couples.

Emerging adults: Do they have time for dating? How do emerging adults balance career obligations and romantic involvement?

It is quite common to describe emerging adults as moving between transitory and inconsistent states and being in and out of relationships (Cohen et al., 2003; European Group for Integrated Social Research [EGRIS], 2001). The vast majority (60%) are involved in short-lived and non-stable relationships (Rauer et al., 2013). Yet, closer inspection suggests a more complex phenomenon. Overall, approaching the age of 30, a clear progress toward stabilization (Cohen et al., 2003) can be observed. Demographics suggest that by the age of 30 a substantial number of young people have married (US Census Bureau, 2017) or cohabit (Settersten & Ray, 2010), and these figure are quite similar in other Western countries (see Chapters 5 and 6 for further details). Considered together, many emerging adults who are involved both in the pursuit of career and in some form of romantic interaction have to find ways to coordinate between work obligations and love in their daily lives. In this chapter we thus explore the different ways emerging adults may employ in addressing both their work (career) and love lives.

At the age of 28–29, in the career interview, our participants were asked to describe how they handle both their career/work and dating (or family) lives. Reading their responses yielded a number of different approaches that young people employed in handling this dilemma, as can be seen in the following sections.

"My work and personal life are more important than being in a relationship"

Roy, 28 years old, was still studying for a degree in business administration and working to support himself. Roy perceived work as a means to earn money, adding that work gives him inner energy. Further, despite his investment, his work allows him to find time for his hobbies. He summarized his response by saying, "I do not currently have a serious relationship, I do not have enough time and *my work and personal life are more important than being in a relationship.*"

Another young man, 29-year-old Gadi, provided a more interesting view on how to balance work and family. He told us that "Work is the most essential part of life. Most of our life we spend and will spend at work not with our partner, and I think this is the way life is." He believes that in the future he will be in a relationship because "we are programmed to bear children" but "family is only for weekends."

These two men describe not having time to invest in a relationship, which they perceive as secondary to career success. Interestingly, we found similar stories among a number of women.

These descriptions emphasize the importance and centrality of work and tend to overlook or underestimate the role a relationship might or should play in a person's life. Being completely invested in career seems natural to them, and they strongly emphasize the need and pressures to progress and attain a career. We also noticed ideas that family is less central than work in a man's life. In addition, being immersed in their careers served as an explanation for these men as to why they were unable to become seriously involved in a romantic relationship.

"Career demands plenty of time and energy and there is not enough time to put too much into a relationship; my wife [currently or in the future] will have to learn to accept this"

Yori, aged 27, works in advertising, which he describes as very demanding and full of pressure. He has been involved in a "distant" romantic relationship for almost a year and a half. Yori is not ready to live with the girl because he needs his space and to invest in his work. He added that keeping this distance is good for them because "it causes us to miss one another, which is good for the relationship." Yori further emphasized that even when they do live together, he will continue to keep his separate space.

Eli, aged 30, elaborated further on the need to keep a distance in the relationship.

> Women expect and wait for their husbands to have more time for them and the children. But a man is always at work. She needs to learn to keep herself busy. She should not disturb. Slowly she will understand that this is good for her, that her husband works for her.

Yoram, aged 28, works as a computer engineer. He was even more drastic in his responses, emphasizing the centrality of work and the woman's need to accept this. Similar to the other men, he emphasized that work is "two thirds of my life" and that he works for the family. He expects his future wife also to be invested in her work—"Otherwise she will go crazy and will drive me crazy. I see my brother. His wife is at home, takes care of the children, does not work and drives him crazy." Yoram expects his wife to be busy with her issues, not with his.

These men echo the traditional approach that it is the man's responsibility to succeed in his career (Greenhaus & Powell, 2006). Yoram stated this quite explicitly, further describing that men are the breadwinners and that this, after all, serves the woman and the family.

"It is not easy at this stage of life, I love my work, even enjoy it, but I would also like to have more time for a relationship [for the family]"

The examples presented in the earlier sections of this chapter represent young people who "removed" the romantic relationship from their lives or saw work and family as two separate domains. Other young adults, however, think that romance or family is an integral part of life and that finding the time and a way to progress toward greater romantic involvement is important. For example, Avi, aged 30, works in high tech and is highly invested in his career. He is not currently involved in a relationship but thinks it is time to start investing in a relationship and progressing toward establishing a family. In a similar way, Noach, aged 27, who is heavily invested in his high-tech job, believes that this is the stage at which he needs to initiate change and become more involved and invested in a relationship.

Varda, aged 28, works in private banking and has a very successful career. The interview with her was conducted 3 weeks after she got married. She told us that she is highly invested in her career but knows that it is going to change because work is not all of life. She expects to spend time with her family and be invested in her family. She concluded, "I want my work to be satisfying, but I won't sacrifice my life for my job. I want to be with my family as well."

Lily, aged 29, heads an office in a construction company, loves her work, and is highly invested. We asked her how she feels about the balance of work and relationship in her life. From her response we could see that she was concerned. "I find myself involved too much in my work and ask myself if this is going to be my life." It was her boss (a female) who calmed her and told her "I had the same feeling you have now but once you will be in a relationship, once you have children, you will see that you will find a better balance, so don't worry."

Considered together, the descriptions presented by these young people demonstrated greater investment in their jobs. This was correct for both men and women. However, they perceive this greater investment in work as temporary. They wish for a relationship and to establish a family and are aware (and expect) that adaptations will have to be made. One young man even added that he would consider changing his workplace in order to find a job where he would have more time for his family.

"This is the time for work—we have to make money, but we do this together"

Overall, most of our interviewees described that at this stage of life they were supposed to complete their education, find a job, and progress toward financial independence. Yet, unlike the previous respondents, there were young people who were aware of the need to coordinate between career and family and the importance of this. Balancing work and family was articulated in their future plans. In addition, a number of young people described how their plans and those of their partners were coordinated during recent years.

Rina, aged 29, is a lawyer in a small firm and in a relationship for 2.5 years, with plans to marry in the near future. She is much invested in her career and describes herself as a career woman, but family is also very important for her. She does not want someone else to take care of and raise her children in the future. Therefore, it was clear to her that she wanted a partner who would also be invested in the family.

Alex, aged 29, whom we described in Chapter 5, met a girl and decided that she was the one he wanted to marry. They got married when he was in his early 20s, and he decided to postpone his studies to start a family. At the same time, he was also invested in his work as a technician, where he was highly regarded and promoted over time. In the interview he was very clear about the dilemma he faced—getting married versus pursuing a degree—and the decisions to be made by himself and his wife:

> We were together for five years, and we used to discuss this issue candidly, without putting pressure on one another. We finally made the decision together; we understood that this was what we wanted [to get married], despite all the difficulties.

He and his future wife decided to alternate in their career development. He was working as a technician, while she studied for a degree in nursing. When she completed her studies and was working, he started his studies at the university. "I said to myself, let's first undertake the project of family and then combine it [with studying]. That's how I moved forwards."

Both cases represent modes of balancing career and family. In both stories, told by a woman and a man, career and family were considered central in their lives; and they acted, or planned to act, to achieve a true balance between work and love. Yet a closer inspection of the two stories also indicates their differences. Reading Rina's story, it sounded more as if she was looking for a partner who would help fulfill her dreams to coordinate career and family. Levinson (1978) describes that a person selects a partner who can be helpful in the pursuit and achievement of one's dream. In contrast, the way Alex and his wife coordinated career and family, her career and his career, echoes Bodenmann's (2005) construct of dyadic coping. The balance Alex and his wife have handled along the years represents an ongoing process of negotiation and joint coping with difficulties that emerged at junctions across the years. Coordination of work and family characterized the balances these two couples negotiated to allow development of each partner together with progress toward their joint creation of their family.

To summarize, the ways that emerging adults described for handling and coordinating career pursuit and progress toward the establishment of a close and committed romantic relationship indicated two major trends. First, the majority of emerging adults prioritized career pursuit over investment in romantic relationships. The prioritization of career could be found in descriptions where investment in a romantic relationship, or even the wish or need for a romantic relationship, does not exist or is suppressed during these years. Others perceived romantic relationships as an important goal that they would start pursuing in the future after they had settled down financially. Even those who were romantically invested described planning their dyadic life in a way that did not interfere with their career aspirations; for example, they met only when it was possible.

Thus, career pursuit was given priority on the individual level as well as on the dyadic level among those who were romantically involved. Only a small number of emerging adults, such as Alex and his girlfriend, planned their lives while coordinating work and love ("I did not want to lose her") and intensively pursuing their careers.

Second, we noticed significant differences between men and women in their attitude toward the need and the time for balancing work and love. Overall, men were more likely to put romantic life aside and become immersed in their careers. The wish to begin a family was more dormant among men. In contrast, women were more aware of and felt the urge to start a family and bear children.

In the following section we will incorporate notions from a life-cycle approach and evolutionary theory to understand why investment in romantic relationships is postponed. The distinctive attitude of women to balancing work and family will be further discussed in Chapter 9, which focuses on the gendered pathways in career pursuit and romantic development.

Focusing on work and postponing investment and commitment in romantic relationships: Perspectives from a life-cycle approach

In his seminal book on human development, Levinson (1978) also underscores the complexity of transition to a long-term partnership and considers the need to coordinate between dyadic commitment and individual life plans (such as career). Levinson writes,

> By 20 [years] most of the mental and bodily characteristics that have been evolving... are at or near their peak levels. The young (wo)man is close to full height, and his maximal level of strength, sexual capability... and general biological vigor. He is close to his peak in intelligence and in those qualities of intellect that have grown so measurably. (p. 21)

According to Levinson, these capabilities enable the young person to form a preliminary individual identity. Unlike the identity attained during adolescence—defined mainly in psychological terms—a young adult is expected to make major first choices such as occupation, marriage, residence, and style of living.

In his theory, Levinson contends that each person constructs an "individual life structure" that represents the "design" that person has for their life. In this structure one has an idea about occupation, love relationships, marriage, children, and role as a citizen in a community and society at large. These aspirations include wishes and anxieties, values, and skills. A person's life structure consists of two basic and central components: work or occupation and love, marriage, and family (Shulman & Nurmi, 2010a). A person's occupation determines income, social level, and prestige in their group. It is the vehicle through which one's aspirations for the future are defined and pursued. Marriage and establishment of family also encompass one's aspirations about the role for oneself as a partner and parent of children. The two basic components of occupation and relationships are highly interconnected. Entering into a relationship and becoming committed are not only about love, romance, and sexuality. A spouse can play a crucial role in one's life plan, for better or worse. Indeed, recent research shows that a romantic partner is the most influential figure in emerging adults' career decision-making process, even compared to parents or best friends (Kvitkovičová et al., 2017). In his theoretical work Levinson describes how a true partner can be like a mentor by helping to live and shape one's life plan, believing in the partner's ability, giving a blessing, and joining the journey wholeheartedly. In connecting to the "dream" (life plan) of one's spouse, one facilitates not only the pursuit of the dream but also entry into the adult world (Levinson, 1978, p. 109). Within this context, entering the adult world also means shifting the center of one's life from the family of origin and consolidation of one's individuality and identity in order to become "a novice adult with a new home base that is more truly his own home" (p. 79). This can be achieved after initial choices about occupation and family life have been made, and these subsequently affect the nature and capabilities of the young person to start a family, bear children, and care for them properly.

The emphasis on the interconnectedness between different life tasks resonates in the recent elaboration of the life-cycle theory into the life-course approach. Macmillan and Copher (2005) outline the complex interdependencies of different roles, of linked lives, and of structural and socio-historical contexts that better approximate the ways in which individuals exist and develop over time. Life course is beyond trajectories or sequential stages but rather points to the dynamic, interconnected unfolding of trajectories and transitions over time. Within this complexity, life courses also define the order and timing of the assumption of different roles across development (Elder, 1998). Thus, events and experiences in one domain, such as work or studies, affect and are affected by events in another domain, such as romantic involvements and commitment.

The literature on the interplay between work and relationship experiences has been quite widely studied in married couples and can shed further light on the difficulties that young adults might face in addressing work and romantic relationships at the same time. Two dynamics were suggested to explain the interconnectedness between events in the realms of work and family. According to Edwards and Rothbard (2000), success or failure in one domain enhances or weakens positive or negative experiences, in turn affecting functioning in another domain. Similarly, difficulties at work or with studies can weaken an individual's capability and enthusiasm for meeting the demands within the family domain as resources used while coping with the demands of one domain are drained, leaving less energy to deal with issues in another domain (Frone et al., 1997). Thus, we suggest that difficulties that a young person encounters in their career pursuit might drain the energy (and time) needed for investing in a romantic relationship.

In the past, parents and societal norms provided greater direction and support to the younger generation. It was common that during their early 20s young people would make the major choices of marriage and occupation and assume an adult life. According to Levinson (1978), "this is the time [for the young person] to pay dues and make his essential contribution to the survival of the species: begetting and raising children, maintaining a marriage and a family, giving his labor to the economy and welfare of the 'tribe'" (p. 22). Becoming an adult was thus one step in a "preprogrammed" process, moving from personal development to reproduction and care for the next generation (Shanahan et al., 2005). Further, in the past, couples came together to build their joint life. For example, pursuit of one's career (mainly the husband's) took place within the dyadic context of the young couple. Nowadays, particularly in Western industrialized societies, young people are raised in a culture that values independence, individualism, and self-expression. Young people prepare themselves for the future individually. Considering that nowadays the mean age of marriage is about 28 for men and 26 for women, it is clear that young people meet potential partners when they are in the process of pursuing their careers. More importantly, a partner might also be valued to the extent that they can help or hinder one's career pursuit. Thus, it is probably only when they feel confident about their own career accomplishments, and are more financially secure, that they will feel confident to move toward a committed relationship, as described very clearly by our interviewees.

Indeed, research supports our contentions. For example, Manning et al. (2011) showed that in making decisions concerning romantic relationships young people highly value the educational and financial achievements of a potential partner. Young adults generally value financial security in a relationship, and the majority think it is important to be in a "financially secure" relationship. In addition, more than half of young people report caring about the financial future of a romantic partner. Sneed and colleagues (2007) also showed how financial success is likely to drive increasing romantic involvement. The more a person has progressed in financial confidence, the more likely they are to make progress in the romantic domain as well. In a similar vein, the level of career success among young men was found to affect the stability of cohabiting unions and the transition to marriage. For a substantial proportion of young men, cohabitation seemed to represent an adaptive strategy during a period of career immaturity. In contrast, marriage was a more likely outcome for both stably employed young men and women (Guzzo, 2014; Oppenheimer, 2003).

Considered together, young people face serious and real dilemmas that are not easily resolved. While they might be psychologically ready to become committed to a relationship, they have to cope simultaneously with occupational and financial demands. Experiencing the variety of challenges in a number of developmental tasks can drain the resources of young people, who might then have less energy to pursue a career while entering a committed relationship (Frone et al., 1997). As described by our participants, it is probably only after individuals have progressed significantly in their careers and attained a greater sense of financial confidence that serious overtures toward romantic intimacy and commitment will begin.

Focusing on work and postponing investment and commitment in romantic relationships: Perspectives from an evolutionary approach

The life-cycle and life-course theories effectively explain the difficulties that young people have in coordinating different life tasks and settling down. The evolutionary approach can help us to explain further the way that economic and educational statuses and aspirations play a role in the timing of romantic commitment.

In his outline of an evolutionary approach to understanding developmental processes, Ellis (2004) attempts to explain different trade-off patterns in the distribution of resources for completing life functions: maintenance, growth, and reproduction (Roff, 2002). Each trade-off constitutes a decision mode in the allocation of resources, and each decision node influences the next decision mode (e.g., at a given time, high investment in self-growth interferes with resources directed toward reproduction). In general, humans have adapted a slow strategy, characterized by prolonged upbringing, late onset of reproduction, and increased investment in the next generation. Yet individuals may differ depending on existing conditions that may accelerate or slow down one's strategy (Belsky et al., 1991; Chisholm, 1999; Ellis, 2004).

Recent developments of the evolutionary theory point to two environmental conditions that impact life-history strategies: the degree of harshness and the degree of unpredictability (Ellis et al., 2009; Roff, 2002; Vigil & Geary, 2006; Worthman, 2003). *Harshness* of an environment describes the level of strain placed upon the organism. *Unpredictability* of environments describes the degree to which there is an unaccounted-for variability in the outcomes of an employed strategy (Winterhalder & Leslie, 2002). Unpredictability of environments is a function of the variation in environmental risks (harshness) and outcome, which itself can become a source of stress (Ellis et al., 2009). Ellis and his colleagues (see Brumbach et al., 2009) also describe uncontrollable events in which the probability of an event is not related to the organism's behavior and whether or not an organism responds. Unpredictable events are more detrimental because they interfere with the ability of the organism to solve the adaptive problem of avoiding or escaping such stressful events in the future.

Brumbach and colleagues (2009) were able to demonstrate the extent to which environmental harshness and unpredictability during adolescence affected levels of functioning and reproductive strategy during young adulthood. By analyzing data from the National Longitudinal Study of Adolescent Health, they showed that environmental unpredictability (measured by frequent changes or ongoing inconsistency such as lack of consistent parental care or provision of food during adolescence) had a direct negative effect on young adult evolutionary strategy. Young adults with a higher history of unpredictability were more likely to be found on a faster-moving life-history track. Experiencing a harsh environment in adolescence (increased exposure to violence) had an indirect effect seen through lower sexual restrictedness during adolescence, which in turn affected the young adulthood life-history track of becoming sexually active.

Much has been written about the complexities and difficulties with which young people must cope nowadays (Arnett, 2004; Côté, 2000; EGRIS, 2001). Mastering the transition to adulthood has, in particular, been complicated by the societal changes and increase in unemployment during the last two decades. Moreover, postmodern societies are characterized by increased risks: economic and health risks, new modes of instability, and new forms of underemployment that do not secure future success (Côté & Bynner, 2008). In addition, in the past, life was more institutionalized, and transitions from one stage to another were clearly regulated by societal norms and rules (Bynner, 2005). Nowadays, young people are left to their own resources and initiatives to cope with difficulties or failures (Shulman et al., 2005; Wallace & Kovatcheva, 1998). Under these circumstances, young people have less control of their career and economic destinies and might find it difficult to realize plans despite efforts (Leccardi, 2006). These current societal and economic conditions undoubtedly reflect conditions of harshness and unpredictability described by the life-history theory (Ellis, 2004). The degree of difficulties and uncertainties experienced with regard to career attainment is likely to affect young people's reproductive strategies.

The works by Belsky and colleagues (1991) and Brumbach and colleagues (2009) focused on explaining early activation of the reproductive system in early adolescence or young adulthood, due to a history of being raised in underprivileged environments. While past experiences lead individuals to enact different reproductive strategies, we believe that within the tenets of the life-history theory we can also look for current factors that may lead individuals to readapt reproduction strategies. Within this understanding, we would like to extend the life-history theory to understand postponed activation of the reproductive system, as evidenced among the majority of young people in the last two decades.

Though postponement of settling down seems to be contrary to the still existing norms and expectations, it might be a better strategy under the current difficult and unpredictable societal and economic conditions. Postponement of commitment and marriage allows a young person to search more effectively for what they will do in life and provide better for their offspring. Therefore, focusing on career and postponement of romantic involvement might be considered adaptive as young adults attempt to keep options open under conditions of uncertainty (Côté & Bynner, 2008) and may serve as a means for individuals to maximize person–environment fit (Heckman, 1994). Thus, postponed settling down can maximize one's potential and increase the chances for better provision for the next generation. Once an individual has the sense that they can provide better (increased professional and economic competence), they will feel more ready to become committed. Some support for this notion can be found in sociological studies that showed the role of economic assets in marital decision-making. Men and women believe a prerequisite for marriage is financial stability (Smock et al., 2005), and economic security has a greater influence on marriage than cohabitation (Brines & Joyner 1999). Across the years between adolescence and young adulthood, individuals need the time to complete their education and explore professional routes while addressing current uncertainties. This prolonged trajectory fits mainly young people with educational capabilities and aspirations. In contrast, those who do not have educational plans are more likely to move more quickly to adulthood, get married, and have children. Postponement of settling down will not improve their earnings and capabilities to provide for the next generation.

Support of the distinction between post–secondary education–bound and non-post–secondary education–bound emerging adults can be found in a number of recent studies. Osgood and colleagues (2005) identified a number of typical paths from adolescence into early adulthood. The most common path was characterized by *educated singles*, young people who invested mainly in education and career and had developed few family obligations. Another smaller group left school early, married in their early 20s, became parents, and entered the labor force. The extensive investment in family life was paralleled without much investment in education or career. This family–education balance was also documented by Macmillan and Copher (2005). They found that the transition to adulthood for a substantial number of young people is largely a school-to-work transition, with only minimal movement into commitment and family roles. The movement into family roles is the main pathway to adulthood for only a smaller number.

Two examples from our participants can demonstrate the late and the early approaches in activating the reproductive system. Yaron, a 28-year-old man, was studying for a degree in technology in the south of the country. He had been in a relationship for about 8 months, which he described as intimate and close but still not committed; and they recently separated. Yaron told us that his girlfriend did not find a job and suggested that they move to the center of the country where jobs are more available. He was not willing to move because his studies and work are in the south. Yaron added that he wished she had not moved, but he understood and accepted her decision. He explained that the decision to separate was mutual, and he understands this is because "we are still not so connected." At this stage both favored their personal development over settling down. Moreover, pursuing one's career and establishing oneself financially were given higher priority over relational needs. Thus, the postponement of serious romantic involvements and marriage is often in the service of maximizing individual professional development, which is seen as a prerequisite for moving to the stage of establishing a family.

In contrast, Sarah, aged 29, had been married for 10 years, which was an exception in our sample. She applied to the college preparatory program when her children were a little older. Sarah described that after graduating from high school she did not have any particular plan.

> But then the knight on the white horse arrived. He was older, had money and bought a house. He proposed. I hesitated to marry, thought maybe I should study a profession. But I decided I wanted to bear children while still young. I would be able to study later in life. And I think it was the right decision.

For Sarah, who had no particular educational or career plans at that time, starting the reproductive cycle early seemed appropriate; and now, 10 years later, she still feels she made the right decision.

The early or late activation of the reproductive system is to some extent gendered, as our interviews suggested. Men were more likely than women to focus on their careers and to perceive this as the center of their life. In contrast, even among women who were focused on and invested in their careers, relationships were on their horizon. These gender differences have also been noticed in the demographic studies reviewed above. The number of women who marry early is almost one and a half times higher than that among men (Uecker & Stokes, 2008; US Census Bureau, 2008). Even with the general documented trend of getting married later, on average and across cultures, women tend to marry 2 or 3 years earlier than men.

To summarize, due to changing societal and economic conditions in the last two decades, young people are faced with shakier prospects and greater uncertainty. In particular, they feel less confident in their ability to support themselves and provide for a family. This has led the majority of young people to adopt a late reproductive strategy. A longer period of time is needed to establish oneself professionally and financially in order to better provide for the next generation. A person is ready to enter relational commitment only after some degree of educational and economic achievement. Only among the less privileged is postponement less likely to make a difference. When no educational and economic achievements are expected or aspired to, marrying early and bearing children take priority.

Finally, putting romantic investment on hold and focusing on career pursuit can further contribute to our understanding of romantic fluctuations that characterize emerging adults. As described in the previous chapters, more than 60% of emerging adults are involved in short-lived and non-stable relationships (Rauer et al., 2013) or in casual sexual encounters (Bogle, 2008; Claxton & van Dulmen, 2013). Moreover, even longer relationships are not necessarily stable over time (Meier & Allen, 2009). Emerging adults who are focused on their career development are possibly driven to casual romantic and sexual encounters by their sexual desires rather than the search for intimacy. This speculation corresponds with our notions in the previous chapters that romantic fluctuations are probably on a par with developmental processes and represent the increased focused on career pursuit. Yet, as we argued above, involvement in casual encounters may also serve, in the long run, for learning about romantic relationships and facilitating the move toward greater interest and involvement in a stable relationship.

Patterns of balancing career: Romantic relationships (family) during emerging adulthood and their future "outcomes" at age 35

In the previous chapter we described that earlier patterns of romantic intimacy and commitment are likely to be carried forward into the future, but change might also take place. Conceptually, Furman and Winkles (2012) contended that patterns of interactions experienced in an earlier romantic relationship are likely to be carried forward and enacted in a future relationship. Earlier patterns might evolve into scripts directing a person's behavior, and the model of the script is expressed in a future relationship (Byng-Hall, 1995a). Yet, considering the developmental progress that emerging adults are likely to experience (see a more detailed explanation in Chapter 10 on personality and emerging adulthood), a person might gain greater reflectivity (Michaeli et al., 2018) and approach the work–family balance in a different manner over time. In addition, a supportive and understanding partner might further serve as an instigator, leading to change of an earlier pattern (Rönkä et al., 2002).

In our 12-year-long study we were able to interview a significant number of our participants again at the age of 35 and asked them to describe their career and family lives and how they currently addressed them. Two patterns, described above, represented emerging adults who were highly invested in their careers. In the first pattern, individuals almost disregarded the need to address the relationship issue, as if a relationship was not really in their scope. In the second pattern, individuals were aware of relationships and family in the life of a person, but the men describing this pattern insisted that a woman needed to understand that her husband was invested in his career and accept this as it was for her benefit. Six years later we were able to interview four of the six interviewees described above.

At age 28 Roy described that his work was the center of his life and was more important than being in a relationship. At the age of 34 Roy was not in a relationship. When asked about his expectations regarding being in a relationship he responded, "Of course I would like to be in a relationship and hope it arrives." However, it was difficult for him to elaborate on how a relationship would "arrive." Later in the discussion he became more open and disclosed that "I do not think too much about this. I have plans about the future but not about a relationship. This is not part of life." He attributed his lower interest in relationships to his parents' divorce. We were quite surprised when he told us what his mother thinks about him getting married: "Is this really what you need? If you want children, find a girl, but why get married?"

At the age of 28 Yossi also described that "Work takes the major chunk of my life. And I hope it stays this way." At the second interview at age 35 Yossi was still much invested in his career and was not married. He had been dating a woman of his age for 3 months. He described that he is highly emotionally involved and was sure that this was a serious relationship and that they would marry. Yossi still sees the husband as the primary breadwinner. However, despite this attitude, he spoke fondly of his current girlfriend, her values, and her work. He added that he would have to make compromises but is happy with her and willing to settle down and start a family. It remains to be learned whether he married his current girlfriend.

The life histories of these two young adults suggested that the pattern of putting emphasis on career was continued until the age of 35, although it was differently expressed. The story of Yoram represents a different pattern. At the age of 28 Yoram also placed strong emphasis on his career and expected his partner to have her own work and not interfere with his plans. However, at the second interview at 35 years old, he had been married for 6 years and had a son almost 2 years old. He was still very career-focused, and when interviewed he was seeking a managerial position. However, though he still felt that he had the greater responsibility to support his family, his attitude toward balancing career and family had changed: "I am not looking for a job where I'll have to invest all my life in it. I want to do more for my family than for my work." In addition, Yoram described that he consults his wife when an important decision concerning his career needs to made and concluded, "I trust her. I think that I have come a long way. I have developed in our relationship both personally and professionally."

To summarize, emerging adults tend to prioritize career over romantic investment (Shulman & Connolly, 2013; Sneed et al., 2007). This is understandable considering the increasing societal and economic instabilities (Furlong & Cartmel, 2007) that have decreased the confidence emerging adults have in achieving financial security. In the past career pursuit (mainly of men) took place within the realm of the family (Levinson, 1978). Nowadays, young people tend to pursue their careers individually and become more practically and emotionally free to explore romantic relationships in a serious manner only once they have progressed in their careers. Stories such as that of Alex and his wife, who had coordinated the progress of their careers already in their mid-20s, were not common among our participants.

We contend that prioritization of career seems to represent the reality that young people must cope with a multitude of tasks they are facing at the same time. However, difficulty in finding time and resources to get romantically involved might reflect not only developmental processes but also difficulty in the capacity for romantic involvement. For example, Roy was overinvolved in his career, and reading the interview at age 35 suggested that prioritization of career also served as an explanation for refraining from romantic involvement.

Overall, the majority of emerging adults at their early and mid-20s indeed tended to prioritize investment in career over romantic commitment. However, following them across their 20s and into their mid-30s showed how they employed different patterns of balancing career and family and provided a variety of explanations for prioritizing work or balancing work and family. Yet, with age the majority learned how to balance career and family and described the centrality of career as well as the importance of family in their lives. Similar to our conclusions outlined in the previous chapters, again we can see how the emerging adulthood years are a period of preparation for settling down when approaching the 30s and how, within this process, young adults learn to balance work and love. Furthermore, in this process most young people change earlier perceptions of the essence of life and learn how to place the establishment of a family center stage. At age 28 Yoram perceived his career as the center of his universe and a future wife as a helpmate to assist his career aspirations. Six years later we met a different man. He truly balanced career and family, enjoyed his involvement with his little son, appreciated his wife's work as a teacher, and cherished the support and advice he receives from his wife, whom he highly trusts.

8
Achieving Life Authorship
The Psychological Challenge of Emerging Adulthood

In the previous chapter we described the variety of routes that emerging adults take toward successfully attaining their career and romantic goals. For the majority, progress toward their goals was a complex task; and along the way, they had to learn what career might serve them better in their lives and provide a sense of success. Although the road toward romantic commitment was not necessarily smooth, the majority of our participants found partners and started family life. Life, however, does not end once a person has successfully achieved a state of "settling down" (Levinson, 1978). Life continues after "settling down," after emerging adulthood. Life is a sequence of events and tasks that evolve and change across the years (Elder et al., 2003). This chapter examines how patterns of progress made during emerging adulthood might serve as models for, or guide future navigation across, life. Put differently, our question is what are the psychological assets that a young person is supposed to acquire during the emerging adulthood years that can affect future behavior and outcomes?

In his seminal work Daniel Levinson (1978) describes that the young person is a "novice" or an "apprentice" in the adult world. Following progress in one's career and family goals, the task is to advance beyond the apprentice stage and become a "full-fledged adult." The goals achieved up to this stage are then supposed to become the base on which one can further plan for the future and identify long-term aspirations. On this base one is supposed to define the "personal enterprise," giving the person a direction later in life. Levinson (1978) describes that "this enterprise contains in some form the imagery of a *ladder*" (p. 141). This ladder, which a person is expected to "climb" to become a senior member of their society, may have few or many rungs. The ladder captures one's aspirations and plans and, as such, is helpful for leading toward the further realization of one's dream. Levinson contended that the ladder is expected to be stable enough to allow accommodations along the way. In sum, this imaginary ladder is likely to serve as the "vehicle" through which young people continue to consolidate their lives.

Levinson's image of the ladder is impressive and appealing. It teaches us that young people are expected to emerge from the 20s with a solid basis and life plan to direct their lives in the years to come. Despite this inspiring image of the ladder, the construct of the ladder is not explicitly explained or defined. It is not informative about the capacities that are expected to be attained in the earlier years and how these might influence future behavior. Recent conceptualization and work within the narrative approaches to identity development framework can be helpful in providing meaning for the "ladder," that is, the capacities of which it might consist and that climbing it should be achieved toward the end of the emerging adulthood years.

Becoming an author of your life

In the preceding chapters on career and romantic development we described how young people progressed on the road to adulthood. In their words, our participants described their struggles and disappointments along the way, the efforts they made to find their way, and the compromises they had to make. Their efforts and struggles helped them to progress and ultimately settle down.

Conceptualized within the framework of the search for identity, Dan McAdams (2013a) suggests that emerging adulthood experiences can serve as the developmental platform for personal growth and construction of meaning and purpose for the future. Throughout life, individuals construct and internalize an evolving story of life (Singer, 2004) from past episodes and periods in their lives. The internalized and evolving amalgam of self-stories—referred to as a *narrative identity* (McAdams & Pals, 2006)—aims to integrate the reconstructed past, experienced present, and imagined future. Yet, becoming the author of one's life requires more than merely telling coherent stories about individual episodes and experiences. Individuals are expected to explain their role in their explorations, choices, and commitments and, more importantly, to become able to articulate what their personal memories mean for them. Through the search for meaning, and subsequently interpreting their memories, individuals can infer who they are, what their lives mean, and how they wish to navigate their lives (Habermas & Bluck, 2000).

It is particularly important to explore negative experiences in depth, to think about what an experience was like, how it happened, to what it could lead, and what role the negative event may play in the person's overall life story. The endeavor to understand what went wrong in the past has the potential to serve as a learning experience for future coping with and handling difficult experiences. In this way, personal stories that emphasize learning, growth, and positive personal transformation (Bauer et al., 2005) capture *self-continuity*, provide direction, and can become a model for future functioning. In this process, selves create stories that in turn create new selves, all in the context of significant interpersonal relationships and experiences (McLean et al., 2007).

Relatedly, Addis and Tippett (2008) described *narrative continuity*, which refers to a constructed sense of the self as a character in the many different scenes that comprise a story, extending back to the past and forward to the future. In narrative continuity, the integrative life story demonstrates continuity by explaining, in a narrative form, how the self has changed and adapted despite difficulties along the way. It is the capacity to continue to be your true self and to grow out of a difficult experience that guides the direction of life in the future.

McAdams (2013a) summarizes the process that takes place during these years:

> Emerging adults sample from the menu in constructing individual life stories, aiming to find narrative forms that capture their own personal experiences, allow for their own limitations and constraints, and convey their aspirations for the future. They appropriate models for living that prevail in the cultures wherein their lives have their constituent meanings. (p. 153)

Narrative identity thus emerges gradually, through daily conversations and social interactions, through decisions young people make regarding work and love, through introspection, and through lessons learned. Together these experiences provide a sense of continuity and meaningful direction in life, purpose for the future, and knowledge on how to navigate through difficult times based on past experiences (McAdams, 2006; McAdams & Cox, 2010; McLean & Pratt, 2006). As such, achieving authorship can be a marker of adaptation to guide a person in future aspirations and behavior. Indeed, a long line of research shows that overcoming adversity and finding meaning are associated with higher levels of psychological well-being, generativity, and other indices of successful adaptation to life (see Greenhoot & McLean, 2013; McAdams & McLean, 2013). Furthermore, McLean and Pratt (2006) emphasized that, in particular, it is the capacity to engage in more elaborate processing of turning points (following a difficult experience) that tended to associate with better future outcomes.

According to Levinson (1978), successful attainment of emerging adulthood tasks sets the basis for the capacity to continue setting goals for the years to come. Conceptually, Levinson's notions are embedded within the classical concept of developmental stages; namely, achieving an earlier stage facilitates progression and successful coping with future developmental stages. Integrating McAdams' concepts of authorship can further clarify and articulate how and what processes that take place during emerging adulthood affect future outcomes. According to McAdams, it is not only the achievement of emerging adulthood tasks that affects future outcomes; the learning experience that accompanies the progression toward attaining tasks is also crucial for future development and adaptation. According to McAdams (2013b), the *ability to draw lessons* from past experiences and, in particular, learning how to overcome difficulties and *grow out of earlier difficulties* are the mechanisms that are expected to be achieved during emerging adulthood; and this attained authorship is likely to shape future outcomes.

Assessment of authorship achievement and its prevalence toward the end of the 20s

McAdams (2013a) described the achievement of authorship as the hallmark of the process that emerging adults are expected to complete toward the end of their 20s. McAdams' conceptualization sheds light on the intensive and sometimes painful processes that emerging adults undergo on the journey to adulthood. For example, reading Barack Obama's life story (McAdams, 2013a) shows how through painful self-exploration and coming to terms with the past and with his identity, the young Barack Obama facilitated the progress toward grappling with the question of *What is my calling in life?* (p. 155). Conceptually, we would like to argue that the process undergone during the earlier years served the basis for the construction of the ladder (Levinson, 1978) that defined and guided the later moves of the older Obama. In his work McAdams mostly conceptualized the construct and presented case studies to demonstrate the construct of authorship. In this chapter we operationalize the construct of authorship and demonstrate empirically how the achievement of authorship is associated with future adaptive outcomes.

At the time of the fourth assessment in our project, when our participants were on average 29 years old, two in-depth interviews, focusing on career development and romantic development, respectively, were conducted with 100 of our participants. We have described the interviews in the preceding chapters when discussing career pursuit and romantic development. Relevant for understanding the development of authorship and its meaning, participants were also asked to reflect on changes and turning points in their recent work and career histories and on adaptations they made or did not make. To capture and address inner processes, participants were further encouraged to talk about and elaborate on the extent to which they felt that they had advanced on their aspired track and made adaptations, whether they were still unsure about what they really wanted to do in life, and the extent to which their job suits their interests and is meaningful to them. In particular, emphasis was placed on capturing the extent to which participants *learned from past experiences and disappointments* and whether these resulted in changes in behavior, future vocational aspirations, and family plans.

Defining and assessing attainment of authorship

In line with McAdams' (McAdams, 2013b; McAdams & McLean, 2013) accounts of life authorship and narrative identity, we used a number of criteria to determine achievement of authorship in the work or love domain. The ability to formulate a meaningful narrative for life was assessed by the following:

1. The presence of a sequencing of personal episodes that provides a coherent story.
2. The existence of positive changes and personal growth during recent years despite having to overcome possible difficult experiences.
3. The ability to reflect on past events and derive lessons and insights from negative emotional scenes in life.
4. The ability to plan ahead and formulate a meaningful narrative for life that sets the stage for future plans.

Identification of these criteria in an individual's career or romantic story determined whether said individual has or has not achieved authorship in the said domain.

During the coding procedure we learned that it was not always easy to identify all four criteria in some stories. In these cases, identification of three of the four criteria determined the achievement of authorship. In contrast, not achieving any criterion or achieving only one or two criteria was determined as not achieving authorship. Reading the interviews suggested that achieving authorship in one domain, such as career, was not necessarily associated with achieving authorship in the other domain. Therefore, we decided that each participant would be rated on whether authorship was achieved in either domain separately.

Two raters independently coded the interviews, and the inter-rater reliability was kappa = .88. and .79 for career and romantic authorship, respectively.

Types of work and relationship authorship and their prevalence

In line with the operationalization and definition of authorship in the work and relationship domains, we explored four types of authorship—authorship in both domains, in neither domain, or in either one of the domains, work or love. The four possible types were found and are described in the following sections. Prevalence is presented for each type of achieving or not achieving authorship.

Achievement of both work and romantic authorship—52 cases

These individuals provided coherent stories of their career and relationship development. Some of these emerging adults described how they set clear goals, and this directed their career pursuit, in which they were persistent and competent. The stories of a substantial number, however, also included experiences of failures and disappointments, which led them to shift to a different field of study or work. Most importantly, they were able to learn from failures, take initiative, reroute their professional plans, and understand what works or does not work for them. Their new plans provided them with direction and meaning for the coming years.

Their romantic stories were also coherent, although they were not necessarily involved in satisfactory relationships across the years. Some described difficult interactions with partners, which did not lead to a sense of failure but taught them to behave differently in a relationship. A recurrent story was the importance of learning to express your voice within a relationship.

Examination of the stories told by members of this type showed a more frequent use of words and phrases such as *aspired*, to *prove to myself* that, to *show that I am capable, learned a lesson, understood, developed, changed, challenge, realized I can do it differently*, and *choose*. In sum, these words—nouns, verbs, and adjectives—as they appeared in the stories told by these emerging adults, reflect an active and consistent attitude of the self to find its way, learn, change, and move forward even when facing obstacles.

Natti's life story represents a clear example of a young man who attained authorship despite his low starting point. Similar to our other participants, Natti applied to the preparatory program because he did not have the grades to apply to university. Natti describes that his entire life he dreamed of working with animals and that during his childhood he often found activities in which he could play or work with animals. Interviewed at age 28, he was a fourth-year student in biology at a university. Natti told us that studies are the center of his life. However, he failed a number of courses in biology in the preparatory program and understood that this would undermine his plans to continue studying at the university. He made a painful decision:

> I repeated these courses at the college. It took me a year. It was a big sacrifice, I knew I could find a good job, get a car, but I would bury myself my whole life. This was a decision [to repeat the year] for *myself* not for the money.

He applied to a dentistry school and was rejected, but his feeling that he could and should do this was strong. He applied the following year after repeating one more course and was accepted. Natti told us that it is his persistence that works for him: "I was always stubborn, focused, never gave up." He added "you have to look forward only." Natti also attributed much of his success to support from his father and close friend.

It can be seen that Natti has developed a coherent life story. Though the description of his stories could sound heroic, he was open enough to describe his failures, his fears, and his disappointments. More important, he was able to draw lessons from his experiences and construct a plan for developing a career to which he had aspired since his childhood.

In the romantic interview, Natti described that he had been in a close relationship for about a year. Being in a stable relationship is a new experience for him. During his 20s he was never in a serious relationship and was mostly involved in casual encounters. He was introduced to M. through a mutual friend. She is attractive but told him at their first meeting that she was looking for a serious relationship and, therefore, that she was not interested in him. Natti was confused and frightened by this unexpected response. He does not know how this reaction did not push him away but added: "She revived something that I did not have. I do not know whether you call this home, but it is like this." Despite this experience of rejection, Natti was ready to continue this experience: "On the one hand I was hurt, but with her I felt confident to open my heart. I learned you might get hurt but you learn something from this and move to a better place." Natti concluded the interview by saying that he is committed to M., he will never hurt her, and he is seriously considering building a future with her.

Considered together, in his romantic accounts Natti also described a process of learning (resembling the pattern of progress from a sporadic to a steady relationship). In his story, Natti was able to describe clearly how, over time, he became more aware of his casual romantic interactions and wished for change, which was accomplished with the help of M., his current partner for over a year. Furthermore, this progress went hand in hand with his career plans, reflecting a coherent life story with articulated future plans. Reading Natti's life story suggested that during the preceding years he constructed a solid base, the ladder that would take him toward and into his 30s.

Failure to achieve work and romantic authorship—22 cases

Individuals belonging to this type were unable to provide a clear and coherent idea through the interview of what they would like to do with their lives and described feeling miserable. They described being driven by forces or dreams stronger than themselves, as a result of which they found themselves in occupational positions or realities that were beyond their control. Their overall feeling was of repeating mistakes or being lost. Their relationship histories were also incoherent. Some described anxieties that led to lack of initiative in their romantic behavior; others described disappointments in their romantic experiences that they were unable to address and overcome. They also did not describe any ability to learn from their negative experiences and felt miserable, repetitively facing disappointments. Their future seemed uncertain, although they did hope to find a suitable job and establish a family.

Examination of the stories told by participants who had not achieved authorship in any domain revealed more common use of words and phrases such as *I have no idea, got lost, do not know what I really want for myself, nothing changes, find myself in the same place again and again, it is my destiny,* and *feeling lost.* All of these words reflect experiences or feelings where one's self lacks the ability to direct or guide one's life.

We have described Nora's life story in the preceding chapters. At age 27 Nora had not completed any degree and had no stable job, no clear career plan. Despite being involved twice in relationships that lasted for a couple of years, these did not develop into a serious relationship, nor was she able to draw lessons from her romantic involvements to direct her in her future relationships. As such, she truly presents those young people who did not successfully develop any authorship of their career development or romantic relationships.

Whenever Nora is exposed to a difficult situation at her workplace, her common reaction is to quit and start a new job, often a job that does not require any qualifications, such as a salesperson in a shop. Watching how her friends developed during the years leads her to ask herself what is wrong with her. And she realizes, "I do not find myself, have no idea. I have no goal, and this is what shatters my life." Nora was involved in two long romantic relationships in recent years, but she does not understand what went wrong: "All my boyfriends wanted to marry, to settle down but I did not feel I was ready." (*"Can you explain how come they proposed and you refused?"*) "I have no idea, this is what I am." Overall, Nora was not able to describe a coherent story of her romantic experiences. These were episodes that did not connect to one another, and she did not learn from one experience to the next.

In sum, Nora showed difficulty developing a coherent story of her occupational and romantic lives. She appeared to lack any plans and, due to her lack of confidence in her capacities, lacked the ability to pursue a career and to become involved in a serious relationship. Her behavior was rather in response to immediate needs such as earning money or being with somebody. Her overtures were not planned ahead. She was also unable to explain to herself the reasons behind her behavior. She was approaching the end of her 20s and had not constructed any ladder for climbing to the next decade of her life.

Achievement of work authorship—22 cases

Individuals in this category described were highly invested in their work but had not been in a relationship that lasted for at least 6 months. Their work stories were coherent, describing high investment in their work and struggles and successes along the years. They described that success was not achieved easily, and they learned that hard work and, in particular, calculated patience (understanding that it takes time to reach your goal) were necessary to find your way in your professional life.

At times, these individuals appeared to perceive career as the *center of their self*, as if to explain why there was no time left for romantic involvement. "How could I develop a relationship if I work very often till 10 pm?" Although they had aspirations to start a family at this stage of their lives, this goal was pushed to some time in the future.

Yoram, age 28, was raised in a working-class family. In high school he did not invest in his studies and did not achieve the requirements to apply for higher studies. After completing his military service, he found a job where he earned a nice salary and hesitated over whether studying would be a waste of time and money. However, his close friends convinced him to join the college preparatory program so that he would have more options in the future. After completing the program, he was still unsure about what he really wanted to study. Again, a close friend convinced him to apply for engineering. Studies at the school of engineering were not easy, and he needed many scholarships to support himself. Thoughts that this place (engineering) was not for him crossed his mind. The support he received from his teachers and friends helped him through the years. Furthermore, Yoram disclosed that studying changed him and his attitude toward life: "They taught me the kind of a person I am and should be. It helped me, it changed my life. And in the future I will help others."

Yoram made impressive progress from where he had started—not only in attaining a degree. He also underwent some inner changes, becoming more introspective about the route he took and developing generativity. Despite these impressive changes, his views about family are still less articulated. Telling us about his next plan, he described, "I have a clear direction. Graduate, take a long trip, start working and establish a family. Soon I will be 30, enough with parties, drinking, I will go dancing but with my wife. To go with your wife adds more spice." However, getting into a serious relationship is, at this point in time, postponed.

In sum, Yoram made impressive progress in the work domain. However, family life or a wife (at age 28 when interviewed) was considered a necessary part of life yet a part that should not interfere with Yoram's major plan—success in his career—suggesting that authorship in the domain of romantic relationships or family had not yet been achieved.

Achievement of romantic authorship—Four cases

Four young mothers were classified as having achieved romantic relationship authorship but not work authorship. Three women who gave birth during the previous year and one who was due to give birth within the coming 2 months described their family and their children as the center of their lives. Family life is not necessarily easy, but they described their efforts and struggles over the years to establish a close and satisfying relationship with their husbands. They perceived their babies, or the baby soon to be born, as a source of strength that led them to understand themselves in a different and a more mature way and that gave meaning to their lives as mothers. In contrast, work was perceived as a non-supportive environment in which one sometimes had to fight for survival. Furthermore, they had no clear goals or plan for the future and rather conveyed a sense of having gotten lost in their professional lives.

Netta has a history of frequent changes in her fields of study and her workplaces. She studied for about three semesters in a program for kindergarten teachers and left to get married. She then moved between what she termed meaningless jobs. Later, she started a course to become a beautician and left when she had learned that she was pregnant. At the age of 29, she started a program for infant daycare workers, but she is still not sure whether this is the direction she wants to take in her life and finds comfort in raising her baby.

Netta's child provides her with stable ground (and probably serves as an excuse for not working). Her relationship with her husband is more complex. On the one hand, she describes that they love one another; but, on the other hand, she disclosed that they had separated twice for a couple of days. We were not sure whether Netta could correctly be identified as having authorship in the relationship domain. Some aspects of her romantic interview were not coherent. However, considering that she was married and in quite a stable relationship and found support in being a mother, we decided to identify her as having attained authorship in the relationship field but not with regard to career.

Considered together, the findings showed that more than half of our 28- to 29-year-old participants were able to provide coherent and reflective accounts of their work and romantic lives, describing the ability to cope with difficult circumstances, to draw lessons from their experiences, to pursue their plans or adapt new plans, and to have articulated meaningful plans for the coming years (McAdams, 2013b). As described in their stories, the previous years were those during which these emerging adults struggled to formulate a meaningful narrative for life, might have lost their way but found a new way that was meaningful for them, and paved the way for future plans (Heckhausen et al., 2010; McAdams, 2013b; McAdams & Cox, 2010).

Yet, not all achieved authorship in both domains. We found that a quarter of our sample achieved work authorship but fell short of authorship with regard to romantic relationships. We suggest that among those who had not yet settled down and were still pursuing their life plans, the tendency to prioritize work over relationships could still be observed. This idea is consistent with our earlier description of previous findings suggesting that during their earlier 20s it is common for young people to prioritize work over romance (Osgood et al., 2005; Seiffge-Krenke et al., 2010). This preference was clearly expressed in the stories of participants belonging to this type. They described that increased investment in their careers left them with little time to invest in their romantic lives. It is possible that the pressure to attain financial security first does not leave enough time and energy to enter into a committed relationship (Almeida, 2002).

Almost a quarter of our sample had not achieved authorship in either the work or the romantic relationship domain. Their stories might reflect the typical descriptions of emerging adults (Arnett, 2004; European Group for Integrated Social Research, 2001). However, a closer inspection of their narratives suggested that these emerging adults were no longer exploring different options, did not have any clear plans, and had difficulty articulating a coherent life story. The impression was that they got lost during the years of pursuit and were unsuccessful at learning from their experiences.

Closer inspection also showed that the majority of participants who had achieved only work authorship were men. In contrast, the few participants who had achieved only family authorship were women. These gender differences call for greater attention to a possible gendered way toward settling down, and this will be further discussed in the next chapter.

Achievement of authorship and successful settling down during the 30s

The major premise of this chapter is that achieving authorship sets the basis on which successful settling down and future progress rest. Authorship of our participants was assessed when they were, on average, 29 years old—the end of emerging adulthood (Arnett, 2004). Six years later, when our participants were about 35 years old, they were given a large battery of questionnaires assessing their functioning and psychological well-being. In addition, we were able to interview 70% of those who were interviewed 6 years earlier. In the following sections we first compare levels of well-being across the three patterns of authorship—achievement of both work and relationship authorship, failure to achieve both work and relationship authorship, and achievement of work authorship only. Due to the small number of participants who had achieved only relationship authorship, $n = 4$, this pattern was not included in the comparisons. In addition, based on the interviews conducted at age 35, we demonstrate how individuals with different constellations of authorship describe their achievements and their lives in general. This is presented in their own words.

Future outcomes: Quantitative accounts

Participants were told the average monthly income in Israel at the time of the 35-year-old assessment. They were then asked to rate whether their monthly income was below the average (1), about the average (2), or above the average (3). An analysis of variance (ANOVA) revealed significant differences between the three patterns of authorship, $F = 7.27$, $p < .001$. Those who had not achieved authorship in either domain reported the lowest income level, $M = 1.23$ ($SD = .77$); those who had achieved only work authorship reported an intermediate level of income, close to the mean state income, $M = 1.71$ ($SD = .96$); and those who had achieved both work and relationship authorship reported an income level above the average. The mean income level for those who had achieved only work authorship was $M = 2.14$ ($SD = .92$). Post hoc comparisons showed that a significant difference was found between those who had and those who had not achieved both work and relationship authorship. Those who had achieved only work authorship were at the intermediate level.

Cross-tabulation of authorship pattern at age 29 and marital status at age 35 also showed a significant association between the two ($\chi^2[4, n = 85] = 22.19$, $p = .000$). Those who had not achieved authorship in any domain were more likely to be single than married at the age of 35. In contrast, and as might be expected, those who had achieved both work and relationship authorship were more likely to be married than single at age 35. The distribution of those who achieved only work authorship at age 29 showed quite similar numbers for those who were married and those who were single. Taken together, we can see that achieving or not achieving authorship at age 29 significantly explained the extent to which an individual has successfully progressed into young adulthood, earned a reasonable salary, and established a family.

To further assess functioning and psychological well-being at age 35, we assessed the extent to which a person identified with their career, accepted themselves, had a purpose in life, and had a sense of flourishing. For this purpose, we administered the following inventories: *Career commitment* was assessed via the Vocational Identity Status Assessment (Porfeli et al., 2011; e.g., "I feel this is the best work for me"); two of Ryff's (1989) Subscales of Psychological Well-Being, *Purpose of Life* (e.g., "For me, life has been a continuous process of learning, changing and growth") and *Self-Acceptance* (e.g., "I like most aspects of my personality"); and *flourishing* was assessed via the EPOCH measure (Kern et al., 2016), which assesses participants' experience that life is going well, namely feeling good and functioning effectively (e.g., "I think good things are going to happen to me," "I am a cheerful person," "When something good happens to me, I have people in my life that I like to share the good news with"). In addition, the number of *depressive and anxiety symptoms* was assessed via the Brief Symptom Inventory (Derogatis & Melisaratos, 1983). Two subscales assessing number of depressive symptoms (e.g., "How often did you feel lonely during the last month?") and number of anxiety symptoms (e.g., "An unexplained feeling of fear") were also administered.

A multivariate ANOVA comparing psychological well-being across the three authorship patterns yielded a significant difference, Wilks $(df, 12, 144) = 2.33$, $p = .006$.

Means, standard deviations, and univariate F values are presented in Table 8.1. As can be seen, emerging adults who achieved both work and relationship authorship at the age of 29 reported consistently greater psychological well-being at age 35 compared to those who had not achieved authorship in either domain. They were committed to their career choice and found meaning in what they did,

Table 8.1 *Levels of Psychosocial Functioning Across the Three Authorship Patterns: M (SD), F Values and Effect Sizes*

	1 No work no romantic authorship	2 Work authorship	3 Work and romantic authorship	F	η^2
Depressive symptoms	1.74 (1.11)$_a$	.65 (.70)$_b$	.65 (.71)$_b$	14.47***	.25
Anxiety symptoms	1.55 (1.13)$_a$	.61 (.42)$_b$	1.02 (.75)$_{a,b}$	7.45**	.15
Hostility symptoms	1.19 (1.14)$_a$	.43 (.43)$_b$	.74 (.69)$_b$	5.23**	.19
Goal attainment	4.28 (1.46)$_a$	5.05 (1.00)$_{a,b}$	5.50 (.85)$_b$	6.81***	.18
Goal importance	5.42 (1.57)$_a$	6.13 (1.02)$_b$	6.34 (.82)$_b$	5.25**	.11

Note. Different subscripts indicate statistically significant differences between types at the $p < .05$ level. Adapted from Shulman, S., Hakhmigari, M. K., Michaeli, Y., Tuval-Mashiach, R., & Dickson, D. J. (2016). Achieving work and love authorship in emerging adulthood: Types, psychosocial correlations, and precursors. *Emerging Adulthood*, 4(4), 258–271. https://doi.org/10.1177/2167696815606563

**$p < .01$. ***$p < .001$.

found more purpose in their lives, and were more self-accepting. In addition, they had a sense that they were flourishing. Finally, and as could be expected, they reported a very low number of depressive symptoms. Emerging adults who achieved only work authorship revealed an inconsistent pattern of functioning at age 35. Despite describing work authorship, they reported a lower level of career commitment and of flourishing. Their levels of psychological well-being, of purpose in life, and of self-acceptance were intermediate. They reported a low number of depressive symptoms. Considered together, the overall achievement of authorship (McAdams, 2013b) paved the way for smoother settling down and greater psychological well-being during the mid-30s. Our findings suggest that achieving only "partial" authorship could not facilitate the building of a solid "ladder" or built a ladder that did not have enough rungs to climb successfully and competently into the later stages of life.

Future outcomes: Narrative accounts

To further learn about individuals with the different patterns of achieving authorship, we will present descriptions in their own words of the process of settling down and what they had achieved 6 years later. At age 34, when the second round of the in-depth interviews took place, Natti had completed dentistry school and started to work in a public clinic. He was married and had three young children. When asked to describe the changes he went through, Natti replied, "Major changes, I have completed my studies, started working and the children were born. During my first year at dental school my older son was born. It was tough, I was fully invested in my studies, only scholarships." I was supported by scholarships helped him to focus on his studies and graduate. Natti emphasizes and values his wife's role in his course of development.

> I met my wife during the last year of my first degree, and we decided that we want a family. After my son was born, I understood that nothing is important, what is important are the children and the rest are means. You wish to achieve your aspirations, for them. What pushed me was not only my wish to be a vet.

Natti further described how his career and family were coordinated and mutually supportive. "Luckily my aspirations also served as means to support my family. I feel these experiences made me more mature, know how to approach life."

Reading Natti's story suggests that career and family are coordinated and integrated. Progress in one domain supports or gives meaning to the other—"I work for my family." In Natti's story we could see the achievement of work and family authorship, and how their coordination led to the building of a "solid structure" that incorporates and integrates family needs as well as individual needs. This structure serves as a secure base and guides behavior and future plans on a daily basis.

In contrast, the life story of Nora, who had not achieved work or relationship authorship, could be best represented as a "structure-less" pattern of life. Overall, Nora feels that she is lost. "I am stuck, romantically, my studies, I always have the feeling that I am a failure, my life is wasted." From one day to the next, Nora looks for consolation, in the form of a good day at work or a compliment from a romantic partner. When asked how she sees herself 5 years from now, she answered, "Only God might know."

Future outcomes for participants who had achieved only work authorship were mixed. Some aspects of outcomes resembled those who had achieved authorship both in work and in relationships, while on other aspects their level of psychological well-being was lower. Reading their interviews at the age of 35 clarified these inconsistencies. In Chapter 6 we described the life story of Yoram, who was not married at age 28 and perceived the establishment of a family as secondary to his career. However, at the age of 34 he was happily married, the father of a 9-month-old daughter, and very supportive of his wife, who was a teacher. Despite the priority he assigned to work in the past, like Natti he learned the importance and centrality of his family for him: "At work all is politics; it is only the family that cares truly for you." In contrast to Yoram, Yehoshua, who also prioritized career, was not married at age 35.

He completed his degree in engineering, and had become professionally and highly valued in the company in which he worked. It was evident from reading the interview that Yehoshua is very competent in "authoring" his career life plan. However, his romantic life resembles the relationship in which he was involved 6 years earlier that was dissolved after 3 years. Yehoshua describes that he is very much dedicated to his girlfriend of the past 2 years, but the relationship does not seem to progress. It appeared to be replicating his former romantic relationship that was dissolved. No process of learning from the former relationship could be traced in his words, which strengthened our impression that he was still not able to develop authorship in the romantic domain.

Conclusions

In sum, guided by McAdams' (McAdams, 2013b; McAdams & McLean, 2013) accounts of life authorship and narrative identity, we were able to classify participants according to the extent to which they had achieved or had not achieved authorship in the work and romantic relationship domains. Reading the in-depth interviews allowed us to learn about the ways in which emerging adults pursue and achieve work and romantic authorship and the coordination of these two developmental tasks. We were also able to show that for the majority of emerging adults approaching the age of 30, work and romantic relationships are interdependent and that most were able to achieve authorship in both domains. They constructed a meaningful story; were able to draw lessons from past experiences, good or bad; and consolidated a sense of competence in the worlds of work and love. This facilitated the construction of a life plan that paved the way for the challenges and opportunities that emerge in the later stages of life (McAdams, 2013b). Reading the interviews and bearing Levinson's (1978) metaphor in mind, we could better understand how these young people constructed the ladder on which they further climbed in their future lives.

Reading the stories carefully suggested that they constructed the basic structure of a ladder. For example, entering his 30s Natti had constructed a clear plan which he had started to implement: He started dental school and started a family. In addition, Natti's story showed how the basic structure continued to evolve over time, "adding rungs to the ladder." Natti found ways to obtain and secure financial support for his growing family, which was coordinated with his career requirements, such as internship. Thus, his life structure at the beginning of his 30s served as a stepping stone to progress toward the future steps. This process recalls Roberts' (B. W. Roberts & Davis, 2016; B. W. Roberts et al., 2006) construct of personality maturity, suggesting that reaching maturity (such as the capacity to construct a life plan) allows greater flexibility in the way environmental pressures are perceived. As a result, this enhances a person's sense of competence to set and pursue additional tasks and complete a successful transition. Metaphorically, we might suggest that rungs are added in order to extend the ladder for new and future tasks. The processes and the complexity in the construction of authorship further support our contention that the 20s might be considered a period of learning how to settle down and of constructing a life plan—a ladder. The attainment of developmental tasks in career and romantic relationship, and the consolidation of inner authorship, can guide a successful transition and progress into young adulthood and later life stages (Cohen et al., 2003).

9
Gendered Pathways in Career Pursuit and Romantic Development

In Chapter 7 we discussed the ways emerging adults negotiate and balance their work and family goals. Reading the life stories of these young people shows that, overall, men are more likely to put romantic life aside and become immersed in their careers. The wish to begin a family was more dormant and perceived as a future goal. In contrast, women are more likely to express the urge to start a family and bear children. Notwithstanding the importance that young people attribute to their careers (Shulman & Connolly, 2013), for many young women establishing a family was a primary goal and not secondary to their career.

Considering that career pursuit and the establishment of a family are considered the two major goals in a person's development, in this chapter we examine the gendered ways that women and men pursue career and family goals. For this purpose, we first present findings that emerged in our longitudinal study comparing the typical career and romantic pathways among women and men during emerging adulthood. We then examine the theoretical concepts that can explain the reasons for the distinctive roads that women and men take during this journey into adulthood. Finally, following the lives of a number of women, we examine possible different patterns of balancing work and family at which young women tend to arrive.

Career and romantic pathways during emerging adulthood— Gendered patterns of progress toward adulthood

Analysis of emerging adults' accounts of their career and romantic life histories (Chapters 3 and 5) indicates the variety of pathways that young people take on the journey to adulthood. We found that almost 60% of our participants reported an adaptive career pursuit history. They were able either to progress competently (the *Consistent* and *Adapted Pursuit* pathways) toward their initial aspired goal or to disengage from an aspired goal in case of failure or disappointment, set a new goal that was meaningful for them, and pursue this successfully. Among the rest, a third of the sample—the *Survivors*—appeared to have settled down and managed their daily lives properly. However, despite their daily functioning, they reported an inner feeling of dissatisfaction with their current occupations and little emotional connection with their jobs. In addition, a smaller number—belonging to the *Confused/Vague* pathway—were young people who either did not have any clear plans or were afraid of aspiring at all. They were only employed periodically and had a sense of being marginalized.

Tabulation of these career pursuit pathways across genders shows that more young men than young women were likely to belong to the more adaptive pathways: the *Consistent Pursuit* pathway (19 of 24 were men) and the *Adapted Pursuit* pathway (21 of 34 were men). In contrast, young women were more likely than young men to belong to the less adaptive pathways: the *Survivors* pathway (18 of 28 were women) and the *Confused/Vague* pathway (10 of 14 were women). Pathway patterns thus varied by gender: χ^2 ($df = 3$, $n = 100$) = 14.36, $p = .001$. These findings clearly suggest that there is a higher likelihood that young men, compared to young women, will find their way in the career world. Young men were more likely to be either focused on their career goals or more capable of overcoming their difficulties, making a shift along the way and finding a career with which they were satisfied and that was meaningful for them (Blustein, 2011).

Women were found less in the adaptive pathways and more in the less adapted pathways. They were more highly represented in the pathway of those who made a compromise concerning their career, finding themselves in jobs that were not their first choice. In addition, the proportion of women was significantly higher among the emerging adults who lost their way. These findings suggesting that, contrary to men, women are less likely to navigate competently toward a meaningful career raise a major question. This data was collected at the beginning of the third millennium, when it could be expected that women have reached equality and that all options are open to them. We believe that these finding suggest that young women still face "invisible" cultural and societal obstacles. This question, which will be discussed across this chapter, is, in fact, its main message.

Analysis of the romantic life histories showed that emerging adults' romantic involvements across the years were characterized by four different pathways of integrating fluidity and stability. The majority of our interviewees—68.5%, comprising the *Sporadic* and *Casual to Steady* involvement pathways—described a variety of fluctuations between casual sexual and romantic experiences, short-lived relationships, and periods of having no romantic interaction and sometimes no interest. Yet half of these young people, the *Casual to Steady* pathway, were able to learn from their short and non-stable romantic experiences and progress toward romantic intimacy and commitment. The rest of our sample associated with two stable pathways. One was a classical pattern of romantic stability—the *Steady Relationship* pathway. These participants were involved in steady relationships that were characterized by a process of learning and development within their relationships over time. In addition, we found the *Lengthy Relationship but Absence of Experiential Learning* pathway, in which young people tended to be involved mainly in long and lasting romantic relationships that did not progress toward real commitment and led nowhere.

Distinctive gender patterns were found again concerning the romantic pathways that emerging adults took. The distribution of romantic pathways across genders showed that young women were more likely to belong to lasting relationship pathways, whereas young men tended more to belong to short relationship pathways or to be only sporadically involved. Women were more likely to belong to the *Steady Relationship* pathway (9 of the 14 were women) and the *Lengthy Relationship but Absence of Experiential Learning* pathway (8 of 10 were women). In contrast, young men were more likely to belong to less stable pathways: the *Sporadic* (22 of 33 were men) and the *Casual to Steady* pathway (21 of 30 were men). Pathway patterns thus varied by gender; χ^2 (df = 3, n = 92) = 15.75, p < .001. Examination of these gendered pathways suggests that men tend to be more involved in sporadic relationships while women are inclined to be involved in a stable relationship. Interestingly, women and men demonstrated distinctive preferences in their romantic interactions. These were either a sporadic or a stable pathway. Of note, each tendency, sporadic or stable, could either progress or not progress toward mature intimacy and commitment.

Considered together, we might thus suggest that emerging adult men prioritize career over romantic investment. Prioritization of career might explain their greater penchant to be involved in sporadic romantic encounters. This pattern of romantic interaction that is short of commitment is less likely to interfere with men's career pursuit (Shulman & Connolly, 2013). In contrast, emerging adult women tend more to become involved in a stable relationship, which might interfere with their availability to be highly invested in their career pursuit. We speculate that the greater tendency to be involved in a stable romantic relationship might take its toll on women. They might feel more pressured to invest in their romantic relationships and less flexible in staying focused on their careers. Still, it is questionable why women feel more pressured to invest in their families and compromise their career aspirations. In 2012, *The Atlantic* published an article with the provocative title "Why Women Still Can't Have It All" (Slaughter, 2012). The writer of the *Atlantic* article, Anne-Marie Slaughter, served as director of policy planning with the US Department of State between 2009 and 2011. She left this position after 2 years and returned to her previous job as a university professor, stating that she wanted to spend more time with her two adolescent sons, who had been adversely affected by her position. In our opinion, Slaughter's personal story epitomizes the dilemma in which women are still trapped. On the one hand, they might be as highly educated, professional, and competent as their male counterparts, yet they feel a heavy responsibility to invest in the upbringing of their children and the well-being of their family. And they are ready to pay the price (Lachover, 2014).

In order to understand why young women, and not young men, are still currently engulfed by this dilemma, we first review the existing gender-related literature that can explain our proposed dialectic of career and romantic pathways among emerging adult women and men. The evolutionary and cultural scripts, as well as current societal laws and regulations, exert more pressure on women. Second, based on our 12 years of data, we examine how this dialectic is expressed by the young people in their own words in their life stories, with the aim of better understanding the inner motivations that directed the young women's behavior and the distinctive ways in which the young women in our study addressed this dilemma.

The gendered dialectic of career and family: Theoretical perspectives

There are a variety of ways to describe, and that characterize, how men and women differ (Fiese & Skillman, 2000). In his personality theory, McAdams (1993) suggested that the themes of affiliation and achievement play an important part in the development of personal identity. Progressing through life, different themes, such as affiliation and achievement, become integrated into the definition of one's self. Theoretically, it has been suggested that women tend to frame experiences along lines of affiliative themes and men tend to frame experiences along lines of achievement (Gilligan, 1982; McAdams & de St. Aubin, 1992). In her work on the stories that parents tell their young children, Fiese (Fiese et al., 1995; Fiese & Skillman, 2000) showed that though parents emphasize the expression of affiliation, in general boys tended to hear stories that included stronger themes of autonomy than girls, and fathers told stories with stronger themes of autonomy than mothers. Furthermore, this gender distinction intensified as children grew older. Compared to early-age children, preschool children were told more stories capturing achievement and, again, boys were told more stories of achievement than girls were (Fiese et al., 1995). Further, fathers more often told stories of achievement, while the focus of stories told by mothers was more on issues of affiliation. Thus, from both the perspective of the storyteller—father or mother—and the perspective of the child listening to a story—boy or girl—there are consistent gender differences. Men are more focused and attuned to achievement, while women are more attuned to relationships. In her seminal work, Maccoby (1990) showed that similar gender differences can be observed among children within their social contexts. Observation of school-age children shows that the two genders engage in different kinds of activities and games.

Girls play in closed areas and form close and intimate friendships with a number of other girls. In contrast, boys play in larger groups, and their play is rougher and more competitive.

Embedded within the broader framework of the socialization theory, Hill and Lynch (1983) outlined the gender intensification theory, suggesting that parents raise their sons and daughters differently: Parents generally encourage autonomy in sons more than they do in daughters and obedience in daughters more than in sons, and mothers and fathers are differentially involved with daughters versus sons. These distinctive attitudes become more pronounced during adolescence. Adolescent males are granted more autonomy than females, while females who date are more likely to be in conflict with their parents (Dowdy & Kliewer, 1998) and to be heavily regulated (Madsen, 2008) or restricted (Kan et al., 2008). Furthermore, to our surprise, we found that the higher regulation of daughters' and greater support of sons' romantic involvements were conducted not only by their fathers but also by their mothers. This can explain why adolescent males were more likely to be observed in non-stable or short-duration relationships, whereas adolescent females were more likely to be involved in stable relationships of longer duration that are easier to control (Shulman, Walsh, et al., 2009).

These distinctive socialization patterns start as early as in infancy, suggesting that women are more socialized to invest in their close and intimate relationships, whereas men are encouraged more to "play rough" and to follow and achieve their goals. This distinction can explain why men focus more on their work, which captures personal achievement, while women place greater value on intimate relationships (Almeida, 2002). This gendered pattern is further enhanced when child care is at stake. Not only fathers but also mothers tend to believe that mothers are more competent at taking care of their children (Sayer et al., 2004). Contrary to men, women's greater investment in and assignment of greater importance to the care of their children can explain why women's work is more likely to be interrupted by family duties such as child care (Blossfeld & Hofmeister, 2006). Indeed, women regarded parenthood and other family issues as turning points more often than men did, whereas men regarded occupational events as turning points more often than women did (Ronka et al., 2003). It is also quite common for women to perceive their husbands as not sufficiently capable of or committed to taking care of a child, which might also lead women toward greater involvement and to perceive their family and parental obligations as their primary role (Dienhart, 2001). In contrast, men tend to perceive their family and paternal roles as secondary to their career (Pedersen, 2012) and to perceive the provider role, closely linked to work, as central for them as parents (e.g., Christiansen & Palkovitz, 2001). It is interesting to note that in our study women were less represented in the *Consistent* and *Adapted Pursuit* pathways and that, despite acclaimed increases in gender equality in many modern societies, they still find themselves in careers that are less demanding (Buchmann & Kriesi, 2009). Thus, different socialization experiences can explain why women might be less able to fulfill their occupational dreams. In addition, there is an implicit (and sometimes an explicit) expectation that a woman identifies first with her role as a spouse and a mother, while her career takes a secondary role (Palladino Schultheiss, 2008). Thus, despite the seeming increases in gender equality, women still face social expectations that might intensify the different socialization experiences and lead them to take greater responsibility for family issues and be the primary caregivers of their children (Palladino Schultheiss, 2008). This gender distinction was mirrored in our findings concerning the types of romantic pathways in which women and men were more likely to be involved. Women were more likely to be found in steady relationships, even when the relationship was not optimal, while men were over-represented in the non-stable pathways. As suggested above, women place high emphasis on relationships and are probably more willing to waive personal preferences in order to have a relationship and maintain this intact. Previous theory and research suggest that women prefer to remain in a continued connection and pay the price (Jordan, 2004). In contrast, men have a greater need to establish feelings of competence, self-definition, and autonomy. Men, contrary to women, tend to refrain from becoming involved and committed when they encounter difficulties in their romantic involvement. In addition, men deliberately tend to invest more in their studies or career and therefore postpone romantic commitment (Manning et al., 2011; Shulman & Connolly, 2013). It is also possible that men deliberately postpone their commitment until they have completed their studies and can more competently provide for a family (Almeida, 2004).

The gendered pathways in career pursuit and romantic development can also be understood within an evolutionary perspective. Evolutionary approaches describe that men and women have evolved mating strategies whereby either gender can benefit in relation to the costs, namely producing and raising healthy offspring (Buss & Schmitt, 1993; Gangestad & Simpson, 2000). Outlining the sexual strategies theory, Buss and Schmitt (1993) suggested that, on average, men can benefit more than women from attempting to attract multiple mates. For men a single act of intercourse can produce an offspring, and more partners can increase the chances of reproduction. This can motivate men to be more open to sex outside a primary partnership and less committed to any single relationship (Buss & Schmitt, 1993; Schmitt & Shackelford, 2003). In contrast, women's minimum investment of a 9-month gestational period produces only one offspring. For a woman the likelihood of survival of her offspring will increase once she is in a long-lasting relationship with a partner who supports her and her child.

Despite the conceptualized distinctive gender mating strategies, long-term pair-bonding appears to be the norm within and across cultures (Quinlan, 2008), questioning the relevance of this evolutionary approach to the understanding of men's and women's attitudes toward romantic investment. In his review of the sexual strategies theory (Buss & Schmitt, 1993), Smiler (2011) suggested that though the vast majority of men are involved in, and committed to, long-term relationships, men might still desire engagement in short-term mating. In fact, this desire can be found among men in their premarital romantic interactions. For example, men reported a desire for more partners than women did (Schmitt et al., 2003) and greater intent to have sex with previously unknown partners than young women did (Maticka-Tyndale et al., 2003). We also described above that emerging adult men, compared to women, reported involvement in short-term relationships and casual sex more often (Claxton & van Dulmen, 2013). Thus, despite the norm of establishing a long-lasting relationship, evolutionary "residuals" might still play a role in the way men and women handle career and family issues in their lives.

Considered together, both socialization and evolutionary approaches can explain why emerging adult men are more focused on their careers and less attuned to becoming committed in their romantic relationships, whereas women prioritize greater investment in their romantic relationships over career pursuit. Unfortunately, these gendered attitudes toward career and family are further intensified when societal rules, regulations, and realities are closely examined. The law in the majority of societies emphasizes gender equality and claims that every girl and boy should have equal chances to succeed and develop in their lives. However, while the laws underscore women's equality, the attitude toward mothers is less clear. Tamar Krichly-Katz and colleagues (2018) show that laws in the United States are still less successful at addressing discrimination of working mothers. For example, working mothers' salaries tend to decrease by 5% per child compared to those of women without children. Thus, progressing toward settling down and bearing children among women is not only "guided" by different cultural and evolutionary scripts. Even the existing laws are not always sufficiently sensitive to the needs of young mothers and expose them to additional difficulties.

In sum, women and men are often differently guided (or programmed by cultural and societal scripts) when progressing toward settling down. For men, it is more clear that they are expected to be invested in their careers and provide for their family. Women, in contrast, hear and learn of the increasing gender equality; but being sensitive to the cultural scripts, they are also aware that making the transition to motherhood is likely to carry a toll on their career aspirations. In the following section, we examine the extent to which the gendered pathways in career pursuit and romantic/family development are carried forward into young adulthood for both men and women. Based on the interviews conducted with our participants at the age of 35, we try to answer this question in their own words.

The gendered dialectic of career and family and its expression at age 35—The story of men: Connected but separate

In our discussion of the coordination of career and romantic relationships in Chapter 7 we described that during emerging adulthood the majority of men tend to prioritize career over romantic commitment. Later, during young adulthood, we expect a new balance to emerge. Indeed, at age 35 the majority of the men in the study were married and had to manage career and family simultaneously. The stories of our male participants make it sound as if they had reached an optimal balance. We have presented the story of Yochanan, who married when he was close to the age of 29. He describes that work and family complement one another: "Had I known that it works so well [family and work], I would have married earlier." According to Yochanan, marriage, which he was afraid would interfere with his career development, emerged as a pillar of support, helping him manage his career issues more efficiently. In fact, a substantial number of men described that they were satisfied with the coordination of work and family in their lives. Over the years, Alex efficiently coordinated between career and family. We asked 35-year-old Alex, by then a senior engineer, if he could describe a difficulty he experienced in handling both career and family. Alex said that nothing came to mind. Asking him again to try to find an example, he offered the following story:

> Often my wife takes our son to nursery. One day she was supposed to leave earlier, and I was to take him. Everything was well organized. At 7:30 I was down with the baby and sat him in the car. He suddenly started crying and I could not calm him. I checked and found out that he did doodie. I had to go back home and change his diaper, and then I was stuck in traffic for almost an hour.

We felt that this "trivial" story was less likely be told by a woman. It sounded as though for Alex, as for Yochanan, work and family go well together; but this could be because they did not have to cope with such "trivial" dilemmas on a regular basis. This could probably give them the feeling that overall their work and family issues are well coordinated.

The following two stories might shed further light on this issue. Yoram, 35 years old, married and the father of a baby, described that his preference is for a job that does not interfere with his commitment to his family. The way he describes this might sound as if he prioritizes family over career: "I am not looking for a job that I'll have to put all my life into. I want to do more for my family than for my work. Of course, it is important for me that my job is interesting and challenging." He further described his wife as a supportive partner, whose advice he values and listens to. He also added, "We do whatever we can to help each other and do things together. She is a teacher and has more flexible hours, but I am always there." These descriptions are impressive considering that in the interview when Yoram was still single he strongly insisted that he was looking for a wife who would not interfere with his career aspirations. Though Yoram might sound like the ideal husband and father, when interviewed at the age of 35 he was between jobs. He had quit his job because he was expecting to be promoted to a managerial role. It was not clear from the interview how he was planning to be a novice at a more demanding job while continuing to be fully invested in his family.

The inevitable tension between career and family is also evident in the story of Natti, a dentist and father of three, who was described in the previous chapter. When asked how he balances his job, his family, and being a parent, he responded,

> No problem, do it perfectly. What I like about my job [is] that I am employed in a public organization, socially minded. All my colleagues are about my age, parents of young children, and it is understood that at a certain hour the clinic closes and we go home. OK. The work is the means, not the end. We are here to do what we love, and we do the best we can. But we are also parents, we have to fetch the children, or stay with a sick child. This is what I love in my job, and I can develop professionally as well."

Natti's wife also has a career, and he added that he values her work and does his best to help her when she needs help. However, despite his investment in his family, he described that "My professional life is my *escape from home*, from the children. Do you understand what I mean? *Here (at work) I turn into a not-father, I become something else*."

Natti, similarly to Yoram, describes how important his wife and children are to him and how much he is ready to do for them and for his wife's professional success. On the other hand, as he describes, this pro-family attitude does not interfere with the importance of his work and its centrality in his life. He is capable of keeping his career separate from his family, as if these are two separate domains and he is not a father at work. Conceptually, it is possible that even men who incorporate family into their lives and for whom family is important are still able to keep their careers as a *separate psychological domain* and to disconnect this from their families. It is important to acknowledge that, unlike men, women are less likely to perceive or less capable of perceiving family and children as separate. As a result, the investable conflict between family and work is more significant for them.

The gendered dialectic of career and family and its expression at age 35—The story of women

Contrary to men, it is not easy for women to separate the worlds of career and family. As discussed above, women are embedded in their relationships and are less able to separate their relationship/family duties from their careers. The transition to motherhood is a life-changing event that not only changes daily routines but has a significant effect on the new mother's personal identity. Psychologically, a woman establishes *maternal identity* as she becomes a mother. Through commitment to and involvement in the care of their babies, mothers define a new self. The maternal identity continues to evolve as the new mother acquires new skills to regain her confidence in self as new challenges arise (Mercer, 2004). In this process a new mother is supposed to incorporate the way she perceives or anticipated motherhood into her sense of self (Choi et al., 2005). Laney and colleagues (2015) described the processes that may explain the changes in self that a woman might undergo following the transition to motherhood. First, after giving birth a woman loses herself for a time while incorporating her child into her identity, and thus reforming her identity. This transformation of identity and self-boundary leads mothers to feel that mothering and the close relationship with their child intensifies their personalities and identities.

Our findings show that emerging adult women are more attuned to their relationships and more likely to invest in their relationships than in career pursuit. The cited literature on the changes in self-identity following the transition to motherhood can further explain this gendered attitude to the balance of career and family, which is likely to intensify. Ward and Wolf-Wendel (2004) suggested that once children are prioritized and incorporated into the mother's sense of identity, a woman's attitude toward career is likely to change as well, and career and its meaning might be re-evaluated. Reading the interviews we conducted with the women who became mothers (who were the majority in our sample) showed clearly that their attitude toward work changed, no matter how important career was earlier in their lives. This change was clearly expressed in the way the young women referred to the changes in their attitude toward life in general, and career in particular:

> After the children were born the family took first place in my priorities. Would I have to choose between career and family, no question. These are my children's critical years, and I make no compromises. (Limor)

> It is clear that family comes first, no question. (Dorit)

> The first stage was when I fell pregnant and felt that life is changing. Then I gave birth and I had to change the way I was handling my job. Family before all, and my daughter before everything. (Navah)

Yet despite the significant psychological changes, life goes on, and nowadays the majority of women (in Israel as well) return to their work after maternity leave or a few months later. In the interviews conducted at the age of 35 we asked the women how they coordinate their family, motherhood, and career. Qualitative analysis of the interviews suggested that these young women were aware of the greater importance they attribute to their children and their family. They were also aware that, despite workplaces or organizations claiming to respect motherhood and secure mothers' rights, the reality might be different. Considering the reality with which women have to cope, we found three different patterns adopted by young women to negotiate and balance motherhood and career.

Career compromised

Kati, 34 years old and a mother of two, works at a daycare center. Before giving birth to her first child, Kati worked in a small firm and was in charge of budget issues. She liked her work and very much enjoyed the company and the friends she had there. At that point in time, Kati was very career-oriented and decided to leave the company and start looking for a higher-level job. However, she then learned that she was pregnant. She could not go back to the former company and knew that the chances of finding a new job during pregnancy were not high. Kati recalls that she regretted the decision to quit the former company, and then

> After giving birth I decided that I did not want to invest in a career that requires long hours and decided to find something else where it would be easier for me to raise the children. It is more important for me to be with the children than to invest in myself.

She started working in daycare, where the salary is lower. However, she does not feel that she gave up something and does not think that she has a "lower" career. She loves her work, which she considers her second home: "This works well for me, my children, my job."

In Chapter 4 we presented the story of Becky, who has a degree in behavioral sciences and had switched between different jobs until, with help from her future husband, she found a job in a bank. Though at the beginning she considered her job in the bank to be one of convenience, she learned to enjoy her work and felt that the chances for promotion were good. When asked at the age of 35 how she balances her work duties and being a mother of a 3-year-old, Becky responded,

> The truth is that I was looking for a job in the bank because of convenience. It is convenient for me as a mother. I do not need to stay late in the evening, and

they cannot change this. I was looking for something long-term *that will work for me as a mother*. In my job at four [p.m.] I leave, and this is the routine. I have tenure and nobody can ask me to stay longer. I do not see myself being a career woman and working long hours.

Despite their investment in their careers, these two women decided to look for a job that would not interfere with their motherhood. Being with their children when they are young is more important for them than to develop their careers further. To this end, they were willing to earn less. These stories echo previous research suggesting that following the transition to motherhood, the role of career in a woman's life might be re-evaluated and that motherhood is likely to become central in the new mother's life. However, despite the high value that both Kati and Becky attributed to becoming a mother, they still value their work and did not have any thoughts of changing their jobs. Furthermore, it was interesting to learn that after a period of time both Kati and Becky started to find meaning in their current jobs (Blustein, 2011), had plans for future development in their current ("compromised") career, and did not feel that they had given up their career aspirations. They had reached a compromise that balances their motherhood and career.

Career-focused combined with investment in motherhood and family

Women belonging to this pattern have developed a significant career or have a meaningful job. Moreover, they do not have any feeling that they gave up their career because of their motherhood. In addition to the importance they attribute to their professional lives, they emphasize the importance of being a mother and a wife. On a daily basis, life is not easy for them. They describe juggling their two roles: investing in their careers and still being an involved mother.

Limor's story exemplifies the complexity of this pattern of life. Limor is head of a municipal department and in charge of 50 employees. "It is a highly demanding job. But at 4:30 p.m. I leave to be with my family—my husband, my three children." After giving birth she was happy to become a mother, but her job was also important for her. She describes that she had to learn to juggle between family and career. Limor added that becoming a mother broadened her perspectives. She is less pressured at work, always thinking of what is more important for her and always learning how to coordinate motherhood and career.

Limor attributed much of her capacity to handle both career and family to the mother-friendly atmosphere at her workplace. She went on, appreciating and describing the extent to which her workplace is very supportive of mothers.

When asked about the role of her husband under these circumstances, she responded,

> I believe that everything is connected to him as well. Of course. I get a lot of support at home. However, he is never required to sacrifice his career because I am flexible, and I manage. It is his support, his pride in me, this is what is important.

Of note, while Limor has found her mode of balancing motherhood and a highly demanding career, her husband was never required to make compromises with regard to his career.

We met Dorit a couple of months after she had started a new job in human resources in a midsize company. She is a mother of two young girls and started this job after being away for maternity leave. Dorit describes that she can invest in her job due to the support of her husband and her boss. Dorit appreciates the company for being willing to wait for her until her return from maternity leave. After giving birth, she stayed in contact with the company and with the person who substituted for her every day "in order to keep hands on." However, going back to work after the maternity leave was not easy for her. "When I was supposed to go back to work I had moments of tears, crying. I had to work on myself, *and my boss was very special, very supportive. She helped me take the step back to work* [for emphasis]."

Dorit's story of her return to work demonstrates how difficult it can be for a mother to leave her newborn and return to work. However, despite the importance she attributes to motherhood, Dorit is also very focused on her career.

Dorit highly appreciates the support of her boss, but in reality from time to time she works long hours and might return at 7 or 8 p.m. On these occasions, she receives the help of her husband, whom she helps on other occasions. "There are days that he returns late. And we understand one another." We got the impression that Dorit is very ambitious about her career but also highly invested in her motherhood, and the support of her husband and her boss encourages her sense that she does the best she can to be with her children and to pursue a career.

Considered together, Limor and Dorit represent a pattern of young women who focus on and invest in their careers. Success at work is important for them. Yet, at the same time, motherhood is also central in their lives. Unlike the earlier pattern, these women do not look for compromises (of course, there are compromises when a conflict between work and family arises occasionally and they need to stay late); but psychologically, they try both to pursue their career and to be a mother who is invested in her children. Of note, an environment supportive of motherhood, in addition to the support of their spouse, plays a major role in their ability to carry on with this pattern of life.

No career, becoming a frustrated mother

Women belonging to this pattern had not developed any significant career or found a meaningful job. For them, becoming a mother is associated with giving up career aspirations and getting frustrated. Their stories are characterized by high self-criticism. However, despite being more involved with their children, motherhood is less described as an enriching experience, and their stories lack the daily joys found among young mothers.

Ada has been working in customer service in a telephone company for almost 7 years. She does not like the job and describes it as

> a compromise, no satisfaction, not even convenient.... I do something that I do not love, I stay here because it is comfortable and the hours are not too long, but I feel that I do not do what I would like to do.

She attributes her being stuck in this job to "not having the brains, I was not brave enough to look for something different." Ada is disappointed with her status and told us that she expected to be in a different position in her life. Interestingly, she blames her motherhood for her failure in her career.

> The fact that I fell pregnant one after the other is what got me stuck. I told myself that it is not the time to go look for a new job as long as the children are babies, here I am more flexible. I told myself I would look for something else during the summer, then after the winter, and the years passed, and I am here.

In her words Ada mostly describes her disappointment at the fact that she is stuck and does a job that is something of a student's job. Unlike other mothers, Ada did not express any satisfaction or sense of accomplishment in being a mother. She did describe herself as very competent in handling her daily duties with the girls. Unfortunately, however, this seemingly competent sense of motherhood did not raise a sense of being an accomplished mother, and she was focused on her sense of failure and the mistakes she made along the way in her career decisions.

Yonit, mother of a boy and girl, both at preschool age, is employed at a call center where hours are flexible. Recently she started to take courses in psychology at the Open University. When asked how she decided to start studying, she answered, "It is very difficult for me to make decisions. I saw a friend who is 40 years old who started to study, and I said to myself, why not me?"

Similar to the vague reason for resuming studies, Yonit's career history is also unclear and unfocused. Like our other participants, Yonit was enrolled in the college prep program. Unfortunately, she did not graduate, and she now regrets "that nobody gave me a kick in the ass and pushed me to complete my studies." Her future plans are vague and to some extent inconsistent. In addition, she says she has no idea what will happen 5 years from now.

Like with Ada, we did not hear any joy about her children in Yonit's interview. The children are described as part of her routine and duties. She described enjoying the quality time she has with her husband when the two of them are together. Considered together, mothers belonging to this pattern described that they are lost in their career and employed in boring and non-challenging jobs. Although they could have been expected to at least find some comfort in being with their children, for the majority of them their children were not a source of fulfillment, at least at this stage of their lives.

Closer examination of the lives of the women belonging to this pattern suggests that their career difficulties did not start after becoming a mother.

Reading Ada's and Yonit's interviews at age 29 carefully showed that neither had any clear career plans, and the issue of family and children was hardly mentioned. For them it appears that career and family were two domains competing over their resources, and it was difficult for them to contain both career and relationship. In contrast, reading the interview with Limor, who at age 35 had a successful career, suggested that as well as having a clear career plan at age 29, she was already dealing with how to balance career and family. She told us then,

> I want my career to play a dominant role in my life, but not to overtake all other aspects of life. I do not wish to leave home at six in the morning and return at midnight. I want a career, it will make me happy, but I want to be with my family too. I will not sacrifice my life for a job.

Considered together, we might suggest that some women try to balance career and family. Some are successful, while others are less successful and search for a job that can be adapted to suit the needs of raising a child, compromising for a job that allows them to invest in their family. In contrast, there are women for whom career and family are probably separate domains emotionally. Unfortunately, they are not too competent in coping with either career or family demands. As a result, they develop a sense of failure, and motherhood does not become a resource from which to draw strength.

Gendered pathways in career pursuit and romantic development—Are they functional for women?

Review of the gendered pathways we found in our study with regard to career pursuit and romantic development might suggest that men are more functional and adaptive when the quality of transition to adulthood across genders is compared. These findings align with gender stereotypes suggesting that men are more programmed toward advancement, promotion, opportunity for high earning, responsibility, and autonomy. In contrast, women are more attuned to cooperation and investment in others and prefer a friendly atmosphere (Hofstede, 2001; Meece et al., 2006). Moreover, Horner (1995) claimed that women might rather be motivated to avoid success because they are likely to expect negative consequences, such as social rejection and/or feeling unfeminine.

Our follow-up of participants until the age of 35 suggests that this issue is more complex. Indeed, though new fathers value their family, their attitude toward work did not change significantly following the transition to fatherhood. This explains why men are more able to stay focused on their careers. In contrast, for women the transition to motherhood is a life-changing event that places new demands and requires reconsidering priorities. Furthermore, it becomes more than balancing work and family. Motherhood becomes an essential part of the woman's identity and requires that the maternal identity be incorporated into the way work is considered, negotiated with the other aspects of the woman's life, and practiced (Mercer, 2004). Indeed, among new mothers the commitment to work might become lower due to reconsideration of priorities (Evertsson, 2012).

Considering the more complex changes women might experience following the birth of a baby, we would like to suggest that the process women undergo is longer, takes more time, and is more complex. Career pursuit pathways, as we have described them, might not tell the full story. Women need to find their own way in the career pursuit process. In addition, a woman needs to incorporate motherhood and integrate this with her professional dream. The two adaptive career pursuit pathways we found (see Chapter 3) were *Consistent Pursuit* and the *Adapted Pursuit*, and women were less represented in these pathways. Following our participants until the age of 35 helped us to understand the ways women pursue career. We found the *Career-Focused Combined with Investment in Motherhood and Family* pattern, in which women are focused on their career and it is important for them to develop professionally. Yet, simultaneously, it was important for them to be an involved mother, and they worked hard to manage their two "commitments." We also found the *Career Compromised* pattern, in which women looked for a job where they would have more time with their child. They seemed to compromise career for the sake of motherhood. However, following the life stories of these women reveals that they had started to find meaning in their compromised career, finding it interesting and a field worth pursuing. These dynamics echo the recent writings in vocational psychology emphasizing the importance of finding meaning in one's career (Blustein, 2011). The tendency to find meaning in a job that was initially a compromise can explain the finding that once the children grow older, mothers are not less committed to their work than non-mothers (Evertsson, 2012).

It is interesting to understand the current findings from a historical perspective. In his seminal work, Levinson (1978) published the book *The Seasons of a Man's Life*, which conceptualized the process of transitioning to adulthood. This influential book, which we have mentioned many times in our discussions, was followed by another book, *The Seasons of a Woman's Life* (Levinson, 1996). In the second book, among women who were interviewed in the 1980s, Levinson described two types—the homemaker and the career woman. The homemaker's aspiration was, as expected by the archetypical tradition, to care for her husband and children. The career woman, in contrast, Levinson (1996) claimed was quite often in conflict between the "internal Traditional Homemaker figure" and the "internal Anti-Traditional figure" (p. 415) that started to move to the center stage at that time. Of note, none of the women in our study, who were interviewed 40 years after Levinson's study was conducted, expressed any aspiration to be a homemaker. The women in our sample had career aspirations, but it was difficult for them to balance their career aspirations and their family obligations. More importantly, we found that the aspiration to become a mother was not less intense than that to pursue a career. Women were thus truly torn between two inner personal aspirations, career and motherhood, and employed different ways to manage this conflict. It is important to note that this conflict was not expressed by men. They wished to start a family, but they did not want to perceive this aspiration to be in conflict with their career aspirations.

Conclusions

Considered together we might suggest that the gendered pathways in career pursuit, as well as in romantic development, should not be perceived from a masculine perspective and that women are less driven to pursue a career. Women indeed aspire to bear children and care for them, but they too have career aspirations. The pathways we found in our study—when women were followed until the age of 35—probably better reflect the longer and more complex processes that women need to undergo in the current society where women are also expected to work. Some women were more capable of balancing career and children, while others tended to compromise. They found jobs that allowed them to spend more time with their children, but over time they were also able to find meaning in their jobs and to further develop their careers. Considering the complexity of these processes, it can be understood that women who lack the skills (the third pattern) have more difficulties coping with the complexities of the two roles in their lives. They had the feeling that due to motherhood they were not able to develop a career, while, in reality, their difficulties started earlier and were connected to lower personal capabilities.

10
Personality Assets and Developmental Outcomes

We met all our participants at age 23 at a similar junction in their lives. They had all started a college preparatory program with the aim of meeting the requirements necessary for college or university studies. Twelve years later a significant number had completed their academic studies; some even had achieved a graduate degree (a few even obtained a PhD) and developed a career. In contrast, there were other individuals who had not completed any degree and were employed in low-level professions. Similarly, the majority had established a family and borne children, while others were still dreaming of establishing a family or starting to realize that their chances of establishing a family were probably low.

Even for those who navigated their lives successfully, life journeys did not develop smoothly. For example, Natti had dreamed of becoming a dentist. He was focused on this dream. However, in the preparatory program he failed a number of classes and could not apply to university. He repeated the courses and was able to proceed with his dream. During his first year at dental school he married and became a father. Coming from a modest background, many efforts were required to be able to continue his studies as well as provide an income for the family he established. Becky completed a degree in behavioral sciences but then realized that it did not provide real options for the future or offer a reasonable career. She started working as a secretary in a large firm, knowing that this was not the job for which she aspired. Through the help of a friend, who later became her husband, she found a job in a bank. At first, the job seemed boring, but over time she found meaning in her job. She learned to love the financial issues with which she dealt and sees her career progressing in the banking system. Furthermore, as shown in the earlier chapters, Becky felt that she has found a job where she will be able to develop a career and be an involved mother.

In contrast, Nora, who took the same route as that taken by Natti and Becky, did not continue to academic studies. At the end of the preparatory program she found a job as a secretary and was happy to earn the money. When interviewed at age 27, comparing herself to her classmates, she described what they had achieved in their lives: "And I, nothing. I think it is because I was always indifferent." Nora added that for her it was always more important to have money

A New Lens on Emerging Adulthood. Shmuel Shulman, Oxford University Press. © Oxford University Press 2024.
DOI: 10.1093/oso/9780190841836.003.0011

and to go out. Over the years, her romantic involvements did not progress into a committed relationship. At age 35 Nora is employed in a company that is likely to close due to financial issues, and she is not involved in a relationship. In contrast, Natti and Becky were proud of their accomplishments at this stage of life and even had plans for the future. When Nora was asked about how she sees the future, she answered,

> First, of course in a relationship, I really want to believe that this will happen. I also hope I'll complete a degree and will not be stuck as now, and in a job that will be good for me... but only God knows what will happen.

Why could Natti and Becky navigate successfully across the emerging adulthood years despite the difficulties that they encountered, while Nora was stuck in her dreams? Her functioning is reminiscent of the typical floundering behavior that was described as characterizing emerging adults. With this purpose, this chapter will discuss the possible moderators that can explain embarking on such different life trajectories. More specifically, the chapter will focus on personality attributes that might explain the ability to be persistent on one's track despite encountering difficulties or to find a new direction following an experience of failure. Based on our longitudinal data, we show how distinctive personality attributes measured earlier can explain embarking on distinctive pathways. In recent years there has been an increasing body of theorizing and research (B. W. Roberts & Davis, 2016) demonstrating that personality also changes during the emerging adulthood years. In the final section of this chapter we thus examine the extent to which changes in personality during emerging adulthood might further contribute to adaptive or maladaptive outcomes.

The role of personality assets in navigating developmental transition: Career pursuit

The search for precursors of successful transition into the world of work has been studied within the framework of vocational psychology. Guided by sociological and social-psychological conceptualizations, the school-to-work (STW) transition body of research has emphasized the significance of personal and social capital in facilitating a smooth transition.

Research on STW transition grew predominantly out of the emerging trend of youth unemployment and declining wages in the early 1970s (see Blustein et al., 2000). The STW body of research outlined that successful transitions are facilitated by two constructs: the first, located within the individual, includes an array of basic relevant vocational skills and a particular array of psychological features such as self-initiative, purposefulness, flexibility, and agency. The second, related to the environment, includes a supportive family and supportive and engaged peers, teachers, counselors, and supervisors.

These constructs of personal skills and support systems resemble the personal capital model and the social capital model that were formulated by sociologists in the study of transitions. Specifically, Côté (1996, 1997, 2002) proposed that several personal resources are crucially important for effective functioning within and between institutions (Morch, 1997) and for developing the means necessary for "fitting in" and "becoming" part of a workplace or community. This requires empowerment of oneself based on one's resources (attained education, agentic personality, advanced forms of psychological development) and meeting the environment in such a way as to benefit from what it has to offer (family support, peer support, etc.). Notwithstanding the changing social and economic conditions that have increased the difficulties that young people experience nowadays, personal and social capital can facilitate coping with the instabilities of the current world (Côté, 2000). (The role of support systems in developmental outcomes will be discussed at length in the following chapter.)

Correspondingly, the ability to persistently remain on one's track when successful or truly endorse a new direction following failure can also be understood within the framework of the role of personality differences in understanding adaptive outcomes and successful transitions. In our 12-year project we focused on Blatt's theory of personality development and psychopathology (Blatt, 2008), which emphasizes the centrality of self-definition in individual development and pathology. Optimally developing individuals are able to pursue their lives and strive for achievement without losing their sense of self. In contrast, individuals who overemphasize self-definition (i.e., achievement of self-esteem and sense of control) might develop a self-critical personality style that interferes with their ability to remain true to themselves and implement their plans. Blatt and his colleagues consistently found that self-criticism, a maladaptive aspect of self-definition, predicted lack of autonomous regulation, which in turn predicted lack of positive life events. Similarly, efficacy, an adaptive aspect of self-definition, predicted elevated autonomous regulation, which in turn predicted encountering more positive events (Blatt, 1998, 2008; Blatt & Zuroff, 1992).

The self-determination theory (SDT) also addresses the antecedents of healthy self-regulation and psychological well-being. The theory postulates that the fulfillment of autonomy, competence, and relatedness (Ryan & Deci, 2000a, 2017) is the essential nutriment for psychological growth. According to the SDT, these psychological needs are fulfilled particularly when individuals' actions are self-initiated or fully self-endorsed, rather than controlled by forces experienced as alien to the self (Ryan, 1993). In domains or circumstances in which any of these needs are neglected, difficulties engaging in autonomously regulated behavior ensue, and well-being is hypothesized to suffer. Behaviors that are extrinsically motivated, such as those based on the instrumental value of acting for or being valued by others, can become a source of increased stress in conditions of an unsupportive and unpredictable environment.

Shahar, Henrich, Blatt, et al. (2003) integrated Blatt's theory of interpersonal self-definition with Deci and Ryan's SDT. They proposed that adaptive and maladaptive models of self-definition, which represent enduring and profound personality traits, give rise to autonomous and controlled regulation, respectively.

Considered together, these understandings led us to assume that young people who are efficacious and low in self-criticism, as well as internally motivated, will be more able to pursue their goals and cope efficiently with difficulties along the way and to make changes and find new and adaptive routes (see the life stories of Natti and Becky). In contrast, we assumed that self-critical individuals will be less likely to define coherent goals and make adaptations along the way (see the life story of Nora). In addition, being extrinsically motivated will further hamper adaptive pursuit. Thus, together we assumed that greater personality capital would explain embarking on a more adaptive career pursuit pathway. In contrast, lesser personal capital such as low efficacy, higher self-criticism, and lower intrinsic motivation would associate with a higher likelihood of embarking on a less adaptive career pursuit pathway. In the two following sections we describe the role personality might play in the ways emerging adults navigate their career and romantic lives.

Personality precursors of the four career pursuit pathways during emerging adulthood

In order to learn about the role of personality in navigating career development, we calculated the longitudinal associations between personality attributes measured at age 23 and alignment with the four career pursuit pathways (described in Chapter 3) at age 29. For this purpose and in line with our conceptual framework, we administered the following personality questionnaires at age 23.

Personality was assessed by the 66-item Depressive Experience Questionnaire (DEQ; Blatt et al., 1976) rated on a 7-point scale (1 [*absolutely does not agree*] and 7 [*absolutely agrees*]). The three scales from the DEQ were administered: Self-Criticism taps preoccupation with achievement, inferiority, and guilt in the face of perceived failure to meet standards (e.g., "It is not who you are but what you have accomplished that counts"); Dependency reflects a wish to be cared for, loved, and protected, as well as a fear of being abandoned (e.g., "Without the support of others who are close to me, I would be helpless"); and Efficacy represents personal resilience and inner strength (e.g., "I have many inner resources"). In line with the guidelines of Blatt et al. (1976), scores were converted into Z scores. A higher score conveys a higher level of self-criticism, dependency, or efficacy. Cronbach alphas for self-criticism, dependency, and efficacy were .82, .73, and .79, respectively. (In line with our assumptions, only the Self-Criticism and Efficacy scales were considered to predict career pathway outcomes.)

Intrinsic and extrinsic motivations were assessed using a modified version of the Client Motivation for Therapy Scale (Pelletier et al., 1997), which is based on the SDT (Deci & Ryan, 1985). Items are rated on a 5-point scale (1 [*does not agree*] and 5 [*strongly agrees*]). While the original scale focuses on respondents' motivations or attitudes toward therapy, in the current version participants were asked to rate the different items referring to their life course and aspirations. Intrinsic motivation was tapped by items such as "because I enjoy pursuing my goals," while items such as "Because it is important to me that my friends will treat me as a serious person" were used to tap extrinsic motivation. Internal consistency estimates for the intrinsic and extrinsic orientations were α = .72 and .87, respectively.

The longitudinal data allowed us to examine the predictors of affiliation to the different career pursuit pathways. For this purpose, a multinomial regression analysis was conducted to predict career pursuit pathway affiliation. Following our assumptions, indices of efficacy and self-criticism and measures of intrinsic and extrinsic motivation were entered as predictors. Considering our assumption that pathway affiliation will differ across gender, gender was also entered into the equation. Finally, in line with the expected role of support systems (Blustein et al., 2000; Côté, 2000), we also expected that parental and maternal support would contribute to alignment with distinctive career pursuit pathways. Of note, the role of support systems in developmental outcome will be further discussed in the next chapter. We will then present a comprehensive model of the precursors of developmental outcomes that refers to the joint contribution of personality attributes and support to future developmental outcomes. For the sake of clarity, in this chapter we focus on the role of personality. However, the contribution of support is also shown in the findings presented in this chapter.

In Chapter 3 we described the four career pursuit pathways we found: *Consistent Pursuit*, *Adapted Pursuit*, *Survivors*, and *Confused/Vague*. In order to examine the extent to which personality attributes such as self-criticism and inner motivation is associated with career pursuit pathways, a multinomial regression was conducted. In this procedure, levels of personality and support indices (that will be discussed in the next chapter) in the three pathways are compared to those of the optimal pathway—the *Consistent Pursuit* pathway. Results of the multinomial regression analysis are presented in Table 10.1.

The results show that pathway affiliation is significantly predicted by gender, efficacy, self-criticism, and extrinsic motivation (as well as maternal and paternal

Table 10.1 *Results of the Multinomial Regression Analysis Predicting Membership in Pathway Patterns (Comparisons of the Three Alternative Pathways to the Steady Involvement Pathway)*

	Sporadic			Lengthy relationships/ absence of learning			Casual to steady		
	B_b	Wald	OR	B_b	Wald	OR	B_b	Wald	OR
Gender	2.80	9.77***	16.49	−0.24	0.04	0.78	2.37	7.59**	10.67
T1 Efficacy	−0.94	6.69**	0.39	−0.25	25	0.29	0.13	0.15	1.14
T1 Immature dependency	1.08	3.22+	2.79	2.12	7.75**	8.32	0.45	0.66	1.57
T1 Psychological symptoms	0.26	0.16	1.29	−1.57	2.27	0.21	0.54	0.75	1.71
T1 Maternal support	−0.46	0.52	0.63	−1.24	4.19*	0.29	−0.48	0.92	0.62
T1 Paternal support	0.27	0.21	1.30	0.11	0.03	1.12	0.32	0.31	1.37

Note: Significant findings are highlighted in bold. Adapted from: Shulman, S., Seiffge-Krenke, I., Scharf, M., Boiangiu, S. B., & Tregubenko, V. (2018). The diversity of romantic pathways during emerging adulthood and their developmental antecedents. *International Journal of Behavioral Development*, 42(2), 167–174. https://doi.org/10.1177/0165025416673474

+$p < .10$. *$p < .05$. **$p < .01$. ***$p < .001$.

support) measured 7 years earlier, $\chi^2 (30, 100) = 59.76, p < .001$. The Cox value is .49, suggesting that a substantial level of the variance is explained. As can be seen in Table 10.1, affiliates of the *Confused/Vague* pathway were more likely to be women. In addition, their level of efficacy was one sixth, and their levels of self-criticism and extrinsic motivation were more than threefold those of members of the *Consistent Pursuit* pathway. The *Survivors*, who were also overrepresented by women, displayed similar trends. They were also less likely to be efficacious— one quarter—and showed an elevated level of self-criticism—more than threefold that of members of the *Consistent Pursuit* pathway. In addition, they showed a tendency ($p < .10$) also to be more extrinsically motivated.

Interestingly, the *Adapted Pursuit* pathway resembled these two less adaptive patterns, reporting a low level of efficacy—one quarter—and a tendency to be more self-critical and extrinsically motivated compared with the *Consistent Pursuit* pathway. Together, taking a personality perspective suggested that the three less adaptive career pathways differed from the optimal *Consistent Pursuit* pattern on indices of personality and motivation orientation and that people with this pattern tended to be less efficacious, higher on self-criticism, and more extrinsically motivated. The provision or absence of parental support further determined the magnitude of the impact of personality deficiencies on future career outcomes for the better or the worse and will be discussed at length in the next chapter. To summarize, in recent years a successful and smooth transition to work has become more complex. Young people can be found more in and out of work, changing directions and having difficulties settling down in a specific career (European Group for Integrated Social Research [EGRIS], 2001). However, the lack of personal capacities such as being less efficacious, having less inner motivation, and being more self-critical probably further undermines their capacity to navigate across the emerging adulthood years successfully. In contrast, greater personal capacities served as an asset for more efficient coping with the age-related career goals.

Narrative demonstrations of the roles of self-criticism, efficacy, and motivation in career life stories

Self-criticism, efficacy, and intrinsic or extrinsic motivation were measured through inventories at age 23. At age 29 participants were interviewed and asked to describe the story of their career development. Reading their stories clearly shows how issues of efficacy and inner motivation (or the lack thereof) were expressed in their own words. Asking them to reflect on their experiences or whether they regretted the road they took echoed the extent to which they tended to criticize themselves or were more accepting and at peace with the decisions they made in the past.

Natti scored low on self-criticism, $Z = -1.46$ (1.5 SD below the average); high in efficacy, $Z = 0.85$ (almost 1 SD above the average); as well as above the average in intrinsic motivation. At the time of the interview he was completing his first degree in biology and had applied to the school of dentistry. When asked how he felt about the way he was pursuing his career, he answered,

> I am happy, because I do what I love. I am happy because *I am true with myself*. I got an offer for a job, nice salary, a car. But I told myself I am not going to bury myself and chase money. My decisions are not directed by money, they are for *me*.

Natti went further, describing that with everything he does, he weighs first "Every little step." He continued, "I am like a *Rottweiler*. I run, nothing stays in place."

Natti is realistic and understands that the way he takes will not be easy (as described previously, he became romantically committed at this time and planned also to get married). Yet he is highly motivated to pursue his dream. He is also very efficacious in his attitude to "fight" his way and to succeed. At the same time, he is realistic about the hurdles along the way; and despite these, he is ready to move on. Relatedly, he is not worried whether he might regret the decision he made because he plans his moves ahead and understands that not every move will necessarily be successful. "This is life, there are difficulties along the way and you have to accept this and carry on."

This efficacious and self-directed attitude and behavior, combined with the capacity to accept that there might be obstacles along the road, was the driving force that led Natti to succeed and achieve his plans. When we met him again at the age of 35 he was a dentist, and very happy with his career. He was also married and had three children. Natti's accomplishments are impressive considering his modest family background and difficulties at high school but can be understood considering his strong inner motivation and lack of fear of failure.

Nora is the complete opposite of Natti. She is very low in efficacy, $Z = -0.85$ (almost 1 SD below the average), as well as above the average in extrinsic motivation and high on self-criticism, $Z = 0.46$. Nora described that her fantasy is to get up happy in the morning and go happily to work, but this terrifies her because she is aware that she cannot attain a good job. She further explained that she would like to be a social worker, but she needs to study for the degree, which terrifies her: "Terrified just to think of starting to study. This terrifies me." For this reason, for most of the years of our study she was employed in temporary jobs that did not require any qualifications. When asked how she sees the future, Nora answered,

> I have no idea. When I feel fed up I leave and move on. I feel I do not work for my goals. I always apply for a job that is open for everybody, low standards. I am afraid of failure, afraid to go through an interview and learn that I was not accepted. For this reason I always find myself in a shoe shop, a clothing shop.

It is heartbreaking to listen to Nora's story. She has some vague ideas of what she would love to do but does not have the skills. Furthermore, she feels terrified to look for a real job. Her behavior, as well as her words, demonstrate her low efficacy, how critical she is about herself, and how she perceives herself as worthless. These personality deficiencies probably prevented her from pursuing a career, and she feels that she is lost. Nora's status had not changed when she was interviewed again at the age of 32. She was still employed in temporary jobs to keep her afloat, with no direction for the future. Both Natti and Nora were typical emerging adults during their early 20s. They came from a modest background, and their starting point did not seem very promising considering the difficulties that young people are likely to encounter nowadays. However, as described in their own words, their personality capacities or deficiencies determined whether they would navigate their 20s successfully or become stuck and remain an "emerging adult" well into their 30s.

The role of personality attributes in navigating developmental transition: Romantic development

The ability to embark on a romantic pathway leading toward stable involvement requires a number of capacities. Individuals need to be sufficiently competent to coordinate the different tasks, in particular career and romantic relationships (Shulman & Connolly, 2013). In addition, individuals are expected to be competent in handling a relationship, resolving conflicts, and balancing issues of intimacy and independence (Orlofsky, 1993). For example, Salvatore and colleagues (2011) found that better recovery after a conflict predicted more positive relationship emotions and greater relationship satisfaction that, in turn, was likely to contribute to the longevity of a relationship.

The complexity of negotiating and balancing self needs and aspirations and the ability to establish a deep and committed relationship with a partner can be understood within the tenets of Blatt's (2008) theory of personality. According to Blatt, optimally developing individuals are able to become involved in relationships without losing their sense of self and strive for achievement and self-definition without neglecting interpersonal relationships. They are able to be aware of their inner motivation while, at the same time, listening to advice and receiving help from others. Blatt and colleagues (1976) proposed that highly self-critical individuals often hold biased perceptions of themselves and others but also tend to misconstrue events and stressors. In particular, self-critical individuals commonly perceive others as indifferent and uncaring and are more likely to respond to daily hassles or negative/traumatic life events with greater distress (e.g., Besser & Priel, 2010; Blatt, 2004; Sherry et al., 2014).

Guided by Blatt's conceptualization, we examined the extent to which individuals who tend to emphasize interpersonal relatedness (i.e., the attainment of close relations) at the expense of self-definition develop a dependent personality style and how their actions may not be autonomously motivated in their romantic experiences. We expected that these individuals might give up independence for the sake of staying in a relationship where their personal needs and wishes are not necessarily respected. Efficacy, an adaptive aspect of self-definition in Blatt's theory, is claimed to be associated with elevated autonomous regulation, which, in turn, was found to predict encountering more positive events and better functioning (Blatt, 2008). Together we assumed that highly dependent individuals with low efficacy are likely to be less competent in handling a romantic relationship and more likely to be only sporadically involved in romantic relationships. Alternatively, these individuals might slide into relationships that are less than optimal in order to escape loneliness (Spielmann et al., 2013). Finally, self-critical individuals might also have difficulties progressing with and deepening their relationships. They might experience doubts about themselves or their partners, which together might interfere with achieving intimacy and growing toward commitment.

Personality precursors of the four romantic development pathways during emerging adulthood

Our longitudinal data allowed us to examine the possible earlier precursors of affiliation to the different romantic pathways across emerging adulthood. For this purpose, an additional multinomial regression analysis was conducted to predict romantic pathway affiliation. In this analysis, each respective pathway was compared to the "optimal" pathway—in this case, to the pathway of *Steady* involvements. In line with our theoretical assumptions, indices of efficacy, self-criticism, and dependency measured at age 23 were entered as predictors. (Paternal and maternal support measured at age 23 were also entered, and the role of parental support will be discussed in the following chapter.) Considering our expectation that pathway affiliation would differ across gender, gender was also entered into the equation.

The findings show that affiliation with a specific romantic pathway was significantly predicted by gender, efficacy, and dependency and marginally predicted by self-criticism and level of parental support measured 7 years earlier, χ^2 (df = 18, n = 92) = 44.03, p < .001. The Cox value, an estimate of the R^2 value, was .39, suggesting that a substantial level of the variance is explained (Tabachnik & Fidell, 2013). The findings are summarized in Table 10.2. As can be seen, affiliation with the *Sporadic* pathway rather than the *Steady* involvements pathway was explained by gender, level of efficacy, and dependency. The chances of young men belonging to this pathway were 16.48 times higher than those of young women. In addition, a lower level of efficacy and a higher level of dependency at age 23 were associated with future likelihood to affiliate with the *Sporadic* pathway: OR = 0.42 and OR = 3.14, respectively. Affiliation with the *Lengthy Relationships but Absence of Experiential Learning* pathway was explained by level of dependency and parental support measured 7 years earlier. A higher level of dependency and lower parental support were associated with higher chances of belonging to the *Lengthy Relationships but Absence of Experiential Learning* pathway, rather than with the chances of belonging to the *Steady Relationship* pathway, with ORs of 8.32 and 0.39, respectively. (As indicated above, the role

Table 10.2 *Results of the Multinomial Regression Analysis Predicting Membership in Pathway Patterns (Comparisons of the Three Alternative Pathways to the Steady Involvement Pathway)*

	Sporadic			Lengthy relationships/ absence of learning			Casual to steady		
	B_b	Wald	OR	B_b	Wald	OR	B_b	Wald	OR
Gender	2.80	**9.77*****	**16.49**	−0.24	0.04	0.78	2.37	**7.59****	**10.67**
T1 Efficacy	−0.94	**6.69****	**0.39**	−0.25	25	0.29	0.13	0.15	1.14
T1 Immature dependency	1.08	**3.22+**	**2.79**	2.12	**7.75****	**8.32**	0.45	0.66	1.57
T1 Psychological symptoms	0.26	0.16	1.29	−1.57	2.27	0.21	0.54	0.75	1.71
T1 Maternal support	−0.46	0.52	0.63	−1.24	**4.19***	**0.29**	−0.48	0.92	0.62
T1 Paternal support	0.27	0.21	1.30	0.11	0.03	1.12	0.32	0.31	1.37

Note: Significant findings are highlighted in bold.
+$p < .10.$ *$p < .05.$ **$p < .01.$ ***$p < .001.$

of parental support will be discussed in the following chapter.) In addition, a lower level of self-criticism was marginally associated with a higher likelihood to affiliate with the *Lengthy Relationships but Absence of Experiential Learning* pathway, OR = 0.27. Finally, affiliation with the *Casual to Steady* involvements pathway rather than the *Steady Relationship* pathway was explained only by gender, suggesting that personality does not explain affiliation with this romantic pathway. The chances of young men belonging to this pathway were 10.67 times higher than those of young women.

Considered together, personality attributes measured at age 23 predicted romantic pathway affiliation at age 29. Emerging adults high on dependency, namely those who had not developed a mature attitude toward relationship and the ability to see the self and the partner in a mature way, were more likely to find themselves in a less adaptive relationship pattern later in life. These young people, who were also low on efficacy, were more likely to belong to the *Sporadic* pathway. They probably had more difficulties managing a relationship over time and tended to be more involved in short or sporadic relationships. In contrast, when low relationship maturity was combined with low earlier parental support, it was more likely to associate with staying in a long-lasting relationship that does not evolve and mature over time. Highly dependent individuals who had not experienced parental support in the past appeared more inclined to become involved in less adaptive long-lasting relationships, even though these relationships might not be intimate and truly supportive.

Narrative demonstrations of the roles of dependency and efficacy in romantic life stories

Tomi was almost 30 years old at the time of the first interview. At age 23 his reported level of dependency was $Z = 0.35$ above the mean, and the level of efficacy was $Z = -1.35$, well below the mean. When asked at age 30 to describe his romantic status, he said, "I am alone. I go out from time to time. There are two girls that I go out with from time to time but this is not serious. I had a few casual relationships but I felt very awkward. This is not for me." Furthermore, at the end of the interview, Tomi added. "I must admit, romantic relationships frighten me."

Despite his behavior, Tomi admits that he craves a close relationship, but then he needs to test whether he is truly loved. His low efficacy further explains his behavior. This is probably related to his difficulties resolving conflicts and learning how to move on, despite the difficulties that might arise in a relationship. Of note, Tomi had recently started therapy, which could explain some of the reflections that were raised in the interview. Nurit, aged 28, is also mostly involved in casual relationships and is also low on efficacy. When asked how she understands her romantic behavior, being mostly involved in casual encounters, she explained,

> I enjoy being in a relationship, and was in relationships, but I learned that relationships do not last forever. I know this happens with everyone, there are separations, this is part of life. But I realized that I was unable to cope with a break-up. I am broken. So I decided not to get involved seriously so that I do not have to experience the suffering.

Thus, low efficacy, in particular among individuals high on dependency (who need, for example, to be assured that they are loved), interferes with the capacity to manage a relationship, draw lessons from different romantic experiences, and move on to a new relationship. Difficult experiences tend to be repeated, which in turn might lead to increased lack of confidence in handling and enjoying a romantic experience and learning how to handle a future relationship more competently.

Nora, who was identified as aligning with another non-adaptive romantic pathway—*Lengthy Relationships but Absence of Experiential Learning*—is also low on efficacy, $Z = -1.14$, and is close to 1 SD above the mean in dependency, $Z = 0.74$. When asked about the history of her romantic experiences, Nora described, "I am a person who is unable not to be in a relationship. I must find somebody and be in a relationship. And I had, I have many ex-es. Most of them were married." We felt that Nora's neediness to be in a relationship led her to be constantly involved in relationships that had no future. Further, she repeated her needy behavior with a number of married men and, overall, was not capable of drawing lessons from her past experiences and becoming involved in a mature, intimate, and committed relationship.

In contrast to Tomi and Nora, Natti had an average level of dependency, $Z = 0.02$, and was high on efficiency, $Z = 0.85$. During most of his emerging adulthood years he was in sporadic relationships. However, at the age of 28, when he was in an advanced stage of his studies, he met his girlfriend (who would later become his wife), to whom he was very attracted. Natti describes that something changed in him when he met this girl. He started to feel that he wanted to get intimate with her and even progress toward commitment.

> This is new for me to be in this kind of a relationship. I realize that I have to give and not only to expect to get from her. I have to accept that sometimes she might be in a mood, she has her wishes and will, and this all comes in your face. But I learned quickly that it is important to respect, this is the anchor on which a relationship can rest on. If you do not respect your partner, and this is what you bring with you into the relationship, there is no chance that something will develop.

As indicated above, we identified Natti as belonging to the *Casual to Steady* pathway.

Natti describes the extra mile he took to learn to accept differences. He learned that respecting the individuality of the other is essential for maintaining a relationship, and he has also learned how to handle differences—an issue that was difficult for Tomi, Nurit, and Nora. Accepting and responding to the needs of your partner does not mean becoming involved in a relationship in which you give up your individuality. Further discussing his relationship, it sounded as if there are aspects of the relationship in which Natti is dependent on his girlfriend. Natti understood our doubts and further elaborated on the relationship with his girlfriend.

> Yes, we are dependent on one another, but this is not that I am dependent, this is *positive dependency*, we do it for both of us, this is not being needy. I think this is the power of a couple, doing things together. This is the way you achieve your goals and progress in life.

Natti provided us with a very deep explanation of cooperation and compromise and how these differ from acting in tandem due to being dependent and fearing to be alone. Nora was also directed by the need for dependency, but applying Natti's definition, Nora's dependency should be considered *negative dependency*, in contrast to Natti's own *positive dependency*.

To summarize, our longitudinal data allows us to demonstrate that indices of personality collected 7 years earlier can explain why some young people were able to embark on adaptive or less adaptive pathways of career pursuit or relationship development. We found that low efficacy, high self-criticism, and high external motivation predicted less adaptive patterns of occupational decision-making processes. In a similar vein, our findings also showed that earlier low efficacy and increased immature dependency predicted affiliation with a sporadic pathway or a lasting relationship that led nowhere pathway. These difficulties were echoed in the stories describing the difficult experiences and disappointments these young people had in their romantic interactions. Conceptually, our findings reiterate the findings of Blatt and colleagues (see review, Blatt, 2008), who showed that deficient personality attributes are associated with increased adjustment problems. Our findings add that personality attributes are associated with the quality of developmental outcomes among emerging adults as well.

Personality development during emerging adulthood: Developmental outcomes and future well-being

Self-criticism is a personality attribute that we showed has the potential to affect the course of emerging adults' development. In our analyses we referred to the initial level of self-criticism measured at age 23. Implicitly we were suggesting that self-criticism, as for other personality traits, probably remains stable over time, a finding that has been reflected in test–retest correlations of personality measures (Caspi et al., 2005). However, in the last two decades there has been increasing evidence that many personality traits change with age. Longitudinal research has largely revealed that personality changes with age, both on the individual level and across populations. These changes appear to be present throughout most stages of life, even into the older years (Caspi et al., 2005; Mroczek & Spiro, 2007; Specht et al., 2011). In a meta-analysis of longitudinal studies, B. W. Roberts and colleagues (2006) demonstrated that while personality changes take place during the adolescent and young adulthood years, during emerging adulthood personality change occurs at double the rate of change during adolescence. Over these years most individuals gradually became more agreeable, conscientious, and emotionally stable (Bleidorn et al.; 2009; Lüdtke et al., 2011; B. W. Roberts & Davis, 2016). In a similar vein, self-esteem also increases from adolescence into the middle adulthood years (Orth et al., 2012).

Adolescents and emerging adults undergo major changes with respect to their views of themselves and their relationships with others, as well as important tasks they often face (Hutteman et al., 2015; Orth et al., 2012). Individuals tend to become more introspective with age, which is probably a culmination of efforts to establish their own identities, to understand how others perceive them, and to discover what roles or jobs they wish to obtain in adulthood (Arnett, 2004). Traditionally, it is thought that this process of assessing and integrating positive and negative characteristics should be resolved by the end of adolescence (Robins & Trzesniewski, 2005); but, in fact, it continues in greater magnitude throughout emerging adulthood. Thus, personality development across the life span is best characterized by a pattern of increasing emotional stability and benevolence that is most pronounced in emerging adults (B. W. Roberts et al., 2006; Hutteman et al., 2015). Increased emotional stability captures increased functional maturity (Donnellan et al., 2007) and, as such, is likely to facilitate a healthy interaction with others and the environment—both of which are important goals that mark successful entry to adulthood with regard to career and romantic development (Van Aken et al., 2006).

Indeed, an increasing number of studies have demonstrated the contribution of personality maturity, such as increase in emotional stability, to better outcomes in various domains. These domains typically include physical health, psychological health (including lower psychopathology), coping behavior, the quality of close relationships, and work behavior (see, e.g., De Bolle et al., 2012; Mroczek & Spiro, 2007; Steiger et al., 2014). These studies highlight the potential mechanisms that account for how increases in positive personality attributes might result in better functioning across different domains. For example, De Bolle and colleagues (2012) described that becoming more benevolent over time leads to a lower likelihood of approaching social situations from one's own perspective, without considering the interests of others, which leads to fewer behavioral problems. In contrast, decreasing benevolence has the potential of damaging interactions with others. In addition, increasing maturity has the potential to promote a more positive and resilient approach to stressors by enhancing active modes of coping and decreasing maladaptive attitudes such as withdrawal or over-focusing on emotions (Connor-Smith & Flachsbart, 2007). It might also enhance more cooperative attitudes when interacting with a romantic partner or a workmate (De Bolle et al., 2012; Hudson et al., 2012).

Within this framework of personality maturity we would like to suggest that this increase in capacities to cope with stressors and address interactions with others could become an asset for emerging adults facing developmental tasks (Hutteman et al., 2014). Such capacities are particularly important considering the multiplicity of tasks that need to be addressed simultaneously (Caspi, 2002; Grob et al., 2001) and the increased social and economic uncertainties evident in recent years (Leccardi, 2005).

Such personality changes may have the potential to facilitate greater flexibility in the perception of environmental pressures and can assist in setting or readapting goals in order to attain one's desired aspirations (Bleidorn et al., 2010; B. W. Roberts et al., 2004). They might also help in becoming more introspective and gaining a better understanding of what young adults want to do and achieve in their lives (Arnett, 2004).

In the earlier sections of this chapter we discussed and demonstrated the long-term effects of personality on outcomes over time with regard to career pursuit and romantic development. Considering the recently conceptualized and documented increasing personality maturity, namely changes in personality during emerging adulthood, we felt that it is important to learn how personality maturity might further contribute to advances in the attainment of age-related goals such as career and romantic relationships. We assumed that decreasing negative emotionality would have the potential to reduce tendencies to construe events in a biased way (Krueger et al., 2000), to respond excessively to minor or even trivial stressors, and to perceive changes in the environment as threats (Donnellan et al., 2005). As a result, coping with issues that arise at a workplace or with a romantic partner should become more manageable.

Personality maturation can also be conducive to individual well-being (De Bolle et al., 2012; Mroczek & Spiro, 2007; Steiger et al., 2014). One's confidence in one's capacity to cope efficiently with developmental tasks can enhance well-being and increase positive mood (Sumner et al., 2015). In contrast, as outlined above, increasing emotional negativity is likely to associate with a higher likelihood of experiencing stress and failure (Donnellan et al., 2005). This can, in turn, result in diminished life satisfaction, a lower sense of well-being, and greater depressive affect (Klimstra et al., 2014; Sherry et al., 2003).

Previous studies on personality development focused on changes in the Big Five and personality traits such as negative emotionality. Self-criticism, the central personality construct we used in our 12-year-long study, is not part of the Big Five but is a lower-order personality characteristic or a personality facet that has much in common with neuroticism (Békés et al., 2015; M. M. Smith et al., 2016). As such, similarly to neuroticism, we examined the amount of decrease in self-criticism and in self-doubts among emerging adults and whether this decreases further affects future outcomes.

Change in self-criticism during emerging adulthood and future outcomes

Our longitudinal data allows us to examine if and how self-criticism changes throughout emerging adulthood, as well as to examine the influence of change in self-criticism on developmental and psychological outcomes. Our participants were approached at 23, 24, 26.5, 29, and 35 years of age. Self-criticism was assessed four times, at the ages of 23, 24, 26.5, and 29, which allowed us to control the baseline of self-criticism from age 23 to 29, while determining how changes in self-criticism over these ages would be associated with important outcomes such as goal attainment, coping with age-related tasks, and well-being at age 35.

The DEQ (Blatt et al., 1976), described and administered at the initial assessment, was administered again at the ages of 24, 26.5, and 29. Reliability of self-criticism at the additional assessment was satisfactory. In addition, the following questionnaires were administered at the age of 35 to assess developmental and psychological outcomes at this age.

Developmental outcomes: Progress in and coping with age-related tasks

Work and romantic goal progress

We asked participants to complete a modified version of Little's (1983) Personal Project Analysis, in which they listed three personal goals and appraised the extent to which they made progress in each goal along several dimensions. In the current study we refer to progress in *Work Goals* and *Romantic Goals* during the previous 5 years. Each was measured four items (i.e., "To what extent have you made progress realizing this goal?") on a scale from 1 (*low*) to 7 (*high*). Cronbach's alphas were .88 and .83, respectively. Item scores for each scale were averaged.

Negative work and romantic experiences

We used the Brief Young Adult Life Events Scale to assess levels of experienced *Negative Work Experiences* and *Negative Romantic Experiences* (adapted for adult samples from Shahar, Henrich, Reiner, & Little, 2003). Participants were asked to report how frequently six negative events had occurred during the previous 4 weeks: three involved a romantic partner (e.g., "I argued with my romantic partner"), and three occurred at work (e.g., "I was criticized at work"). Responses for each ranged from 1 (*never*) to 4 (*quite frequently*). Cronbach's alphas were acceptable (α = .83–.89). Item scores for each were averaged.

Psychological outcomes

Self-acceptance was assessed by Ryff's (1989) scale of self-acceptance (e.g., "I like most aspects of my personality"). This scale consists of six items rated from 1 (*incorrect*) to 6 (*correct*). The Cronbach alpha for this scale was .85. Item scores were averaged.

Satisfying relationships with others were measured with the Connectedness subscale of the EPOCH measure (Kern et al., 2016). The Connectedness subscale includes five items (e.g., "There are people in my life who really care about me") rated from 1 (*incorrect*) to 5 (*correct*). Cronbach's alpha was .86. Item scores were averaged.

Life satisfaction

We asked participants to complete a 7-item measure that assessed their *Life Satisfaction* with regard to different domains such as social relationships and leisure activities (Zullig et al., 2009). Items were rated on a scale from 1 (*not satisfied*) to 5 (*very satisfied*). Cronbach's alpha was .88. Item scores were averaged.

Depressive symptoms

We asked participants to complete the Brief Symptom Inventory (Derogatis & Melisaratos, 1983), a 53-item inventory that measures psychological symptoms in eight domains. The current study focused on the 6-item Depression subscale (e.g., "How often did you feel lonely during the last month?"). Items were rated on a 5-point scale (1 [*little or no symptoms*], 5 [*many symptoms*]). Cronbach's alpha was .92. Item scores were averaged.

Analysis of the data and results

First, a univariate linear growth curve analysis was conducted for self-criticism in order to examine whether self-criticism changes significantly across time. The growth curve fits the data, $\chi^2(7, N = 168) = 11.15, p = .132$; comparative fit index (CFI) = .981, root-mean-square error (RMSEA) = .059. The growth curve of self-criticism increased linearly over time ($\beta = .03$/year, $p = .011$). The means of the intercept ($M_{intercept} = -0.34$; 95% confidence interval [CI] [−0.48, −0.20]) and slope ($M_{slope} = -0.06$; 95% CI [−0.08, −0.03]) were statistically significant ($p < .001$), as were their variances (0.63 and 0.04, respectively; $p < .023$). Thus, self-criticism significantly decreased from age 23 ($M = -0.31$) to age 29 ($M = -0.67$). Importantly, the correlation between the intercept and slope functions (between the level of mean and the change) did not reach statistical significance, $r = .13, p = .53$. This suggests that decrease in self-criticism over time was not associated with initial level of self-criticism. Change could be found among those who were low at the initial assessment and those who were high.

In order to assess associations between the initial level of self-criticism and its change, and future outcomes, two path models were conducted. The first model

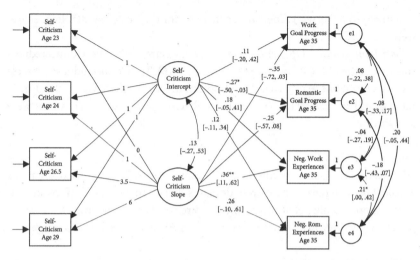

Figure 10.1 Over-time associations from the intercept and slope of self-criticism to coping with age-related tasks at age 35

Note: N = 168. Unstandardized factor loadings are depicted for the intercept and slope latent factors. Estimates for all other associations are standardized. 95% confidence intervals are presented in brackets. *$p < .05$. **$p < .01$ (two-tailed).

examined the extent to which changes in self-criticism were associated with better coping with age-related tasks throughout early adulthood. In this analysis both the baseline levels (intercepts) and trajectories (slopes) of self-criticism were entered as predictors of progress in, and coping with, age-related tasks at age 35. The results are presented in Figure 10.1. The model fit was acceptable, $\chi^2(15, N = 168) = 17.04$, $p = .317$, CFI = .993, RMSEA = .028.

Baseline levels of self-criticism (the intercepts) were negatively associated with romantic goal progress at age 35 ($\beta = -.27$, $p < .027$). Lower baseline levels of self-criticism were associated with greater romantic goal progress 12 years later. The slopes of self-criticism were positively associated with negative work experiences at age 35 ($\beta = .36$, $p = .005$). The greater the linear decreases in self-criticism from age 23 to age 29, the fewer the number of negative work experiences at age 35.

The second model examined the associations between changes in self-criticism and psychological outcomes at age 35. As can be seen in Figure 10.2, both the baseline levels (intercepts) and trajectories (slopes) of self-criticism were associated with psychological outcomes at age 35. Model fit was acceptable, $\chi^2(15, N = 168) = 22.25$, $p = .101$, CFI = .984, RMSEA = .054.

At age 35 baseline levels (the intercepts) of self-criticism were significantly negatively associated with self-acceptance, connectedness, and life satisfaction ($\beta = -.28$ to $-.51$, $p < .003$) and positively associated with depressive symptoms ($\beta = .48$, $p < .001$). Lower baseline levels of self-criticism were associated with better

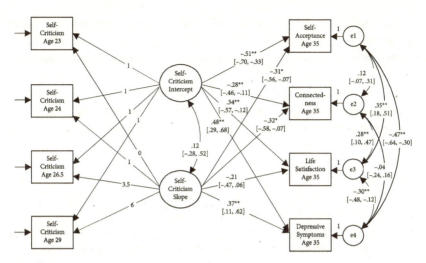

Figure 10.2 Over-time associations from the intercept and slope of self-criticism to psychological outcomes at age 35

Note: N = 168. Unstandardized factor loadings are depicted for the intercept and slope latent variables. Estimates for all other associations are standardized. 95% confidence intervals are presented in brackets. *p < .05. **p < .01 (two-tailed).

self-acceptance, greater connectedness, higher life satisfaction, and lower levels of depressive symptoms 12 years later. At age 35 the slopes of self-criticism were negatively associated with self-acceptance ($\beta = -.31$, $p = .011$) and connectedness ($\beta = -.32$, $p = .012$) and positively associated with depressive symptoms ($\beta = .37$, $p = .006$). The greater the linear decrease in self-criticism from age 23 to age 29, the higher the levels of self-acceptance and connectedness at age 35 and the lower the levels of depressive symptoms at age 35.

Considered together, we found a consistent decrease in self-criticism over a period of 6 years between the ages of 23 and 29 years. In addition, our findings showed that both baseline levels of self-criticism and the magnitude of its decrease explained developmental and psychological outcomes at age 35. Conceptually, we believe, the effects of the initial levels and the change in self-criticism capture the dialectic of stability and change in personality during the emerging adulthood years.

At the beginning of this chapter we discussed the adverse effect of self-criticism on individual functioning in great detail. A self-critical personality style interferes with a one's ability to remain true to oneself and to implement and pursue one's plans. In addition, elevated self-criticism leads to biased perceptions of oneself and others, resulting in misconstruction of events and stressors (Blatt, 2008). This explains the long-term adverse effects of self-criticism on the affiliation with adaptive or less adaptive developmental pathways. The additional findings indicating the change in self-criticism across emerging adulthood add to our understanding of developmental processes. Although personality is stable, it appears also to change as part of a comprehensive maturity principle (Caspi et al., 2005). Positive changes in personality could be helpful for reducing individuals' tendencies to perceive events negatively (Robins & Trzesniewski, 2005) and facilitating positive interaction with others and with the environment (Van Aken et al., 2006). In addition, decrease in self-criticism could increase one's capacity to reflect on one's own thoughts, allowing individuals to acknowledge or recognize their own mental states and those of others better (Fonagy et al., 2002).

Changes in personality should be consistent with the development and maintenance of useful traits and characteristics that support the acquisition of adult responsibilities, such as family or career roles, and reduce traits that might hamper progression. Considered together, transition to adulthood is characterized by both stability and change. The increased penchant for change found during emerging adulthood (B. W. Roberts & Davis, 2016) is probably aimed at facilitating a smoother transition to adulthood and the assumption of adult career and family roles.

Conclusion

We started this chapter asking why some individuals successfully achieve their goals, make the transition to adulthood, and assume an adult role, while others fail. Emerging from Blatt's (2008) theory of personality and the SDT (Ryan & Deci, 2000a, 2017), we were able to show that efficacy, low self-criticism, and being internally motivated have the potential to facilitate smoother career pursuit. In addition, having the capacity to relate to others in a mature manner explained a successful progression toward romantic intimacy and commitment. Thus, a person's personality traits play a role in the capacity to navigate successfully toward adulthood. In addition, we were able to show that together with the lasting effects of personality, personality changes during emerging adulthood and that these changes are geared toward facilitating coping with developmental tasks in career success and romantic development.

Existing theory and research have focused mainly on the difficulties that emerging adults experience nowadays in the transition to adulthood (Arnett, 2004; EGRIS, 2001; Settersten & Ray, 2010). Many of the difficulties were attributed to the major social and economic changes of the last three decades and the need to address multiple tasks simultaneously (Caspi, 2002; Grob et al., 2001). Notwithstanding that nowadays it has become more difficult than in the past to complete the transition to adulthood, based on our findings we suggest that the process is more complex. Personality might play a significant role in the process of this transition. "Positive" personality traits have the potential to facilitate a smoother transition in our changing world. A person with a "positive" personality might have greater capacity to cope with stressors and address hurdles that come up along the way successfully. In contrast, "difficult" personality traits, such as an elevated level of self-criticism, could hamper one's capacity to address uncertainties and even lead to biased perception of reality. Thus, among individuals with a "difficult" personality, difficulties navigating emerging adulthood might be exacerbated by personal deficiencies.

11
Support Systems and Their Role in Developmental Processes During Emerging Adulthood

In the preceding chapters we discussed the changes in the lives of young people as observed during the last decades. Due to extensive economic and social changes, the transition to adulthood has become more difficult for most of the current generations (Bynner, 2012; Furlong & Cartmel, 2007). All of these changes, described in detail in the previous chapters, suggest that nowadays young people are far less likely to have completed education, begun full-time employment, or entered a partnership than in the past. As a result, young people are also less likely to be living on their own (Schoeni & Ross, 2005) and more likely to continue living with their parents (Seiffge-Krenke, 2013), unlike in former years when they were more likely to live on their own.

Relatedly, the changes in the life patterns of young people are associated with changes in the relationship young adult children have with their parents. These changes are expressed in aspects such as co-residence, frequency of contact, and the provision of tangible and non-tangible support (Fingerman & Yahirun, 2016). For example, in contrast to the past, an increasing number of young people can be found living with their parents (Seiffge-Krenke, 2013); and today, most are in closer and more frequent contact with their parents (Arnett & Schwab, 2013). Due to the delay in completing the transition to adulthood, young adults in particular may need support and evaluate it favorably (Schoeni & Ross, 2005). It is not clear, however, whether the increasing provision of support is beneficial or might interfere with a successful transition that traditionally signaled adult status and independence (Fussell & Furstenberg, 2005). Fingerman and her colleagues (2012) found that continued parental support is indeed one marker of the prolonged period of dependence that characterizes young adults nowadays. While it is understandable that continued parental support could lead to a delay in assumption of adult roles, it was found overall that grown children who reported extensive support reported better psychological adjustment and life satisfaction than young adults who had not received extensive parental support (Fingerman et al. 2012).

Conceptually, these findings align basic tenets in developmental psychology that when parents support their offspring in earlier years as well as during young adulthood, children meet their developmental tasks more successfully (Seiffge-Krenke et al., 2010; Shulman, Kalnitzki, & Shahar, 2009). However, the majority of the existing studies suggesting that parental support is associated with better functioning were cross-sectional and conducted with young adults during their earlier 20s. It is clear that significant changes occur in existing relationships during emerging adulthood (Arnett, 2004). The importance of parents may decrease, while relationships outside of the family may become more meaningful (Seiffge-Krenke, 2009). Thus, the extent to which parental support will continue to affect future outcomes during emerging adulthood positively is questionable. Furthermore, over time romantic partners are likely to become the most important figures in the life of a young person, and the centrality of parents is likely to decrease. It is thus questionable whether parental support will continue to serve as an important source of support. Considering the expected change in the hierarchy of support sources during emerging adulthood, a more comprehensive examination of relationships with parents, their course over time, and their potential role in future outcomes is needed.

This chapter aims to address these questions. Based on our longitudinal data, we first describe the amount of support that young adults reported receiving from their parents and friends over the period of 12 years. We show that despite the changes in parent–child relationships during emerging adulthood, parents remain a primary source of support. Furthermore, we show that availability of parental support contributed to affiliation with more adaptive developmental pathways, both career and romantic development. These findings are supported by the narrative accounts of our participants describing their relationship with their parents across the years and the ways their parents provided (or did not provide) support. Careful reading of these interviews suggested that over the years emerging adults tended to develop a more mature and reflective understanding of their parents. More importantly, we show that a more mature understanding of one's parents at age 29 associated with better developmental and psychological outcomes at age 35. Finally, the chapter examines the role of mentors in emerging adults' success in meeting developmental tasks. Of note, in this chapter we do not discuss the role of romantic partners as a support system. As discussed in much detail in Chapters 5 and 6, romantic partners are not necessarily stable figures in the life of an emerging adult until later into their 20s, when an intimate and committed relationship has been established.

Support systems across emerging adulthood

In order to assess the level of support emerging adults receive from different sources, at each assessment they were asked to complete the Network of

Relationship Inventory (NRI; Furman & Buhrmester, 1985) with regard to support provided by mother, father, close friend, romantic partner, and another non-parental adult such as a family or a non-family member (e.g., a mentor). For each support figure participants rated the quality of support across eight items (i.e., "I can rely on..." and "... gives the feeling that I am of worth"). Items were rated on a 5-point scale (1 [*low support*], 5 [*high support*]). This procedure was replicated five times at ages 23, 24, 26.5, 29, and 35. Thus, five assessments of support were collected for each support figure. Cronbach alphas for perceived support from the different support figures across the five assessments were in the range between .88 and .93.

As can be seen in Figure 11.1, mothers are the primary source of support across the years. Although there is a significant, though slight, decrease in the level of support provided by mothers as emerging adults approach age 30, overall mothers continue to be evaluated as a significant source of support. At the earlier stages fathers are also evaluated as an important source of support, but approaching the age of 30, fathers are described as providing less support. Of note, the decrease is substantial. Friends are described as providing a high amount of support. During the earlier stages of emerging adulthood, they are rated as providing even higher support compared to parents. Again, approaching the age of 30 there is a significant decrease in the level of support provided by friends, though this remains high.

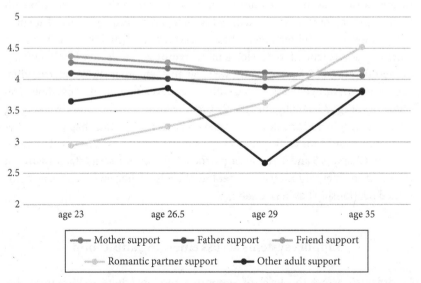

Figure 11.1 Level of support received from different significant figures across the age range of 23 to 35

The decrease in the amount of support provided by mothers, fathers, and close friends toward the age of 30 parallels the importance assigned to the support provided by romantic partners across the years. In the earlier stages, many emerging adults did not have a romantic partner. In addition, considering the lower stability of romantic relationships in the earlier stages of emerging adulthood, romantic partners were less likely to be perceived as providing a high level of support. However, after the age of 30 and having settled down, romantic partners were described as providing the highest level of support. This dialectic between level of support provided by parents and close friends and that provided by romantic partners resembles earlier findings by Laursen and Williams (1997) and Sroufe and colleagues (2005), who also showed that the importance of romantic partners increases with age and replaces that of parents.

Finally, across the years emerging adults also reported on support they received from other non-family adults. Overall, the level provided by other adults was lower than that provided by parents and close friends and remained low over the years. At the end of this chapter we will discuss the role of mentors in development during emerging adulthood in greater detail.

Support systems and attainment of developmental tasks

The role of parental support and relational experiences within the family for future relationships of offspring has been widely discussed and demonstrated across the various stages of child development. Attachment theorists have argued that parent–child relationships form the basis of children's internalized "working models" of close relationships and that these patterns are carried forward into new relationships (Sroufe & Fleeson, 1986). Embedded within socialization theory, Elder and Giele (2009) showed that parents' behavior toward the child, as well as the couple's relationship, influence children's behavior by serving as a model for future relationships with a partner (Bandura, 1977). Indeed, Conger and colleagues (2000) demonstrated that adolescents reared in nurturing and supportive families displayed more supportive and less hostile behaviors toward their romantic partners in young adulthood. Additional studies have also shown that continued availability of parental support, combined with the young person's increased personal capabilities, are essential for meeting developmental tasks and establishing future adaptive relationships as these serve as models for future relationships (Scharf et al., 2004; Seiffge-Krenke et al., 2010). In contrast, lack of parental modeling and support could result in deficient family models and, in turn, lead to greater relationship difficulties. Parental support is also important for enhancing a personal sense of efficacy. The lack of support is also likely to lead to lack of validation of true thoughts, feelings, and aspirations and to the development of a self that is oriented toward pleasing others at the expense of self-assertion or refraining from establishing an intimate relationship (Harter et al., 1997).

Theorizing and research in vocational psychology have also examined the role of parental support in facilitating vocational exploration and career decision-making among adolescents (Blustein et al., 1995; Lent et al., 2002). This is achieved by providing emotional support, enhancing the sense of security and self-efficacy of offspring, and helping them master educational and vocational challenges (Raque-Bogdan et al., 2013; Whiston & Keller, 2004). Whiston and Keller (2004) described the importance of parents in the career development of young people, indicating that parental emotional support and encouragement are likely to be associated with more adaptive career development.

Together, when parents give their offspring their blessing and support, young people are more successful in meeting the developmental tasks of this transitional stage (Seiffge-Krenke et al., 2010; Shulman, Kalnitzki, & Shahar, 2009). Notwithstanding the documented important role of parental support in the development of their children, most of the existing research was conducted on families with young children and adolescents. The studies conducted on young adults mostly assessed parental support during adolescence and examined its effect over time during young adulthood. During emerging adulthood, as described earlier in this chapter, relationships with parents undergo major changes (Lowe & Dotterer, 2018; Fingerman & Yahirun, 2016), and less is known about the extent to which parental support continues to play a role in developmental outcomes. In addition, the role of peer support cannot be underestimated in terms of a young person's self-esteem and adaptation (Galambos et al., 2006). Thus, learning more about the role of parental or peer support in future outcomes among emerging adults could further inform us about the contribution of support systems during emerging adulthood.

Our longitudinal data allowed us to examine this question. Emerging adults' perception of paternal, maternal, peer, and romantic partner support was assessed at age 23. Six years later, at the age of 29, participants were asked to appraise their career goal progress ("to what extent have you made progress realizing this project," three items) with regard to progress in academic, career (work), and romantic goals. In addition, employing the Brief Symptom Inventory, the number of depressive behaviors was assessed via six items, such as "Losing hope about the future." Correlation levels of support provided by parents, peers, and romantic partners at age 23 and developmental outcomes at age 29 are presented in Table 11.1.

As can be seen, attainment of academic goals at age 29 was associated with earlier support by both parents and peers. However, the association of earlier paternal support with academic achievement was more than twice as high as the

Table 11.1 *Age 23 Support Provided by Mothers, Fathers, Close Friends, and Romantic Partners at Age 23 and Attainment of Developmental Tasks and Depressive Affect at Age 29*

	Achievement of academic goal	Achievement of career goal	Achievement of romantic goal	Depressive symptoms
Paternal support	.47**	.40**	.30**	−.26**
Maternal support	.37**	.39**	.16	−.27**
Friend support	.22	.39**	.32**	−.18*
Romantic partner support	.14	.10	.37**	−.17

*$p < .05$. **$p < .01$.

association with peer support, $r = .47$ versus $r = .22$. Associations between earlier provision of support and future achievement of career goal were quite similar for fathers, mothers, and peers. In contrast, achievement of romantic goals associated with earlier paternal and peer support but not maternal support. Level of depressive symptoms at age 29 was negatively associated with earlier support provided by the three figures above. Interestingly, earlier support of a romantic partner associated only with future achievement of romantic goals but not with the other goals or level of depression. To summarize, earlier paternal, maternal, and peer support associated with higher future likelihood of achieving age-related goals and with a lower level of depressive symptoms. In addition, it appeared that the association between earlier support and future academic achievement was stronger for fathers than for peers. Conceptually, it might be suggested that support provided by parents, even during emerging adulthood when young people might be less involved with their parents, still explains future outcomes (Fingerman & Yahirun, 2016).

Career and romantic pathways and earlier parental support

Reading the in-depth career history interviews (see Chapter 3) led to the identification of four career pathways. The first, *Consistent Pursuit*, was characterized by individuals with a clear and articulated life plan that was complex, diversified, and connected to inner aspirations who successfully pursued their dream. The second, *Adapted Pursuit*, consisted of individuals who experienced disappointments or failures along the way that led them to a change in the area of study and/or a shift to a different field of work. However, despite the difficulties experienced along the way, they were able to find a new way and adapt successfully. The third, *Survivors*, consisted of individuals who were not able to successfully pursue their goal but, despite their disappointment and ongoing dream, were employed in steady jobs and had seemingly settled daily lives. The fourth, *Confused/Vague*, were not able to provide a clear and coherent idea of what they wanted to do with their lives and appeared to feel miserable.

In the search for the possible precursors of the different career pathways, we looked for personality attributes and quality of earlier support to explain affiliation to a particular pathway. The role of personality was discussed in the previous chapter, which showed that elevated self-criticism, lower efficacy, and being more extrinsically motivated associated with less optimal future pathways. In addition, and relevant to the current discussion, affiliates of the *Confused/Vague* pathway reported a lower level of maternal support 6 years earlier, compared to that reported by *Consistent Pursuit* affiliates. In addition, the *Adapted Pursuit* pathway resembled the less adaptive pathways on personality attributes, reporting a low level of efficacy and being more self-critical and extrinsically motivated compared with the *Consistent Pursuit* pathway. Yet, they differed from the two least adaptive patterns with regard to paternal support. Members of this pathway reported a sevenfold higher level of paternal support compared with members of the *Consistent Pursuit* pattern. Considered together, low maternal support was a risk factor that associated with higher likelihood of losing one's way in career pursuit. In addition, earlier paternal support served as a protective factor, helping young people to find a new goal following failure and pursue it successfully. Of note, peer support was not associated with affiliation for a particular type of career pathway (see statistics in Table 10.1 in the previous chapter).

The importance of maternal support in explaining affiliation with a less adaptive romantic pathway was also demonstrated. The role of personality attributes, such as high dependency, in explaining future romantic development was discussed in Chapter 10. In addition, earlier low maternal support explained affiliation with the *Lengthy Relationships but Absence of Experiential Learning* pathway. Earlier maternal support reported among members of this pathway was only one third compared to those affiliated with the optimal *Steady Relationship* pathway (see Table 10.2). It is possible that the combination of a dependent personality and lack of maternal support led to the search for an alternative support figure on which to rely and further explains the tendency to remain in a relationship that does not become committed over time.

Conceptually, the finding that low maternal support was associated with a higher likelihood of belonging to the least adaptive pathway 7 years later, the *Confused/Vague* pathway, is in line with the vast body of literature emphasizing the role of mothers in the development of their offspring (e.g., J. P. Allen & Hauser, 1996; Steele et al., 1999; van IJzendoorn & De Wolff, 1997). Yet, findings that paternal support served as a protective factor need further explanation. A closer inspection of the *Adapted Pursuit* affiliates suggests that these young people reported a low level of efficacy, and it was likely that increased paternal support facilitated these young people in overcoming their difficulties to make a shift and find a career with which they were satisfied and that was meaningful for them.

This finding calls for a different understanding of the role of paternal support in the later stages of development. Adolescents described their fathers as expressing respect for their penchant for independence more than their mothers and relying on their emerging capabilities (Shulman & Seiffge-Krenke, 1997). More specifically, Snarey (1993) found that fathers were more sensitive than mothers in providing support that addresses age-related tasks. Thus, fathers might be more attuned to their young adult children in the process of career pursuit, and their support may thus play a role in career development. Within a broader developmental framework, we may suggest that while mothers tend to provide the "secure base," fathers provide "secure exploration" (Grossmann et al., 2002). The lack of maternal support, as reported by the *Confused/Vague* affiliates, was associated with major difficulties in pursuing one's way. In contrast, paternal support, which is probably sensitive to the age-related needs of a young person (Shulman & Seiffge-Krenke, 1997), had the potential for helping a young person find their niche. In sum, we might suggest that maternal support is essential for child development, as has been widely documented in developmental psychology; and this associates with better future outcomes. Yet, paternal support might have an additional unique role in helping a young person find their way within the occupational domain.

Parental support: Narrative accounts

In our study we found significant associations between parental support assessed at age 23 and future career and romantic outcomes at age 29. Support was measured using eight items adapted from the NRI (Furman & Buhrmester, 1985). Conceptually, the eight items captured two aspects of support: emotional support and supporting offspring's self-worth. In the in-depth interviews conducted with participants at age 29, they were asked to talk about their relationship with their parents, the support received from them, and the role parents played in their development. Reading the interviews provided us with an additional lens to understand the ways parental support was provided during emerging adulthood and how parental behavior and attitudes were understood by the children. This is presented verbatim from the interviews with individuals belonging to the different pathways.

Alex successfully and consistently pursued his career. At age 29 he was working as an engineer and planned to continue to graduate studies. Alex's memories of his relationship with his parents echo the differences found between mothers and fathers. He described a good and close relationship with his mother. However, "With Dad I always expected him to give a smile, and it was an impossible mission. He is this sort of person and I learned to live with this." Yet, later he learned through his friends that his father praises him and thinks highly of him, "and this gave me the whole picture." It appears that although Alex's father seemed remote, he was proud of his son's academic accomplishment. Alex further told us that his parents supported him even when he made a decision to switch schools during adolescence—a decision that could have been criticized by parents.

Eitan, who grew up in an immigrant family, also described an encouraging parental environment despite the difficulties his parents faced as new immigrants.

> They were new in the country, did not speak the language. They worked hard. My father worked hard so we could study. And gave me what I needed, a computer for example when not everybody had a computer. When we moved to Ashdod I went to a private school, and this was expensive and not easy for them [financially]. But this changed my life.

In his story, Eitan emphasized that although his parents were not familiar with the schools and studies in their new environment, they provided the support and the environment that allowed him to go on; and they did this in the best way.

The stories of these two successful young men described a supportive family environment that was "mobilized" to serve the progress of their children. Though parents did not necessarily understand exactly what their son was studying, they supported their child's decision, were encouraging, and did all they could to allow their child to advance. Natti, who graduated as a dentist, told a somewhat different story of his relationship with his parents when he was in his first year at the school of dentistry. His parents did not understand why he did not take an easier track, and they had disagreements. However, he speaks warmly of his parents. First, he added that despite disagreements he felt the communication with his parents was always open and respectful. More importantly, he developed a mature understanding of his parents and what they did in their life and for their children.

> I always tell myself that I have the privilege to do [what I want], and my parents did not have this privilege. They worked hard and were invested in their jobs, though they could probably do better. But they did it so that we could succeed. I saw how committed they were to their work, and they were happy with their

jobs, though life was not easy at the beginning. And this drives me with my career and with building my own family.

In addition to the support Natti received during the years, he emphasized the model his parents provided for him. He learned that once you have a family your attitude toward work does not have to serve only your wishes. He saw his parents happy in their jobs, though they could have done something better, because their worked allowed them to raise their family and advance their children. Natti described taking this experience with him to serve as a model of how to approach work and family in a serious manner and do the best you can for yourself and for your family. (The capacity to develop a mature perception of one's parents will be further discussed toward the end of this chapter.)

Perceiving the commitment of parents and adopting this as a model for one's own development and progress are further demonstrated in the life story of Oren, who is about to complete a degree in technical management. Oren comes from a poor family and grew up in a difficult neighborhood. His father was employed as a custodian in a school. Oren remembers his father as never missing a day of work. Life was difficult, but his father did not complain. Speaking about his father, Oren described, "I admire my father, his high work ethics. He felt that he needed to support a family and he succeeded, really succeeded. And we, the children, are successful—each in his field." Thus, in addition to parental support, the father's attitude toward work serves as a model for his son and can explain his persistence.

Becky was identified as belonging to the *Adapted Pursuit* pathway. She changed the course of her career. At first she hoped to become a psychologist, changed to human resources, was floundering for a while, but ended up working in a bank. Though at the beginning banking seemed boring to her, over time she learned to love it and is developing a career in banking. Becky, who found her way over time and found meaning in her work, also describes her relationship with her parents as close. Her relationship with her mother was closer, but when the issue of career arose, her father was more significant. In addition, she spoke highly of her parents' commitment to their work, which continues to serve as a model for her. Thus, parental support and her father's guidance probably helped Becky find meaning in the work she ended up doing, though it was not what she had originally planned.

Roni was identified as belonging to the *Survivors* pathway. Roni works steadily for a weekly publication, which she considers not as a career but more as a way to support herself. It is difficult for her to articulate what exactly she would like to do or study. Roni also describes a close and supportive relationship with her parents. However, Roni feels that her parents did not provide her with direction in her life. She attributes this to the fact that they are old. "She [her mother] never guided me. Never took me to or from school. She was not involved in this. I think that recently this is a direction that I get from my boyfriend."

Tami was also identified as belonging to the *Survivors* pathway. She also describes that her parents cared for her. However, when she asked for support in a decision (with regard to work) her mother tended to be more critical. "My mother said to me, *what*? And what will happen in the future, are you sure? Instead of telling me, OK do it, it is not the end of the world. This led me not to trust myself." Her father was always supportive. He was always involved and did everything for her, which also hurt her self-confidence.

Considered together, *Survivors* appear to describe a supportive family background. However, unlike the emerging adults who belonged to the more adapted pathways, their parents provided less guidance and, through their continued help, might have interfered with the development of their children's sense of competence. Nora was identified as belonging to the *Confused/Vague* pathway. She described a relationship with her parents that was not easy; they were, at the time, absorbed in their own problems. Though continuing to live under the same roof, they were not living together. Lacking parental support, Nora regularly turned to friends for support and guidance. Furthermore, in recent years, Nora feels that her mother needs *her* support with things like cleaning the house, and she comes to help them but flees right after finishing, telling her mother she has to leave.

To summarize, there are a number of aspects that could be derived from the interviews. First, the narrative accounts align with the quantitative findings. Both mothers and fathers are described as central support figures during emerging adulthood. In addition, both female and male participants described their mothers as being the closest person to them, and fathers were described as less involved in the lives of their children. Fathers tended to play a more important role when addressing career issues. Of note, friends were not mentioned often as support figures, but their support was mentioned when relationships with parents were not close. Reading the stories showed that, in addition to emotional support, participants emphasized other components of parents' behavior they considered important. Parents were described as offering guidance. More importantly, young adults highly regarded parental encouragement and enhancement of their offspring's sense of self-worth. Of note, emerging adults who had successfully achieved their developmental goals described that parents respected their decisions and continued to support them even when their choices were not necessarily recommended by the parents. In contrast, emerging adults who achieved their goals less successfully were more likely to describe parents who were more critical and undermined their adult children's sense of self-worth.

The difficulty in balancing between support and encouragement of individuality and exploration is demonstrated in the stories of those belonging to the

Survivors pathway. Both Roni's and Tami's parents were described as supportive and providing a sense of being available. However, their parents undermined their sense of confidence and self-worth that, in turn, probably affected their capacity to cope efficiently with developmental tasks. For example, Tami described that her father is ready and willing to do everything for her but, in addition, tries to push her into decisions "that left me with the feeling that I was worth nothing." Thus, in addition to the centrality of support, the stories highlight the importance of parents in encouraging the confidence and self-worth of their offspring while navigating their 20s. The least optimal are the cases where parents were not able to provide support. Nora, who belonged to the least optimal pathways, the *Confused/Vague* career pathway and the *Lengthy Relationships but Absence of Experiential Learning* romantic pathway, indeed described a personal history lacking parental support, which could explain her non-adaptive outcomes in both the career and romantic domains.

Reading the stories carefully suggests that the accounts provide a new, additional perspective for understanding the role of parents during emerging adulthood. Indeed, the provision of support and the way support is provided are important. Reading the stories suggests that participants also described their parents as serving as models for their lives. Past research in developmental psychology and vocational psychology has described parents as role models (T. D. Allen et al., 2004; Raque-Bogdan et al., 2013). However, our participants described a more complex process that they took with them from their parents. It was not parental behavior per se that served as a model. Participants belonging to the adaptive pathways described an increasing capacity to understand the behavior of their parents. They were capable of reflecting on parental behavior (Fonagy et al., 1998). For example, though their parents were employed in jobs that were not highly regarded, Oren and Natti were able to recognize the mental states of their parents, the compromises they made. This led to high regard for the efforts parents made to adjust, considering the conditions in which they were living (poverty, immigration). Understanding their parents from a different and valued perspective helped these two young people to understand life more comprehensively and to learn from their parents.

Conceptually, we thus suggest an additional component in parent–child relationships during emerging adulthood: the ability to reflect on the behavior of their parents, which can be expected to be achieved toward the later years of emerging adulthood. We suggest that achieving the capacity to develop a reflective understanding of one's own parents (Fonagy et al., 2002) would contribute to further adaptive development, as was shown in the cases of Oren and Natti. For this purpose, we decided to assess participants' reflective capacity to perceive parents at age 29 methodically and to examine its association with future career and romantic outcomes at age 35. This is described in greater detail in the next section.

Reflective capacity at age 29 and career and romantic outcomes at age 35

Both our quantitative and qualitative findings clearly showed that parental support experienced at age 23 associated with more adaptive outcomes at age 29. In addition, parental support associated with the type of career and romantic pathways on which emerging adults embarked. Notwithstanding the importance of parental support, relationships with parents might undergo significant changes during emerging adulthood in relation to housing, closeness, support, and intimacy (Lowe & Dotterer, 2018). Contact and shared activities between parents and emerging adults tended to decline (Fingerman & Yahirun, 2016; Parker et al., 2012). Our findings also showed a significant decrease in parental support between ages 23 and 29 for both fathers and mothers (see Figure 11.1). Lowe and Dotterer (2018) suggested that these changes in parent–child relationships increase the awareness of family members to one another's separate needs and priorities, while maintaining their relationships. The increasing awareness of one another results in greater synchronization between parents and children, and relationships are more beneficial. In his description and theory of emerging adulthood, Arnett (2004) suggested that changes in parent–child relationships can lead to a broader understanding of the relationships one has or had with one's parents and in one's family. Potentially, this can lead to the development of a more comprehensive perspective of a person's family narrative in a more coherent manner (Fiese & Pratt, 2004).

The ability to achieve awareness of relationships in one's family conceptually represents an increase in reflectivity. Attributing reasons to self and others allows one to understand that one's own or others' behavior arises from internal states. This, in turn, enables the individual to give meaning to people's behavior and to understand others' thoughts and feelings (Bouchard et al., 2008; Fonagy et al., 2002). The better understanding of relationships within the family and between parents themselves can thus serve as a model for understanding the behavioral motives of other family members and for addressing the complexity of relationships, for example, how to be close while acknowledging one's (or the other's) individuality and separate needs. As such, greater reflectivity can be conducive to learning how to coordinate personal aspirations within a relationship, while considering the aspirations of one's partner (Levinson, 1978). Greater reflectivity might also lead to a more comprehensive understanding of parents' work-related behavior. What were the reasons behind staying in a particular job, and what function did that work serve for the parents? In addition, increasing reflectivity can lead to better understanding of the ways parents handled their dyadic and family relationships and serve as an adaptive model for one's own family life (Byng-Hall, 1995a). In sum, developing a reflective understanding can be a helpful model not only for pursuing and achieving intimacy and commitment (Eyre et al., 2012) but also for better handling of family and career issues, how to navigate through career dilemmas, and how to find meaning in one's work (Blustein, 2011).

In line with this conceptualization, we set out to examine the associations between reflective capacity at age 29 and career and romantic outcomes at age 35. This procedure was conducted twice. First, we examined the role of reflective capacity concerning parents' career in work and future career-related outcomes. Second, we examined the associations between greater reflectivity concerning one's family of origin and future handling of romantic and family issues.

Reflective capacity at age 29 concerning parents' career and work and future career-related outcomes at age 35

As part of the interview about their own career history at age 29, participants were also interviewed about their parents' work history. This section consisted of two stages: first, a spontaneous story was told, after which the questions were presented (Rosenthal, 1993). In the opening question, participants were asked to tell the story of their parents' work, as they remembered it from their childhood and during recent years, in their own words and from their own point of view. The second stage was comprised of questions that attempted to reference specific topics raised by the participants themselves more accurately. In line with the study questions, participants were probed about how their parents perceived their work, what their attitudes were toward their work, and what changes their parents had made over the years with regard to their careers. In particular, participants were asked to explain how they understood their parents' behavior and decisions about work and how their parents balanced work and family. Interviews were recorded, transcribed, and rated on the degree of reflectivity in participants' descriptions of their parents' career over the years.

To assess reflectivity concerning parental work history, the scoring system developed by Fonagy and colleagues (1998) was applied and adapted for the scoring of the Parent Development Interview (PDI; Slade et al., 2005) to denote reflectivity regarding oneself and others. Participants' transcribed stories and answers to the questions were rated on a scale from −1 (*no reflectivity*) to 5 (*full or exceptional reflectivity*). Low level of reflectivity consisted of superficial and concrete descriptions of parents' work, difficulty providing explanations, and lack of awareness of parents' feelings about their work. Even when explanations were provided, they were rather concrete, remained at a descriptive level, and did not reflect parents' motives. In contrast, high reflectivity consisted of descriptions characterized by profound understanding of the objective and subjective reasons that led to the parents' career history. Descriptions referred to emotions and internal states more than to concrete behaviors. Within this context there is reference to processes, decisions, prices that were paid, compromises, and the meaning the parents' work had for the child (the interviewee).

Age 35 outcomes

The following career-related indices were assessed:

Career goal attainment. As reported in the previous chapters, participants were asked to assess career goal progress ("to what extent have you made progress realizing this goal") using a modified version of Little's (1983) Personal Project Analysis.

Career commitment. Participants completed the Vocational Identity Status Assessment (Porfeli et al., 2011), which measures participants' level of career development. Two subscales were used for the current study. Eight items assessed participants' *Career Commitment* (e.g., "I feel this is the best work for me"). Cronbach's alpha was .88. Six items were used to assess participants' *Career Reconsideration* (e.g., "I ask myself whether this is really the work I want"). Cronbach's alpha was .81. For both measures, items were rated on a 5-point scale (1 [*strongly disagree*], 5 [*strongly agree*]). Item scores were averaged for both measures.

Negative work events. Participants completed the Brief Young Adult Life Events Scale, which assesses levels of experienced negative events in work (Shahar, Henrich, Reiner, & Little, 2003). Participants were asked to report how frequently three negative events occurred during the previous 4 weeks ("I was criticized at work"). Items were rated on a 1 (*never*) to 5 (*quite frequently*) scale. Cronbach's alphas were .87. and .89, respectively.

Satisfaction with work. Participants completed a 3-item measure assessing satisfaction with their work and level of income (Zullig et al., 2009). Items were rated on a 1 (*not satisfied*) to 5 (*very satisfied*) scale. Cronbach's alpha was .83.

We first assessed the associations of parental support at age 23 and at age 29 and reflective capacity in relation to parents' career at age 29 with future career-related outcomes at age 35. No associations between paternal or maternal support at age 23 and paternal or maternal support at age 29 and career-related outcomes at age 35 were found. Level of reflectivity at age 29, however, associated with future greater satisfaction with work, $r = .30$, $p = .001$; greater career commitment, $r = .25$, $p = .011$; and lesser career reconsideration, $r = -.32$, $p = .008$.

To further and more accurately assess the contribution of reflectivity to future career outcomes, a set of hierarchical regressions were conducted. We assessed the contribution of reflectivity after controlling for personality (self-criticism and efficacy) and earlier parental support. The findings showed that reflectivity at age 29 contributed to future career-related outcomes above and beyond the contribution of personality and earlier parental support. Reflectivity explained greater career goal attainment, $\beta = .19$, $p = .041$; greater satisfaction with work, $\beta = .33$, $p = .011$; greater career commitment, $\beta = .24$, $p = .032$; and lesser career reconsideration, $\beta = -.31$, $p = .01$. In sum, achieving a reflective understanding of parents' career-related behaviors and motives toward the end of emerging adulthood (at age 29) could serve as a model for young people in approaching and addressing their own career issues following settling down (at age 35). Conceptually, we thus suggest that in addition to parental support at earlier stages of development, reflective understanding of parents' career-related behavior can serve as a model for children in addressing their careers in young adulthood.

Reflective capacity at age 29 regarding parents' marital and family relationships and future career-related outcomes at age 35

In addition to the interview about parents' career history, a second interview was conducted with participants to assess their understanding of their parents' marital and family relationships (Rosenthal, 1993). Again, participants were first asked to tell the story of their parents' marriage and of family life in general during recent years, in their own words and from their own point of view. Subsequently, participants were probed about how their parents handled their relationship and how they coped when disagreements or conflicts arose. To capture and address inner processes and, in particular, to assess their level of reflectivity, the participants were encouraged to talk about, and elaborate on, their various experiences in their family and while observing their parents. In particular, they were encouraged to describe how they currently understand what they observed between their parents in the past. Interviews were recorded, transcribed, and rated on the degree of reflectivity in participants' descriptions of their parents and family.

To assess reflectivity regarding one's family, we again applied the scoring system developed by Fonagy and colleagues (1998) and adapted for the scoring of the PDI (Slade et al., 2005) to assess reflective understanding of parents' marital and family life. Participants' transcribed stories and answers to the questions were rated on a scale from −1 (*low reflectivity*) to 5 (*full or exceptional reflectivity*). The scales are conceptually similar to the scales that were developed to assess reflectivity of parents' career-related behavior but were adapted to assess family issues. Again, low reflectivity consisted of superficial, very concrete description of parents' relationships and difficulty providing further descriptions or elaborations when requested. When explanations were provided, they were banal and lacked efforts to understand motives that led to parents behaving as they did. In contrast, high reflectivity included descriptions characterized by profound understanding of the mutual influences of each parent on the other, as well as reference to events and processes that preceded the relationships and those that led to changes in parents' relationships. Descriptions also referred to emotions and internal states more than to concrete behaviors. Of note, participants did not necessarily describe an ideal family of origin. Developing a reflective capacity of the difficulties that their parents experienced might have led participants to become more aware of their own lives and how to handle their relationships better.

Age 35 outcomes

The following relationship/family-related indices were assessed:

Satisfaction with current romantic/marital relationship. Participants were asked to rate four items to assess the extent to which they were satisfied with different aspects of their romantic/marital relationships (i.e., daily interactions with partner, sexual life). Cronbach's alpha was .92.

Romantic partner support. Partner support was assessed using the NRI (Furman & Buhrmester, 1985) described above. Items were similar to those used to assess parental support. Cronbach's alpha was .91.

Progress in attainment of romantic goal. Using the Little (1983) Personal Project Analysis, participants were asked to rate four items assessing their sense of progress in the pursuit of their romantic goal (e.g., "to what extent have you made progress realizing this [romantic] goal"). Cronbach's alpha was .91.

Work–family balance. The Work–Family Spillover Scale was used to assess four distinct dimensions of work–family spillover (Grzywacz & Marks, 2000). Two scales were used to assess negative and positive spillover from work to family ("Job worries or problems distract me when I am at home" and "Things that I do at work help me deal with personal and practical issues at home"). Two additional scales were used to assess negative and positive spillover from family to work ("My investment in my relationship reduces my commitment to my work" and "A discussion with my partner helps me to cope with issues that come up at work"). Alphas for the four scales ranged between .82 and .93.

Correlations between parental support at ages 23 and 29 and reflective functioning at age 29 and relationship/family-related outcomes at age 35 appear in Table 11.2. As can be seen, maternal and paternal support at age 23 explained higher likelihood of attaining romantic/family goals at age 35. In addition, paternal support at age 23 explained other indices: relationship satisfaction, support of romantic partner, and positive spillover from family to work and vice versa at age 35. Additionally, greater maternal support at age 29 explained greater support by offspring's partner. Paternal support at age 29 explained relationship satisfaction, support of romantic partner, and positive spillover from family to work at age 35. Finally, greater reflective understanding of parents' marital and family relationships at age 35 explained greater likelihood of attainment of romantic/family goals at age 35, as well as greater positive spillover from family to work and from work to family at age 35.

Again, in order to further and more accurately assess the contribution of reflectivity to future romantic/family outcomes, a set of hierarchical regressions was conducted. We assessed the contribution of reflectivity after controlling for personality (self-criticism and dependency) and earlier parental support. The findings showed that reflectivity at age 29 contributed to future romantic/family outcomes above and beyond the contribution of personality and earlier parental support. Reflectivity explained greater romantic/family goal attainment ($\beta = .28$,

Table 11.2 *Associations Between Parental Support at Age 23 and Age 29 and Reflective Perception of Parents at Age 29 and Outcomes at Age 35*

	Satisfaction with one's relationships	Achievement of family goals	Romantic partner support	Positive spillover work to family	Positive spillover family to work
Maternal support (age 23)	.16	.21*	.13	.04	.16
Paternal support (age 23)	.22*	.22*	.21*	.20*	.174
Maternal support (age 29)	.1	.17	.29**	.02	.15
Paternal support (age 29)	.24*	.09	.27*	.16	.28**
Reflective perception of parents	.17	.38**	.16	.28**	.37**

*$p < .05$. **$p < .01$.

$p = .032$) and greater positive spillover from family to work and from work to family ($\beta = .29, p = .021$ and $\beta = .31, p = .009$, respectively).

In sum, earlier maternal support at ages 23 and 29 explained only two romantic/family outcomes at age 35: romantic/family goal attainment and support of romantic partner. Earlier paternal support, however, explained these two indices as well as better handling of the balance between family and work. The lesser contribution of maternal support compared to paternal support needs further explanation. Maternal support might be perceived more as interfering with offspring's progress toward autonomy (Fingerman & Yahirun, 2016). Support of fathers who are less involved (we saw earlier that paternal support was perceived to decrease significantly across ages compared to maternal support) might be perceived as less interfering with emerging adults' penchant for independence. Conceptually, fathers were considered more respectful of children's aspirations for individuality (Shulman & Seiffge-Krenke, 1997).

Notwithstanding the role of earlier parental support, our findings also suggest that in the later stages of emerging adulthood individuals might develop a capacity to better understand the behavior and motives of their parents. This asset, conceptualized as reflectivity (Fonagy et al., 1998), represents a capacity to perceive and understand parents in a mature mode, is probably a marker of the psychological development of an individual, and can serve as a model for development and progress to maturity.

Non-family support systems: Friends and mentors

In the previous sections we have shown that parental support continues to play a significant role in individual development through the 20s and even the 30s, despite the changes these relationships undergo. In addition to parents, friends, in particular close friends, are described as a major source of support during adolescence and emerging adulthood (Sroufe et al., 2005). Friends provide emotional support, enhance sense of security and self-efficacy, and help cope with social issues.

Research in educational and vocational psychology has shown that teachers, counselors, and senior co-workers can also become influential figures in the career-related decision-making processes and outcomes (Kidd et al., 2004; Phillips et al., 2001) of adolescents and college students. Most studies exploring the beneficial effects of non-parental career-related support have been conducted on adolescents, college students, or adults in a workplace environment (T. D. Allen et al., 2004; McDonald et al., 2007). However, less is known about the roles of these support systems during the transition to adulthood.

In our project, participants were asked to rate the support that they received from other (non-family) adults in addition to the support of parents and peers. We have shown above that close friend support at age 23 associated with higher likelihood of achieving developmental tasks at age 29 (see Table 11.1). However, close friend support at age 29 was minimally associated with outcomes at age 35 and not associated with any future career-related outcomes. Close friend support only associated with future greater satisfaction within one's relationships and greater positive spillover from family to work.

Similar to the assessment of parental and peer support, support of other non-family adults, such as a senior co-worker, was also measured using the NRI (Furman & Buhrmester, 1985) but did not associate with any future outcomes. To further examine the possible contribution of the support from non-family/mentors, we read the work history interviews again, where interviewees were asked to describe other figures who might also have played a role in their career development. We found that 49 of 100 interviewees described that they received professional help from others such as a manager or a senior co-worker. Twenty-one reported that they also received emotional support from a manager or a senior co-worker. Reports on receiving professional support or guidance at age 29 associated with greater satisfaction at work at age 35, $r = .263$, $p = .014$.

Reading the interviews further demonstrated how the presence or absence of support systems differentiated between the developmental pathways. Roni works for a weekly publication, but she does not like her work and hopes to do something else. However, she is still not sure what exactly she would like to do in the future. When asked whether any significant persons had influenced her, she responded, "I don't think so . . . that somebody . . . was [interested in] what I do."

In contrast, Limor, who was about to finish her internship in a law office, responded to the same question differently. Limor admires her boss: "She taught me a lot. The way she handles issues. I learned to follow her and how to approach issues [the need to be taken care of]. I learned a lot from everything that happened around me."

Others were able to describe a specific point in time or meeting with a person who made a significant impact on them. Becky, who is developing a career in banking, described a specific event that happened the first time she was looking for a job. She was interviewed for work at a hotel in a remote town. On her way to the bus station after the interview, she realized that she missed the last bus.

> It got late and there were no buses any more to get home. I was choked by tears. I went to the person in charge of human resources. And she was there for me. She resolved everything. I felt so bad and she gave me a good feeling. And when I started working there, she was always there for me. She invited me to her office. I saw her degrees on the wall, and she talked with me about the importance

of studying. She told [me] what she studied. And I felt I wanted to be like her. I think this is something that stays with you. I remember her well.

Becky's personal story shows that there are individuals who know how to seek help when they are in need, which in turn further intensifies their capacity to draw from resources around them. This tendency aligns with the research on resilience showing that proactive individuals naturally seek out developmental opportunities through relationships (Werner & Smith, 1982). They cultivate their skills for managing interactions and building trusting relationships (Dougherty et al., 2008). They know how and make efforts to form mutually beneficial relationships, and they engage in appropriate levels of follow-up to keep their mentors informed of how helpful their assistance has been (Chandler et al., 2010).

In contrast, others might lack the capacity to seek help when needed and might question the motives behind the willingness of others to provide help. For example, Aron works in a large firm. However, when asked about figures who helped him, he responded, "I cannot say that anybody did anything special for me, or that anybody destroyed me." Interestingly, despite being promoted at his workplace, he lives with a feeling that his position is insecure and is afraid that he might be laid off.

Thus, while friends were described as an important source of support during development (Sroufe et al., 2005), our findings focusing on emerging adults did not show friends to be a major source of support in addition to parents. We found, however, that support provided by adults other than parents, such as a manager at a workplace, might play a significant role in occupational adequacy and sense of well-being of emerging adults, thereby emphasizing the increasing importance of non-family support in the third decade of life. We believe that considering the current unfavorable societal and economic conditions (Furlong & Cartmel, 2007), the capacity to seek and to accept support from non-family figures could become an asset at this stage of life.

Conclusions

Conceptualization and research on parent–child relationships during emerging adulthood have documented changes in frequency, modes, and quality of these relationships. Despite these changes, for example, the decrease in parental support during the 20s, we showed that parental support continues to play a role in the career and romantic adaptation of their adult children. Thus, the role of parental support that was described as a major factor in children's development continues in the later stages of development, such as emerging adulthood, by providing support and advice. Of note, we found that while maternal support associated more with romantic life–related outcomes, paternal support was more likely to explain future career-related outcomes, probably reflecting the distinctive role of fathers in supporting independence.

In addition, we found that probably due to the changes in parent–child relationships during emerging adulthood, a new and broader perspective in understanding parental behavior could be expected. We termed this new perspective *reflectivity*, namely developing a capacity to better understand the behavior and motives of one's parents. Our longitudinal data revealed that achieving greater capacity to understand parents' own career and family behavior could serve as a model for better adaptation later during young adulthood. Conceptually, we thus propose that in addition to serving as a support system, mature understanding of parental behavior could further serve as a model to guide one during the transition to adulthood. Understanding parents' motives could serve as a model for offspring to address their own dilemmas better and facilitate the transition to an adult role. Finally, in addition to the role of parental support (direct support and through serving as models), non-family adults, such as a manager or senior co-worker, might also be considered an important factor in making a successful transition to the adult world.

12
Patterns of Mental Health During Emerging Adulthood and Their Association With the Success or Failure to Attain Developmental Tasks

Accumulating data about mental health during emerging adulthood, ages 18 to 29, presents contradictory directions. On the one hand, there is evidence of improvement in mental health and a decrease in problem behavior. For example, drawing from the Monitoring the Future study based on nationally representative samples, John Schulenberg and Nicole Zarrett (2006) showed a significant increase in well-being and decreases in depressive affect, risk-taking behavior, and conduct problems. These findings were replicated in a number of other studies (Galambos et al., 2006; Meadows et al., 2006; Schulenberg et al., 2005; Tanner et al., 2007), suggesting an overall improvement in mental health during emerging adulthood. On the other hand, the onset of severe psychopathology increases during emerging adulthood. Major depressive disorders, schizophrenia, bipolar disorder, and borderline personality disorders, for example, typically appear during late adolescence and early adulthood (Cicchetti & Rogosch, 2002). For example, Ronald Kessler and colleagues (2005) showed that the likelihood of the onset of mood disorders or impulse-control disorders is significantly higher during the emerging adulthood years than in other age groups across the life span.

These conflicting trends in the course of psychological problems and the onset of severe psychopathology raise a number of questions, for example, why mental health improves and problem behavior decreases in the general population, while the onset of severe psychopathology occurs during the emerging adulthood years. In addition, these trends reflect the average tendencies in the general population. However, in the previous chapters we have shown that emerging adults embark on different pathways in their pursuit of career and romantic tasks. Given this heterogeneity in the life paths of emerging adults, could we expect heterogeneity in the trajectories of mental health as well? The trends reported in the literature are mostly illustrative, and a more comprehensive understanding of mental health among emerging adults is warranted.

To address this question, this chapter will first embed the understanding of mental health in emerging adulthood and its manifestations and changes over time within a developmental psychopathology perspective. Within this conceptual framework, psychopathology is understood within the context of development over the life span (Cicchetti, 2006); that is, psychopathology is not disconnected from normative development. Failure to attain a developmental milestone is then likely to associate with the manifestation of psychopathology. Building on the previous chapters, we thus suggest that failure to achieve developmental tasks of emerging adulthood (such as career or romantic relationships) is likely to associate with the expression of psychological problems. To support our notion, we will present data from our longitudinal study demonstrating the interplay between success or failure to attain developmental tasks and the increase or decrease in depressive affect over a period of 12 years. Qualitative data will be incorporated to better demonstrate and understand associations between career and romantic developmental pathways and the developmental course of depressive affect.

Extending our findings on the heterogenic developmental pathways during emerging adulthood and in line with the advances in statistical methodology, we also explore possible different trajectories of depressive affect across the emerging adulthood years (Masten & Kalstabakken, 2018). Employing techniques such as latent growth modeling, we explore possible divergent pathways of depressive affect, their meaning, their antecedents, and their role in later developmental and psychological outcomes. Together, we will present in this chapter a more comprehensive approach for understanding mental health during emerging adulthood.

Transition to adulthood: The contribution of developmental psychopathology to understanding adaptive and maladaptive courses and outcomes

Emerging adulthood is a transitional period when individuals are expected to pursue and reach developmental tasks and to settle down and assume an adult role. Young people might strive for multiple goals in different domains of life but have to prioritize which goals to pursue first and which to put aside (Tomasik, 2016). Traditionally, the two major developmental goals are developing a career and establishing a romantic relationship (Burt & Masten, 2010; Shulman & Nurmi, 2010a). Although the way of coordinating between the two major tasks might be affected by personal inclinations (Shulman & Connolly, 2013), it is also well set in a sociocultural context and related to norms, available resources, and support systems (Nurmi, 2004). While emerging adults might prioritize one developmental task over another, the need to coordinate between different goals and set priorities is challenging and can become a source of additional stress (Schulenberg & Zarrett, 2006).

In the previous chapters we have described and discussed the difficulties that young people might face nowadays when pursuing their goals (Côté & Levine, 2002; Furlong & Cartmel, 2007) due to the recent major social and economic changes. These current increasing societal and economic uncertainties and instabilities might lead to increasing stress for emerging adults. Greater worries about the future, fewer opportunities, and more obstacles might hamper emerging adults' emotional resources, undermining their capacities to cope effectively with developmental tasks and leading, in turn, to more psychological symptoms. Thus, psychological difficulties can be understood to relate to the individual way of handling developmental tasks and the extent to which an individual is successful or fails to pursue and achieve developmental tasks (Burt & Masten, 2010).

This understanding of psychological problems representing difficulties or failure in developmental thriving is embedded within the conceptual framework of developmental psychopathology (Sroufe, 2013). Developmental psychopathology has been developed in the study of children, and its basic tenet is that psychopathology in children is best understood in relation to the changes—progressions, regressions, deviations, successes, and failures—that occur in the course of children's attempts to master the developmental tasks they face. Indeed, in his seminal and pioneering work, Sroufe (1989) contended that a psychological disorder can be viewed as *developmental deviation*—namely, the deviation from normal development. Thus, in understanding psychopathology, the focus of interest should not be limited to the description and assessment of a disorder. It is important also to focus on the course and causes of individual patterns of behavioral maladaptation and on transformations in the manifestation of disordered behaviors across development (Masten, 2006; Sroufe & Rutter, 1984). In addition, developmental psychopathology looks not only at those individuals who have developed a disorder but also at those individuals who have developed the capacity to deviate from a maladaptive pathway, embarked on a normative path, and achieved adequate adaptation despite earlier adversity, namely become resilient.

The research on resilience is conceptually linked to these concepts of developmental psychopathology as it also focuses on understanding processes that contribute to positive adjustment under conditions of adversity (Luthar & Cicchetti, 2000). *Resilience* refers to the capacity for successful adaptation or development in the context of significant threats to the life or function of the person (Burt & Masten, 2010; Masten, 2016). Within this understanding, resilience research requires a number of elements to understand the complexity of developmental processes and their outcomes: What personality traits or environmental conditions might serve as protective factors; what risk factors might hinder adaptive development; and finally, what are adaptive and less adaptive outcomes, and how are these assessed?

Developmental psychopathology, as well as the earlier body of resilience research, was developed from the study of children. We believe that the years of emerging adulthood offer an additional lens for understanding developmental processes, which can explain the success or failure of achieving mental health among young individuals. Due to the recent social and economic changes (Furlong & Cartmel, 2007), emerging adulthood can be perceived as a period of adversity (Masten, 2006). The question is which emerging adults will successfully navigate through these years, which will experience increasing difficulties and exhibit psychological problems, and finally, which will be able to find their way and display reasonable adaptability despite earlier setbacks? Assuming a developmental psychopathology approach would first suggest pathology across time develops in a lawful manner. Therefore, it should be possible to identify precursors and pathways leading to disorder, together with factors that drive individuals along such pathways or direct them back toward a normative and functional path. In addition, considering the developmental course of disorders, it might be possible to identify earlier factors that could prevent the development of problems in the future when facing stressful conditions.

To summarize, we suggest that the question to be addressed is not whether psychopathology increases or decreases across emerging adulthood or the incidence of the emergence of specific disorders during this age period. We should rather explore the age-related developmental processes and pathways and learn which pathways are associated with an increase or decrease in psychopathology and which individuals are more or less likely to exhibit psychological problems during this transitional period.

In line with these assumptions, we first examine the association between career pursuit pathways (described in Chapter 3) and patterns of increase or decrease in depressive affect over a period of 12 years. We then examine the extent to which affiliation with the different romantic pathways (described in Chapter 5) is associated with patterns of increase or decrease in depressive affect.

Career pursuit pathways and changes in depressive affect across 12 years

Reading the career stories of the participants reiterated to us the difficulties that emerging adults face when taking the first steps into the adult world. While

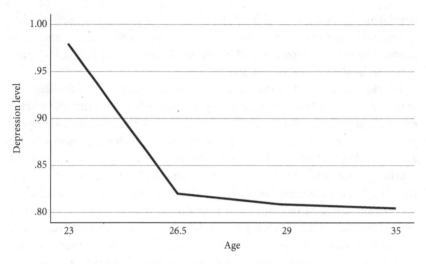

Figure 12.1 Level of depressive affect between ages 23 and 35

the majority of our participants had career aspirations, pursuit of aspired goals was never an easy task. The majority, as could be expected, had to cope with disappointments, failures, and unexpected changing circumstances. However, plotting the level of depressive symptoms for the entire sample, as depicted in Figure 12.1, showed a significant decrease in depressive affect over the years. Does this significant "mean" decrease in depressive affect across emerging adulthood truly represent what happened to the majority of participants who described difficulties they encountered along the years?

Examination of the changes in level of depressive symptoms across the four career pursuit pathways, as depicted in Figure 12.2, shows a different phenomenon. (In Figure 12.2, levels of depressive affect are plotted for the ages 23, 26.5, 29, and 35 across the four career pursuit pathways.) About a quarter of the participants were classified as belonging to the *Consistent Pursuit* pathway. Despite having a clear goal that they pursued consistently, these young people also encountered obstacles along the way. They might have encountered difficulties at a workplace or had to make compromises. However, they felt that they had successfully attained their aspired goal. In their accounts they described their efforts and the persistence they invested to progress in their career field. For example, Natti described,

> I am a big boy and I passed many difficulties, but I am stubborn. Someone else would have given up but I go on pushing until I get what I wish to get. Step after step. I applied to dentistry school. I was anxious, but I knew, I succeeded in the past, and will do it in the future.

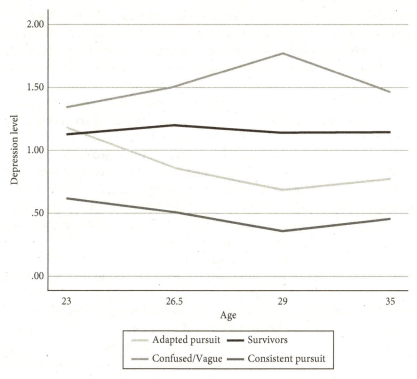

Figure 12.2 Level of depressive affect between ages 23 and 35 across the four career pathways

Indeed, as can be seen in Figure 12.2, level of depressive affect among members of the *Consistent Pursuit* pathway was low across the four measurements, suggesting that despite the inevitable difficulties expected during these years, these young people perceived themselves as competent to cope with the difficulties. Accordingly, their level of depressive affect remained low across the years.

Those belonging to the *Adapted Pursuit* pathway described greater difficulties along the way: failures and disappointments that led them to change course, find a different career, and start pursuing the new goal. As can be understood, the earlier years were difficult and frustrating for these young people. Yet, they had found their way. Indeed, this is reflected in the change in level of depressive affect among the members of the *Adapted Pursuit* pathway. Depressive affect was high at their first assessment but decreased later. Of note, we can clearly see the association between the changes in depressive affect in this pathway and the career pursuit of its members. At the earlier stages (before the age of 26) they lost their way and had to readapt and find a new goal. Indeed, at the earlier assessment their depressive affect was high, but after they found their way their depressive affect decreased and was quite similar to that of those belonging to the *Consistent Pursuit* pathway. For example, Becky described how difficult it was for her at the time she was looking for a job that could develop into a career. In the meantime she took a job that was available. "But it was boring. Nothing interesting and no future options in this company. And this was not easy." It took a year and half until she found a job in a bank that evolved into an aspired career. Taken together, the level of depression in the *Consistent Pursuit* and the *Adapted Pursuit* pathways corresponded to their success in dealing with their career goals. This tendency recalls the Burt and Masten (2010) contention that psychological difficulties relate to the way an individual manages developmental tasks. Developmental success is likely to associate with increased well-being, while failure to achieve a developmental marker is likely to lead to decreased well-being, as is well expressed in Becky's description of her career history.

The association between developmental success and psychological well-being is further and more strongly demonstrated when observing the trajectory of depressive affect among members of the *Confused/Vague* pathway. Confused emerging adults had difficulties setting clear goals from the outset. The lack of a clear goal further complicated their capacity to address developmental tasks. Nora, who was identified as belonging to this pathway, provided a very gloomy description of her life as she approached the age of 30: "I am in a very bad place. I work in something I do not like. Awfully dislike.... And when I go to work it is awful, I feel very bad and I hate myself." Indeed, as can be seen in Figure 12.2, depressive affect among members of this career pursuit pathway steadily increased over time.

Interestingly, number of depressive symptoms among *Survivors* did not change significantly over time. At the initial assessment their level of depressive affect was similar to that of members of the *Consistent Pursuit* and the *Adapted Pursuit* pathways. However, while level of depressive affect among the members of the other two pathways increased or decreased according to their success or failure in attaining their career goals, depressive affect among *Survivors* did not change over time. The "stability" in the level of their depressive affect needs further explanation, and we will address this aspect toward the end of this chapter.

Romantic pathways and changes in depressive affect across 12 years

Changes in depressive affect over time across the four romantic pathways (described in detail in Chapter 5) are depicted in Figure 12.3. Again, and similar to the trends found with regard to career pursuit pathways, direction of change

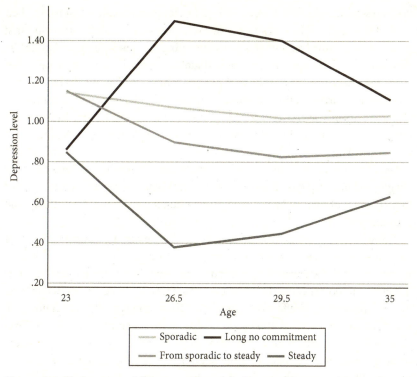

Figure 12.3 Trajectories of depressive symptoms between the ages of 23 and 35 across the four romantic pathways

Note: Adapted from Shulman, S., Yonatan-Leus, R., & Silberberg, O. (2023). Understanding stability and change in depressive symptom trajectories across young adulthood through the lens of career development: A mixed-methods study. *International Journal of Behavioral Development*, 47(2), 169–179. https://doi.org/10.1177/01650254221146416

in depressive affect corresponded with affiliation with a romantic pathway. Emerging adults belonging to the *Sporadic* pathway reported an above average level of depressive affect consistently across the different assessments. In contrast, members of the *Steady Relationships* pathway reported a low level of depressive affect at the first assessment at age 23, which further decreased consistently across the years. At the first assessment members of the *Casual to Steady* pathway reported depressive symptoms at the same level as their *Sporadic* counterparts. However, their progress toward steady involvement was parallel to a consistent decrease in depressive affect. Thus, being involved in sporadic and non-steady romantic encounters associated with elevated depressive affect. Progression toward steady romantic involvement resulted in a decrease in depressive affect.

The fluctuations in level of depressive affect among the members of the *Lengthy Relationship but Absence of Experiential Learning* pathway are interesting. At the first assessment, when they were involved in a long and steady relationship, their level of depressive affect was low. However, over time, probably realizing that their romantic involvement was not developing into an intimate relationship, their sense of depressive affect almost doubled. Nora's reflections explain why, over time, she started to feel bad in the relationship in which she was involved: "I met him at a party and this was not easy for me, but I felt attracted to him. I had butterflies in my belly. I told myself, I would try, though I knew for sure that this was not for me and would not work." Nora stayed in this relationship for a year and half, knowing that the relationship was going nowhere. Again, it can be seen how the depressive affect over time found among those belonging to the *Lengthy Relationship but Absence of Experiential Learning* pathway corresponded to their sense of success or failure in progressing toward romantic intimacy and commitment.

Taken together, progress or failure to progress toward attainment of career or romantic goals was found to correspond with increase in mental health. Developmental progression paralleled a decrease in depressive affect, while difficulties in progressing toward career or romantic goals corresponded with an increase in depressive affect over the years. Thus, conceptually and in line with a developmental psychopathology perspective, we suggest that changes in psychological well-being among emerging adults are affected by success or failure in progressing toward achieving the age-related developmental tasks (Burt & Masten, 2010). Although our findings point to an association between development and mental health, it is nevertheless important to understand how developmental progression leads to better mental health. In the following section we present the stories of participants who succeeded or failed in their developmental pursuits. Reading their stories can be helpful by offering a unique window into the processes and emotions that participants experienced during the journey to adulthood which might have influenced their affect.

Success or failure in meeting developmental tasks and sense of well-being among emerging adults: What can be learned from their personal stories

In Chapter 10 we discussed the changes in personality during emerging adulthood and their association with better developmental outcomes. Within the framework of the personality maturity principle (Donnellan et al., 2015; B. W. Roberts et al., 2001), Caspi and Shiner (2006) outlined how the maturity principle operates. In their view, positive changes in personality are associated with (or even driven by) the increasing "capacity to become a productive and involved contributor to society, with the process of becoming more planful, deliberate, and decisive" (p. 336). Thus, it is the developmental achievements that lead to change with regard to self and other, resulting in the strengthening of positive personality traits. Extending the maturity principle to understanding changes in well-being, we suggest that success in the achievement of developmental tasks increases the feeling of self-efficacy and capacity to direct one's life that, in turn, leads to greater positive affect. In contrast, failure to achieve an aspired developmental goal is detrimental to one's sense of well-being. Reading the stories of our participants further illustrates these processes.

At the age of 35, Alex is living in Canada where he represents an Israeli engineering firm. He feels that he has accomplished his dreams. The higher sense of well-being could be captured when Alex was asked to give three words related to his work and he said,

> Fun, and more fun and self-actualization. Fun because I really like what I do; every day I [can't] wait to get to work. And more fun because I love the people working with me. And self-actualization because I was focused and achieved what I dreamed about. I feel that I contribute to my field and the company, and this makes me happy.

Becky was identified as belonging to the *Adapted Pursuit* pathway. We described above that she lost her way for a number of years but later found a job in a bank with which she is satisfied and in which she is advancing. Becky also sees her job in the bank as fun, as well as challenging:

> It is fun working here. Some people think that working in a bank is boring, but it is challenging. Nowadays, banking is marketing, a lot of work, it is psychology of customers, I enjoy seeing the results. It is a lot of work, hard work, in particular when you care for your customers, but then they are satisfied and this gives me a lot of pleasure. I am happy to get to work.

Becky further explained what makes her happy at work:

> I am happy because there is action, and people value what I do. I am very dynamic at work. I move things, make changes. You know, I have also many things to do at home that I really love [Becky is married and is a mother] but it is also fun to go to work. I get up in the morning and go happily.

Becky describes similar feelings when talking about her family.

> I have a wonderful husband, love and a family. He is very helpful and considerate, he invests in our relationship, in the family. We love each other. And my

family is so important to me. It is my little place, happy to be here, happy to get back home. The best place on earth, my HOME."

Both Alex's and Becky's descriptions of their lives show that their success at work and establishing a loving family has given them a sense of happiness. They enjoy their family life as well as their career life. In addition to this positive affect, their stories suggest that their success provided them with a sense of self-actualization.

Yoram also described the extent to which he loves his job, particularly considering his modest family background. He was able to study based on scholarships he received over the years. He graduated as an engineer and does well. He described that his studies changed him. "As an engineer I will help people who are in need. The studies *changed me*, taught me what kind of a person I am and should be. It helped me, it changed my life." Yoram described the sense of change and personal growth. Furthermore, he emphasized the development of generativity, encompassing a higher stage of development, and capacity to care for others (Pratt & Matsuba, 2018) that increase his sense of success and accomplishment. Thus, extending the maturity principle, we suggest that success in accomplishing aspired career and family goals contributes to the "process of becoming more planful, deliberate, and decisive" (Caspi & Shiner, 2006, p. 336), as well as to the sense of self-actualization, and drives further progress toward generativity. This contributes overall to an increasing sense of well-being and further explains the decrease in negative affect among the young people who were successful in their transition to adulthood.

Contrary to these successful young adults (who navigated their way directly or experienced some difficulties along the way but were able to overcome several obstacles), the less successful young adults described a sad and gloomy life. Nora, who was not successful in developing a career or establishing a stable relationship, summed up her experience as, "It is *sad*, I don't know what will happen in the future." Roni described her disappointment with her current career and romantic status in more detail and emphasized the feelings of regret she experiences:

> I regret that I did not study, I regret that I studied a topic I liked but has no future. I am not getting younger and I have to decide what I will do with the rest of my life. . . . but who knows whether I'll realize in the future that this is not for me.

Roni's story is that she finds herself in conditions she did not plan. After a while she becomes disappointed and lives with the feeling that things go wrong for her. She would prefer to be in a "stable position," knowing what she wants to do with herself and feeling secure, but does not know whether she will be able to find herself in such a position. This explains the low mood that characterizes her life.

Like Roni, Aron was identified as belonging to the *Survivors* pathway. He has a stable job and earns well. In Chapter 4 we described that Aron found his current job by chance and is employed as head of security in a large retail firm. Though he earns well, he is not sure that this is the type of work he wants to do. "I am confused, but mostly I am concerned about the future and have no idea what the next day will bring.... I am always dissatisfied. At work, in life." Interestingly, though Aron has a stable and well-paid job, he lacks the feeling that he is the master of his life. This increases his sense of insecurity and leads to frequent ruminations about the future.

Considered together, the emerging adults who navigated their way during the years competently and successfully gained a sense of self-actualization and an increased sense of confidence that associated with greater positive emotional affect. In contrast, regret and disappointment with their current status were more common among those who were less capable or successful in leading their lives. Moreover, even holding a stable job (that was not aspired for) might not enhance their sense of security. Feelings of failure and worries about the future reduced their inner sense of confidence. To summarize, reading the personal stories of our participants demonstrated that individual well-being during emerging adulthood is not disconnected from the capacity to navigate through the years and is associated with progress or failure in meeting developmental tasks.

Depressive trajectories among emerging adults

In the earlier sections of this chapter we were able to show that success or failure in achieving career or romantic developmental tasks associates with change in depressive affect over time. Conceptually, these findings align with the *vulnerability* model, suggesting that ineffectively dealing with developmental tasks might lead individuals to develop depressive symptoms over time (Durbin & Hicks, 2014). For example, it was shown that adolescents with an identity status characterized by lower commitment levels and higher levels of identity reconsideration or ruminative exploration reported higher levels of depressive symptoms compared with adolescents with stronger identity commitments and lower levels of reconsideration and ruminative exploration (i.e., Luyckx et al., 2010; Meeus et al., 2012). In a recent study, Becht and colleagues (2019) also showed that ruminative exploration and reconsideration of identity commitment predicted the development of depressive symptoms over a period of 5 years.

Notwithstanding the vulnerability model, there is also evidence for substantial earlier variation in depressive affect among adolescents and young adults.

Namely, the degree and development of depressive symptoms are not necessarily associated with the attainment of developmental tasks and might, at least in part, be determined by earlier patterns of individual risk and protective factors (Costello et al., 2008). Thus, conceptually, it might be possible to find different depressive trajectories that are not necessarily determined by developmental success or failure across the years. For example, it is accepted that depressive symptoms increase during adolescence and tend to decline in late adolescence and early adulthood (Ge et al., 2006). However, within this trend in the "population" of increase and later decrease in depression, boys' trajectories of depressive symptoms tended to be relatively stable, while symptom trajectories among girls exhibited greater increases over time (Cole et al., 2002; Garber et al., 2002). These gender difference raised the question as to whether there is room to explore different trajectories within the "population." In addition, the developing conceptual framework of developmental psychopathology suggests that depressive disorders are best understood as "heterogeneous conditions that are likely to eventuate through a variety of developmental pathways" (Cicchetti & Toth, 1998, p. 221). Relatedly, the recently developed group-based trajectory model examines the existence of clusters or groupings of distinctive developmental trajectories of symptomatology that themselves may reflect distinctive etiologies (Nagin & Tremblay, 2005).

Inspired by these approaches, earlier studies used person-centered techniques and identified patterns of depressive symptoms over time. Some studies reported evidence for three (Rodriguez et al., 2005) and others four (Brendgen et al., 2005; Stoolmiller et al., 2005) trajectory groups. Trajectory groups that were common across these studies were characterized by (1) consistently low and (2) consistently high depressive symptoms. Other trajectory groups showed consistently moderate, increasing, and decreasing depressive symptoms. The study by Costello and colleagues (2008), who draw on data from the National Longitudinal Study of Adolescent Health, is the most relevant for our understanding of the depressive trajectories among emerging adults. They found four distinct trajectories to characterize patterns of depression between ages 12 and 25: no depressed mood, stable low depressed mood, early high declining depressed mood, and late escalating depressed mood.

Guided by the framework of developmental psychopathology and applying the methodological approach that permits the empirical identification of trajectories (Nagin & Tremblay, 2005), we also searched for the possible depressive trajectories in our sample that followed participants between the ages 23 and 35. Our participants reported on the level of depressive affect via the Brief Symptoms Inventory (Derogatis & Melisaratos, 1983). They reported on their level of depressive affect at five assessments at ages 23, 24, 26.5, 29, and 35. A latent profile analysis was carried out, and three distinctive trajectories of

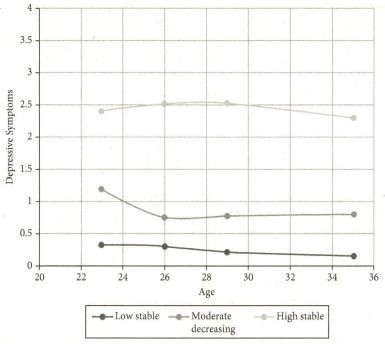

Figure 12.4 Trajectories of Depressive Symptoms.

depressive affect were identified. As can be seen in Figure 12.4, the first trajectory was stable low depressive affect across all the years of emerging adulthood, which accounted for 38.8% of the sample; the second trajectory was moderate and decreasing depressive affect, which accounted for 43.2% of the sample; and the third trajectory was stable high depressive affect, which accounted for 18% of the sample. Our findings corroborate earlier studies that found three or four distinctive trajectories of depressive affect (Brendgen et al., 2005; Rodriguez at al., 2005; Stoolmiller et al., 2005). More importantly, it reiterates the importance of exploring individual differences in the course of depressive affect during emerging adulthood, beyond the general trend of decrease in depressive affect during these years. From a clinical perspective it is important to note that among approximately 20% of emerging adults, their depressive affect remained high and stable during these years, and no decrease in psychopathology was observed among them. In addition, 43.2% reported a change in level of depressive affect, decreasing from moderate to low. Finally, only 36.8% of emerging adults reported a stable low depressive affect across the 12 years of study. These findings are, to some extent, contrary to former studies that reported a much higher percentage of subjects with a stable low depressive affect. We believe that these figures mirror emerging adulthood development. Many emerging adults have difficulties taking their first steps into the adult world (Arnett, 2004). However, emerging adults undergo major changes with respect to their views of themselves, their aspired career goals and future tasks, and their relationships with others (Hutteman et al., 2015); and, as we have shown, many find their way. This can explain an initial higher level of depressive affect that decreases later.

Precursors of trajectories of depressive affect during emerging adulthood and their future outcomes

Our findings pointing to three depressive trajectories during emerging adulthood resemble other recent findings (see, e.g., Costello et al., 2008). However, the developmental and clinical meanings of these three psychometrically derived trajectories are still questionable. In order to address this question, we first searched for the possible precursors that could explain embarking on an adaptive or a less adaptive trajectory. In addition, considering the extensive assessment of our participants at the age of 35, we were interested in learning of the possible association between trajectories and future outcomes.

Comparing the precursors of the depressed to those of the non-depressed groups, Costello and her colleagues (2008) showed that being female, belonging to a minority group, having a low socioeconomic status, and earlier addictive behavior associated with higher likelihood to affiliate with the depressed trajectory group during the transition to adulthood. In contrast, belonging to an intact family; feeling connected to parents, peers, or school; and high self-esteem served as protective factors and associated with greater likelihood of membership in the non-depressed trajectory. Additional studies reported similar predictors of depressed versus non-depressed trajectories. One bulk of predictors included lower self-esteem, lower grade point average (Repetto et al., 2004), and poor academic achievement (Stoolmiller et al., 2005). The other bulk of predictors referred to available support: existence or lack of parental support (Meadows et al., 2006; Stoolmiller et al., 2005), secure attachment to friends (Cook et al., 2016), or the quality of interactional skills (Stoolmiller et al., 2005).

Conceptually, these studies attest to the role of personal and social capital as protective or risk factors in embarking on a depressive trajectory during adolescence and the transition to adulthood. In our project we also assessed the extent to which personal and social capital might predict alignment with depressive trajectories across the years of emerging adulthood. Guided by Blatt's (2008) theory of personality and psychopathology, we focused on the personality constructs that might explain embarking on a depressive or a non-depressive trajectory. Blatt (2008) focuses on personality characteristics that are believed to foster optimal development and well-being throughout the life span. Central to this study is *self-definition*, or the maintenance of a coherent, realistic, and positive sense of self. Positive self-definition, such as high dispositional efficacy and confidence in oneself, fosters adaptive functioning. In contrast, negative self-definition, such as high self-criticism, leads to maladaptive functioning (Blatt, 2008). High self-criticism is characterized by a preoccupation with achievement and negative appraisals of the self, including guilt and fear of losing approval when failing to live up to certain standards. Nevertheless, low and reasonable levels of self-criticism could serve as a compass facilitating adaptive behavior, while a total absence of self-criticism might indicate maladjustment. Blatt and his colleagues consistently found that self-criticism, a maladaptive aspect of self-definition, predicted lack of autonomous regulation, which in turn predicted lack of positive life events and higher likelihood to develop depressive symptoms. In contrast, efficacy, an adaptive aspect of self-definition, predicted elevated autonomous regulation, which in turn predicted encountering more positive events and lesser likelihood of experiencing depressive affect (Blatt, 1998, 2008; Blatt & Zuroff, 1992). Relatedly, we assumed that greater inner motivation might also be a protective factor against depressive affect (Ryan & Deci, 2000b; Shahar, Henrich, Blatt, et al., 2003).

An additional factor in Blatt's (2008) personality theory is dependency, which reflects a wish to be cared for, loved, and protected and fear of being abandoned (e.g., "Without the support of others who are close to me, I would be helpless"). The dependency factor corroborates earlier-mentioned studies emphasizing the role of support systems, supportive parenting, and adaptive peer relationships as protective factors against depression (Cook et al., 2016; Meadows et al., 2006; Stoolmiller et al., 2005).

Guided by these understandings, we examined the extent to which earlier lower self-criticism, inner motivation, and higher efficacy would explain a lower likelihood of embarking on a depressive trajectory. In addition, we examined the extent to which lower dependency (as measured in line with Blatt's theory) combined with greater parental and peer support would serve as a protective factor against the acceleration of depressive affect. As described above, we assessed personality and quality of parental and peer support at age 23 and the extent to which the availability of support might further explain embarking or not embarking on a depressive trajectory.

For this purpose, a multinomial regression analysis was conducted to predict depressive trajectory affiliation. Following our assumptions, indices of self-criticism, efficacy, dependency, level of inner motivation, and levels of maternal, paternal, and peer support assessed at age 23 were entered as predictors. In addition, considering the role of gender in depression, gender was entered as a control variable. Finally, at the end of the college preparatory program participants

Table 12.1 *Results of the Multinomial Regression Analysis Predicting Membership in Depressive Affect Comparisons of the Two Alternative Depressive Trajectories to the Low Depressive Trajectory*

	High depressive affect			Moderate and decreasing		
	B_b	Wald	OR	B_b	Wald	OR
Gender	.48	.04	1.61	.80	2.05	2.24
Age 23 self-criticism	**2.84**	**23.51*****	**17.15**	**2.29**	**23.01*****	**9.88**
Age 23 Efficacy	−.76	3.66	.055[+]	−.42	1.78	.66
Age 23 Immature dependency	.55	1.68	1.73	.35	.30	1.42
Age 23 Intrinsic motivation	−.18	.06	.83	**−1.18**	**5.12***	**.30**
Age 23 Maternal support	−.07	.07	.93	.08	.06	.1.08
Age 23 Paternal support	−.31	.41	.73	−.07	.03	.93
Age 23 peer support	−.10	.03	.90	**1.02**	**4.58***	**2.77**
Success at the prep program	−.05	1.67	.95	−.01	.35	.98

Note: Significant findings are highlighted in bold.
[+]$p < .10$. *$p < .05$. **$p < .01$. ***$p < .001$.

were asked to rate how successful they perceived the program to be for them, on a scale from 1 to 6. We believe that a sense of success could protect against increase in the level of depressive affect. This sense of success was therefore additionally entered as a control variable. As can be seen in Table 12.1, depressive trajectory membership was significantly predicted by self-criticism, efficacy, level of intrinsic motivation, and peer support measured at age 23, $\chi^2(18, 178) = 98.69$, $p < .001$. The Cox value is .501, suggesting that a substantial level of the variance of depressive trajectory affiliation is explained.

In the multinomial regression procedure the *high stable* depressive affect and *moderate and decreasing* depressive affect trajectories are compared to the least depressive trajectory, *low stable*. As can further be seen in Table 12.1, members of the *high stable* trajectory reported a 17.15 times higher level of self-criticism compared to members of the *low stable* trajectory. In addition, they reported a lower by half level of efficacy at age 23 than the efficacy level reported by members of the *low stable* trajectory (this was significant only at the $p = .055$ level). This finding replicates the above-cited studies and is in line with our

Table 12.2 *Tabulation of Marital Status Across Depressive Trajectories*

	Low depressive affect	Moderate and decreasing	High depressive affect
Single	4	18	11
Married	37	34	13
Divorced	0	6	1

conceptualization. Increased self-criticism leads to elevated preoccupation with achievement and negative appraisals of the self and can explain the persistent higher depressive affect across the years of emerging adulthood. In addition, a lower sense of self efficacy is likely to further solidify the sense of depression, which stayed stable across the 12 years.

Comparison of the *moderate and decreasing* trajectory to the *low stable* trajectory also revealed that they were 9.88 times more self-critical compared to the *low stable* trajectory. In addition, level of intrinsic motivation among the *moderate and decreasing* was about half of that among the members of the *low stable* trajectory. These findings explain the difficulty experienced by members of this trajectory during the earlier years of emerging adulthood. However, members of the *moderate and decreasing* trajectory reported a higher level of peer support during those years, which might explain the decrease in the level of depressive affect over time. Support systems are known to serve as a protective factor against depression. Considered together, close to 60% of our participants reported an overall stable or almost stable depressive affect across the 12 years of assessment. Almost 40% of them reported a *low stable* depressive affect, and the additional 17.7% reported a *high stable* depressive affect. Only 43.3% were characterized by change in depressive affect over time. At age 23 they reported a moderate level of depressive affect, which later decreased.

Affiliation with a particular trajectory associated with level of income and marital status at age 35. At age 35 participants rated whether their level of income was below the national average (1), at about the national average (2), or above the national average (3). Comparison among the three trajectories showed that level of salary among the *high stable* and the *moderate and decreasing* groups was $M = 1.50$ ($SD = 1.10$) and $M = 1.65$ ($SD = .89$), respectively, whereas level of income among the *low stable* was $M = 2.15$ ($SD = .97$), $F = 4.21, p < .02$.

Comparison of the marital status of members of the three trajectories revealed a similar tendency. Shown in Table 12.2, and as could be expected, members of the *high stable* depressive trajectory were the least likely to be married at age 35. Members of the *low stable* depressive trajectory reported the least likelihood to be single or divorced and the highest likelihood to be married at age 35. Although

Table 12.3 *Depressive Trajectories and Outcomes at Age 35*

	High depressive affect	Moderate and decreasing	Low depressive affect
Level of income	1.5	1.68	2.15
Career commitment	2.91	3.20	3.28
Self-acceptance	3.58	4.83	5.56
Purpose of life	4.40	4.49	5.66
Flourishing	3.92	4.26	4.56
Satisfaction with life	3.34	3.73	3.40

most members of the *moderate and decreasing* group were married, a significant number were single. In addition, the majority of those who had divorced (which were not many) was associated with this trajectory.

Members of the three trajectories also differed on indices of psychological well-being at the age of 35. Members of the three trajectories were compared on indices of self-acceptance and purpose of life (taken from Ryff scales of psychological well-being; Ryff & Keyes, 1995), flourishing (the EPOCH measure; Kern et al., 2016), and satisfaction with life. As can be seen in Table 12.3, members of the *low stable* depressive trajectory, as could be expected, reported the highest levels of psychological well-being at age 35. Members of the *low stable* trajectory differed from those of the *high stable* trajectory on all indices. They reported higher levels of self-acceptance, purpose of life, flourishing, and satisfaction with life. Members of the *moderate and decreasing* trajectory reported overall an intermediate level of psychological well-being at age 35. They reported a low level only on the index of purpose of life, similar to that reported by members of the *low stable* trajectory.

To summarize, employing person-centered techniques, we were able to identify three different trajectories of depressive affect among emerging adults. Affiliation with a specific trajectory was determined by both personality makeup and protective factors. In addition, embarking on different trajectories associated with future distinctive outcomes. The *high stable* depressive trajectory associated with greatest future difficulties compared to the *low stable* trajectory, while members of the *moderate and decreasing* trajectory reported an intermediate level of psychological well-being. Conceptually, these findings corroborate the scar model, suggesting that experiencing depressive symptoms may affect individuals' capacity to address age-related tasks (Durbin & Hicks, 2014; Klimstra & Denissen, 2017). Previous studies showed that adolescents who experience depressive symptoms also often feel less agency and motivation to pursue valued goals. Because goal directedness and motivation to pursue valued goals are important capacities in forming strong commitments (Becht et al., 2018; Burrow & Hill, 2011), more depressed individuals might also be less able to develop strong commitments over time, as predicted by the scar model.

The scar model can explain the different precursors and future psychological outcomes of the three depressive trajectories that emerged in our project. Yet, it is interesting to further understand the distinction between the *low stable* and the *moderate and decreasing* trajectories. This can be understood when comparing the stories of Yafa, who was affiliated with the *moderate and decreasing* trajectory, and Natti, who was affiliated with the *low stable* trajectory. Yafa graduated from college with a degree in social sciences and started to look for a job. Once she learned that jobs in her field would be available only in a few months, she decided to start working as a secretary in a small company. She was advised to study bookkeeping, a field in which she is still working, and became responsible for financial matters. When asked at age 29 how she understands the development of her career, she responded,

> Sometimes I regret that I did not leave. I tell myself I should have left this position. But it meant leaving and going to the unknown. But to be honest with myself I am *not really sorry*. After all, what is bad for me in the company? It is good that I stayed. It is comfortable, very convenient and I found that it is fine with me to be here.

Yafa was identified as belonging to the *moderate and decreasing* trajectory. Yafa did not find a suitable job after she graduated. She needed to work and compromised for a job that she did not like, which could explain her moderate level of depressive affect. However, over time she started to see the potential in a bookkeeping career and probably found more meaning in her job, which could explain the decrease in depressive affect over time.

In contrast to Yafa, Natti, whose story we have presented in great detail, was identified as belonging to the *low stable* trajectory. At age 35 he is very satisfied with his accomplishments as a dentist. Contrary to Yafa, he was more ready to face uncertainties and cope with challenges and lives at peace with his earlier decisions. When asked to describe whether he has any questions or reservations about the decisions he made in the past, Natti responded,

> I wish I could be sure that every decision I made was correct. But I do not dwell on the past. At that point in time I probably made the calculation before making the decision. So I do not dwell on what I did in the past. It was probably the best decision under those circumstances. Considering where I am today, I probably

made good decisions. And I want to believe that in the future I will again do my best.

The persistent sense of competence and lack of self-criticism can explain Natti's stable low depressive affect.

Furthermore, due to his lower level of self-criticism and higher sense of inner motivation, Natti was probably more capable of learning lessons from his past experiences and accepting and living at peace with earlier decisions (Pratt & Lawford, 2014). The lesser self-doubt about one's decisions and actions (low self-criticism) could explain his stable sense of low depressive affect. He was more willing to face stressors knowing that he has the capacity to address challenges and move forward. Meadows and colleagues (2006) describe a similar phenomenon. By encountering (and not retreating from) stressful life events, individuals can learn how to cope with inevitable stressors during this period of life. Consequently, earlier coping repertoires and past experiences enable individuals to make better use of the coping strategies they acquired when addressing future developmental tasks and goals, as reflected in Natti's higher level of psychological well-being at age 35. Overall, Yafa also currently functions well, has found her way, and reported a decreasing level of depressive affect.

Conceptually, we thus suggest extending the scar model (Durbin & Hicks, 2014). Simply put, the greater the scar, or depressive affect, the lesser an individual will have the capacity to cope with age-related tasks. Consequently, future psychological outcomes are likely to be lower. However, considering the normative challenges that individuals face during developmental stages, it is likely that refraining from coping for the sake of convenience might become counterproductive. Addressing challenges, even at the price of a moderate depressive affect, might bear benefits for the future. Conceptually, we suggest that understanding the effects of the scar model should not be disconnected from resiliency processes. If the "scar" is not too deep, for some individuals, encountering challenges, though stressful, might be beneficial after all, through the simultaneous enhancement of resiliency (Burt & Masten, 2010).

Summary

Research on the incidence and changes in mental health during emerging adulthood has not provided a clear picture. Some studies have reported a decrease in psychological problems and an increase in well-being (see, e.g., Schulenberg & Zarrett, 2006). On the other hand, there is an increase in the onset of severe psychopathology during emerging adulthood (Cicchetti & Rogosch, 2002).

Taking a developmental psychopathology perspective, we claim that psychopathology can be better understood within the context of development over the life span (Cicchetti, 2006), suggesting that psychopathology is not disconnected from normative development. Based on our 12-year longitudinal data, we were able to show the parallels between attainment of developmental tasks (in the domains of career and romantic relationships) and the course of depressive affect over this long period of time. Those who were successful in their career and established a stable and committed relationship reported a decrease in depressive affect over the years. In contrast, those who failed to develop a successful career or establish a stable relationship reported an increase in depressive affect.

Applying the group-based trajectory model that assesses trajectories of symptomatology (Nagin & Tremblay, 2005), we were also able to demonstrate the existence of three distinctive depressive trajectories. A small number of individuals reported a stable elevated depressive affect across all the years of emerging adulthood until the age of 35. The rest were divided equally between individuals who reported a *low stable* depressive affect and those who reported a moderate depressive affect that started to decrease a few years later. These trajectories, which might reflect distinctive etiologies (Nagin & Tremblay, 2005), mirror coping with developmental changes and are associated with different future career, relationship, and psychological outcomes.

Considered together, we thus suggest that understanding psychopathology within a developmental period and, in particular, a transitional period such as emerging adulthood cannot be disconnected from developmental processes. Success or failure to achieve developmental tasks is likely to affect the course of depressive affect. In addition, trajectories of depressive affect (that might emerge due to earlier etiological factors) are likely to affect age-related outcomes. Of note, in the current chapter we focus on the course of depressive affect during emerging adulthood. It is possible that the association between other psychopathologies and developmental outcomes might be different and is worthy of further exploration.

13
Developmental Pathways During Emerging Adulthood
A Cross-Cultural Perspective

The major aim of this book is to propose a new lens for understanding development during emerging adulthood by understanding the pathways taken by young people in their pursuit of work and love aspirations. In the previous chapters we were able to show the diverse ways that young people take, and the efforts they make, in order to successfully attain their goals. Relatedly, we showed the circumstances that associated with failure to attain one's goals, the adjustments that might be made in search of an alternative goal, and the despair into which a person might be drawn. Overall, the personal stories told by these young people echoed the endeavors they made until they found (or did not find) their way. Contrary to earlier research reports and theory that highlighted the fluctuations and instabilities among emerging adults (Arnett, 2004; Côté, 2000; Settersten & Ray, 2010), our findings, based on a 12-year longitudinal study, rather pointed to the possibility that what might seem chaos or disorder to the outside observer encapsulates normative processes of variability and instability in which new ways are learned. These are aimed toward finding one's niche (Mayes, 2001) and achieving aspirations in work and love.

Our study was conducted on a sample of Israeli emerging adults. In the first chapter we argued that overall Israel is a Western society. Despite the uniqueness of the Israeli society and culture (as each society is) described in Chapter 1, overall young Israelis live in an economy and a society that resemble the mainstream societies and culture in North America and Europe. Although our findings call for a different understanding of the main processes during the emerging adulthood years, it is still questionable whether our findings capture and are relevant for non-Western and less developed societies. This question echoes the existing debate questioning the relevance of the emerging adulthood theory to non-Western cultures (Arnett, 2007; Côté, 2006, 2014). The aim of this chapter is not to join this debate. In line with the main tenets of this book, we would rather like to understand how young people in different societies and economies address the challenges of developing a career and establishing a love relationship in their own society. We believe that listening to their life histories could shed further light on the mechanisms and processes that young people from non-Western societies might take in pursuit of their work and love aspirations. In the following sections we first review the work and marital statuses of young people in societies across the globe to obtain a better picture of the current life contexts of young people. We then examine the extent to which the emerging adulthood literature and research address and explain the extended process of settling down in different societies. In order to further understand the ways young people cope with increasing societal uncertainties, we focus on three "case stories" that richly document and describe the current lives of young people in two different, hard-hit societies. First, we present the "story" of young people in Greece. Greece experienced a major economic crisis in recent years which affected drastically the lives of young people. Second, we discuss the story of young people on the island of Sardinia. Though Sardinia is part of Italy, it is an island that is remote from the Italian mainland and can be considered an "extreme" case of uncertainty in Europe (Bello & Cuzzocrea, 2018). Finally, we focus on the Arab world, North Africa and Africa at large, which represent societies that have been dramatically affected economically and politically in recent years and where young people face a high level of uncertainty. For this purpose, we examine sociological, historical, and political processes taking place in these societies and their significant impact on the lives of young people. Within the unique contexts of the different societies we will examine how emerging adults cope with the transition to adulthood.

Work and marital statuses of young people around the globe and their relevance for understanding the emerging adulthood years

The last two decades, and particularly following the 2008 recession, recent years have witnessed a slower workforce growth (Karoly, 2009) and increasing levels of uncertainty and job insecurity. Due to these constantly changing and worsening circumstances in economies and societies, it has become more difficult to find a job. In particular, finding a meaningful job in one's field of training has become even more crucial for young people nowadays (Fadjukoff et al., 2010).

A recent report by the World Bank (International Labour Organization, 2019) shows that the mean global percentage of youth (defined by the World Bank as between ages 15 and 24) unemployment was 12.8%, lower than the figures for adults. As can be seen in Figure 13.1, this global mean level of unemployment is quite similar to the unemployment levels in central Europe, North America, China, East Asia, and the Pacific, suggesting that these regions were quite capable of coping with and overcoming the 2008 recession to some extent. However, there are still some major regional differences in

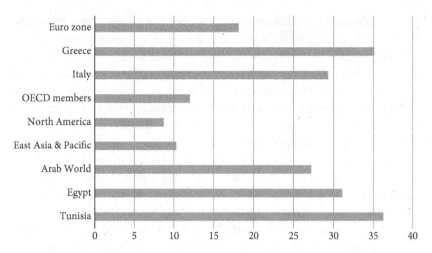

Figure 13.1 Youth unemployment (percentage) across regions and in a number of hard-hit countries—2019

Note: OECD = Organisation for Economic Co-operation and Development.

youth unemployment. Unemployment levels in the economies that were hard hit by the economic crisis are significantly higher. For example, in European Mediterranean countries such as Italy, Spain, and Greece the level of youth unemployment was very high: 28.7%, 33.2%, and 39.3%, respectively. In the Middle East and North Africa the figure was 26.2%, and in Egypt it reached 32.4%. Average percentage of youth unemployment in Latin America was 17.6%, somewhat higher than the mean global level. Of note, in addition to significant differences between countries belonging to the same region, there are regional differences within countries, representing the more and less developed parts of a country. In addition to regional differences, differences in unemployment levels can be found between low-skilled youth and youth with higher education in the same society. For example, in China low-skilled workers with a primary and junior secondary education, especially young migrants from rural China, can easily find jobs in the transportation, construction, and catering industries. In contrast, college graduates have difficulties finding the jobs that they desire and are unwilling to take low-quality, low-paid jobs. These young graduates might rather stay at home and rely on their parents to survive than go out to work (Zhao & Huang, 2010).

These figures represent an increasing difficulty among young people nowadays to embark on a successful transition into work and developing a career. Finding work and developing one's career are prerequisites for being able to support oneself and a family (Shulman & Connolly, 2013). This explains the recent documentation of postponement of marriage among the younger generation, which has become a global phenomenon. Across different societies young people face similar challenges. The decision to marry made by an individual (or by their family) cannot be disconnected from the need for financial resources required to make this transition (Shulman & Connolly, 2013).

In the previous chapters on romantic pathways we discussed that fewer young people in Western societies are involved in long-lasting and committed relationships and that the age of marriage has been postponed to toward the end of the 20s (Shulman & Connolly, 2013). The vast majority of young people get married only when approaching the age of 30 (Arnett, 2007). For example, the mean age at first marriage in the United States in 2017 was 27.4 for women and 29.5 for men. In Israel, the mean age at first marriage in 2015 was 26.1 for women and 28.0 for men. However, in a number of European countries the age at first marriage has passed 30 for both women and men (Buchholz, 2019). Indeed, as with the rates of unemployment, there are significant regional differences in the age at first marriage (Buchholz, 2019). Accordingly, review of marital timetables indicates that a number of distinctive contextual and cultural patterns of the transition to marriage can be found across regions and nations.

Statistics from nine countries in Pacific Asia show a consistent trend in delaying marriage, or even a failure to marry at all, since 1970. Countries affected by this new behavior include Japan, Thailand, Myanmar, Singapore, Malaysia, Taiwan, the Philippines, and, to a more limited extent, South Korea and Indonesia. Interestingly, this trend is as common in affluent as in less developed countries (Jones, 2007). Yet, while in the West young people can be observed in different patterns of non-committed romantic and sexual behavior, this is not the case in Asian countries. In addition, cohabitation, which could be perceived as a form of pre-marriage relationship, is not common and might even be socially prohibited (Jones, 2004). An increasing number of young people cohabiting has been observed only in Japan and the Philippines, which cannot be considered representative of these countries. Each of these countries has coined a term to describe this non-marital relationship—the "live-in" pattern in the Philippines (Raymundo & Cruz, 2004) and "living apart together" in Japan (Kiernan, 2000).

Yet, as in the West, cohabitation does not necessarily lead to marriage (Stanley et al., 2006). When Japanese men and women aged 25–34 who were cohabiting or had an intimate partner were asked why they had not married, the most common answers for men were that they "felt no need" and "can't afford marriage." For women, the most frequent answers were that they "felt no need" and "can't meet an appropriate partner," followed by "dedicated to work or study" (Jones, 2007).

Pacific Asia has been undergoing major economic and social changes, and these changes are reflected in the delay of marriage and establishing a family of their own among adolescents and emerging adults (Rosenberger, 2007).

Summarizing the trends across the region, Jones (2007) wrote, "The key element shared by the rapidly growing economies of the region, heavily affected by globalization, and the more stagnant economies may be that job security in all of them is now generally tenuous" (p. 463). Under these circumstances, women are reluctant to marry men whose economic prospects are uncertain, and men are reluctant to marry under such circumstances. In many of these societies, remaining single has become a common phenomenon among urban youth. Furthermore, even in societies where cohabitation is found, this might not necessarily lead to marriage due to economic constraints or career dedication.

Figures from India are different, where the mean age at marriage remains below 20 for women (Desai & Andrist, 2010). However, it is the diversity in age at marriage that characterizes India. Age at marriage in India may range from 16 to 25 years, depending on the region and social economic background. The large differences in age at the time of marriage are affected by education, with women with higher secondary and college education marrying 4.9 years later than less-educated women (Desai & Andrist, 2010). As in Western societies, the pursuit of higher education is likely to lead to delay in marriage. Interestingly, among the poor, employment in casual labor (such as seasonal work in agriculture), which could have been expected to associate with later marriage, is, in fact, associated with earlier marriage. It appears that among the educated the prospect of higher education and future status and earning leads to later marriage, while among the poorest the realization that the chances for better prospects are low might lead young people and their families to marry under conditions of minimal substance as they do not see any brighter future.

In many traditional societies marriage was a crucial step in a ritualized journey to adulthood. A man would be granted a piece of land or work, and a woman was offered the means to become a wife and a mother. This traditional path to adulthood has gradually been eroded by urbanization, modernization, and globalization as youths increasingly migrate to urban centers for schooling or employment. Today, African and Arab countries are struggling with economic decline, strained educational systems, high unemployment rates, and insecure livelihoods, all of which seriously weaken the social fabric. As a result, these societies are no longer able to endow young people with the social, economic, and cultural resources they need to embark on a secure pathway to adulthood (Hownana, 2012). For example, as in China, urban and educated young Egyptians have significant difficulties finding a job that suits their qualifications and meets their expectations. As a result, in Egypt, which is a traditional society, nearly 34% of urban males marry for the first time between the ages of 30 and 40, and about 22% of young women marry after age 25 (Singerman, 2007). Furthermore, the number of unmarried young adults into their 40s in Egypt has increased significantly in recent years (Tzoreff, 2010).

These demographic and sociological changes clearly demonstrate that in hard-hit societies young people face major difficulties finding a job and, consequently, making the transition into marriage. This has led to a significant postponement in the age at marriage. Studying the lives of emerging adults in non-Western societies or in societies that have gone through an economic crisis might then inform us of the mechanisms that young people employ in order to cope with the difficulties and make their way into adulthood.

Research on emerging adulthood in Western depressed economies and in non-Western societies

Studies of emerging adults in non-Western societies, as well as in European countries that were hard hit by the economic recession, were mainly conceptualized and guided by the emerging adulthood theory. Close inspection of these studies shows that they were mostly conducted on college students. In addition, emerging adults were assessed via the conceptual tools and instruments derived from the emerging adulthood theory, such as identity development and criteria of adulthood or life choices (see, e.g., Galanaki & Sideridis, 2019; Mitra & Arnett, 2021; Nelson et al., 2013; Ozer et al., 2019).

Emerging adults in Greece

A recent study by Galanaki and Sideridis (2019) examined the "existence of emerging adulthood" among college students in Greece, a society that has gone through major economic and social crises in recent years. The crisis in Greece led to restricted social welfare, job insecurity, high unemployment and underemployment rates, and income inequality. European statistics show that the crisis has, in particular, drastically affected young people (see Eurostat, 2017). The unemployment level among young people is 49.0%, including among recent graduates; 71.5% of young adults aged 20–29 live with their parents, and 41.5% attend tertiary education, which is free in Greece. Age at marriage has climbed to 32.8 years for men and 28.6 years for women. Overall, these figures suggest that the majority of young people continue living with their parents and rely on their financial help. This "solution" that young Greeks have adopted reflects Greek traditional values that emphasize strong family ties and solidarity (Iannelli & Smyth, 2008).

Galanaki and Sideridis (2019) examined the in-between feeling, dimensions of emerging adulthood such as exploration, and the perceived criteria for adulthood. Within the framework of the emerging adulthood theory they found that a significant proportion of Greek college students felt in between adolescence and adulthood. In addition, they were addressing questions of identity exploration, experimentation/possibilities, self-focus, and feeling in between. In their conclusion, the authors suggested that their findings provide support for the existence of emerging adulthood as a distinct life period in a southern European country, suggesting that even within the context of a major crisis, emerging adults continue to address issues of the definition of adulthood and identity exploration.

To their credit, Galanaki and Sideridis (2019) also conducted person-focused analyses and were able to find distinct profiles of identity exploration that seem to capture the economic and social crises and the conditions under which young Greeks live. Their analyses showed that only about one third of their subjects described lower financial adversity and were characterized by more productive and less troubled pathways to adult life (adult committers). In contrast, the majority, the remaining two thirds (i.e., anxious explorers in between, immature explorers, and blocked in transition) reported anxious identity exploration, fewer commitment experiences, fewer accomplishments in terms of adult roles, and/or a weak perception of the transition process. These young people described the extent to which financial constraints and concerns blocked and negatively affected their transition to adulthood.

These findings suggesting that two thirds of Greek youth felt that they were stuck in their lives clearly echo reports on the impact of the economic recession on Greek youth. A report by the European Parliament in 2015 described that at the peak of the crisis Greece experienced an alarming youth unemployment rate of 59.5% in the first quarter of 2013. Since then, youth have benefited more than adults from an improving labor market situation, though youth unemployment is still more than double the rate before the crisis. The youth unemployment rate dropped to 50.1% in January 2015 (European Parliament, 2015). As a result, one in two young people in Greece was at risk of poverty. The report attributed these difficulties also to "skills mismatches." Universities and institutes of higher education prepared graduates for a limited range of qualifications.

In sum, the share of NEETs (not in employment, education, or training) among Greek young people increased significantly during the recession (Cholezas, 2014). Yet, despite the high rate of unemployment, the adverse conditions into which young people were drawn were less visible. One explanation for the diminished visibility is the strong family safety net. Most NEETs live with their parents, brothers, or sisters; and many have health insurance provided by their parents' place of employment. Reliance on the family for financial support reduced youth autonomy as many remained living with their parents (Cholezas, 2014). Though these figures reflect the difficulties that young Greeks face in their daily lives, it is less clear how they cope with these difficulties.

A review of a number of media reports can shed light on the ways that young people in Greece cope with this severe economic crisis on a daily basis. Stories of being unemployed for extended periods of time are common in these reports. Howden and Baboulias (2015) present the story of Maria Armakola, who left school early and has been working since she was 14. She noticed that since the crisis work pays less than it used to and money disappears a lot faster. "I used to get €20 and not really know what to do with it. Now it's gone straightaway." During all her years in the workforce she has never been able to get a secure job as employers have always paid her under the table. At the time, she was working uninsured in a local café, where a 9-hour shift earns her just €20. "But that is a good day." More often the owner tells her to go home after 6 hours to get away with paying her only €10. The work is hard, and the customers are freer with their hands than they are with tips; but she adds that she needs the money. She has to help her family, where her retired father's pension has been cut and her mother can only find occasional work as a cleaner.

The conditions for university graduates are not much better. Bateman (2019) presents the story of Areti Stabelou from Athens, who, since graduating university with a degree in political science in 2011, was unable to find a job that suited her training. She was recently laid off from a call center where she had been working for a while, a job that was hard and demanding. She hated this job: "I was just there for the money—it didn't give me anything else." In the interview she described the difficulty in finding a job that is secure, well paid, or suited to one's skills. This left many bright graduates working as bartenders or servers in the service industry or doing promotional work such as handing out flyers in the streets, where they might earn as little as €3 per hour. These young people have no option other than taking any offer that comes up as this is the only way they can support themselves or help their family with whom they continue to live. Other graduates gave up their professional dreams and decided to retrain in practical trades, such as hairdressing or the nail industry. Fenia, another young woman, was working in a European Union–funded program. When this program was closed, she did not find another job and was still looking for a job. She described how on some days she felt that there was no reason to get up. Nothing was waiting for her. In the meantime, she does all she can to stop spending altogether (Howden & Baboulias, 2015).

Realizing that the crisis has been going on for a number of years, talk of leaving the country can be heard from many young people. Leaving the country and looking for a job in another country in Europe or across the Atlantic has become an option for young Greeks, particularly for capable university graduates. A young person about to leave for Paris described, "Most of my friends also want to go and work or study abroad because youth unemployment is at its highest level in Greek contemporary history. It's creating a suffocating environment for young people who do not have the opportunity to get a job here" (Farand, 2017). It is estimated that anywhere between 170,000 and 200,000 people have left the country. A headline in the *Independent* (Farand, 2017) ran as follows: "The Brain Drain and Youth Depression Taking Over Greece." Only a small number of young people take the initiative and navigate their way. For example, Vasileios Karavasilis, 25, co-founder of a game development company, eNVy Softworks, described, "My dad was without work for several years and it made me realize I couldn't just wait to finish my studies and find a job—I had to do things for myself, from early on" ((Batemen, 2019). He and his classmates started to make video games alongside their studies and see their future in this enterprise.

In sum, due to an unprecedented economic crisis, Greek emerging adults face harsh conditions that prevent them from attaining career and romantic goals and assuming adulthood. This setback is not a result of increased confusion or unlimited exploration but rather the response to a dire situation. Interestingly, despite the impossible conditions, the majority have not given up. Many are willing to readjust their expectations and compromise for a lower-level profession or temporary job in order to support themselves. Many others plan to leave or have already left Greece to look for opportunities abroad. Only a small number of young people were able to take an initiative and develop a new path for themselves. Conceptually, the ways that young Greeks cope with the unprecedented crisis point to the inner capacities of emerging adults and the mechanisms they employ to find their way. We cannot be sure whether the ways described by these youths are unique to Greece considering the fact that these young people know that they are part of the European Union and can easily move to a different country or might expect that the rescue plan offered to Greece would work and the situation would improve.

Emerging adulthood in Sardinia—The impossibilities of transitioning to adulthood in a peripheral and underdeveloped region

Sardinia is the second-largest island in the Mediterranean Sea after Sicily and is located west of the Italian peninsula and to the immediate south of the French island of Corsica. Sardinia is a region of Italy that enjoys some degree of domestic autonomy. Until recently the Sardinian economy was oriented primarily to subsistence; it was based mainly on agriculture, and industry was limited to household handicrafts. Today, the traditional subsistence economy has been replaced by a market economy, and tourism has become a major source of income. The social economic legacy of the island, and the change into a market economy, severely affected the young generation. According to the Italian Institute of

Statistics (2015), the level of youth unemployment is higher in Sardinia than in the rest of the country (54% vs. 42.4% nationally). After a period between the end of the 1990s and the early 2000s, which was dominated by the hope and promise of a new economy (Ferrucci & Porcheddu, 2004; Mongili, 2015) that was channeled through specific experiences of temporality (Mandich, 2009), the conditions for Sardinian youth have once again become stagnant. Indeed, the unemployment rate among young people in Sardinia is 56.4% (Eurostat, 2017). The few jobs available are temporary, of low quality, and badly paid. Young people often lack the right skills. Thus, young people in Sardinia face one of the "extreme" cases of uncertainty in Europe (Bello & Cuzzocrea, 2018).

Thus, it is not only that the economy in Sardinia is not yet ready to offer solutions to the younger generation but also that young people lack the skills required for a job in a modern society. In the previous section we described that a significant number of young Greeks have left the country. A story in the *Guardian* (Davies, 2014) described the initiative taken by a young mayor in a Sardinian town to help young people search for work somewhere else:

> Now, in a struggling corner of Italy, one mayor thinks he has found an answer to his town's chronic lack of work—although, rather than a solution, it appears to some to be more of an admission of defeat. Valter Piscedda, the centre-left mayor of Elmas, a small town near Sardinia's capital, Cagliari, wants to pay residents to leave. The council will pay for 10 unemployed locals to take intensive English lessons, board a cheap flight and look for jobs elsewhere in Europe.

Why do the young people in Sardinia lack the skills, or maybe the will, to take the initiative and search for work somewhere else? Cuzzocrea (2019), a sociologist from Cagliari (the capital of Sardinia), discussed the Sardinian case within the framework of Erikson's theory of identity experimentation and the theory of social acceleration that emphasizes the pressure on young people to find positions in the labor market and become active citizens (Rosa, 2013).

Emerging adulthood has been much conceptualized with the Eriksonian theory (Arnett, 2004). According to Erikson (1968), psychosocial moratorium exemplifies exploration through self-experimentation. Adult obligations are postponed, and during the "gap years" between adolescence and adulthood, emerging adults search for their optimal "niche" in the adult world. As a result, periods of confusion, changes between careers, and less goal-directed behavior are understood as part of the developmental process. Cuzzocrea (2019) contrasts this understanding with the social acceleration theory (Rosa, 2013), emphasizing the inherent drive for success and adaptation to societal requirements. Indeed, the current job market is difficult, the security of future employment is unforeseeable, and not all plans can be materialized. However, if a person is open enough, opportunities can be found. Therefore, taking a proactive attitude in the face of the challenging demands of a competitive economy can become an advantage (Rosa, 2003).

Within the acceleration theory framework a person is expected to "accelerate" toward the future. *Dead times*, when a person is not pursuing future goals, are perceived as pathological (Leccardi, 2009). In addition, acceleration assigns meaning to the frame of time, which can be subjective and objective (Rosa, 2003). The subjective dimension may determine feelings of time being scarce, while the objective dimension relates to the intensity of action taken—the more you do, the better. Incorporating the Eriksonian notion of moratorium and notions from acceleration theory, Cuzzocrea (2019) suggests that it is important to understand better the meaning, motivation, and emotions that accompany periods of being "in between." Are such periods meant to explore and prepare for a better future, or do they carry a somewhat different meaning?

To understand the attitudes toward the future and learn about the plans of young people in Sardinia, Cuzzocrea (2019) analyzed narratives provided by 341 subjects. Based on this analysis, she described two main forms of moratorium that she found among Sardinian youth. The first she termed the *classic moratorium*, which is characterized by elements of experimentation, a struggle that is combined with fulfillment of one's plans and a sense of achievement. Cuzzocrea (2019) presents an example of a young person who took initiative and left for England in search of a better future:

> As a 19-year-old I left, something I had always wished to do, and it was a bit complicated initially. The first step was England, we stopped in London and we accepted all jobs that were proposed to us. Every month we moved to a different place and so our CVs improved and grew full of marvelous experience and positive notes. Fun was already around, and despite the fact that I missed my parents, I realised I had never felt so good and complete as I had then. (p. 577)

The other form of a less adaptive moratorium was *waiting* for something to happen—either for an opportunity to present itself or for someone to intervene for the benefit of the young person. These young people live in the present. They might be employed in temporary or undeclared jobs in order to support themselves and have a minor income for survival. However, they have no particular plans, nor do they take any initiative to change the situation. There is a hope that at some point in time things will improve, and they wait for a "miracle" to change their lives. For example, a young man described, "After having attended a Degree Course (which was a short training), then fortune knocked at my door offering me the occasion to work in an airport."

In sum, there are young people in Sardinia who take the initiative to change their routine of life and search actively for a niche that suits them. However, others lack intrinsic exploratory motivation. They prefer to *wait* for an event or a person that will change their lives, offer them a job, and help them join the adult world. *Waiting* resembles the term *waithood* coined to explain the conditions of young people in the Arab and North African countries (Hownana, 2012; Singerman, 2007). The meaning of *waithood* will be discussed in the following section. As in the case of young people in the Arab world, in response to the impossible economic and social conditions that lack opportunities for change, the younger generation might enter a period of suspension—waiting for some miracle to save them. Cuzzocrea (2019) summarizes that waithood, unlike moratorium, is not a period of preparing for life. It is emptiness and waiting for a "miracle," rather than accumulation of skills or experience of any kind. In comparison to the young people in Sardinia, it is possible that, despite the dire crisis in Greece, young people are still hopeful and waiting for the situation to change, at which time they will be able to mobilize their capacities again and move forward (Galanaki & Sideridis, 2019). In contrast, it seems that in Sardinia, considering the structural problems of this society, part of the younger generation has lost hope and is less likely to make future plans. They prefer to wait for some person to save them personally and lead them to a brighter future, questioning whether this is not their response to the conditions under which they live.

Emerging adulthood in the Arab and North African countries—A period of waithood

At the beginning of this chapter we presented the figures of youth unemployment around the globe. The figures clearly show that the rates of unemployment among young people in the Arab world, and in North Africa and Africa at large, are very high. The majority of Arab and African youths today are grappling with job scarcity and deficient education. After they leave school with few skills, they are unable to obtain a stable and satisfactory job. Frustration is particularly high among the majority of university graduates, whose education has not prepared them well and who lack the qualifications required in the few available prestigious jobs (Honwana, 2014). Living in traditional societies, young people wish to build, buy, or rent a house for themselves; support their relatives; get married; and establish families, which will allow them to gain social recognition as adults—and this has become almost impossible. These economic and social conditions led to a significant suspension in the transition from adolescence to adulthood. Singerman (2007) coined the term *waithood*—waiting for adulthood—to describe the suspended process of transition. Young people are forced to continue living with their families and depend on their parents for financial support. One of the significant consequences is that they remain single, and marriage is delayed.

Singerman (2007) focused mainly on the phenomenon of delayed marriage in Egyptian society, due to the lack of resources required from men to obtain the approval of a bride's parents for marriage. Many young men perceive the period of waithood as the time for saving money to buy a house and get married. Unfortunately, although there are many young people struggling to find employment, opportunities are few. Honwana (2014) suggested that, despite the dire circumstances, waithood does not mean that young people sit and wait—they look for ways to support themselves. Their daily strategies might be street vending and cross-border trade. Others look for every opportunity and accept jobs that are far below their qualifications. Al Sherbini (2015) described the many efforts made by a young Egyptian man, which only led to greater sense of despair. Four years after his graduation from law school, Islam Ali has no permanent job, a situation that has dimmed his chances of tying the knot in the near future. "Marriage? Not on my agenda. Two years ago, I went to the family of the girl I wanted to marry. They rejected my proposal for her because I have no fixed job and do not have enough money for the cost of marriage." Ali, 25 years old, had tried his hand at several casual jobs to help his father, who is a government employee.

> I have worked as a wall painter, an assistant to an electrician and a salesman at a supermarket. I could not continue in any of these jobs for more than months. Maybe I bear part of the blame for this because I haven't been determined enough to prove myself. However, my bosses, who hardly knew how to read and write, would scold me for the slightest mistake.

Ali started considering leaving the country and looking for opportunities elsewhere. Others might choose to overcome their pride and support themselves through temporary positions while hoping that the desired government position would eventually open up. For example, a young Egyptian university graduate tried to convince the journalist who interviewed him as follows: "This is temporary work; I am waiting for a response from a government office where I applied for the position of deputy department manager." But this person had been waiting for an answer for over 3 years (Tzoreff, 2010).

A few might search for and come up with creative solutions. Sabri, aged 29, graduated with a degree in science. He was looking for a job at a medical lab or a pharmaceutical company, but he was not successful. It took him 7 years to change his plans and establish his own business. He now owns a small shop selling perfumes, which he produces. "I started my business three years ago with a bank loan guaranteed by my family's house. Gradually, my shop attracted customers because of the cheap prices of products and their good quality" (Tzoreff, 2010). Having his own business and earning money allowed him to get married, and he is the father of a 2-month-old baby. Yet not all young people have the capabilities required to change paths or be creative enough to establish their own business. Masquelier (2019), describing *waithood* among university-educated young men in Niger, wrote, "they are waiting for career opportunities that rarely materialize. They spend their time in spaces called fadas, or 'tea circles,' to pass time and tap into supportive male social networks."

Singerman (2007) and Tzoreff (2010) suggested that increasing numbers of young unemployed men and women can lead to social unrest, due to unmaterialized energies. The criticism of the desperate younger generation is echoed by Tzoreff (2010, p. 18): "When you have studied for five years in an elementary school, three years in middle school, an equal amount in high school and four or five years in university to work afterwards in the vegetable market, do not despair—you are in an Arab country." Criticism such as this raised by a young Arab man can explain the outbreak of the Arab Spring.

Other young people might find solace in religion. Tzoreff (2010) presents the life story of Amad Muammad Sayyid, age 28, who has a degree in tourism and hotel management but was not successful at finding a job in his field of study; he works from time to time as a driver. Amad Muammad Sayyid was engaged for 2 years. During this period he was supposed to purchase an apartment and furniture for himself and his fiancée and even save enough money to pay for the wedding party. However, his meager monthly salary was not enough, and the engagement was canceled due to pressure from the bride's family. The young man, who lives with his mother, a 45-year-old divorcee, has drawn closer to religion as his disappointments became more frequent, his dignity was lost, and his frustration increased. For many months he has been isolating himself in his house. Next to his bed lie two books: a large Qur'an and a small Qur'an. He spends most of his time listening to the daily chapters of the Qur'an broadcast on the radio. "I can't find a workplace that suits my training and my skills. I do not have money, and I cannot get married. What else can I say?"

The role of waithood in the breakout of the Arab Spring or in religious radicalization is beyond the scope of this chapter and book. However, we can see that despite the impossible circumstances in undeveloped or crisis-hit societies, many young people might make many efforts to survive daily and are ready to accept jobs that are considered demeaning. Others use their agency and creativity to navigate their lives toward more satisfactory outcomes. We would like to suggest that the search for ways of coping with their impossible life conditions is further demonstrated in the creative ways that some young Egyptians have started to utilize in addressing the delay in marriage and in the societal sanctioning of premarital relationships between men and women.

In addition to the difficulties young people have finding suitable jobs or work, there has been a constant rise in marriage costs in Egypt. For example, in 1999 it cost $6000 to get married—11 times the per capita annual income. Five years later, in 2004, the overall cost had increased by 25%. A groom is expected to own a house (or at least to be able to rent an apartment), to have a permanent workplace, and to pay the wedding expenses (Tzoreff, 2010). Considering the economic instabilities, the investable result was a delay in marrying. While in the past the mean age at marriage for men was in the mid-20s, in recent years it has reached 31.3 years. In Western societies the delay of marriage associated—as described in Chapter 5—with the increasing phenomena of casual sex, friends with benefits, and cohabitation that does not lead to marriage (Claxton van Dulmen, 2013; Stanley et al., 2006). This solution is unacceptable in a traditional Muslim society such as Egypt. Young people are not expected to meet each other before the potential bride or groom has been "screened" by the parents.

Despite the strict traditional prohibition of meeting the other gender privately or having sex before marriage, young Egyptians have found a way to address this dilemma. In Shiite Islam there is a tradition of *mut'ah* weddings, which are temporary unions simply for sexual purposes. These marriages have the oral consent of the partners for a period that can range from 1 hour to 99 years. Importantly, these weddings take place without any official documentation. Traditionally, this type of marriage was criticized by Sunni religious scholars. Despite Egypt being a Sunni country, *urfi* or *misyar* weddings, which are secretive and undocumented, have become a solution to the inability to get married. *Urfi* or *misyar* weddings take place in private, without the knowledge of the couple's parents. Witnesses are unlikely to attend this ceremony, which undermines the validity of these marriages. Thus, secretive weddings have become the Sunni version of the Shiite *mut'ah* weddings: pleasure marriages that allow young men and women to realize their love. Tzoreff (2010) described that at the beginning of June 2007 the Al-Azhar Supreme Council for Islamic Affairs confirmed the validity of *misyar* and *urfi* weddings as a solution for the hardships the young people face.

Yet, Tzoreff (2010) argues that while there are those who view the council's step as a display of flexibility and adoption of a pragmatic view of reality, this new pattern of marriage cannot be a solution to, but is rather a means of bypassing, the wider problem. Furthermore, this might even be perceived as further deterioration of basic conditions, which might lead to unexpected and unfavorable results (Singerman, 2007). For example, the husband is not contractually and legally obligated to provide housing for the wife but only visits her. This pattern of secretive marriage is, in particular, less favorable for young women, who might pay a heavier price than the men as the loss of virginity will make it more difficult for them to remarry in the future. In addition, according to Muslim law, the woman cannot sue her husband for a divorce if he chooses to deny this undocumented marriage and might remain "chained," forbidden from remarrying. The press and popular media have reported cases where the young woman became pregnant and was abandoned by her husband. This explains the increasing opposition to this pattern of relationship by feminist organizations that claim that these secretive marriages are only one step above prostitution.

Considered together, review of the lives of emerging adults in Arab and North African countries clearly shows that due to the great economic hardships, as well as social and religious traditions and norms, successful transition to adulthood has become, to some extent, an impossible task. The chances of finding a reasonable job, not to mention developing a career, are low. As a result, the likelihood of getting married has also decreased, and young people remain unmarried for many years. Despite these dire conditions, a closer examination of the lives of emerging adults by sociologists (e.g., Singerman, 2007) and social historians (e.g., Tzoreff, 2010) called our attention to the many strategies these young people search for, and invent, in order to make their living and survive from one day to the next. Within this framework, it is also impressive to observe the ways that these young people have invented to address their romantic and sexual desires in a society that has strict moral codes but has fallen short of facilitating their transition to marriage. Thus, despite the hardships, it is difficult to overlook the motivations and energies of this young generation that cannot be appropriately utilized in their societies.

Conclusion

The study of cross-cultural differences (or comparisons) has been widely influenced by the seminal work of Hofstede (1991). This conceptual framework shows the effects of a society's culture on the values of its members and how these values relate to behavior. Review of the existing research comparing the development of emerging adults in different cultures suggests, however, that a different approach was taken in conceptualizing and conducting these studies. Most studies assessed non-American emerging adults on "Western" dimensions such as identity development and dimensions or criteria of adulthood that were examined in American and European samples (Galanaki & Sideridis, 2019; Ozer et al., 2019). These types of studies can provide information on the extent to which emerging adults in a particular culture are similar to or different from their American counterparts but consider the distinctive features of a certain culture or context less. For example, above we described the findings of the Galanaki and Sideridis (2019) study showing that a significant portion of Greek college students felt in between adolescence and adulthood and were addressing questions of identity exploration and experimentation. However, closely examining the lives of Greek emerging adults showed that they live in an extreme economic crisis in which close to half are unemployed and do not foresee change in the near future. These dire conditions explain well why they feel in between, have less accomplished adult roles, and are anxious with regard to identity exploration. Thus, it is likely that their identity status represents their response to their economic context rather than their psychological development. Furthermore, and contrary to emerging adulthood theory, review of economic and social reports from Greece and the European Union suggests that, despite these dire conditions, Greek emerging adults are not paralyzed or necessarily confused. They look for ways to support themselves on a daily basis, they make plans and search for opportunities in other countries, and some are even creative in finding their niche in their own country.

This understanding of the story of young Greeks guided us in our attempts to understand the ways that emerging adults cope under difficult and impossible economic conditions. We presented the cases of emerging adults in Sardinia, a remote island off the coast of Italy that is less developed and was also hit hard by the recent recession, as well as the case of emerging adults in the Arab world. The conditions in Sardinia are more difficult than those in Greece, and a significant number of young people have entered a state of waiting for something to change. Many others, however, try to take some initiative to change the direction of their lives.

Arabic and North African youth live under even more dire conditions, where monthly income might be a mere $100. Yet again, although these young people also feel that they are in a period of waithood, they make great efforts for daily survival and are ready to accept jobs that are below their expectations. Others, similar to their counterparts in Greece, are creative in finding their own way and starting successful businesses. Only a small number drew closer to religion to regain their dignity. The creative ways that young Egyptians have developed to form romantic and sexual relationships in a traditional society that does not provide them with the means required for marrying and establishing a family are more impressive.

In sum, economic and social conditions have changed radically over recent decades, and young people's chances of completing a successful transition to adulthood have decreased (Furlong & Cartmel, 2007). This situation has worsened since the recession of 2008 and has affected youth around the globe, resulting in possible perception of emerging adults as a lost generation. However, examination of the stories and lives of young people, in particular those in hard-hit societies, shows that, despite the enormous hardships, many emerging adults have not lost hope. Indeed, although some have regressed into a condition of waithood, many act differently. They mobilize their inner strengths for daily survival or to search for and find creative ways out of the misery. Interestingly, these understandings drawn from societies that are in crisis correspond to our findings in our Israeli sample, which is an advanced economy. We showed that the majority of our participants were actively pursuing their way toward adulthood. Further, in the preceding chapters we have presented and emphasized the different ways that young people take to navigate the emerging adulthood years. Considering the major findings of our project and the cross-cultural data presented in this chapter together, we suggest perceiving emerging adulthood as a dynamic period of life during which young people actively pursue their developmental goals aimed at settling down. These new understandings of emerging adulthood will be further discussed in the concluding chapter.

14
Emerging Adulthood Revisited
A New Conceptualization for Understanding Fluctuations, Changes, and Processes

There is no dispute on how young people in their 20s, the emerging adulthood years, behave.

There is, however, a dispute as to how to understand and, in particular, how to conceptualize patterns of fluctuations that have become quite common among many young people (European Group for Integrated Social Research, 2001). How do young people make the move from instability to settling down? Indeed, past research conceptualized emerging adulthood as a period of extended identity exploration. Yet, it is unclear whether and how these processes of identity exploration are associated with future outcomes. It is also less clear how young people successfully complete the transition to adulthood after all, despite increasing contextual hardships.

Our study moves toward answers to these questions. Focusing through the lens of career development and romantic commitment (two major tasks of the transition to adulthood) and following a sample of young people for a period of approximately 12 years provided us with a better understanding of the journey that young people might take and the ways they navigate through these years. In the following sections we summarize our major findings and embed these within theoretical frameworks.

Conceptual frameworks for understanding emerging adulthood

Developmental progression during the emerging adulthood years—Going back and forth: A developmental systems theory perspective

Developmental and motivational conceptualization has emphasized the centrality of setting goals as the starting point for coping during transitional periods (Fleeson & Cantor, 1995; Nurmi, 2004). Goals serve as a road map that guides the life paths of individuals by directing and regulating their behavior (Haase et al., 2008) and leading them through their own development. Successively assessing the goals set by the participants in our study over the period of 12 years showed that half had clear goals. They had plans regarding what they wished to achieve in their lives. Some had more elaborated goals, while others' goals were less elaborated; but nevertheless, they had ideas of how to carry on with their lives. A little more than a third also described having goals in the major domains of education, career, and establishing a family. However, despite having appropriate goals, these individuals were preoccupied with concerns of whether they would find the right job or partner and whether they would succeed in their lives. Only about 14% found it difficult to set goals that related clearly to the common age-related goals of career development or establishing a significant romantic relationship. In addition, it was difficult to see coherent developmental patterns of their goals, and the goals they set seemed to reflect momentary interests or preoccupations.

A close inspection of these goal development patterns thus suggests that only the 14% who had difficulty setting goals might be considered "typical emerging adults" (Arnett, 2000, 2007). Our 12-year span of observation showed quite clearly that these individuals were not "cured" of the "emerging adult" characteristics; their functioning at the age of 35 was below average, and they were less likely to be married. Among those who were concerned at the earlier assessments as to whether they would be able to achieve their goals, some change was observed. These participants had clearer goals in the later assessments, focused on career and family, and had increased adaptation with age. Yet, it is important to emphasize that at large more than half of our participants were able to draw clear goals that directed their progression to adulthood and that, overall, they reached their goals when approaching the age of 30.

Considered together, observation of the majority of emerging adult participants in our study through the lens of goal setting does not suggest a "story" of confusion or extended exploration. On the contrary, the majority of the young people knew their life plans well at the age of 23 and were able to elaborate on them. A closer inspection of the stories of participants' actual career pursuit was even more surprising. Almost 60% of our participants reported an adaptive career pursuit history. They were able to either progress consistently and directly toward their initial aspired goal or disengage from an aspired goal in case of failure or disappointment and to set and successfully pursue a new goal that was meaningful for them. Career pursuit was not necessarily easy. Many who had successfully attained a successful career described significant difficulties along the way. They either failed in their efforts to achieve an aspired goal or were disappointed with their choice and had to give up their initially aspired life plan. However, it was impressive to learn of their efforts to re-find their way, to set and successfully pursue a new goal, and to re-embark toward successful settling down.

About a third of the participants described difficulties in achieving their aspired goal. The goal they had set was either unattainable for them or even unrealistic considering their capabilities or circumstances. However, despite this sense of disappointment, they managed to handle their daily lives properly. They kept a stable job and made their living. Despite their unfulfilled dreams and being employed in an occupation that was not actually their first choice, some reported that they were progressing at their workplace. They appeared to have realized that they would not get anything better and, therefore, compromised. Yet, interestingly, assessing these young people at the age of 35 showed that some of them had started to find meaning in what they do (Blustein, 2011). To enrich their lives, others had become involved in hobbies that became important to them, and they found joy in the families they had established. Thus, despite having to make compromises, they still found strength to make their lives more meaningful, albeit not via their careers. Again, only about 14% had lost their way. These "lost" young people were only employed periodically and had a sense of being marginalized. In fact, some were demonstrating a variety of adjustment problems that prevented them from properly addressing age-related tasks.

Together, our findings suggest that being lost and confused is not necessarily the norm. More important, reading the career histories of the young people clearly demonstrates that they were active in setting their life path. First, in the early years of emerging adulthood many had set clear goals, although encountering difficulties while pursuing their aspired goal was a fairly common phenomenon. Difficulties could be either external—realizing that it is difficult to find a job in their aspired field (and acquired education)—or internal—being disappointed with one's first choice. It was impressive to learn about young people's capacity to re-find their way and even more impressive to learn of those who had to make compromises and, after a period of time, started to find meaning in their jobs or looked for other activities to enrich their lives.

In Chapters 3 and 4 we conceptualized the endeavors our participants described within Heckhausen's motivational theory of life-span development, which we found to be of great relevance for understanding the meaning of fluctuations and change (Heckhausen, 1999; Heckhausen et al., 2010). Successful goal pursuit is not always direct, and failures are part of life. In the face of failure, it is crucial to learn to disengage from an unattainable goal and pursue an alternative goal. While relinquishing one's aspired goal may seem to be a drawback, Heckhausen suggested that in reality this strategy reflects self-mastery and is beneficial to well-being. The ability to come to terms with loss or failure facilitates compromise and the formulation of a new and different goal and brings an individual back on track (Wrosch et al., 2003). We could argue that the process of finding meaning in one's occupation (Blustein, 2011) or searching for satisfaction in other domains of life (such as a hobby) might be understood as an additional mechanism of adaptation when navigating through a transitional period. In sum, we thus suggest understanding fluctuations as functional. Periods of instability, or fluctuations, can be understood as an arena for learning how to pursue one's way through the challenges of life. Furthermore, it is through the failure, and the efforts made to address and overcome the failure, that the way is paved for successful attainment of one's goal (either the original or a new aspired goal). Thus, despite emerging adulthood seeming to be aimless years of confusion and exploration, a closer inspection of individual life histories during these years suggests that these years can be understood as a period of active personal coping, growth, and maturation, notwithstanding unfavorable societal contexts.

This understanding was even further substantiated when we learned about the romantic development of the participants in the current study. In Chapter 5 we described that analyzing the romantic histories of our participants in greater detail showed that close to 70% of them described involvement in pathways characterized by *Sporadic* and *Casual to Steady* involvements. These pathways consisted of a variety of fluctuations between casual sexual and romantic experiences, short-lived relationships, and periods of having no romantic interaction and, sometimes, interest. However, a substantial number of participants, which accounted for half of the fluid cases of our sample, were able to learn from their short and non-stable romantic experiences. They were able to overcome failures and disappointments and progress toward establishing stable and intimate relationships. Their earlier non-stable romantic and sexual experiences thus served as an arena for learning how to interact within, and solidify, a close romantic relationship (te Riele, 2004).

Considered together, accounts of career pursuit pathways and romantic development pathways indeed suggest that many of the emerging adults in our study could be characterized as unstable and fluid (Arnett, 2000, 2007; Settersten & Ray, 2010). Their behavior could be described as ranging between chaos and order (Mayes, 2001). However, looking into the processes and dynamics of both their career and romantic pathways over time (obtained through the in-depth interviews) suggested that a variety of the unstable experiences in fact served as an arena for learning. In earlier chapters we suggested that perceiving the variety of emerging adulthood experiences as a possible arena for learning can be embedded within the developmental systems theory (Thelen & Smith, 1998).

Development is intuitively perceived as a linear process—one growing, learning, maturing, and becoming bigger and better. This explains the tendency to perceive emerging adults in "deficit" terms (Arnett, 2000, 2007; Settersten & Ray, 2010) or as "arrested" (Côté, 2000). The delay in the assumption of adult roles and, in particular, fluidity is perceived as a drawback. However, within the conceptual framework of the developmental systems theory, development is not necessarily always linear, and fluidity also characterizes children's course of development (Thelen & Smith, 1998). As children grow, they have to adjust to changing circumstances, new information, and changing capabilities that need to be slowly transformed into new structures. In their seminal work, Thelen and Smith (1998) described, inter alia, the transition from crawling to walking. This progress to walking is not necessarily gradual or linear, and children may exhibit different forms of behavior in this process. At times, a child may still crawl, although they could have been expected to reach the capacity to walk. Thelen and Smith (1998) articulated how different, and sometimes contradictory, "pieces" of behavior need to be organized into a new structure. Behavior might seem unstable and even chaotic only until new forms of organization are consolidated. New structures or forms of behavior only become stable following the completion of change in an old function and reorganization of different functions into a new integrated function or ability (Mayes, 2001).

In sum, unlike previous conceptualizations of emerging adulthood and the transition to adulthood from a deficit perspective or an extension of adolescence, we propose that periods of instabilities, and even regressions, during the emerging adulthood years can be part of developmental reorganization and might be aimed at finding and developing new forms of behavior that address the need and potential for change and growth (Knight, 2011; Mayes, 2001; Thelen & Smith, 1998). Closer inspection of young people's accounts of their career and romantic lives enabled us to reach this understanding. Overall, individuals' actions were geared toward progress in the attainment of their aspired tasks. There might have been back-and-forth movements along the way in order to find a more suitable path. Subsequently, successful endeavors are likely to be repeated, and the recurrent patterns of behavior lay the basis of self-organization (Granic, 2005; Thelen & Smith, 1998). The transition to the next step (in our case, settling down) can be completed once the variety of different "pieces" of behavior organization is reached and consolidated and the individual is ready for the next stage (Spencer et al., 2011). Thus, embedding our findings and conceptualization within the developmental systems theory can explain how the non-stable and sometimes inconsistent behaviors are the route through which the transition to adulthood can be completed and guide the young adult toward settling down. Extending the developmental systems theory and applying it to the study of emerging adulthood, we thus suggest that understanding the dynamic back-and-forth processes is of great relevance for capturing developmental processes during transitional periods. During a transitional period, earlier patterns of behavior have to be relinquished and new patterns of behavior learned. This can be accomplished only through back-and-forth movements or trial and error.

Conceptually, we suggest that, similar to young children who are "programmed" to progress toward walking, emerging adults are "programmed" to progress toward settling down. They might take different paths, might make changes along the road; but overall they are tuned toward attaining the age-related tasks and undergo a process of self-organization (Granic, 2005; Thelen & Smith, 1998). We thus propose understanding the emerging adulthood years as a period of growth and progression, though not linear growth.

In the following section we discuss the recent conceptualization of personality development and show the parallel process of personality maturity that takes place during these years. Together, considering increasing findings that indicate a process of personality development during emerging adulthood, we suggest focusing on the progression that emerging adults undergo and learning more about the mechanisms that can explain this expression of growth.

The emerging adulthood years, personality development, and adaptive outcomes

Examination of the way in which personality changes during the emerging adulthood years can further demonstrate that a comprehensive process of progression does operate during these years. In Chapter 10 we discussed the recent conceptualization and findings suggesting an increase in personality maturity during the third decade of life. Recent theoretical work and empirical studies have shown that, despite the rank-order stability of personality, levels of personality traits, such as neuroticism, change to a fair degree in people throughout the life span (B. W. Roberts et al., 2008; Specht et al., 2014). Personality development appears to accelerate during early adulthood, as evidenced by pronounced increases in emotional stability, conscientiousness, self-control, self-esteem, and agreeableness (Bleidorn, 2015; Orth et al., 2012; B. W. Roberts et al., 2006). During these years most individuals gradually became more agreeable, conscientious, and emotionally stable (Bleidorn et al., 2009; Lüdtke et al., 2011; B. W. Roberts & Davis, 2016). Relatedly, accumulating research indicates evidence of age-related changes indicative of increases in self-esteem (Hutteman et al., 2015; Steiger et al., 2014).

Following our participants through their 20s, we were also able to show a significant decrease in level of self-criticism during these years. Across the years we found that emerging adults became less preoccupied with achievement and negative appraisals of their self. They felt less guilt and less fear about losing approval when failing to live up to certain standards (Michaeli et al., 2019). In another study we were able to document a decrease in rejection sensitivity. Rejection sensitivity is a relational schema (Furman & Wehner, 1997) that affects the lenses through which individuals see their interactions with others (Downey & Feldman, 1996). Rejection-sensitive individuals are highly sensitive to signs of disagreement and rejection, and this affects the quality of relationships with peers, romantic partners, and a future spouse. Following individuals from adolescence into emerging adulthood, we, and others, showed a significant decrease in level of rejection sensitivity during these years (Hafen et al., 2014; Norona et al., 2018).

Past studies demonstrated the contribution of personality maturity, such as greater emotional stability, to better outcomes in various domains. These domains typically include physical health, psychological health (including lower psychopathology), coping behavior, the quality of close relationships, and work behavior (see, e.g., De Bolle et al., 2012; Mroczek & Spiro, 2007; Steiger et al., 2015). Conceptualized within a developmental framework, we showed that a decrease in self-criticism explained better future coping with age-related tasks as well as psychological well-being, such as satisfaction with life and flourishing (see in more detail in Chapter 10). Relatedly, we (Norona et al., 2018) and Hafen and colleagues (2014) were also able to show that decrease in rejection sensitivity associated with greater quality of romantic relationships in the future and more adaptive coping with relationship stressors. Considered together, this accumulating evidence suggests significant personality changes during the emerging adulthood years. Individuals become more positive and emotionally stable, and these positive changes associate with more adaptive outcomes. As we have shown, the increasing capacity for more efficient coping facilitates greater success in addressing age-related developmental tasks such as career and romantic development.

In addition to more efficient coping with age-related tasks, positive changes in personality can facilitate positive interaction with others and with the environment (Van Aken et al., 2006). More specifically, becoming better at interacting positively with others often results in a variety of positive outcomes such as increasing one's understanding of others' perspectives, gaining greater awareness about oneself and one's capacities, and learning to balance the needs of oneself and others (Shulman et al., 2006). Indeed, individuals tend to become more introspective with age, which is probably the culmination of efforts to understand how others perceive them and to discover what roles or jobs they want to obtain in adulthood (Arnett, 2004).

In a seminal work, Fonagy and colleagues (2002) termed these metacognitive abilities to think about the thoughts and feelings of both themselves and others *reflectivity*. Reflectivity includes an intrapersonal dimension (self-awareness and understanding), as well as an interpersonal dimension (the ability to see others as psychological entities with thoughts, emotions, and needs). As such, reflectivity involves both a cognitive process akin to psychological insight and perspective-taking and an emotional process based on the capacity to regulate and understand one's own mental states and deduce the emotional and mental states of others (Slade, 2005). Within this context, gaining greater awareness can also facilitate the capability to draw lessons from past experiences, which in turn may facilitate better handling of developmental tasks and promote mental health. In a recent study we were indeed able to show that decreases in self-criticism during the emerging adulthood years anticipated a higher level of reflective capabilities at age 29, which can be considered indicative of maturation. Reflective capabilities at age 29 in turn explained a greater likelihood of adaptive settling down and more positive psychological well-being (Michaeli et al., 2019). Considered together, we suggest that a significant process of personality maturation takes place during the emerging adulthood years. This is seen in a decrease in emotional negativity and an increase in emotional stability and consequently higher levels of reflective capacity. Together these increases in personality maturity set the stage for a smoother transition toward the attainment of developmental tasks and promote future psychological health.

There is a debate regarding what stimulates the changes in personality during the emerging adulthood years. Are these changes biologically driven, or are they in response to the increase in the assumption of an adult role (McCrae & Costa, 2008; B. W. Roberts et al., 2006)? Although this debate is beyond the focus of our book, it is generally agreed that the majority of these changes in personality take place during the third decade of life and, in turn, facilitate coping with age-related tasks. Thus, taking a personality development perspective also suggests that an active process of positive change takes place during the emerging adulthood years. In this process personality becomes less negative and less critical, and as a result, better coping with age-related tasks is facilitated. In sum, incorporating the recent findings of personality development further supports our notion that the emerging adulthood years are not necessarily a period of confusion and extended exploration. The emerging adulthood years can be understood as a period in life that is programed toward an increased penchant for adaptation and maturation. Of note, we suggest that the focus of emerging adulthood is not limited to the attainment of major goals such as career and love. Attainment of goals and accompanying personality maturation set the stage for the capacities that allow further development, guiding one's way into later adulthood. This can be achieved by the attainment of authorship, as discussed in the next section.

Emerging adulthood—Progress toward and attainment of life authorship

Throughout this book we have repeatedly examined the tasks of emerging adulthood through the lens of career development and the establishment of an intimate and committed romantic relationship. Career and romantic development can be perceived as "practical" tasks that are expected to be achieved. We might ask what the "inner" psychological processes are that can explain the progression during these years and, ultimately, the achievement of the two central tasks of work and love.

Following the work of McAdams (2013a), we have discussed the development of authorship or, in McAdams' words, becoming "an author of your life," which is expected to be achieved during the years of emerging adulthood. Conceptualized within the framework of the search for identity, narrative identity (McAdams & Pals, 2006) integrates the *reconstructed past, experienced present*, and *imagined future*. Integrating past and present experiences is important for establishing a sense of self-continuity, which is the base for well-being.

Similar to our suggestion to perceive emerging adulthood as a process that is geared toward progression (though not necessarily in a linear mode), McAdams (2013a) suggests that the ability to draw lessons from past experiences and, in particular, learning how to overcome difficulties and grow out of earlier difficulties is the mechanism that is expected to be achieved during emerging adulthood. Furthermore, attainment of this capacity can shape future outcomes.

The sense of self-continuity not only is the nucleus of mental health but also serves as a guide for future development. McAdams (2013a) wrote,

> Emerging adults sample from the menu in constructing individual life stories, aiming to find narrative forms that capture their own personal experiences, allow for their own limitations and constraints, and convey their aspirations for the future. They appropriate models for living that prevail in the cultures wherein their lives have their constituent meanings. (p. 153)

Conceptually, we thus argue that during emerging adulthood, through the process of finding what suits one with regard to career development and the processes involved in the development of a stable relationship, the sense of self is consolidated. This coherent self, integrating past and present, serves as the base for one's future life. In a similar vein, in his seminal book Levinson (1978) described that a person is supposed to set the "personal enterprise," which gives the person a direction later in life. Levinson described this enterprise using the image of a ladder that the person is expected to "climb" in order to continue their life into the future. In Chapter 8 we indeed showed that those who had achieved a higher level of authorship at age 29 were more likely to be married, to be committed to their career, to earn a higher salary, and to exhibit higher levels of psychological well-being. Considered together, we thus suggest that during the emerging adulthood years, based on personal experiences and the lessons learned from them, the young person is expected to develop personal authorship and that attainment of authorship serves as a road map for future development and adaptation.

To summarize, we suggest a different understanding of the processes that characterize the emerging adulthood years. Young people are not necessarily confused or in a state of extended exploration during their 20s. We have shown that the majority of the younger generation has aspirations concerning their future and sets goals to achieve these aspirations. Based on following our sample for 12 years, we propose that emerging adulthood can be perceived as a dynamic period of time during which three important processes take place. First, young people actively search for their way in life and are geared toward setting and achieving their life plans. Second, through the fluctuations and changes along the way, individuals learn what they can achieve, when compromises need to be made, and finally to be open enough to find meaning in a career they might not have dreamed of initially. Finally, the capacity to compromise and adapt oneself to the circumstances is facilitated by the processes of personality change expressed by an "easier" and more stable personality. Together, the increased capacity to draw lessons combined with an "easier" personality contributes to a sense of continuity that sets the stage for developing a sense of authorship. We suggest understanding emerging adulthood as a dynamic period "programmed" toward settling down. "Settling down" can be considered the major task of this age period (Levinson, 1978). Within this process, individuals might take different routes on their journey, and settling down might take different forms.

Distinctive pathways to adulthood

The variety and complexity of pathways taken on the journey to adulthood

Through our in-depth interviews we found that there is no single route to adulthood. Individuals might embark on a variety of pathways when pursuing their career or in the process of developing romantic relationships. Throughout the book we have described the different career development pathways and the different romantic development pathways in detail. Examining career development, we found four distinctive career pursuit pathways. The first, *Consistent Pursuit*, was characterized by individuals with a clear and articulated life plan that was complex, diversified, and connected to inner aspirations; and these individuals were successful in pursuing their dream. The second, *Adapted Pursuit*, consisted of individuals who had experienced disappointments or failures along the way that led them to a change in the area of studies and/or a shift to a different field of work. However, despite the difficulties experienced along the way, they were competent in finding a new way and adapted successfully. The third, *Survivors*, consisted of individuals who had a goal that they did not pursue successfully. Yet, despite their disappointment and continued dream of an unattained goal, they were steadily employed, and their daily lives seemed settled. They appeared to have compromised. The fourth, *Confused/Vague*, pathway included individuals who were not able to provide a clear and coherent idea of what they would like to do with their lives and appeared to feel miserable.

Similarly, we found that emerging adults' romantic involvements across the years could also be characterized by four different pathways. The first, *Sporadic*, is characterized by romantic fluctuations that never moved toward, or developed into, steady and long-lasting relationships. The second, *Casual to Steady*, is characterized by individuals who could also be described by instabilities and fluctuations across the years. However, following them over a long period of time showed that these emerging adults were moving toward a steady involvement after a period of exploration. Most importantly, they were able to reflect on their past romantic involvements and described a process of learning from their experience in non-stable romantic encounters. The third, *Lengthy Relationships but Absence of Experiential Learning*, includes individuals who reported involvement in lasting relationships that were not necessarily intimate and mutually respectful. Relationships were described as part of a routine, and no will or capacity to change this condition was raised by these young people. Finally, the fourth pathway, *Steady Relationships*, consisted of individuals who described a tendency to form and maintain long-lasting relationships. In addition, they tended to describe a process of learning and development in their relationships that led to the solidification of an intimate and committed relationship.

Our findings clearly suggest that the transition to adulthood is characterized by different routes, with some leading to adaptive outcomes and others being characterized more by difficulties. There are, however, emerging adults who might have embarked on a less adaptive pathway but are able to find internal (as well as external) resources, change direction, and embark on a more adaptive route in either career or romantic development. The variety of ways, as well as the capacity to change route and find a different and adaptive route, demonstrates again the dynamics of the emerging adulthood years and the resilience of this period. Overall, emerging adults are active in setting their direction in life and navigate to adulthood successfully or, at least, make compromises and find their niche in life.

Gendered pathways to adulthood
An additional example of the complexity and richness of the nature of progress to adulthood is reflected by the differences in the distinctive routes that men and women take on their journey to adulthood. In Chapter 9 we showed that men and women tend to take different career pursuit pathways. Young men were more likely than young women to belong to the more adaptive pathways: the *Consistent*

pathway and the *Adapted* pathway. In contrast, young women were more likely than young men to belong to the less adaptive pathways: the *Survivors* pathway and the *Confused/Vague* pathway. Thus, young men appeared to be more focused on their career goals or more capable of overcoming their difficulties, making a shift along the way and finding a career with which they were satisfied and that was meaningful for them. In contrast, women had a greater tendency to make compromises and stay in jobs that they did not necessarily enjoy.

Distinctive gender patterns were also found concerning the romantic pathways taken by emerging adults. Young women were more likely to belong to lasting relationships, whereas young men tended more to belong to short relationships, whose members were sporadically involved in casual encounters. Of note, women were more likely to remain for longer periods of time in relationships that did not lead to true intimacy and future commitment. Discussing these gender differences, we suggested that emerging adult men appear to prioritize career over romantic investment, while emerging adult women prioritize romantic involvement at the expense of developing their own careers.

These gender differences seem to suggest that women are less likely to navigate competently through the emerging adulthood years, particularly with regard to their career development. However, the interviews we conducted with our participants at the age of 35 suggested that the process is more complex. We learned that men are as interested as women in establishing a family but that, despite the importance of establishing a family, they are more focused on their careers. In contrast, women assign a higher priority to becoming a mother. For this reason, it is more difficult for a woman to find the balance between being a mother (in their words, a good and invested mother) and developing a successful career. Some women find a way to balance the two successfully, to invest in their children and to develop professionally. However, we noticed that for the majority of the women in our study it was difficult to find a professional context that supports their dream to integrate motherhood and career. As a result, there are women who are more ready to make compromises at the expense of their professional development.

Conceptually, we thus suggest that it is not that women are less career-oriented or capable of succeeding professionally. They are. Yet, unlike men, they are also child- and family-oriented. Becoming a mother is perceived by many women as part of their identity, and they have to consider this central aspect of their lives and identity more seriously than men when navigating toward settling down. The road to adulthood is thus more complex for young women. Without entering a discussion of the extent to which society nowadays is truly supportive of women (which is beyond the scope of this book), it was impressive to learn of the efforts that young women made and the ways they chose on their journey to adulthood. Observing the efforts and the struggles of young women on their path to adulthood again demonstrates the complex dynamics of the emerging adulthood years. To summarize, emerging adults in general, and women in particular, are active and struggle while determining their route and navigating their way to adulthood. Some are more successful, while others have to make compromises. Of note, despite these complexities, we found that the majority of emerging adults are not confused. Moreover, the majority in our sample were not preoccupied with issues of self-exploration—what fits my identity or is my dream. They were exploring to find their way as mothers and materialize their dream within the changing social and economic worlds in which they live.

What can cross-cultural differences teach us about emerging adults?

Examination of emerging adults in Western or economically developed societies shows clear social and demographic changes pointing to a delay in assumption of adult roles such as career and marriage. This undisputed observation led to the perception of the emerging adulthood years as a period of fluctuations and instabilities. Review of the majority of the existing research on this phenomenon within the framework of "emerging adulthood" attributed these instabilities to an extended process of identity exploration into the third decade of life.

We have argued that attempts to understand the lives and dynamics of emerging adults in developing societies (or societies under crisis) along the yardstick of Western societies falls short of teaching us about the true dynamics of their emerging adulthood years. The number of studies that were conducted within the conceptual framework of emerging adulthood could only teach us about the extent of identity exploration or feeling versus not feeling as an adult among young people in non-Western societies. The approach we took, described in the previous chapter, led us to examine the works of demographers, sociologists, anthropologists, and social historians and to learn how they perceive and understand the younger generation in their societies.

We have focused on two European societies currently suffering a severe economic crisis: Greece and the island of Sardinia, an underdeveloped part of Italy. In addition, we examine the Arab and North African world, focusing particularly on Egypt. In all these societies in recent or continuous crisis, the majority of young people were not confused and, more importantly, had not given up their aspiration to progress to adulthood. Many among them realized the impossible conditions they faced and were willing to readjust their expectations and compromise for a lower-level profession or temporary jobs in order to support themselves and survive. Others had plans to leave, or had already left, their country in search of opportunities abroad. Only a few did not function. They lost hope and waited for salvation, while, in the meantime, they retreated into idleness or turned to religion (in the Muslim world). Thus, a conceptual review of emerging adulthood in societies in crisis suggests that, despite the enormous hardships, most had not lost hope. Many tended to mobilize their inner strengths for daily survival, for ways to leave their country, or to search, and sometimes find, creative ways to escape the misery.

The competence and creativity of emerging adults could further be demonstrated by examining the romantic lives of young people in Egypt and certain other Arab countries. We were not able to find information about the romantic and sexual lives of emerging adults in countries such as Greece and Sardinia. It is possible that due to the delay in the age at marriage young people are romantically and sexually involved similarly to their counterparts in other Western societies. In contrast, Egypt is a traditional society, and sex before marriage is socially and religiously unacceptable. It was interesting to learn of the creative way the young Egyptians developed to address this issue. To stay within the cultural norms of their society, an increasing number of young Egyptians started to adopt the tradition of *mut'ah* weddings, which are temporary unions simply for sexual purposes. These "weddings" are secret, are undocumented, and take place in private without the knowledge of the couple's parents. A closer understanding of the development and implementation of this form of secret weddings further highlights the competence that emerging adults have developed and employ in order to cope with the unfavorable and impossible conditions under which they live. Interestingly, these understandings align with our conceptualization which emphasizes the efforts that young people make to navigate across the emerging adulthood years.

Furthermore, we were able to learn that, even under dire conditions, the majority of emerging adults know what they want and to where they are heading.

Thus, as we have suggested, it may appear that emerging adulthood is "programmed" toward settling down successfully.

Developmental transitions—An evolutionary perspective

A basic tenet in developmental psychology is that stressful conditions are associated with less adaptive outcomes (see, e.g., G. W. Evans et al., 2013). Recent theorizing and research have documented the increasing difficulties in making a smooth transition to adulthood due to major societal changes and increases in unemployment (Arnett, 2004; Côté, 2000). Considering these societal changes, it might be reasonable to question whether taking the traditional linear route to adulthood—early commitment to career and establishing a family at an earlier age—is the best option for a young person nowadays. Debarking from an expected linear route, such as quitting a job or terminating a relationship, might be the preferable way considering the possible benefits and costs of the specific route. This dilemma is basic for understanding development within an evolutionary perspective.

In understanding reaction to stress, the evolutionary conceptualization suggests that it is unlikely that there is a single strategy for survival and reproduction when facing stressful conditions. Instead, it is possible that different strategies are developed to cope under stressful conditions, and the strategies vary as a function of three factors (Ellis & Del Giudice, 2019). First, the costs and benefits of a certain strategy depend on the likelihood of successfully surviving and flourishing in the specific environment (e.g., food availability, availability or lack of jobs in the specific field). Second, the success or failure of a specific strategy depends on an organism's internal capacities to cope successfully and achieve the aspired outcome. Some organisms, contrary to others, might have the skills or be able to develop new skills to address the stress to which they are exposed. Finally, an organism's gender is additionally likely to affect the strategy taken, considering the extent to which gender plays a role in the chances of success of a particular strategy (Ellis & Del Giudice, 2019, p. 113). Our findings correspond to these three basic evolutionary tenets. We found that in response to current societal stressors, the majority of emerging adults are not necessarily confused or involved in an extended (and sometimes aimless) process of exploration considering the significant societal changes and increased uncertainty. We found that emerging adults tend to embark on different pathways when pursuing a career or romantic development. In addition, we showed that affiliation with a specific pathway was affected by personality attributes. For example, we found that individuals adopted a specific pathway that suited their capacity or lack of capacity to cope with the age-related developmental task. For example, low self-criticism associated with higher likelihood to progress directly in one's career development. Finally, we also showed that men and women tended to take different pathways. For women, in particular, the likelihood of "reproductive success" (having time to invest in your child) played a role when making career choices.

The evolutionary framework can also shed further light on the complexity of the dynamics in the comprehensive process of pursuing developmental tasks. We described, and claimed, that the fluctuations in both career and romantic development could serve as a learning arena on the road to adulthood and embedded our notions within the developmental systems theory. Interestingly, these understandings echo similar processes described by evolutionary thinkers. Organisms tend to employ different strategies aimed at balancing costs and benefits in order to maximize their expected fitness or reproductive outcomes. A strategy taken is built upon the organism's capacities, the particular environment, and the fit between these. We showed that a strategy can be flexible and adjustments can be made along the process in order to reach a better balance. The selection of a specific strategy, and the flexibility to make adjustments across time within the strategy that was selected, recall the concept of *adaptive developmental plasticity* (Del Giudice & Belsky, 2011; Ellis et al., 2006) and capture the dynamics employed to achieve better outcomes. Thus, we suggest that by taking an evolutionary perspective we can further understand the back-and-forth movements across the developmental course of emerging adulthood that we have described in our model. The process of making adjustments is geared toward finding the better balance between cost and benefit in a changing, and sometimes unpredictable, environment and could be understood as part of a progression process aimed at maximizing personal fitness and reproductive outcomes. Conceptually, understanding emerging adulthood as a period geared toward maximizing optimal settling down entails an additional important aspect. Settling down and assuming an adult role is not the end of the line. As we have hinted above, an additional aim is to set the stage and direction for the following years of adulthood.

The emerging adulthood years—Laying the ground for future adulthood years

Our observations led us to understand the emerging adulthood years as a period during which dynamic processes take place in the navigation to adulthood. As a rule, the majority of young people actively pursue career and romantic goals. They mobilize their inner capacities and are open and willing to accept support from parents, family, and non-family figures. Personal capacities and social capital, together, enable young people to search competently, find their niche, and achieve their aspired goals. In addition to the achievement of work and love goals during this dynamic process of development, capacities that are needed for future development and adaptation are refined, strengthened, and consolidated. These capacities include facilitating interaction with others, coping with stressors, and developing a more mature perception of oneself and others. Extending Levinson's metaphor of a ladder, we suggest that during emerging adulthood new rungs are expected to be added to the ladder to facilitate continuing one's road into adulthood. Relatedly, the consolidation of a "personal enterprise" provides the person with a direction later in life (Levinson, 1978) that serves as the basis for development in the coming years. We believe that these fluctuations can provide a richer, more complex, and more stable structure. Achieving this stable structure serves as the base for future development that is expected to foster the emergence of the next stage of life—adulthood.

Future directions and policy implications

Further empirical work is required to assess and replicate our suggestion to perceive emerging adulthood as a period of growth and integration. More evidence is needed to show whether, and how, behaviors that explicitly represent instability and fluctuations can serve as an arena for learning and future development. For this purpose, longitudinal studies and reanalysis of existing longitudinal data can be helpful for assessing when and what changes along the way are beneficial and when they signify difficulties in progression and finding one's way. In addition, personal life stories can provide insights into the routes taken on the journey to adulthood. We believe that, considering the dynamics of transitional periods, cross-sectional studies are too short to provide a clear account of the complexity of a developmental course.

Finally, emerging adulthood has been portrayed as a period of youth instability and narcissism, which has led to increased criticism of the younger generation in the Western world and non-Western societies alike. Criticism raised by traditional circles perceives the younger generation as rebellious and unwilling to accept the "good old" values. Our findings indicate that matters are more complex. The majority of young people in different societies wish to develop a career or at least make their living and start their family. However, major changes in the economy undermine young people's smooth transition. The older generation and, in particular, social institutions need to take initiative to mobilize resources and find ways to support the younger generation in their wish to progress to adulthood in their societies. Our findings over 12 years suggest that it is not the young generation's fault that it is "lost in transition." On the contrary, young people try hard to find their way, leaving their families and possibly their country of origin in search of a better future. Honestly acknowledging the current more difficult, and in some societies dire, conditions that the young generation faces could be the first step in the direction of change that needs to be made.

References

Addis, D. R., & Tippett, L. J. (2008). The contributions of autobiographical memory to the content and continuity of identity: A social-cognitive neuroscience approach. In F. Sani (Ed.), *Self continuity: Individual and collective perspectives* (pp. 71–84). Psychology Press.

Allen, J. P., & Hauser, S. T. (1996). Autonomy and relatedness in adolescent–family interactions as predictors of young adults' states of mind regarding attachment. *Development and Psychopathology, 8*(4), 793–809.

Allen, T. D., Eby, L. T., Poteet, M. L., Lentz, E., & Lima, L. (2004). Career benefits associated with mentoring for protégés: A meta-analysis. *Journal of Applied Psychology, 89*(1), 127–136.

Almeida, D. M. (2002). Using daily diaries to assess temporal friction between work and family. In A. C. Crouter & A. Booth (Eds.), *Work–family challenges for low income parents and their children* (pp. 127–136). Erlbaum.

Almeida, D. M. (2004). Using daily diaries to assess temporal friction between work and family. In A. C. Crouter & A. Booth (Eds.), *Work–family challenges for low income parents and their children* (pp. 127–136). Routledge.

Almog, O. (2000). *The Sabra the Creation of the New Jew*. Berkley, CA: University of California Press.

Al Sherbini, R. (2015, November 17). Egypt youth in perpetual state of "waithood." *Gulf News*. https://gulfnews.com/world/mena/egypt-youth-in-perpetual-state-of-waithood-1.1620733

Arlozorov, M. (2012, Oct 29). The good luck of young people in Israel. themarker.com. https://www.themarker.com › caree

Arnett, J. J. (2000). Emerging adulthood—A theory of development from the late teens through the twenties. *American Psychologist, 55*, 469–480.

Arnett, J. J. (2004). *Emerging adulthood: The winding road from the late teens through the twenties*. Oxford University Press.

Arnett, J. J. (2006). The psychology of emerging adulthood: What is known, and what remains to be known? In J. J. Arnett & J. L. Tanner (Eds.), *Emerging adults in America: Coming of age in the 21st century* (pp. 303–330). American Psychological Association. https://doi.org/10.1037/11381-013

Arnett, J. J. (2007). Emerging adulthood: What is it, and what is it good for? *Child Development Perspectives, 1*(2), 68–73.

Arnett, J. J., & Schwab, J. (2013). *The Clark University Poll of Emerging Adults, 2012: Thriving, struggling, and hopeful*. Worcester, MA: Clark University.

Arnett, J. J., & Tanner, J. L. (2011). Themes and variations in emerging adulthood across social classes. In Debating emerging adulthood: Stage or process (pp. 31–50). Oxford University Press.

Azaryahu, M. (2020). *Tel Aviv: Mythography of a City*. Syracuse, NY: Syracuse University Press.Baker, S. R. (2004). Intrinsic, extrinsic, and amotivational orientations: Their role in university adjustment, stress, well-being, and subsequent academic performance. *Current Psychology, 23*, 189–202.

Bandura, A. (1977). Self-efficacy: Toward a unifying theory of behavioral change. *Psychological Review, 84*(2), 191–215.

Bateman, J. (2019, May 4). *How Greek crisis helped removed taboo on mental health*. BBC News. https://www.bbc.com/news/world-europe-48069644

Bauer, J. J., McAdams, D. P., & Sakaeda, A. R. (2005). Interpreting the good life: Growth memories in the lives of mature, happy people. *Journal of Personality and Social Psychology, 88*(1), 203–217.

Becht, A. I., Bos, M. G., Nelemans, S. A., Peters, S., Vollebergh, W. A., Branje, S. J., Meeus, W. H. J., & Crone, E. A. (2018). Goal-directed correlates and neurobiological underpinnings of adolescent identity: A multimethod multisample longitudinal approach. *Child Development, 89*(3), 823–836.

Becht, A. I., Luyckx, K., Nelemans, S. A., Goossens, L., Branje, S. J., Vollebergh, W. A., & Meeus, W. H. (2019). Linking identity and depressive symptoms across adolescence: A multisample longitudinal study testing within-person effects. *Developmental Psychology, 55*(8), 1733–1742.

Békés, V., Dunkley, D., Taylor, G., Zuroff, D., Lewkowski, M., Foley, J., Myhr, G., & Westreich, R. (2015). Chronic stress and attenuated improvement in depression over 1 year: The moderating role of perfectionism. *Behavior Therapy, 46*, 479–492.

Bello, B. G., & Cuzzocrea, V. (2018). Introducing the need to study young people in contemporary Italy. *Journal of Modern Italian Studies, 23*(1), 1–7.

Belsky, J., Steinberg, L., & Draper, P. (1991). Childhood experience, interpersonal development, and reproductive strategy: An evolutionary theory of socialization. *Child Development, 62*(4), 647–670.

Besser, A. V. I., & Priel, B. (2010). Personality vulnerability, low social support, and maladaptive cognitive emotion regulation under ongoing exposure to terrorist attacks. *Journal of Social and Clinical Psychology, 29*(2), 166–201.

Blatt, S. J. (1998). Contributions of psychoanalysis to the understanding and treatment of depression. *Journal of the American Psychoanalytic Association, 46*(3), 723–752.

Blatt, S. J. (2004). *Experiences of depression: Theoretical, clinical, and research perspectives*. American Psychological Association.

Blatt, S. J. (2008). *Polarities of experience, relatedness and self-definition in personality development, psychopathology, and the therapeutic process*. American Psychological Association.

Blatt, S. J., D'Afflitti, J. P., & Quinlan, D. M. (1976). Experiences of depression in normal young adults. *Journal of Abnormal Psychology, 85*(4), 383–389.

Blatt, S. J., & Zuroff, D. C. (1992). Interpersonal relatedness and self-definition: Two prototypes for depression. *Clinical Psychology Review, 12*(5), 527–562.

Bleidorn, W. (2015). What accounts for personality maturation in early adulthood? *Current Directions in Psychological Science, 24*(3), 245–252.

Bleidorn, W., Kandler, C., Hülsheger, U. R., Riemann, R., Angleitner, A., & Spinath, F. M. (2010). Nature and nurture of the interplay between personality traits and major life goals. *Journal of Personality and Social Psychology, 99*(2), 366–379.

Bleidorn, W., Kandler, C., Riemann, R., Angleitner, A., & Spinath, F. M. (2009). Patterns and sources of adult personality development: Growth curve analyses of the NEO PI-R scales in a longitudinal twin study. *Journal of Personality and Social Psychology, 97*(1), 142–155.

Blossfeld, H. P., & Hofmeister, H. (Eds.). (2006). *Globalization, uncertainty and women's careers: An international comparison*. Edward Elgar Publishing.

Blustein, D. L. (2011). A relational theory of working. *Journal of Vocational Behavior, 79*(1), 1–17.

Blustein, D. L., Juntunen, C. L., & Worthington, R. L. (2000). The school-to-work transition: Adjustment challenges of the forgotten half. In S. D. Brown & R. W. Lent (Eds.), *Handbook of counseling psychology* (pp. 435–470). John Wiley & Sons.

Blustein, D. L., Prezioso, M. S., & Schultheiss, D. P. (1995). Attachment theory and career development: Current status and future directions. *The Counseling Psychologist, 23*(3), 416–432.

Bodenmann, G. (2005). Dyadic coping and its significance for marital functioning. In T. A. Revenson, K. Kayser, & G. Bodenmann (Eds.), *Decade of behavior. Couples coping with stress: Emerging perspectives on dyadic coping* (pp. 33–49). American Psychological Association. https://doi.org/10.1037/11031-002

Bogle, K. A. (2008). *Hooking up: Sex, dating, and relationships on campus* (Vol. 1). New York University Press.

Bouchard, M. A., Target, M., Lecours, S., Fonagy, P., Tremblay, L. M., Schachter, A., & Stein, H. (2008). Mentalization in adult attachment narratives: Reflective functioning, mental states, and affect elaboration compared. *Psychoanalytic Psychology, 25*(1), 47–66.

Brandtstädter, J. (1998). Action perspectives on human development. In W. Damon & R. M. Richard (Eds.), *Handbook of child psychology: Vol. 1. Theoretical models of human development* (5th ed., pp. 807–863). John Wiley & Sons.

Brandtstadter, J., & Lerner, R. M. (Eds.). (1999). *Action and self-development*. Sage.

Brandtstädter, J., & Rothermund, K. (2002). The life-course dynamics of goal pursuit and goal adjustment: A two-process framework. *Developmental Review, 22*, 117–150.

Brannen, J., & Nilsen, A. (2002). Young people's time perspectives: From youth to adulthood. *Sociology, 36*(3), 513–537.

Brendgen, M., Wanner, B., Morin, A. J., & Vitaro, F. (2005). Relations with parents and with peers, temperament, and trajectories of depressed mood during early adolescence. *Journal of Abnormal Child Psychology, 33*(5), 579–594.

Brines, J., & Joyner, K. (1999). The ties that bind: Principles of cohesion in cohabitation and marriage. *American Sociological Review, 64*(3), 333–355.

Briscoe, J. P., Hall, D. T., & DeMuth, R. L. F. (2006). Protean and boundaryless careers: An empirical exploration. *Journal of Vocational Behavior, 69*(1), 30–47.

Brown, B. B. (1999). "You're going out with whom?" Peer group influences on adolescent romantic relationships. In W. Furman, B. B. Brown, & C. Feiring (Eds.), *The development of romantic relationships in adolescence* (pp. 291–329). Cambridge University Press.

Brumbach, B. H., Figueredo, A. J., & Ellis, B. J. (2009). Effects of harsh and unpredictable environments in adolescence on development of life history strategies. *Human Nature, 20*(1), 25–51.Buchholz, K. (2019). *When people get married around the world*. Retrieved from https://www.statista.com

Buchmann, M., & Kriesi, I. (2009). Escaping the gender trap: Young women's transition into nontraditional occupations. In I. Schoon & R. K. Silbereisen (Eds.), *Transitions from school to work: Globalization, individualization, and patterns of diversity* (pp. 193–215). Cambridge University Press. https://doi.org/10.1017/CBO9780511605369.009

Bumpass, L., & Lu, H. H. (2000). Trends in cohabitation and implications for children's family contexts in the United States. *Population Studies, 54*(1), 29–41.

Becht, A. I., Luyckx, K., Nelemans, S. A., Goossens, L., Branje, S. J. T., Vollebergh, W. A. M., & Meeus, W. H. J. (2019). Linking identity and depressive symptoms across adolescence: A multisample longitudinal study testing within-person effects. *Developmental Psychology, 55*(8), 1733–1742. https://doi.org/10.1037/dev0000742

Bleidorn, W., Kandler, C., Riemann, R., Angleitner, A., & Spinath, F. M. (2009). Patterns and sources of adult personality development: Growth curve analyses of the NEO PI-R scales in a longitudinal twin study. *Journal of Personality and Social Psychology, 97*(1), 142–155. https://doi.org/10.1037/a0015434

Brines, J., & Joyner, K. (1999). The ties that bind: Principles of cohesion in cohabitation and marriage. *American Sociological Review, 64*(3), 333–355. https://doi.org/10.2307/2657490

Burrow, A. L., & Hill, P. L. (2011). Purpose as a form of identity capital for positive youth adjustment. *Developmental Psychology, 47*(4), 1196–1206.

Burt, K. B., & Masten, A. S. (2010). Development in the transition to adulthood: Vulnerabilities and opportunities. In J. E. Grant & M. N. Potenza (Eds.), *Young adult mental health* (pp. 5–18). Oxford University Press.

Buss, D. M., & Schmitt, D. P. (1993). Sexual strategies theory: An evolutionary perspective on human mating. *Psychological Review, 100*(2), 204–232.

Byng-Hall, J. (1995a). Creating a secure family base: Some implications of attachment theory for family therapy. *Family Process, 34*(1), 45–58.

Byng-Hall, J. (1995b). *Rewriting family scripts: Improvisation and systems change*. Guilford Press.

Bynner, J. (2005). Rethinking the youth phase of the life-course: The case for emerging adulthood? *Journal of Youth Studies, 8*(4), 367–384.

Bynner, J. (2012). Role statuses and transitions in adolescence and young adulthood: Reflections and implications. *Longitudinal and Life Course Studies, 3*(2), 243–253.

Bynner, J., Ferri, E., & Shepherd, P. (1997). *Getting on, getting by, getting nowhere: Twenty something in Great Britain*. Ashgate.

Carroll, J. S., Willoughby, B., Badger, S., Nelson, L. J., McNamara Barry, C., & Madsen, S. D. (2007). So close, yet so far away: The impact of varying marital horizons on emerging adulthood. *Journal of Adolescent Research, 22*(3), 219–247.

Carver, K., Joyner, K., & Udry, J. R. (2003). National estimates of adolescent romantic relationships. In P. Florsheim (Ed.), *Adolescent romantic relations and sexual behavior: Theory, research, and practical implications* (pp. 23–56). Lawrence Erlbaum Associates.

Caspi, A. (2002). Social selection, social causation, and developmental pathways: Empirical strategies for better understanding how individuals and environments are linked across the life-course. In L. Pulkkinen & A. Caspi (Eds.), *Paths to successful development: Personality in the life course* (pp. 281–301). Cambridge University Press.

Caspi, A., Roberts, B. W., & Shiner, R. L. (2005). Personality development: Stability and change. *Annual Review of Psychology, 56*, 453–484.

Caspi, A., & Shiner, R. L. (2006). Personality development. In W. Damon & R. M. Lerner (Eds.), Handbook of child psychology: Social, emotional, and personality development (6th ed., Vol. 3, pp. 300–365). Hoboken, NJ: John Wiley & Sons.

CBS News. (2008, 21 July). *The Next Generation: How They Differ from Boomers, X and Y.* https://www.cbsnews.com/news/gen-x-fight-back-heres-how/

Chandler, D. E., Hall, D. T. T., & Kram, K. E. (2010). A developmental network & relational savvy approach to talent development: A low-cost alternative. *Organizational Dynamics, 39*(1), 48–56.

Chisholm, J. S. (1999). *Death, hope and sex: Steps to an evolutionary ecology of mind and morality.* Cambridge University Press.

Choi, P., Henshaw, C., Baker, S., & Tree, J. (2005). Supermum, superwife, supereverything: Performing femininity in the transition to motherhood. *Journal of Reproductive and Infant Psychology, 23*(2), 167–180.

Cholezas, I. (2014). *The economic impact of the recession on Greek youth.* Social Situation Monitor.

Christiansen, S. L., & Palkovitz, R. (2001). Why the "good provider" role still matters: Providing as a form of paternal involvement. *Journal of Family Issues, 22*(1), 84–106.

Cicchetti, D. (2006). Preface. In *Developmental psychopathology: Vol. 3. Risk, disorder, and adaptation* (2nd ed., pp. xi–xiii). John Wiley & Sons. https://doi.org/10.1002/9780470939406

Cicchetti, D., & Rogosch, F. A. (2002). A developmental psychopathology perspective on adolescence. *Journal of Consulting and Clinical Psychology, 70*(1), 6–20.

Cicchetti, D., & Toth, S. L. (1998). The development of depression in children and adolescents. *American Psychologist, 53*(2), 221–241.

Claxton, S. E., & van Dulmen, M. H. (2013). Casual sexual relationships and experiences in emerging adulthood. *Emerging Adulthood, 1(2),* 138–150. https://doi.org/10.1177/2167696813487181

Cohen, P., Kasen, S., Chen, H., Hartmark, C., & Gordon, K. (2003). Variations in patterns of developmental transitions in the emerging adulthood period. *Developmental Psychology, 39*(4), 657–669. https://doi.org/10.1037/0012-1649.39.4.657

Cole, D. A., Tram, J. M., Martin, J. M., Hoffman, K. B., Ruiz, M. D., Jacquez, F. M., & Maschman, T. L. (2002). Individual differences in the emergence of depressive symptoms in children and adolescents: A longitudinal investigation of parent and child reports. *Journal of Abnormal Psychology, 111*(1), 156–165.

Conger, R. D., Cui, M., Bryant, C. M., & Elder, G. H., Jr. (2000). Competence in early adult romantic relationships: A developmental perspective on family influences. *Journal of Personality and Social Psychology, 79*(2), 224–237.

Connolly, J., & Goldberg, A. (1999). Romantic relationships in adolescence: The role of friends and peers in their emergence and development. In W. Furman, B. B. Brown, & C. Feiring (Eds.), *The development of romantic relationships in adolescence* (pp. 266–290). Cambridge University Press. https://doi.org/10.1017/CBO9781316182185.012

Connolly, J., & McIsaac, C. (2009). Romantic relationships in adolescence. In R. M. Lerner & L. Steinberg (Eds.), *Handbook of adolescent psychology: Vol. 2. Contextual influences on adolescent development* (3rd ed., pp. 104–151). John Wiley & Sons.

Connor-Smith, J. K., & Flachsbart, C. (2007). Relations between personality and coping: A meta-analysis. *Journal of Personality and Social Psychology, 93*(6), 1080–1107.

Cook, S. H., Heinze, J. E., Miller, A. L., & Zimmerman, M. A. (2016). Transitions in friendship attachment during adolescence are associated with developmental trajectories of depression through adulthood. *Journal of Adolescent Health, 58*(3), 260–266.

Costello, D. M., Swendsen, J., Rose, J. S., & Dierker, L. C. (2008). Risk and protective factors associated with trajectories of depressed mood from adolescence to early adulthood. *Journal of Consulting and Clinical Psychology, 76*(2), 173–183.

Côté, J. E. (1996). Sociological perspectives on identity formation: The culture–identity link and identity capital. *Journal of Adolescence, 19*(5), 417–428.

Côté, J. E. (1997). An empirical test of the identity capital model. *Journal of Adolescence, 20*(5), 577–597.

Côté, J. E. (2000). *Arrested adulthood: The changing nature of maturity and identity.* New York University Press.

Côté, J. E. (2002). The role of identity capital in the transition to adulthood: The individualization thesis examined. *Journal of Youth Studies, 5*(2), 117–134.

Côté, J. E. (2006). Emerging adulthood as an institutionalized moratorium: Risks and benefits to identity formation. In J. J. Arnett & J. L. Tanner (Eds.), *Emerging adults in America: Coming of age in the 21st century* (pp. 85–116). American Psychological Association. https://doi.org/10.1037/11381-004

Côté, J. E. (2014). The dangerous myth of emerging adulthood: An evidence-based critique of a flawed developmental theory. *Applied Developmental Science, 18*(4), 177–188.

Côté, J. E., & Bynner, J. M. (2008). Changes in the transition to adulthood in the UK and Canada: The role of structure and agency in emerging adulthood. *Journal of Youth Studies, 11*(3), 251–268.

Côté, J. E., & Levine, C. G. (2002). *Identity, formation, agency, and culture: A social psychological synthesis.* Lawrence Erlbaum Associates.

Creed, P. A., Fallon, T., & Hood, M. (2009). The relationship between career adaptability, person and situation variables, and career concerns in young adults. *Journal of Vocational Behavior, 74*(2), 219–229.

Creed, P., Patton, W., & Prideaux, L.-A. (2006). Causal relationship between career indecision and career decision-making self-efficacy: A longitudinal cross-lagged analysis. *Journal of Career Development, 33*(1), 47–65. https://doi.org/10.1177/0894845306289535

Crittenden, P. M. (2006). Why do inadequate parents do what they do? In O. Mayseless (Ed.), *Parenting representations: Theory, research, and clinical applications* (pp. 388–433). Cambridge University Press.

Crittenden, P. M., Lang, C., Claussen, A. H., & Partridge, M. F. (2000). Relations among mothers' dispositional representations of parenting. In P. M. Crittenden & A. H. Claussen (Eds.), *The organization of attachment relationships: Maturation, culture, and context* (pp. 214–233). Cambridge University Press.

Cuzzocrea, V. (2019). Moratorium or waithood? Forms of time-taking and the changing shape of youth. *Time & Society, 28*(2), 567–586.

Davies, L. (2014, September 23). Sardinian town finds novel way to cut unemployment: Pay people to leave. *The Guardian.* https://www.theguardian.com/world/2014/sep/23/sardinian-town-novel-way-cut-unemployment-pay-people-to-leave

De Bolle, M., Beyers, W., De Clercq, B., & De Fruyt, F. (2012). General personality and psychopathology in referred and nonreferred children and adolescents: An investigation of continuity, pathoplasty, and complication models. *Journal of Abnormal Psychology, 121*(4), 958–970.

Deci, E. L., & Ryan, R. M. (1985). The general causality orientations scale: Self-determination in personality. *Journal of Research in Personality, 19*(2), 109–134.

Del Corso, J., & Rehfuss, M. C. (2011). The role of narrative in career construction theory. *Journal of Vocational Behavior, 79*(2), 334–339.

Del Giudice, M., & Belsky, J. (2011). The development of life history strategies: Toward a multi-stage theory. In D. M. Buss & P. H. Hawley (Eds.), *The evolution of personality and individual differences* (pp. 154–176). Oxford University Press.

Derogatis, L. R., & Melisaratos, N. (1983). The Brief Symptom Inventory: An introductory report. *Psychological Medicine, 13*, 595–605.

Desai, S., & Andrist, L. (2010). Gender scripts and age at marriage in India. *Demography, 47*(3), 667–687.

Dhariwal, A., Connolly, J., Paciello, M., & Caprara, G. V. (2009). Adolescent peer relationships and emerging adult romantic styles: A longitudinal study of youth in an Italian community. *Journal of Adolescent Research, 24*(5), 579–600.

Dienhart, A. (2001). Make room for daddy: The pragmatic potentials of a tag-team structure for sharing parenting. *Journal of Family Issues, 22*(8), 973–999.

Dietrich, J., Jokisaari, M., & Nurmi, J. E. (2012). Work-related goal appraisals and stress during the transition from education to work. *Journal of Vocational Behavior, 80*(1), 82–92.

Dietrich, J., Parker, P., & Salmela-Aro, K. (2012). Phase-adequate engagement at the post-school transition. *Developmental Psychology, 48*, 1575–1593.

Dietrich, J., Shulman, S., & Nurmi, J. E. (2013). Goal pursuit in young adulthood: The role of personality and motivation in goal appraisal trajectories across 6 years. *Journal of Research in Personality, 47*(6), 728–737.

Donnellan, M. B., Conger, R. D., & Burzette, R. G. (2007). Personality development from late adolescence to young adulthood: Differential stability, normative maturity, and evidence for the maturity–stability hypothesis. *Journal of Personality, 75*(2), 237–264.

Donnellan, M. B., Hill, P. L., & Roberts, B. W. (2015). Personality development across the life span: Current findings and future directions. In *APA handbook of personality and social psychology: Vol. 4. Personality processes and individual differences* (pp. 107–126). American Psychological Association.

Donnellan, M. B., Larsen-Rife, D., & Conger, R. D. (2005). Personality, family history, and competence in early adult romantic relationships. *Journal of Personality and Social Psychology, 88*(3), 562–576.

Dougherty, T. W., Cheung, Y. H., & Florea, L. (2008). The role of personality in employee developmental networks. *Journal of Managerial Psychology, 23*(6), 653–669.

Dowdy, B. B., & Kliewer, W. (1998). Dating, parent–adolescent conflict, and behavioral autonomy. *Journal of Youth and Adolescence, 27*(4), 473–492.

Downey, G., & Feldman, S. I. (1996). Implications of rejection sensitivity for intimate relationships. *Journal of Personality and Social Psychology, 70*(6), 1327–1343.

Duffy, R. D., & Blustein, D. L. (2005). The relationship between spirituality, religiousness, and career adaptability. *Journal of Vocational Behavior, 67*(3), 429–440.

Duncan, M. J., Eyre, E. L., Bryant, E., Seghers, J., Galbraith, N., & Nevill, A. M. (2017). Autonomous motivation mediates the relation between goals for physical activity and physical activity behavior in adolescents. *Journal of Health Psychology, 22*(5), 595–604. https://doi.org/10.1177/1359105315609089

Durbin, C. E., & Hicks, B. M. (2014). Personality and psychopathology: A stagnant field in need of development. *European Journal of Personality, 28*(4), 362–386.

Edwards, J. R., & Rothbard, N. P. (2000). Mechanisms linking work and family: Clarifying the relationship between work and family constructs. *Academy of Management Review, 25*(1), 178–199.

Elder, G. H. (1998). The life course as developmental theory. *Child Development, 69*(1), 1–12.

Elder, G. H., & Giele, J. Z. (2009). *The craft of life course research*. Guilford Press.
Elder, G. H., Johnson, M. K., & Crosnoe, R. (2003). The emergence and development of life course theory. In J. T. Mortimer & M. J. Shanahan (Eds.), *Handbook of the life course* (pp. 3–19). Springer.
Ellis, B. J. (2004). Timing of pubertal maturation in girls: An integrated life history approach. *Psychological Bulletin, 130*(6), 920–958.
Ellis, B. J., & Del Giudice, M. (2019). Developmental adaptation to stress: An evolutionary perspective. *Annual Review of Psychology, 70*, 111–139.
Ellis, B. J., Figueredo, A. J., Brumbach, B. H., & Schlomer, G. L. (2009). Fundamental dimensions of environmental risk. *Human Nature, 20*(2), 204–268.
Ellis, B. J., Jackson, J. J., & Boyce, W. T. (2006). The stress response systems: Universality and adaptive individual differences. *Developmental Review, 26*(2), 175–212.
Erikson, E. (1968). *Identity: Youth and crisis*. W. W. Norton.
European Group for Integrated Social Research. (2001). Misleading trajectories: Transition dilemmas of young adults in Europe. *Journal of Youth Studies, 4*, 101–118.
European Parliament. (2015). Youth unemployment in Greece: Situation before the government change. Europa. Ea. https://www.europarl.europa.eu
Eurostat. (2017). *Europe in figures—Eurostat yearbook*. Retrieved from http://ec.europa.eu/eurostat/statistics-explained/index.php/Europe_in_figures_-_Eurostat_yearbook
Evans, G. W., Li, D., & Whipple, S. S. (2013). Cumulative risk and child development. *Psychological Bulletin, 139*(6), 1342–1396.
Evans, K., & Heinz, W. R. (1994). *Becoming adults in the 1990s*. Anglo German Foundation.
Evertsson, M. (2012). The importance of work: Changing work commitment following the transition to motherhood. *Acta Sociologica, 56*(2), 139–153.
Eyre, S. L., Flythe, M., Hoffman, V., & Fraser, A. E. (2012). Primary relationship scripts among lower-income, African American young adults. *Family Process, 51*(2), 234–249.
Fadjukoff, P., Kokko, K., & Pulkkinen, L. (2010). Changing economic conditions and identity formation in adulthood. *European Psychologist, 15*(4), 293–303. https://doi.org/10.1027/1016-9040/a000061
Farand, C. (2017, July 13). The brain drain and youth depression taking over Greece. *The Independent*. https://www.independent.co.uk/news/long_reads/greece-austerity-cuts-pensions-athens-a7838756.html
Ferrucci, L., & Porcheddu, D. (2004). *La new economy nel Mezzogiorno: Istituzioni e imprese fra progettualità e contingencies in Sardegna*. Il mulino. Fiese, B. H., Hooker, K. A., Kotary, L., Schwagler, J., & Rimmer, M. (1995). Family stories in the early stages of parenthood. *Journal of Marriage and the Family, 57*, 763–770. https://doi.org/10.2307/353930
Fiese, B. H., & Pratt, M. W. (2004). Metaphors and meanings of family stories: Integrating life course and systems perspectives on narrative. In M. W. Pratt & B. H. Fiese (Eds.), *Family stories and the life course: Across time and generations* (pp. 401–418). Lawrence Erlbaum Associates.
Fiese, B. H., & Skillman, G. (2000). Gender differences in family stories: Moderating influence of parent gender role and child gender. *Sex Roles, 43*(5–6), 267–283. Fingerman, K. L., Cheng, Y. P., Wesselmann, E. D., Zarit, S., Furstenberg, F., & Birditt, K. S. (2012). Helicopter parents and landing pad kids: Intense parental support of grown children. *Journal of Marriage and Family, 74*(4), 880–896.
Fingerman, K. L., & Yahirun, J. J. (2016). Emerging adulthood in the context of family: Young adults' relationships with parents. In J. J. Arnett (Ed.), *Oxford handbook of emerging adulthood* (pp. 163–176). New York: Oxford University Press.

Fleeson, W., & Cantor, N. (1995). Goal relevance and the affective experience of daily life: Ruling out situational explanations. *Motivation and Emotion, 19*, 25-57.

Fonagy, P., Gergely, G., Jurist, E. L., & Target, M. (2002). *Affect regulation, mentalization, and the development of the self*. Other Press.

Fonagy, P., & Target, M. (2005). Bridging the transmission gap: An end to an important mystery of attachment research? *Attachment & Human Development, 7*(3), 333-343. https://doi.org/10.1080/14616730500269278

Fonagy, P., Target, M., Steele, H., & Steele, M. (1998). *Reflective-functioning manual, version 5.0, for application to adult attachment interviews*. University College London.

Freund, A. M., & Baltes, P. B. (2002). Life-management strategies of selection, optimization and compensation: Measurement by self-report and construct validity. *Journal of Personality and Social Psychology, 82*(4), 642-662.

Frone, M. R., Yardley, J. K., & Markel, K. S. (1997). Developing and testing an integrative model of the work-family interface. *Journal of Vocational Behavior, 50*(2), 145-167.

Furlong, A., & Cartmel, F. (2007). *Young people and social change: Individualization and risk in late modernity* (2nd ed.). Open University Press.

Furman, W., & Buhrmester, D. (1985). Children's perceptions of the personal relationships in their social networks. *Developmental Psychology, 21*, 1016-1024. https://doi.org/10.1037/0012-1649.21.6.1016

Furman, W., & Wehner, E. A. (1997). Adolescent romantic relationships: A developmental perspective. *New Directions for Child and Adolescent Development, 1997*(78), 21-36.

Furman, W., & Winkles, J. K. (2012). Transformations in heterosexual romantic relationships across the transition into adulthood. In B. Laursen & W. A. Collins (Eds.), *Relationship pathways: From adolescence to young adulthood* (pp. 191-213). Sage Publications.Fussell, E., & Furstenberg, F. F., Jr. (2005). *The transition to adulthood during the twentieth century: Race, nativity, and gender*. University of Chicago Press.

Galambos, N. L., Barker, E. T., & Krahn, H. J. (2006). Depression, self-esteem, and anger in emerging adulthood: Seven-year trajectories. *Developmental Psychology, 42*(2), 350-365.

Galanaki, E., & Sideridis, G. (2019). Dimensions of emerging adulthood, criteria for adulthood, and identity development in Greek studying youth: A person-centered approach. *Emerging Adulthood, 7*(6), 411-431.

Gangestad, S. W., & Simpson, J. A. (2000). The evolution of human mating: Trade-offs and strategic pluralism. *Behavioral and Brain Sciences, 23*(4), 573-587.

Garber, J., Keiley, M. K., & Martin, N. C. (2002). Developmental trajectories of adolescents' depressive symptoms: Predictors of change. *Journal of Consulting and Clinical Psychology, 70*(1), 79-95.

Ge, X., Natsuaki, M. N., & Conger, R. D. (2006). Trajectories of depressive symptoms and stressful life events among male and female adolescents in divorced and nondivorced families. *Development and Psychopathology, 18*(1), 253-273.

Gilligan, C. (1982). Adult development and women's development: Arrangements for a marriage. In *Women in the middle years* (pp. 89-114). John Wiley & Sons.

Gollwitzer, P. M. (1999). Implementation intentions: Strong effects of simple plans. *American Psychologist, 54*(7), 493-503.

Granic, I. (2005). Timing is everything: Developmental psychopathology from a dynamic systems perspective. *Developmental Review, 25*(3-4), 386-407.

Greenhaus, J. H., & Powell, G. N. (2006). When work and family are allies: A theory of work-family enrichment. *Academy of Management Review, 31*(1), 72-92.

Greenhoot, A. F., & McLean, K. C. (2013). Introduction to this Special Issue Meaning in personal memories: Is more always better? *Memory, 21*(1), 2–9.

Grob, A., Krings, F., & Bangerte, A. (2001). Life markers in biographical narratives of people from three cohorts: A life span perspective in its historical context. *Human Development, 44*, 171–190.

Grossmann, K., Grossmann, K. E., Fremmer-Bombik, E., Kindler, H., Scheuerer-Englisch, H., & Zimmermann, A. P. (2002). The uniqueness of the child–father attachment relationship: Fathers' sensitive and challenging play as a pivotal variable in a 16-year longitudinal study. *Social Development, 11*(3), 301–337.

Grzywacz, J. G., & Marks, N. F. (2000). Family, work, work–family spillover, and problem drinking during midlife. *Journal of Marriage and Family, 62*(2), 336–348.

Guzzo, K. B. (2014). Trends in cohabitation outcomes: Compositional changes and engagement among never-married young adults. *Journal of Marriage and the Family, 76*(4), 826–842. https://doi.org/10.1111/jomf.12123

Haase, C. M., Heckhausen, J., & Köller, O. (2008). Goal engagement during the school-work transition: Beneficial for all, particularly for girls. *Journal of Research on Adolescence, 18*(4), 671–698.

Habermas, T., & Bluck, S. (2000). Getting a life: The emergence of the life story in adolescence. *Psychological Bulletin, 126*(5), 748–769. Hafen, C. A., Spilker, A., Chango, J., Marston, E. S., & Allen, J. P. (2014). To accept or reject? The impact of adolescent rejection sensitivity on early adult romantic relationships. *Journal of Research on Adolescence, 24*(1), 55–64.

Halpern-Meekin, S., Manning, W. D., Giordano, P. C., & Longmore, M. A. (2013). Relationship churning in emerging adulthood: On/off relationships and sex with an ex. *Journal of Adolescent Research, 28*(2), 166–188.

Harter, S., Bresnick, S., Bouchey, H. A., & Whitesell, N. R. (1997). The development of multiple role-related selves during adolescence. *Development and Psychopathology, 9*(4), 835–853.

Hauser, S. T., & Greene, W. M. (1991). Passages from late adolescence to early adulthood. In S. I. Greenspan & G. H. Pollock (Eds.), *The course of life: Vol. 4. Adolescence* (pp. 377–405). International Universities Press.

Heckhausen, J. (1999). *Developmental regulation in adulthood: Age-normative and sociostructural constraints as adaptive challenges.* Cambridge University Press.

Heckhausen, J., Wrosch, C., & Schulz, R. (2010). A motivational theory of life-span development. *Psychological Review, 117*(1), 32–60.

Heckman, J. (1994). Is job training oversold? *The Public Interest, 115*, 91–115.

Heinz, W. R. (1999). Introduction: Transitions to employment in a cross-national perspective. In W. R. Heinz (Ed.), *From education to work: Cross-national perspectives* (pp. 1–24). Cambridge University Press. Heinz, W. R. (2001). Work and the life course: A cosmopolitan-local perspective. In V. W. Marshall, H. Krueger, W. R. Heinz, & A. Verma (Eds.), *Restructuring work and the life course* (pp. 3–22). University of Toronto Press.

Heinz, W. R. (2002). Transition discontinuities and the biographical shaping of early work careers. *Journal of Vocational Behavior, 60*(2), 220–240.

Hendry, L. B., & Kloep, M. (2007). Conceptualizing emerging adulthood: Inspecting the emperor's new clothes? *Child Development Perspectives, 1*(2), 74–79.

Hill, J. P., & Lynch, M. E. (1983). The intensification of gender-related role expectations during early adolescence. In J. Brooks-Gunn & A. C. Petersen (Eds.), *Girls at puberty: Biological and psychosocial perspectives* (pp. 201–228). Springer.

Hofstede, G. (1991). Empirical models of cultural differences. In N. Bleichrodt & P. J. D. Drenth (Eds.), *Contemporary issues in cross-cultural psychology* (pp. 4–20). Swets & Zeitlinger.

Hofstede, G. (2001). *Culture's consequences: Comparing values, behaviors, institutions and organizations across nations.* Sage Publications.

Honwana, A. (2014). "Waithood": Youth transitions and social change. In D. Foeken, T. Dietz, L. de Haan, & L. Johnson (Eds.), *Development and equity: An interdisciplinary exploration* (pp. 28–40). Brill.

Horner, M. S. (1972). Toward an understanding of achievement-related conflicts in women. *Journal of Social Issues, 28*, 157–175.

Hownana, A. (2012). "Desenrascar a vida": Youth employment and transitions to adulthood. In *III Conferência Internacional do IESE "Moçambique: Acumulação e transformação em contexto de crise internacional,"* Maputo, Mozambique, September (pp. 4–5).

Howden, D., & Baboulias, Y. (2015, July 26). Who'd be young and Greek? Searching for a future after the debt crisis. *The Guardian.* https://www.theguardian.com/global/2015/jul/26/greece-youth-unemployment-debt-crisis-eurozone

Hudson, N. W., Roberts, B. W., & Lodi-Smith, J. (2012). Personality trait development and social investment in work. *Journal of Research in Personality, 46*(3), 334–344.

Hutteman, R., Hennecke, M., Orth, U., Reitz, A. K., & Specht, J. (2014). Developmental tasks as a framework to study personality development in adulthood and old age. *European Journal of Personality, 28*(3), 267–278.

Hutteman, R., Nestler, S., Wagner, J., Egloff, B., & Back, M. D. (2015). Wherever I may roam: Processes of self-esteem development from adolescence to emerging adulthood in the context of international student exchange. *Journal of Personality and Social Psychology, 108*(5), 767–783.

Iannelli, C., & Smyth, E. (2008). Mapping gender and social background differences in education and youth transitions across Europe. *Journal of Youth Studies, 11*, 213–232.

International Labour Organization. (2019). *Unemployment, youth total (% of total labor force ages 15–24).* Retrieved from https://data.worldbank.org

Italian Institute of Statistics. (2015). *Italy in figures 2014.* Retrieved from https://www.istat.it/it/files//2015/03/07-labour-market.pdf

Jack, D. C. (1991). *Silencing the self: Women and depression.* Harvard University Press.

Jones, G. W. (2004). Not "when to marry" but "whether to marry": The changing context of marriage decisions in East and Southeast Asia. In G. W. Jones & K. Ramdas (Eds.), *Untying the knot: Ideal and reality in Asian marriage* (pp. 3–56). Asia Research Institute, National University of Singapore.

Jones, G. W. (2007). Delayed marriage and very low fertility in Pacific Asia. *Population and Development Review, 33*(3), 453–478.

Jordan, J. V. (2004). Toward competence and connection. In J. V. Jordan, M. Walker, & L. M. Hartling (Eds.), *The complexity of connection: Writings from the Stone Center's Jean Baker Miller Training Institute* (pp. 11–27). Guilford Press.

Kan, M. L., McHale, S. M., & Crouter, A. C. (2008). Parental involvement in adolescent romantic relationships: Patterns and correlates. *Journal of Youth and Adolescence, 37*(2), 168–179.

Karoly, L. A. (2009). The future at work: Labor-market realities and the transition to adulthood. In I. Schoon & R. K. Silbereisen (Eds.), *Transitions from school to work: Globalization, individualization, and patterns of diversity* (pp. 352–384). Cambridge University Press.

Kern, M. L., Benson, L., Steinberg, E. A., & Steinberg, L. (2016). The EPOCH measure of adolescent well-being. *Psychological Assessment*, *28*(5), 586–597. https://doi.org/10.1037/pas0000201

Kessler, R. C., Berglund, P., Demler, O., Jin, R., Merikangas, K. R., & Walters, E. E. (2005). Lifetime prevalence and age-of-onset distributions of DSM-IV disorders in the National Comorbidity Survey Replication. *Archives of General Psychiatry*, *62*(6), 593–602.

Kidd, J. M., Hirsh, W., & Jackson, C. (2004). Straight talking: The nature of effective career discussion at work. *Journal of Career Development*, *30*(4), 231–245.

Kiernan, K. (2000). European perspective on union formation. In L. J. Waite (Ed.), *The ties that bind* (pp. 40–58). Aldine de Gruyter.

Klimstra, T. A., & Denissen, J. J. (2017). A theoretical framework for the associations between identity and psychopathology. *Developmental Psychology*, *53*(11), 2052–2065.

Klimstra, T. A., Luyckx, K., Hale, W. W., III, & Goossens, L. (2014). Personality and externalizing behavior in the transition to young adulthood: The additive value of personality facets. *Social Psychiatry and Psychiatric Epidemiology*, *49*(8), 1319–1333.

Knight, R. (2011). Fragmentation, fluidity and transformation Nonlinear development in middle childhood. *The Psychoanalytic Study of the Child*, *65*, 19–47.

Koestner, R., Otis, N., Powers, T. A., Pelletier, L., & Gagnon, H. (2008). Autonomous motivation, controlled motivation, and goal progress. *Journal of Personality*, *76*(5), 1201–1230.

Krahn, H. J., Howard, A. L., & Galambos, N. L. (2013). Exploring or floundering? The meaning of employment and educational fluctuations in emerging adulthood. *Youth & Society*, *47*(2), 245–266. https://doi.org/10.1177/0044118X12459061

Krichly-Katz, T., Rosen-Zvi, I., & Ziv, N. (2018). Hierarchy and stratification in the Israeli legal profession. *Law & Society Review*, *52*(2), 436–464. https://doi.org/10.1111/lasr.12325

Krueger, R. F., Caspi, A., & Moffitt, T. E. (2000). Epidemiological personology: The unifying role of personality in population-based research on problem behaviors. *Journal of Personality*, *68*(6), 967–998.

Kvitkovičová, L., Umemura, T., & Macek, P. (2017). Roles of attachment relationships in emerging adults' career decision-making process: A two-year longitudinal research design. *Journal of Vocational Behavior*, *101*, 119–132.

Lachover, A. (2014). "Why women still can't have it all": Israeli media discourse on motherhood vs. career. HAGAR—Studies in culture, polity and identities. Special issue. *Women and Work from Feminist Perspectives*, *11*(2), 105–126.

Laney, E. K., Hall, M. E. L., Anderson, T. L., & Willingham, M. M. (2015). Becoming a mother: The influence of motherhood on women's identity development. *Identity*, *15*(2), 126–145.

Laursen, B., & Williams, V. A. (1997). Perceptions of interdependence and closeness in family and peer relationships among adolescents with and without romantic partners. *New Directions for Child and Adolescent Development*, *1997*(78), 3–20.

Leccardi, C. (2005). Facing uncertainty: Temporality and biographies in the new century. *Young*, *13*(2), 123–146.

Leccardi, C. (2006). Redefining the future: Youthful biographical constructions in the 21st century. *New Directions for Child and Adolescent Development*, *2006*(113), 37–48.

Leccardi, C. (2009). Widersprüchliche zeiten: Beschleunigung und verlangsamung in biographien junger frauen und männer. In V. King & G. Gerisch (Eds.), *Zeitgewinn und selbstverlust. Folgen und grenzen der beschleunigung* (pp. 242–260). Campus Verlag.

REFERENCES

Legault, L., Green-Demers, I., & Pelletier, L. (2006). Why do high school students lack motivation in the classroom? Toward an understanding of academic amotivation and the role of social support. *Journal of Educational Psychology, 98*(3), 567–582.

Lent, R. W., & Brown, S. D. (2006). Integrating person and situation perspectives on work satisfaction: A social-cognitive view, *Journal of Vocational Behavior, 69*(2), 236–247.

Lent, R. W., Brown, S. D., & Hackett, G. (2002). Social cognitive career theory. *Career Choice and Development, 4*, 255–311.

Lerner, R. M. (1982). Children and adolescents are producers of their development. *Developmental Review, 2*, 242–309.

Lerner, R. M. (1998). Theories of human development: Contemporary perspectives. In W. Damon & R. M. Lerner (Eds.), *Handbook of child psychology: Theoretical models of human development* (p. 1–24). John Wiley & Sons.

Levinson, D. J. (1978). *The seasons of a man's life*. Ballantine Books.

Levinson, D. J. (1996). *The seasons of a woman's life*. Alfred A. Knopf.

Lewis, D. M. (2011). *Intimacy, passion, and commitment as predictors of couples' relationship satisfaction*. ProQuest Dissertations Publishing.

Lichter, D. T., Turner, R. N., & Sassler, S. (2010). National estimates of the rise in serial cohabitation. *Social Science Research, 39*(5), 754–765.

Lieblich, A., Tuval-Mashiach, R., & Zilber, T. (1998). *Narrative research: Reading, analysis, and interpretation*. Sage.

Liem, G. A. D. (2016). Academic and social achievement goals: Their additive, interactive, and specialized effects on school functioning. *British Journal of Educational Psychology, 86*(1), 37–56.

Little, B. R. (1983). Personal projects: A rationale and method for investigation. *Environment and Behavior, 15*(3), 273–309. https://doi.org/10.1177/0013916583153002

Little, B. R., Salmela-Aro, K., & Phillips, S. D. (Eds.). (2007). *Personal project pursuit: Goals, action, and human flourishing*. Lawrence Erlbaum Associates.

Locke, E. A., & Latham, G. P. (2002). Building a practically useful theory of goal setting and task motivation: A 35-year odyssey. *American Psychologist, 57*(9), 705–717.

Lowe, K., & Dotterer, A. M. (2018). Parental involvement during the college transition: A review and suggestion for its conceptual definition. *Adolescent Research Review, 3*(1), 29–42.

Lüdtke, O., Roberts, B. W., Trautwein, U., & Nagy, G. (2011). A random walk down university avenue: Life paths, life events, and personality trait change at the transition to university life. *Journal of Personality and Social Psychology, 101*(3), 620–637.

Luthar, S. S., & Cicchetti, D. (2000). The construct of resilience: Implications for interventions and social policies. *Development and Psychopathology, 12*(4), 857–885.

Luthar, S. S., Cicchetti, D., & Becker, B. (2000). The construct of resilience: A critical evaluation and guidelines for future work. *Child Development, 71*(3), 543–562. https://doi.org/10.1111/1467-8624.00164

Luyckx, K., Duriez, B., Klimstra, T. A., & De Witte, H. (2010). Identity statuses in young adult employees: Prospective relations with work engagement and burnout. *Journal of Vocational Behavior, 77*(3), 339–349.

Luyckx, K., Goossens, L., Soenens, B., & Beyers, W. (2006). Unpacking commitment and exploration: Preliminary validation of an integrative model of late adolescent identity formation. *Journal of Adolescence, 29*(3), 361–378.

Macapagal, K., Greene, G. J., Rivera, Z., & Mustanski, B. (2015). "The best is always yet to come": Relationship stages and processes among young LGBT couples. *Journal of Family Psychology, 29*(3), 309–320. https://doi.org/10.1037/fam0000094

Maccoby, E. E. (1990). Gender and relationships: A developmental account. *American Psychologist*, 45(4), 513–520.

Macmillan, R., & Copher, R. (2005). Families in the life course: Interdependency of roles, role configurations, and pathways. *Journal of Marriage and Family*, 67(4), 858–879.

Maddux, J. E., & Volkmann, J. R. (2010). Self-efficacy and self-regulation. In R. H. Hoyle (Ed.), *Handbook of personality and self-regulation* (pp. 315–331). Wiley-Blackwell.

Madsen, S. D. (2008). Parents' management of adolescents' romantic relationships through dating rules: Gender variations and correlates of relationship qualities. *Journal of Youth and Adolescence*, 37(9), 1044–1058.

Mandich, G. (2009). *Quotidiano flessibile. L'esperienza del tempo nella sardegna della new economy*. AM&D Edizioni.

Manning, W. D. (2013). Trends in cohabitation: Over twenty years of change, 1987–2010. *Studies*, 54, 29–41.

Manning, W. D., Giordano, P. S., Longmore, M. A., & Hocevar, A. (2011). Romantic relationships and academic/career trajectories in early adulthood. In F. D. Fincham & M. Cui (Eds.), *Romantic relationships in emerging adulthood* (pp. 317–333). Cambridge University Press.

Manning, W. D., & Smock, P. A. J. (2005). Measuring and modeling cohabitation: New perspectives from qualitative data. *Journal of Marriage and Family*, 67(4), 989–1002. https://doi.org/10.1111/j.1741-3737.2005.00189.x

Marcia, J. E. (1980). Identity in adolescence. In J. Adelson (Ed.), *Handbook of adolescent psychology* (pp. 159–187). John Wiley & Sons.

Marcia, J. E. (2002). Identity and psychosocial development in adulthood. *Identity: An International Journal of Theory and Research*, 2(1), 7–28.

Masquelier, A. (2019). *Fada: Boredom and belonging in Niger*. University of Chicago Press.

Masten, A. S. (2006). Developmental psychopathology: Pathways to the future. *International Journal of Behavioral Development*, 30(1), 47–54.

Masten, A. S. (2016). Resilience in developing systems: The promise of integrated approaches. *European Journal of Developmental Psychology*, 13(3), 297–312.

Masten, A. S., Hubbard, J. J., Gest, S. D., Tellegen, A., Garmezy, N., & Ramirez, M. (1999). Competence in the context of adversity: Pathways to resilience and maladaptation from childhood to late adolescence. *Development and Psychopathology*, 11(1), 143–169.

Masten, A. S., & Kalstabakken, A. W. (2018). Developmental perspectives on psychopathology in children and adolescents. In J. N. Butcher & P. C. Kendall (Eds.), *APA handbook of psychopathology: Child and adolescent psychopathology* (pp. 15–36). American Psychological Association. https://doi.org/10.1037/0000065-002

Maticka-Tyndale, E., Herold, E. S., & Oppermann, M. (2003). Casual sex among Australian schoolies. *Journal of Sex Research*, 40(2), 158–169.

Mayes, L. C. (2001). The twin poles of order and chaos: Development as a dynamic, self-ordering system. *The Psychoanalytic Study of the Child*, 56(1), 137–170.

Mayseless, O., & Scharf, M. (2003). What does it mean to be an adult? The Israeli experience. *New Directions for Child and Adolescent Development*, (100), 5–20. https://doi.org/10.1002/cd.71

McAdams, D. P. (1993). *The stories we live by: Personal myths and the making of the self*. Guilford Press.

McAdams, D. P. (2001). The Psychology of Life Stories. *Review of General Psychology*, 5(2), 100–122. https://doi.org/10.1037/1089-2680.5.2.100

McAdams, D. P. (2006). The redemptive self: Generativity and the stories Americans live by. *Research in Human Development, 3*(2-3), 81-100. McAdams, D. P. (2013a). Life authorship: A psychological challenge for emerging adulthood, as illustrated in two notable case studies. *Emerging Adulthood, 1*(2), 151-158.

McAdams, D. P. (2013b). The psychological self as actor, agent, and author. *Perspectives on Psychological Science, 8*(3), 272-295.

McAdams, D. P., & Cox, K. S. (2010). Self and identity across the life span. In R. M. Lerner, M. E. Lamb, & A. M. Freund (Eds.), *The handbook of life-span development* (pp. 158-207). John Wiley & Sons. https://doi.org/10.1002/9780470880166.hlsd002006

McAdams, D. P., & de St. Aubin, E. D. (1992). A theory of generativity and its assessment through self-report, behavioral acts, and narrative themes in autobiography. *Journal of Personality and Social Psychology, 62*(6), 1003-1015.

McAdams, D. P., & McLean, K. C. (2013). Narrative identity. *Current Directions in Psychological Science, 22*(3), 233-238.

McAdams, D. P., & Pals, J. L. (2006). A new Big Five: Fundamental principles for an integrative science of personality. *American Psychologist, 61*(3), 204-217.

McCrae, R. R., & Costa, P. T., Jr. (2008). The five-factor theory of personality. In O. P. John, R. W. Robins, & L. A. Pervin (Eds.), *Handbook of personality: Theory and research* (pp. 159-181). Guilford Press.

McDonald, S., Erickson, L. D., Johnson, M. K., & Elder, G. H. (2007). Informal mentoring and young adult employment. *Social Science Research, 36*(4), 1328-1347.

McLean, K. C., Pasupathi, M., & Pals, J. L. (2007). Selves creating stories creating selves: A process model of self-development. *Personality and Social Psychology Review, 11*(3), 262-278.

McLean, K. C., & Pratt, M. W. (2006). Life's little (and big) lessons: Identity statuses and meaning-making in the turning point narratives of emerging adults. *Developmental Psychology, 42*(4), 714-722.

Meadows, S. O., Brown, J. S., & Elder, G. H. (2006). Depressive symptoms, stress, and support: Gendered trajectories from adolescence to young adulthood. *Journal of Youth and Adolescence, 35*(1), 89-99.

Meece, J. L., Glienke, B. B., & Burg, S. (2006). Gender and motivation. *Journal of School Psychology, 44*(5), 351-373.

Meeus, W., van de Schoot, R., Keijsers, L., & Branje, S. (2012). Identity statuses as developmental trajectories: A five-wave longitudinal study in early-to-middle and middle-to-late adolescents. *Journal of Youth and Adolescence, 41*(8), 1008-1021.

Meier, A., & Allen, G. (2009). Romantic relationships from adolescence to young adulthood: Evidence from the National Longitudinal Study of Adolescent Health. *The Sociological Quarterly, 50*(2), 308-335.

Mercer, R. T. (2004). Becoming a mother versus maternal role attainment. *Journal of Nursing Scholarship, 36*(3), 226-232.

Michaeli, Y., Dickson, D. J., Hakhmigari, M. K., Scharf, M., & Shulman, S. (2022). Change in self-criticism across emerging adulthood and psychological well-being at age 35: The mediating role of reflectivity. *Emerging Adulthood, 10*(2), 323-334.

Michaeli, Y., Kalfon Hakhmigari, M., Scharf, M., & Shulman, S. (2018). Romantic outcomes in young adulthood: The role of dependency, parental support, and reflective functioning. *Journal of Family Psychology, 32*(7), 873-881.

Mitra, D., & Arnett, J. J. (2021). Life choices of emerging adults in India. *Emerging Adulthood, 9(3),* 229-239. https://doi.org/10.1177/2167696819851891

Mongili, A. (2015). Modelli di innovazione e politiche dell'innovazione. Il caso del Parco scientifico e tecnologico della Sardegna. In A. Mongili (Ed.), *Topologie postcoloniali innovazione e modernizzazione in Sardegna* (pp. 283–301). Condaghes.

Morch, S. (1997). Youth and activity theory. In L. Bynner, L. Chisholm, & A. Furlong (Eds.), *Youth citizenship and social change in European context* (pp. 245–261). Ashgate.

Mortimer, J. T., & Johnson, M. K. (1998). New perspectives on adolescent work and the transition to adulthood. In R. Jessor (Ed.), *New perspectives on adolescent risk behavior* (pp. 425–496). Cambridge University Press.

Mroczek, D. K., & Spiro, A. (2007). Personality change influences mortality in older men. *Psychological Science, 18*(5), 371–376.

Nagin, D. S., & Tremblay, R. E. (2005). What has been learned from group-based trajectory modeling? Examples from physical aggression and other problem behaviors. *The Annals of the American Academy of Political and Social Science, 602*(1), 82–117.

Nelson, L. J., Duan, X. x., Padilla-Walker, L. M., & Luster, S. S. (2013). Facing adulthood: Comparing the criteria that Chinese emerging adults and their parents have for adulthood. *Journal of Adolescent Research, 28*(2), 189–208. https://doi.org/10.1177/0743558412467685

Nelson, L. J., & Padilla-Walker, L. M. (2013). Flourishing and floundering in emerging adult college students. *Emerging Adulthood, 1*(1), 67–78.

Norona, J. C., Tregubenko, V., Boiangiu, S. B., Levy, G., Scharf, M., Welsh, D. P., & Shulman, S. (2018). Changes in rejection sensitivity across adolescence and emerging adulthood: Associations with relationship involvement, quality, and coping. *Journal of Adolescence, 63*, 96–106.

Nurmi, J.-E. (2004). *Socialization and self-development: Channeling, selection, adjustment, and reflection.* In R. M. Lerner & L. Steinberg (Eds.), *Handbook of adolescent psychology* (pp. 85–124). John Wiley & Sons.

O'Connor, T. G., Allen, J. P., Bell, K. L., & Hauser, S. T. (1996). Adolescent–parent relationships and leaving home in young adulthood. *New Directions for Child and Adolescent Development, 1996*(71), 39–52.

OECD (2021). Israel Education at a Glance 2021: OECD Indicators. https://www.oecd-ilibrary.org

Oppenheimer, V. K. (2003). Cohabiting and marriage during young men's career-development process. *Demography, 40*(1), 127–149.

Organisation for Economic Co-operation and Development. (2022). *OECD labour force statistics 2021.* https://doi.org/10.1787/177e93b9-en

Orlofsky, J. L. (1993). Intimacy status: Theory and research. In *Ego identity: A handbook for psychosocial research* (pp. 111–133). Springer.

Orlofsky, J. L., & Roades, L. A. (1993). Intimacy status interview and rating scales. In *Ego identity: A handbook for psychosocial research* (pp. 334–358). Springer.

Orth, U., Robins, R. W., & Widaman, K. F. (2012). Life-span development of self-esteem and its effects on important life outcomes. *Journal of Personality and Social Psychology, 102*(6), 1271–1288.

Osgood, D. W., Ruth, G., Eccles, J. S., Jacobs, J. E., & Barber, B. L. (2005). Six paths to adulthood: Fast starters, parents without careers, educated partners, educated singles, working singles, and slow starters. In R. A. Settersten, Jr., F. F. Furstenberg, Jr., & R. G. Rumbaut (Eds.), *On the frontier of adulthood: Theory, research, and public policy* (pp. 320–355). University of Chicago Press.

Owen, J., & Fincham, F. D. (2011). Effects of gender and psychosocial factors on "friends with benefits" relationships among young adults. *Archives of Sexual Behavior*, 40(2), 311–320.

Ozer, S., Meca, A., & Schwartz, S. J. (2019). Globalization and identity development among emerging adults from Ladakh. *Cultural Diversity and Ethnic Minority Psychology*, 25(4), 515–526.

Palladino Schultheiss, D. (2008). Current status and future agenda for the theory, research, and practice of childhood career development. *Career Development Quarterly*, 57, 7–24.

Parker, P. D., Lüdtke, O., Trautwein, U., & Roberts, B. W. (2012). Personality and relationship quality during the transition from high school to early adulthood. *Journal of Personality*, 80(4), 1061–1089.

Paulsen, J. A., Syed, M., Trzesniewski, K. H., & Donnellan, M. B. (2016). Generational perspectives on emerging adulthood: A focus on narcissism. In J. J. Arnett (Ed.), *The Oxford handbook of emerging adulthood* (pp. 26–44). Oxford University Press.Pedersen, D. P. (2012). The good mother, the good father, and the good parent: Gendered definitions of parenting. *Journal of Feminist Family Therapy*, 24, 230–246.

Pelletier, L. G., Fortier, M. S., Vallerand, R. J., & Briere, N. M. (2001). Associations among perceived autonomy support, forms of self-regulation, and persistence: A prospective study. *Motivation and Emotion*, 25(4), 279–306.

Pelletier, L. G., Tuson, K. M., & Haddad, N. K. (1997). Client motivation for therapy scale: A measure of intrinsic motivation, extrinsic motivation, and amotivation for therapy. *Journal of Personality Assessment*, 68(2), 414–435.

Phillips, S. D., Christopher-Sisk, E. K., & Gravino, K. L. (2001). Making career decisions in a relational context. *The Counseling Psychologist*, 29(2), 193–214.

Pinquart, M., Silbereisen, R. K., & Wiesner, M. (2004). Changes in discrepancies between desired and present states of developmental tasks in adolescence: A 4-process model. *Journal of Youth and Adolescence*, 33(6), 467–477.

Porfeli, E. J., Lee, B., Vondracek, F. W., & Weigold, I. K. (2011). A multi-dimensional measure of vocational identity status. *Journal of Adolescence*, 34(5), 853–871.

Powers, T. A., Koestner, R., Lacaille, N., Kwan, L., & Zuroff, D. C. (2009). Self-criticism, motivation, and goal progress of athletes and musicians: A prospective study. *Personality and Individual Differences*, 47(4), 279–283.

Pratt, M. W., & Lawford, H. L. (2014). Early generativity and types of civic engagement in adolescence and emerging adulthood. In L. M. Padilla-Walker & G. Carlo (Eds.), *Prosocial development: A multidimensional approach* (pp. 410–436). Oxford University Press. https://doi.org/10.1093/acprof:oso/9780199964772.003.0020

Pratt, M. W., & Matsuba, M. K. (2018). *The life story, domains of identity, and personality development in emerging adulthood: Integrating narrative and traditional approaches*. Oxford University Press. Puentes, J., Knox, D., & Zusman, M. E. (2008). Participants in "friends with benefits" relationships. *College Student Journal*, 42(1), 176–180.

Quenqua, D. (2013, Aug 5). Seeing Narcissists Everywhere. *The New York Times*. https://www.nytimes.com › 2013/08/06

Quinlan, R. J. (2008). Human pair-bonds: Evolutionary functions, ecological variation, and adaptive development. *Evolutionary Anthropology*, 17, 227–238.

Ranta, M., Dietrich, J., & Salmela-Aro, K. (2014). Career and romantic relationship goals and concerns during emerging adulthood. *Emerging Adulthood*, 2(1), 17–26.

Raque-Bogdan, T. L., Klingaman, E. A., Martin, H. M., & Lucas, M. S. (2013). Career-related parent support and career barriers: An investigation of contextual variables. *The Career Development Quarterly*, *61*(4), 339–353.

Rauer, A. J., Pettit, G. S., Lansford, J. E., Bates, J. E., & Dodge, K. A. (2013). Romantic relationship patterns in young adulthood and their developmental antecedents. *Developmental Psychology*, *49*(11), 2159–2171. https://doi.org/10.1037/a0031845

Ravert, R. D. (2009). "You're only young once": Things college students report doing now before it is too late. *Journal of Adolescent Research*, *24*(3), 376–396.

Raymundo, C. M., & Cruz, G. T. (2004). *Youth, sex, and risk behaviors in the Philippines. A report on a nationwide study: 2002 Young Adult Fertility and Sexuality Study (YAFS3)*. Demographic Research and Development Foundation, University of the Philippines Population Institute.

Repetto, P. B., Caldwell, C. H., & Zimmerman, M. A. (2004). Trajectories of depressive symptoms among high risk African-American adolescents. *Journal of Adolescent Health*, *35*(6), 468–477.

Rhoades, G. K., Stanley, S. M., & Markman, H. J. (2006). Pre-engagement cohabitation and gender asymmetry in marital commitment. *Journal of Family Psychology*, *20*(4), 553–560. Roberts, B. W., Caspi, A., & Moffitt, T. E. (2001). The kids are alright: Growth and stability in personality development from adolescence to adulthood. *Journal of Personality and Social Psychology*, *81*(4), 670–683.

Roberts, B. W., & Davis, J. P. (2016). Young adulthood is the crucible of personality development. *Emerging Adulthood*, *4*(5), 318–326. https://doi.org/10.1177/2167696816653052

Roberts, B. W., O'Donnell, M., & Robins, R. W. (2004). Goal and personality trait development in emerging adulthood. *Journal of Personality and Social Psychology*, *87*(4), 541–550. Roberts, B. W., Walton, K. E., & Viechtbauer, W. (2006). Patterns of mean-level change in personality traits across the life course: A meta-analysis of longitudinal studies. *Psychological Bulletin*, *132*(1), 1–25.

Roberts, B. W., Wood, D., & Caspi, A. (2008). The development of personality traits in adulthood. In O. P. John, R. W. Robins, & L. A. Pervin (Eds.), *Handbook of personality: Theory and research* (pp. 375–398). Guilford Press.

Roberts, K., Osadchaya, G. I., Dsuzev, K. V., Gorodyanenko, V. G., & Tholen, J. (2003). Economic conditions, and the family and housing transitions of young adults in Russia and Ukraine. *Journal of Youth Studies*, *6*(1), 71–88.

Robins, R. W., & Trzesniewski, K. H. (2005). Self-esteem development across the lifespan. *Current Directions in Psychological Science*, *14*(3), 158–162.

Rodriguez, D., Moss, H. B., & Audrain-McGovern, J. (2005). Developmental heterogeneity in adolescent depressive symptoms: Associations with smoking behavior. *Psychosomatic Medicine*, *67*(2), 200–210. Roff, D. A. (2002). *Life history evolution*. Sinauer Associates.Roisman, G. I., Masten, A. S., Coatsworth, J. D., & Tellegen, A. (2004). Salient and emerging developmental tasks in the transition to adulthood. *Child Development*, *75*(1), 123–133.

Rönkä, A., Kinnunen, U., & Pulkkinen, L. (2001). Continuity in problems of social functioning in adulthood: A cumulative perspective. *Journal of Adult Development*, *8*(3), 161–171. Rönkä, A., Oravala, S., & Pulkkinen, L. (2002). "I met this wife of mine and things got onto a better track": Turning points in risk development. *Journal of Adolescence*, *25*(1), 47–63.

Ronka, A., Oravala, S., & Pulkkinen, L. (2003). Turning points in adults' lives: The effects of gender and the amount of choice. *Journal of Adult Development*, *10*, 203–215.

https://doi.org/10.1023/A:1023418414709Rosa, H. (2003). Social acceleration: Ethical and political consequences of a desynchronized high-speed society. *Constellations*, *10*(1), 3–33.

Rosa, H. (2013). *Social acceleration: A new theory of modernity*. Columbia University Press.

Rosenberger, N. (2007). Rethinking emerging adulthood in Japan: Perspectives from long-term single women. *Child Development Perspectives*, *1*, 92–95.

Rosenthal, G. (1993). Reconstruction of life stories: Principles of selection in generating stories for narrative biographical interviews. In R. Josselson & A. Lieblich (Eds.), *The narrative study of lives* (Vol. 1, pp. 59–91). Sage Publications.

Ryan, R. M. (1993). Agency and organization: Intrinsic motivation, autonomy, and the self in psychological development. In J. E. Jacobs (Ed.), *Nebraska symposium on motivation, 1992: Developmental perspectives on motivation* (pp. 1–56). University of Nebraska Press.

Ryan, R. M., & Deci, E. L. (2000a). Intrinsic and extrinsic motivations: Classic definitions and new directions. *Contemporary Educational Psychology*, *25*(1), 54–67.

Ryan, R. M., & Deci, E. L. (2000b). Self-determination theory and the facilitation of intrinsic motivation, social development, and well-being. *American Psychologist*, *55*(1), 68–78.

Ryan, R. M., & Deci, E. L. (2017). *Self-determination theory: Basic psychological needs in motivation, development, and wellness*. The Guilford Press. https://doi.org/10.1521/978.14625/28806

Ryff, C. D. (1989). Happiness is everything, or is it? Explorations on the meaning of psychological well-being. *Journal of Personality and Social Psychology*, *57*(6), 1069–1081.

Ryff, C. D., & Keyes, C. L. M. (1995). The structure of psychological well-being revisited. *Journal of Personality and Social Psychology*, *69*(4), 719–727.

Salmela-Aro, K. (2010). Personal goals and well-being: How do young people navigate their lives? *New Directions for Child and Adolescent Development*, *2010*(130), 13–26.

Salmela-Aro, K., Kiuru, N., Nurmi, J. E., & Eerola, M. (2011). Mapping pathways to adulthood among Finnish university students: Sequences, patterns, variations in family- and work-related role. *Advances in Life Course Research*, *16*(1), 25–41.

Salmela-Aro, K., Nurmi, J. E., Saisto, T., & Halmesmaki, E. (2001). Goal construction and depressive symptoms during the transition to motherhood: Evidence from two cross-lagged longitudinal studies. *Journal of Personality and Social Psychology*, *81*, 1144–1159.

Salvatore, J. E., Kuo, S. I., Steele, R. D., Simpson, J. A., & Collins, W. A. (2011). Recovering from conflict in romantic relationships: A developmental perspective. *Psychological Science*, *22*(3), 376–383. https://doi.org/10.1177/0956797610397055

Savickas, M. L. (1997). Career adaptability: An integrative construct for life-span, life-space theory. *The Career Development Quarterly*, *45*(3), 247–259.

Savickas, M. L. (2005). The theory and practice of career construction. In S. D. Brown & R. W. Lent (Eds.), *Career development and counseling: Putting theory and research to work* (pp. 42–70). John Wiley & Sons.

Savickas, M. L. (2011). New questions for vocational psychology: Premises, paradigms, and practices. *Journal of Career Assessment*, *19*(3), 251–258. https://doi.org/10.1177/1069072710395532

Savickas, M. L., Nota, L., Rossier, J., Dauwalder, J. P., Duarte, M. E., Guichard, J., Soresi, S., Van Esbroeck, R., & Van Vianen, A. E. (2009). Life designing: A paradigm for career construction in the 21st century. *Journal of Vocational Behavior*, *75*(3), 239–250.

Sayer, L. C., Bianchi, S. M., & Robinson, J. P. (2004). Are parents investing less in children? Trends in mothers' and fathers' time with children. *American Journal of Sociology*, *110*(1), 1–43. https://doi.org/10.1086/386270

Scharf, M., Mayseless, O., & Kivenson-Baron, I. (2004). Adolescents' attachment representations and developmental tasks in emerging adulthood. *Developmental Psychology*, *40*(3), 430–444.

Schmitt, D. P., & International Sexuality Description Project. (2003). Universal sex differences in the desire for sexual variety: Tests from 52 nations, 6 continents, and 13 islands. *Journal of Personality and Social Psychology*, *85*(1), 85–104. https://doi.org/10.1037/0022-3514.85.1.85

Schmitt, D. P., & Shackelford, T. K. (2003). Nifty ways to leave your lover: The tactics people use to entice and disguise the process of human mate poaching. *Personality and Social Psychology Bulletin*, *29*(8), 1018–1035. https://doi.org/10.1177/0146167203253471

Schoeni, R. F., & Ross, K. E. (2005). *Material assistance from families during the transition to adulthood*. University of Chicago Press.

Schulenberg, J., O'Malley, P. M., Bachman, J. G., & Johnston, L. D. (2005). Early adult transitions and their relation to well-being and substance use. In R. A. Settersten, Jr., F. F. Furstenberg, Jr., & R. G. Rumbaut (Eds.), *On the frontier of adulthood: Theory, research, and public policy* (pp. 417–453). University of Chicago Press. https://doi.org/10.7208/chicago/9780226748924.003.0013

Schulenberg, J. E., & Zarrett, N. R. (2006). Mental health during emerging adulthood: Continuity and discontinuity in courses, causes, and functions. In J. J. Arnett & J. L. Tanner (Eds.), *Emerging adults in America: Coming of age in the 21st century* (pp. 135–172). American Psychological Association. https://doi.org/10.1037/11381-006

Schwartz, S. H. (1994). Beyond individualism/collectivism: New cultural dimensions of values. In U. Kim, H. C. Triandis, Ç. Kâğitçibaşi, S.-C. Choi, & G. Yoon (Eds.), *Individualism and collectivism: Theory, method, and applications* (pp. 85–119). Sage Publications, Inc.

Seiffge-Krenke, I. (1995). *Stress, coping, and relationships in adolescence*. Lawrence Erlbaum Associates.

Seiffge-Krenke, I. (2003). Testing theories of romantic development from adolescence to young adulthood: Evidence of a developmental sequence. *International Journal of Behavioral Development*, *27*(6), 519–531. https://doi.org/10.1080/01650250344000145

Seiffge-Krenke, I. (2009). Leaving home patterns in emerging adults: The impact of earlier parental support and developmental task progression. *European Psychologist*, *14*(3), 238–248.Seiffge-Krenke, I. (2013). "She's Leaving Home . . ." Antecedents, consequences, and cultural patterns in the leaving home process. *Emerging Adulthood*, *1*(2), 114–124.

Seiffge-Krenke, I., Luyckx, K., & Salmela-Aro, K. (2014). Work and love during emerging adulthood: Introduction to the special issue. *Emerging Adulthood*, *2*(1), 3–5. https://doi.org/10.1177/2167696813516091

Seiffge-Krenke, I., Overbeek, G., & Vermulst, A. (2010). Parent–child relationship trajectories during adolescence: Longitudinal associations with romantic outcomes in emerging adulthood. *Journal of Adolescence*, *33*(1), 159–171.

Settersten, R. A., Jr., & Ray, B. (2010). What's going on with young people today? The long and twisting path to adulthood. *The Future of Children*, *20*, 19–41. https://doi.org/10.1353/foc.0.0044

Shahar, G., Henrich, C. C., Blatt, S. J., Ryan, R., & Little, T. D. (2003). Interpersonal relatedness, self-definition, and their motivational orientation during adolescence: A theoretical and empirical integration. *Developmental Psychology, 39*(3), 470–483. https://doi.org/10.1037/0012-1649.39.3.470

Shahar, G., Henrich, C. C., Reiner, I. C., & Little, T. D. (2003). Development and initial validation of the Brief Adolescent Life Event Scale (BALES). *Anxiety, Stress & Coping, 16*(1), 119–128.

Shanahan, M. J. (2000). Pathways to adulthood in changing societies: Variability and mechanisms in life course perspective. *Annual Review of Sociology, 26*, 667–692.

Shanahan, M. J., Porfeli, E. J., Mortimer, J. T., & Erickson, L. D. (2005). *Subjective age identity and the transition to adulthood: When do adolescents become adults?* University of Chicago Press.

Sheldon, K. M. (2002). The self-concordance model of healthy goal striving: When personal goals correctly represent the person. In E. L. Deci & R. M. Ryan (Eds.), *Handbook of self-determination research* (pp. 65–86). University of Rochester Press.

Sheldon, K. M., & Elliot, A. J. (1999). Goal striving, need satisfaction, and longitudinal well-being: The self-concordance model. *Journal of Personality and Social Psychology, 76*(3), 482–497.

Sherry, S. B., Gautreau, C. M., Mushquash, A. R., Sherry, D. L., & Allen, S. L. (2014). Self-critical perfectionism confers vulnerability to depression after controlling for neuroticism: A longitudinal study of middle-aged, community-dwelling women. *Personality and Individual Differences, 69*, 1–4.

Sherry, S. B., Hewitt, P. L., Flett, G. L., & Harvey, M. (2003). Perfectionism dimensions, perfectionistic attitudes, dependent attitudes, and depression in psychiatric patients and university students. *Journal of Counseling Psychology, 50*(3), 373–386.

Shulman, S., & Ben-Artzi, E. (2003). Age-related differences in the transition from adolescence to adulthood and links with family relationships. *Journal of Adult Development, 10*(4), 217–226.

Shulman, S., Blatt, S. J., & Feldman, B. (2006). Vicissitudes of the impetus for growth and change among emerging adults. *Psychoanalytic Psychology, 23*(1), 159–180.

Shulman, S., & Connolly, J. (2013). The challenge of romantic relationships in emerging adulthood: Reconceptualization of the field. *Emerging Adulthood, 1*(1), 27–39.

Shulman, S., Davila, J., & Shachar-Shapira, L. (2011). Assessing romantic competence among older adolescents. *Journal of Adolescence, 34*(3), 397–406. https://doi.org/10.1016/j.adolescence.2010.08.002

Shulman, S., Feldman, B., Blatt, S. J. Cohen, O., & Mahler, A. (2005). Emerging adulthood: Age-related tasks and underlying self processes. *Journal of Adolescent Research, 20*, 577–603.

Shulman, S., Hakhmigari, M. K., Michaeli, Y., Tuval-Mashiach, R., & Dickson, D. J. (2016). Achieving work and love authorship in emerging adulthood: Types, psychosocial correlations, and precursors. *Emerging Adulthood, 4*(4), 258–271. https://doi.org/10.1177/2167696815606563

Shulman, S., Kalnitzki, E., & Shahar, G. (2009). Meeting developmental challenges during emerging adulthood: The role of personality and social resources. *Journal of Adolescent Research, 24*(2), 242–267. https://doi.org/10.1177/0743558408329303Shulman, S., & Nurmi, J. E. (2010a). Understanding emerging adulthood from a goal-setting perspective. *New Directions for Child and Adolescent Development, 2010*(130), 1–11.

Shulman, S., & Nurmi, J. E. (2010b). Dynamics of goal pursuit and personality make-up among emerging adults: Typology, change over time, and adaptation. *New Directions for Child and Adolescent Development, 2010*(130), 57–70.

Shulman, S., Scharf, M., Livne, Y., & Barr, T. (2013). Patterns of romantic involvement among emerging adults: Psychosocial correlates and precursors. *International Journal of Behavioral Development, 37*(5), 460–467. https://doi.org/10.1177/0165025413491371

Shulman, S., & Seiffge-Krenke, I. (1997). *Fathers and adolescents: Developmental and clinical perspectives*. Routledge.

Shulman, S., Seiffge-Krenke, I., Scharf, M., Boiangiu, S. B., & Tregubenko, V. (2018). The diversity of romantic pathways during emerging adulthood and their developmental antecedents. *International Journal of Behavioral Development, 42*(2), 167–174.

Shulman, S., Seiffge-Krenke, I., Scharf, M., Lev-Ari, L., & Levy, G. (2017). Adolescent depressive symptoms and breakup distress during early emerging adulthood: Associations with the quality of romantic interactions. *Emerging Adulthood, 5*(4), 251–258. https://doi.org/10.1177/2167696817698900

Shulman, S., Walsh, S. D., Weisman, O., & Schelyer, M. (2009). Romantic contexts, sexual behavior, and depressive symptoms among adolescent males and females. *Sex Roles, 61*(11–12), 850–863.

Shulman, S., Yonatan-Leus, R., & Silberberg, O. (2023). Understanding stability and change in depressive symptom trajectories across young adulthood through the lens of career development: A mixed-methods study. *International Journal of Behavioral Development, 47*(2), 169–179. https://doi.org/10.1177/01650254221146416

Singer, J. A. (2004). Narrative identity and meaning making across the adult lifespan: An introduction. *Journal of Personality, 72*(3), 437–460.

Singerman, D. (2007). *The economic imperatives of marriage: Emerging practices and identities among youth in the Middle East* [Working paper 6]. Middle East Youth Initiative, Wolfensohn Center for Development.

Slade, A. (2005). Parental reflective functioning: An introduction. *Attachment & Human Development, 7*(3), 269–281.

Slade, A., Grienenberger, J., Bernbach, E., Levy, D., & Locker, A. (2005). Maternal reflective functioning, attachment, and the transmission gap: A preliminary study. *Attachment & Human Devlopment, 7*(3), 283–298.

Slaughter, A.-M. (2012, July/August). Why women still can't have it all. *The Atlantic*.

Smiler, A. P. (2011). Sexual strategies theory: Built for the short term or the long term? *Sex Roles, 64*(9–10), 603–612.

Smith, C., Christoffersen, K., Davidson, H., & Herzog, P. S. (2011). *Lost in transition: The dark side of emerging adulthood*. Oxford University Press.

Smith, M. M., Sherry, S. B., Rnic, K., Saklofske, D. H., Enns, M., & Gralnick, T. (2016). Are perfectionism dimensions vulnerability factors for depressive symptoms after controlling for neuroticism? A meta-analysis of 10 longitudinal studies. *European Journal of Personality, 30*(2), 201–212.

Smock, P. J., Manning, W. D., & Porter, M. (2005). "Everything's there except money": How money shapes decisions to marry among cohabitors. *Journal of Marriage and Family, 67*(3), 680–696.

Snarey, J. R. (1993). *How fathers care for the next generation: A four-decade study*. Harvard University Press.

Sneed, J. R., Hamagami, F., McArdle, J. J., Cohen, P., & Chen, H. (2007). The dynamic interdependence of developmental domains across emerging adulthood. *Journal of Youth and Adolescence, 36*(3), 351–362. Specht, J., Bleidorn, W., Denissen, J. J., Hennecke, M., Hutteman, R., Luhmann, M., Orth, U., Reitz, A. K., & Zimmermann, J. (2014). What drives adult personality development? A comparison of theoretical perspectives and empirical evidence. *European Journal of Personality, 28*(3), 216–230.

Specht, J., Egloff, B., & Schmukle, S. C. (2011). Stability and change of personality across the life course: The impact of age and major life events on mean-level and rank-order stability of the Big Five. *Journal of Personality and Social Psychology, 101*(4), 862–882.

Spencer, J. P., Perone, S., & Buss, A. T. (2011). Twenty years and going strong: A dynamic systems revolution in motor and cognitive development. *Child Development Perspectives, 5*(4), 260–266.

Spielmann, S. S., MacDonald, G., Maxwell, J. A., Joel, S., Peragine, D., Muise, A., & Impett, E. A. (2013). Settling for less out of fear of being single. *Journal of Personality and Social Psychology, 105*(6), 1049–1073.

Sroufe, L. A. (1989). Relationships, self, and individual adaptation. In A. J. Sameroff, R. N. Emde, & T. F. Anders (Eds.), *Relationship disturbances in early childhood: A developmental approach* (pp. 70–94). Basic Books.

Sroufe, L. A. (2013). The promise of developmental psychopathology: Past and present. *Development and Psychopathology, 25*(4, Pt. 2), 1215–1224.

Sroufe, L. A., Egeland, B., Carlson, E. A., & Collins, W. A. (2005). *The development of the person: The Minnesota study of risk and adaptation from birth to adulthood.* Guilford Publications.

Sroufe, L. A., & Fleeson, J. (1986). Attachment and the construction of relationships. In W. Hartup & Z. Rubin (Eds.), *Relationships and development* (pp. 57–71). Lawrence Erlbaum Associates.

Sroufe, L. A., & Rutter, M. (1984). The domain of developmental psychopathology. *Child Development, 55*(1), 17–29.

Stanley, S. M., Rhoades, G. K., & Markman, H. J. (2006). Sliding versus deciding: Inertia and the premarital cohabitation effect. *Family Relations, 55*(4), 499–509.

Steele, H., Steele, M., Croft, C., & Fonagy, P. (1999). Infant–mother attachment at one year predicts children's understanding of mixed emotions at six years. *Social Development, 8*(2), 161–178.

Steiger, A. E., Allemand, M., Robins, R. W., & Fend, H. A. (2014). Low and decreasing self-esteem during adolescence predict adult depression two decades later. *Journal of Personality and Social Psychology, 106*, 325–338.

Steiger, A. E., Fend, H. A., & Allemand, M. (2015). Testing the vulnerability and scar models of self-esteem and depressive symptoms from adolescence to middle adulthood and across generations. *Developmental Psychology, 51*(2), 236–247.

Stoolmiller, M., Kim, H. K., & Capaldi, D. M. (2005). The course of depressive symptoms in men from early adolescence to young adulthood: Identifying latent trajectories and early predictors. *Journal of Abnormal Psychology, 114*(3), 331–345.

Sumner, R., Burrow, A. L., & Hill, P. L. (2015). Identity and purpose as predictors of subjective well-being in emerging adulthood. *Emerging Adulthood, 3*(1), 46–54.

Tabachnik, B. G., & Fidell, S. L. (2013). *Using multivariate statistics* (6th ed.). Pearson Education.

Tanner, J. L., Reinherz, H. Z., Beardslee, W. R., Fitzmaurice, G. M., Leis, J. A., & Berger, S. R. (2007). Change in prevalence of psychiatric disorders from ages 21 to 30 in a community sample. *The Journal of Nervous and Mental Disease, 195*(4), 298–306.

te Riele, K. (2004). Youth transition in Australia: Challenging assumptions of linearity and choice. *Journal of Youth Studies, 7*(3), 243–257. https://doi.org/10.1080/1367626042000268908

te Riele, K. T. (2006). Youth "at risk": Further marginalizing the marginalized? *Journal of Education Policy, 21*(2), 129–145.

Thelen, E., & Smith, L. B. (1996). *A dynamic systems approach to the development of cognition and action.* MIT Press.

Thelen, E., & Smith, L. B. (1998). Dynamic systems theories. In W. Damon & R. M. Lerner (Eds.), *Handbook of child psychology: Vol. 1. Theoretical models of human development* (5th ed., pp. 563–634). John Wiley & Sons.

Tomasik, M. J. (2016). Orchestrating multiple goals across adulthood: From solo to tutti. *Research in Human Development, 13*(4), 273–279.

Tuval-Mashiach, R., & Shulman, S. (2006). Resolution of disagreements between romantic partners, among adolescents, and young adults: Qualitative analysis of interaction discourses. *Journal of Research on Adolescence, 16*(4), 561–588.

Tuval-Mashiach, R., Hanson, J., & Shulman, S. (2014). Turning points in the romantic history of emerging adults. *Journal of Youth Studies, 18*(4), 434–450. doi:10.1080/13676261.2014.963533

Twenge, J. M. (2013). The evidence for generation me and against generation we. *Emerging Adulthood, 1*(1), 11–16.

Tzoreff, Y. (2010). Barriers to resolution of the conflict with Israel—The Palestinian perspective. In Y. Bar-Siman-Tov (Ed.), *Barriers to peace in the Israeli-Palestinian conflict* (pp. 58–98). Konrad-Adenauer-Stiftung Israel and The Jerusalem Institute for Israel Studies.

Uecker, J. E., & Stokes, C. E. (2008). Early marriage in the United States. *Journal of Marriage and Family, 70*(4), 835–846.

US Census Bureau. (2008). *Statistical abstract of the United States.* US Government Printing Office.

US Census Bureau. (2017). *Statistical abstract of the United States.* US Government Printing Office.

US Census Bureau. (2021). *Statistical abstract of the United States.* US Government Printing Office.

Van Aken, M. A., Denissen, J. J., Branje, S. J., Dubas, J. S., & Goossens, L. (2006). Midlife concerns and short-term personality change in middle adulthood. *European Journal of Personality, 20*(6), 497–513.

Van IJzendoorn, M. H., & De Wolff, M. S. (1997). In search of the absent father—Meta-analyses of infant–father attachment: A rejoinder to our discussants. *Child Development, 68*(4), 604–609.

Vespa, J. (2014). Historical trends in the marital intentions of one-time and serial cohabitors. *Journal of Marriage and Family, 76*(1), 207–217.

Vigil, J. M., & Geary, D. C. (2006). Parenting and community background and variation in women's life-history development. *Journal of Family Psychology, 20*(4), 597–604.

Wallace, C., & Kovatcheva, S. (1998). *Changing times, changing lives: The construction and deconstruction of youth in east and west Europe* [Working paper 22]. Institut für Höhere Studien. https://nbn-resolving.org/urn:nbn:de:0168-ssoar-222010

Ward, K., & Wolf-Wendel, L. (2004). Academic motherhood: Managing complex roles in research universities. *The Review of Higher Education, 27*(2), 233–257.

Wentzel, K. R. (2000). What is it that I'm trying to achieve? Classroom goals from a content perspective. *Contemporary Educational Psychology*, 25(1), 105–115.
Werner, E., & Smith, R. (1982). *Vulnerable but invincible: A longitudinal study of resilient children and youth*. McGraw-Hill.
Whiston, S. C., & Keller, B. K. (2004). The influences of the family of origin on career development: A review and analysis. *The Counseling Psychologist*, 32(4), 493–568.
Williamson, D. S., & Bray, J. H. (1988). Family development and change across the generations: An intergenerational perspective. In C. J. Falicov (Ed.), *Family transitions: Continuity and change over the life cycle* (pp. 357–384). Guilford Press.
Winterhalder, B., & Leslie, P. (2002). Risk-sensitive fertility: The variance compensation hypothesis. *Evolution and Human Behavior*, 23(1), 59–82. Worthman, C. M. (2003). Energetics, sociality, and human reproduction: Life history theory in real life. In K. W. Wachter & R. A. Bulatao (Eds.), *Offspring: Human fertility behavior in biodemographic perspective* (pp. 289–321). National Academies Press.
Wrosch, C., & Heckhausen, J. (1999). Control processes before and after passing a developmental deadline: Activation and deactivation of intimate relationship goals. *Journal of Personality and Social Psychology*, 77, 415–427.
Wrosch, C., Scheier, M. F., Carver, C. S., & Schulz, R. (2003). The importance of goal disengagement in adaptive self-regulation: When giving up is beneficial. *Self and Identity*, 2, 1–20.
Wynne, L. C. (1984). The epigenesis of relational systems: A model for understanding family development. *Family Process*, 23(3), 297–318.
Zhao, L., & Huang, Y. (2010). *Unemployment problem of China's youth*. East Asian Institute, National University of Singapore.
Zullig, K. J., Huebner, E. S., Patton, J. M., & Murray, K. A. (2009). The brief multidimensional students' life satisfaction scale-college version. *American Journal of Health Behavior*, 33(5), 483–493.

Index

For the benefit of digital users, indexed terms that span two pages (e.g., 52–53) may, on occasion, appear on only one of those pages.

Tables and figures are indicated by *t* and *f* following the page number

Ada (study participant), 160
Adapted Pursuit pathway, 51–53, 56–57, 59–61, 60*t*, 257–58
    career adaptability and, 65–66
    level of depressive affect among members of, 213*f*, 213–14
    men vs. women, 147–48, 151–52, 162, 168–70, 258–59
    parental support and, 191–93, 195
adaptive developmental plasticity, 262–63
Addis, D. R., 133
adolescence/adolescents
    depressive trajectories, 219–20, 226–27
    effect of parental support during, 190
    gender intensification theory, 151
    goals and plans, 27, 29
    National Longitudinal Study of Adolescent Health, 125, 220
    paternal vs. maternal support, 193
    personality development, 178
    romantic relationships, 79–80
Alex (study participant)
    career adaptability, 63–65, 66
    career pathway, 48–50, 56
    gendered pathways, 154
    mental health patterns, 217, 218
    romantic pathway, 88, 119–21, 130
    support systems, 194
Allen, G., 91–92
ambiguous, developmentally unrelated, and disorganized goals pattern, 35–37
amotivation, 14–15, 19–20, 21
analysis of variance (ANOVA), authorship, 142–44, 143*t*
Arab emerging adults, 241–45, 246
Ariel (study participant)
    career adaptability, 70–71, 76
    goals, 41–42, 42*t*, 44–45
Aristotle, 11
Armakola, Maria, 237

Arnett, Jeffrey, 10–11, 198
Aron (study participant)
    career adaptability, 68–69, 71, 75
    mental health patterns, 219
    support systems, 206
assumption of adulthood, 7–8. *See also* conceptual frameworks
attributes, personality. *See* personality attributes
authorship
    attainment of in 30s, 141–45
    attainment of in late 20s, 134–35
    narrative accounts, 144–45
    narrative continuity, 133
    narrative identity, 132–34
    overview, 4, 131–32
    psychosocial functioning, 143*t*
    quantitative accounts, 142–44
    romantic authorship, 140–41
    self-continuity, 132–33
    work and romantic authorship, 136–38
    work authorship, 139–40
autonomous motivational orientation, 19–20
Avi (study participant), 118

Baboulias, Y., 237
Bateman, J., 237
Becky (study participant)
    career adaptability, 65–66, 73
    career pathway, 51–53, 56–57
    gendered pathways, 157–58
    mental health patterns, 213–14, 217–18
    personality assets, 164–65
    support systems, 195, 205–6
Belsky, J., 125–26
biographical agency, 24
Blatt, S. J., 14, 167, 172, 222–23. *See also* theory of personality
Brandtstädter, Jochen, 23, 40
Brief Symptoms Inventory, 142–44, 181, 220–22
Brief Young Adult Life Events Scale, 180, 200

Brumbach, B. H., 125–26
Burt, K. B., 213–14
Buss, D. M., 152
Bynner, John, 11–12

career adaptability
 adaptations and compromises, 66–71
 Compromised pattern, 75, 76–78, 77t, 157–58, 162
 coping skills, 73–74
 finding meaning in work, 73–74
 Integrated pattern, 74, 76–78, 77t
 living from one day to the next, 71–72
 overview, 62–63
 refinding one's way and flourishing, 63–66
 self-regulation and, 73–74
 Vague pattern, 75–78, 77t
 well-being and, 76–78
career commitment inventory, 142–43
career development pathways. *See also* Adapted Pursuit pathway; Confused/Vague pathway; Consistent Pursuit pathway; gendered pathways; Survivor pathway
 exploring and floundering, 56–59
 goal achievement, 59–61
 goal readjustment, 51
 identifying, 48
 overview, 46–47
 parental support and, 191–93
 relationship between work status and marital status, 231–35
 variety and complexity of, 257–60
 youth unemployment, 231–33, 232f
Career-focused combined with investment in motherhood and family pattern, 158–59, 162
career history interview, 47
career pursuit. *See* career adaptability; career development pathways; work-family balance
Caspi, A., 216–17
Casual to Steady romantic pathway, 88, 93, 94
 changes in depressive affect, 94f
 fluctuations, 258
 fluidity and, 90–91
 level of depressive affect among members of, 214–15, 215f
 men vs. women, 148–49
 multinomial regression analysis predicting membership in, 173–74, 174t
 non-heterosexual young adults, 89–90
 overview, 86–88
 romantic goals and life satisfaction, 93t

change over time, goals and plans, 30–34, 32f
Client Motivation for Therapy Scale, 19–20, 168
cohabitation, 9–10, 79–97, 233
commitment, lack of, 9–10, 95. *See also* intimacy status
Compromised pattern of career adaptability, 75, 76–78, 77t, 157–58, 162
conceptual frameworks
 career development pathways, 257–60
 cross-cultural perspective, 260–61
 developmental psychology, 261–64
 developmental systems theory perspective, 248–53
 evolutionary perspective, 261–64
 gendered pathways, 258–60
 ladder metaphor, 131–32, 143–44, 145–46, 263
 life authorship, 255–57
 personality development and adaptive outcomes, 253–55
 romantic development pathways, 257–60
Conflictual but Committed intimacy status, 99
Confused/Vague pathway, 55–56, 58, 59–60, 60t, 257–58
 career adaptability and, 68–71
 level of depressive affect among members of, 213f, 214
 men vs. women, 147–48, 168–69, 258–59
 parental support and, 191–93, 196–97
Conger, R. D., 189–90
Connectedness subscale, 181
Consistent Pursuit pathway, 48–51, 56–57, 59–61, 60t, 257–58
 career adaptability and, 63–65
 level of depressive affect among members of, 212–13, 213f
 men vs. women, 147–48, 151–52, 162, 168–70, 258–59
 parental support and, 191–92
continuity
 intimacy status and, 103–5
 narrative continuity, 133
 self-continuity, 132–33, 256
controlled motivational orientation, 19–20
Copher, R., 122
coping skills, 73–74, 75, 100, 125, 178, 179, 184–85, 228
Costello, D. M., 220, 222
Côté, James, 11, 13, 166
Crittenden, P. M., 107
cross-cultural perspective
 Arab and North African emerging adults, 241–45, 246

cohabitation, 233
Greek emerging adults, 235–38, 245–46
overview, 260–61
relationship between work status and marital status, 231–35, 245–46
Sardinian emerging adults, 238–41
Cuzzocrea, V., 239–40, 241

Dan (study participant), 37t, 101
Daria (study participant)
intimacy status, 106–7, 108
romantic pathway, 83, 84
data analysis, 181–84
dating. *See also* romantic development
career pursuit and, 116–21
romantic pathways and attainment of romantic goals, 92–94
David (study participant), 38–39, 39t
dead times, social acceleration theory, 240
De Bolle, M., 178
Deci, Edward, 14
deficit model, 11
demographics of emerging adulthood, 2, 79–97, 116–17, 235, 260
dependency
defined, 19, 167–68, 223
negative vs. positive, 176–77
role in romantic life stories, 175–77
depressive affect
between ages 23 and 35, 212f
Brief Symptom Inventory, 142–44, 181
career pursuit pathways and, 59–61, 60t, 211–14, 213f
depressive trajectories and outcomes, 222–28, 226t
high stable trajectory, 224–28, 224t, 225t, 226t
low stable trajectory, 224–28, 225t, 226t, 229
marital status and, 225–26, 225t
moderate and decreasing trajectory, 224–28, 224t, 225t, 226t
person-centered techniques for, 220–22, 223–27
precursors of trajectories of, 222–28
predictors for depressive trajectory membership, 223–25, 224t
romantic pathways and, 214–16, 215f
Depressive Experiences Questionnaire (DEQ), 19, 167–68, 180
developmental deviation, 210
developmental goals. *See also* goal pattern framework
ambiguous, developmentally unrelated, and disorganized goals pattern, 35–37, 43

elaborated and progressing life goals, 40–42, 43
means, standard deviations, and significance of differences, 44t
overview, 34–42
pursuit of goals accompanied by underlying insecurities and concerns, 37–38
realistic and orderly career and family goals, 38–40, 43
developmental outcomes, measuring, 20
developmental pathways
Arab and North African emerging adults, 241–45, 246
Greek emerging adults, 235–38, 245–46
overview, 230–31
relationship between work status and marital status, 231–35
Sardinian emerging adults, 238–41, 246
youth unemployment, 231–33, 232f
developmental psychopathology. *See also* depressive affect
developmental deviation, 210
group-based trajectory model, 219–20, 229
overview, 208–9
personality maturity, 216–19
role in understanding adaptive and maladaptive courses and outcomes, 209–11
scar model, 6, 226–28
theory of personality, 14, 150–51, 166, 172, 184, 222–23
vulnerability model, 219–20
developmental success
defined, 14
psychological well-being and, 213–14
developmental systems theory, 81, 91–92, 248–53
Dietrich, J., 20–21
dispositional representations, 107
divided lives, 9
Dorit (study participant), 156, 159
Dotterer, A. M., 198
dynamic systems theory, 257, 260, 262–63

Edwards, J. R., 122–23
efficacy, 14, 166
defined, 19, 167–68
goal attainment and, 21
role in career life stories, 170–72
role in romantic life stories, 175–77
self-definition and, 172–73
EGRIS (European Group for Integrated Social Research), 9

Eitan (study participant), 194
elaborated and progressing life goals pattern, 40–42
Elchanan (study participant), 89–90
Elder, G. H., 189–90
Eli (study participant), 118
Ellis, B. J., 124–25
emerging adulthood
  defined, 11
  economic factors, 11–12
  feeling-in between, 11
  identity exploration, 11
  instability, 11
  possibilities, 11
  self-focus, 11
emotional autonomy, 15–16
environmental conditions, life-history theory, 124–25
Erikson, E., 97, 239–40
Eriksonian theory, 97–98, 104, 239–40
European Group for Integrated Social Research (EGRIS), 9
evolutionary perspective, 261–64
  career and romance, 124–28
  gendered pathways, 152–53
  overview, 7–8
extrinsic motivation, 166–67, 168

family–education balance, 126–27
Fiese, B. H., 150–51
Fingerman, K. L., 186
floundering, 44–57, 58–59, 77–78
fluctuations and changes in life path
  career pathways, 51, 58–59
  depressive affect, 215–16
  developmental systems theory, 92
  functional, 80–81
  motivational theory of life-span development, 24, 250–51, 257, 258, 262–64
  romantic pathways, 82, 83, 90, 95, 104, 128
fluidity
  developmental systems theory perspective, 251–52
  in life task commitments, 80
  perception of, 1–2
  progression of romantic involvement and, 90–92
  self-socialization, 24
Fonagy, P., 199–200, 201–2
friends as social support, 13, 15–16, 204–5
Furman, W., 107, 128–29
future outcomes
  authorship and, 4, 142–45
  change in self-criticism during emerging adulthood and, 179–81
  conceptual meanings and, 42–45
  depressive trajectories and, 222–28
  Intimate but not Committed status and, 111–13
  parental support and, 186–87, 190, 203t
  peer support and, 190
  person–environment fit, 12–13, 23
  precursors of trajectories of depressive affect during emerging adulthood and, 222–28
  psychological assets and, 256
  reflective capacity and, 198–204
  romantic pathways and, 3–4, 105–6

Gadi (study participant), 117
Galanaki, E., 235–36
gendered pathways, 127, 141, 258–60
  Career-focused combined with investment in motherhood and family pattern, 158–59, 162
  career pursuit, 147–48
  Compromised pattern of career adaptability, 157–58, 162
  Connected but separate pattern, 154–55
  evolutionary perspective, 152–53
  gender intensification theory, 151
  historical perspective, 163
  maternal identity, 156–57
  men, 154–55
  No career, frustrated mother pattern, 160–61
  overview, 5, 147
  personal identity, 151–52
  priorities and, 149–50
  romantic pathways, 148–49
  sexual strategies theory, 152–53
  socialization theory, 150–52
  stereotypes, 161–62
  theoretical perspectives, 150–53
  theory of personality, 150–51
  women, 156–63
"Generation Me," 1, 10–11
Gideon (study participant), 87–88
Giele, J. Z., 189–90
goal achievement and attainment
  career pursuit pathways, 59–61, 60t, 191t
  personal resources and, 21
  reflectivity and, 201, 203–4
  romantic pathways, 92–94, 93t, 191t
  support systems and, 21, 204
goal constellations
  change over time, 30–34
  conceptual meanings and future outcomes, 42–45

developmental patterns, 34–42, 44t
interdependence, 30–34
priorities, 30–34
goal pattern framework
   adolescents, 29
   age-appropriate goals, 40
   Ariel's major goals, 42t
   arrested pattern, 22–23
   change over time, 32f
   coordination of goals, 27
   Dan's major goals, 37t
   David's major goals, 39t
   descriptive statistics for personal goal, 31t
   developmental systems theory perspective, 248–50
   flexibility, 39–40
   floundering, 44
   goal descriptions, 21–22
   goal investment, 14, 20
   goal progress, 14, 20
   goal stress, 14
   Limor's major goals, 41t
   love arrested pattern, 22–23
   motivational theory of life-span development, 250–51
   Noam's major goals, 39t
   Nora's major goals, 36t
   personal characteristics and capabilities and, 30
   progressive pattern, 22–23
   qualitative approach, 27
   Roni's major goals, 38t
   sequential ordering of, 33–34
   sociocultural environment and, 29–30
   trajectories of academic, career, and romantic importance across age, 32f
   transitional periods, 27, 29
   unattainable goals, 24
goal readjustment
   Adapted pursuit pathway, 51–53, 57, 59–61
   Consistent pursuit pathway, 50–51
goal-setting theory, 14
goal stress, 20
Greek emerging adults, 235–38, 245–46
Guardian, 239

harshness of environment, life-history theory, 124–25
Heckhausen, Jutta, 24, 51, 56, 250–51
Heinz, Walter, 12–13, 23–24
Henrich, C. C., 167
high stable trajectory, depressive affect, 224–28, 224t, 225t, 226t

Hill, J. P., 151
historical perspective, gendered pathways, 163
Howden, D., 237

identity exploration, 11, 235–36, 245–46, 248, 260
Independent, 237–38
Integrated pattern of career adaptability, 74, 76–78, 77t
interdependence of goals, 30–34
intimacy status
   cohabitation, 96–97
   Conflictual but Committed, 99
   continuity, 103–5
   difficulties in successfully integrating intimacy and commitment, 103–5
   Eriksonian theory, 97–98
   Intimacy Status Interview, 98–99
   Intimate but not Committed pattern, 99, 101–2, 103, 106t, 111–13
   Intimately Committed pattern, 99, 100, 104–5, 106t
   Isolate status, 99
   Lengthy relationships romantic pathway, 110–11
   Mergers/Committed status, 99
   Mergers/Uncommitted status, 99
   Non-intimate Commitment pattern, 99, 102–3, 110–11
   Non-stable pattern, 99, 100, 106–9
   overview, 96–99
   Pre-intimate status, 99
   Pseudo-intimate status, 99
   romantic pathways and, 105–6, 106t
   Sporadic romantic pathway and, 106–9
   Stereotype status, 99
Intimacy Status Interview, 98–99
intrinsic motivation, 167, 168
Isolate intimacy status, 99
Israeli society, 17–19

Joel (study participant), 109
Joseph (study participant)
   intimacy status, 108–9
   romantic pathway, 83–84

Kalnitzki, E., 20–21
Karavasilis, Vasileios, 237–38
Kati (study participant), 157, 158
Katy (study participant), 100
Keller, B. K., 190
Kessler, Ronald, 208
Krahn, H. J., 57
Krichly-Katz, Tamar, 153

ladder metaphor, 131–32, 143–44, 145–46, 263
Laney, E. K., 156
Latham, Gary, 14
Laursen, B., 189
learning from experiences, 133–34. *See also* authorship
Lengthy Relationships but Absence of Experiential Learning pathway, 84–86, 91, 93–94, 93*t*, 258
    depressive affect and, 94*f*, 215*f*, 215–16
    men vs. women, 148–49
    multinomial regression analysis predicting membership in, 173–74, 174*t*
    Non-intimate Commitment pattern, 110–11
    parental support and, 192
Lerner, Richard, 23
Levinson, Daniel, 121–22, 123, 133–34, 163
    importance of dreams, 46
    ladder metaphor, 131–32, 145–46, 263
    personal enterprise, 256
    romantic partner as mentor, 32–33
life authorship, 255–57
    analysis of variance, 142–44, 143*t*
    attainment of in 30s, 141–45
    attainment of in late 20s, 134–35
    narrative accounts, 144–45
    narrative continuity, 133
    narrative identity, 132–34
    overview, 4, 131–32
    psychosocial functioning, 143*t*
    quantitative accounts, 142–44
    romantic authorship, 140–41
    self-continuity, 132–33
    work and romantic authorship, 136–38
    work authorship, 139–40
life-course approach, career and romance, 122
life-cycle approach, career and romance, 121–24
life-history theory, 124–25
life path, fluctuations and changes in
    career pathways, 51, 58–59
    depressive affect, 215–16
    developmental systems theory, 92
    functional, 80–81
    motivational theory of life-span development, 24, 250–51, 257, 258, 262–64
    romantic pathways, 82, 83, 90, 95, 104, 128
life satisfaction, 92–94, 93*t*, 181
Lily (study participant), 119
Limor (study participant)
    gendered pathways, 156, 158–59, 161
    goals, 40–41, 41*t*
    support systems, 205
Little, B. R., 20, 59, 92–93, 180, 202

living from one day to the next, 71–72
Locke, Edwin, 14
Lost in Transition (Smith, et al.), 10–11
Lowe, K., 198
low stable trajectory, depressive affect, 224–28, 225*t*, 226*t*, 229
Luthar, Suniya, 13
Lynch, M. E., 151

Macmillan, R., 122
Manning, W. D., 33, 123–24
market economy
    effect on Israeli society, 18–19
    OECD, 18
    Sardinia, 238–39
Masten, A. S., 13, 213–14
maternal identity, 156–57
maternal support, 192–93, 200, 203, 203*t*, 204, 206–7
maturity principle. *See* personality maturity
Maya (study participant), 107–8, 109
Mayer (study participant), 107, 108
Mayes, Linda, 91–92
McAdams, Dan, 4, 25, 132, 133–34, 150–51, 256
McLean, K. C., 133
Meadows, S. O., 228
meaning in work and life, 44–45, 66, 250–51
    career adaptability and, 76, 77
    finding, 73–74
    gendered pathways, 162, 163
    importance of, 41–42
    Survivors pathway, 71
Meier, A., 91–92
mental health. *See also* psychopathology
    Brief Symptom Inventory, 142–44, 181
    career pursuit pathways and, 59–61, 60*t*, 211–14, 213*f*
    depressive affect between ages 23 and 35, 212*f*
    Depressive Experiences Questionnaire, 19, 167–68, 180
    depressive trajectories and outcomes, 219–22, 226, 226*t*
    marital status and, 225–26, 225*t*
    person-centered techniques for depression, 220–22, 223–27
    precursors of trajectories of depression, 222–28
    predictors for depressive trajectory membership, 223–25, 224*t*
    romantic pathways and, 214–16, 215*f*
mentors, 205–6
Mergers/Committed intimacy status, 99
Millennials, 10–11

moderate and decreasing trajectory, depressive
    affect, 224–28, 224t, 225t, 226t
Monitoring the Future study, 208
moratorium
    classic moratorium, 240
    waithood vs., 241
    waiting, 240–41
motivation
    intrinsic vs. extrinsic, 166–67, 168
    motivational orientations, 14–15, 19–20
    role in career life stories, 170–72
motivational theory of life-span
        development, 51, 56
    fluctuations and changes in life path, 24, 250–51, 257, 258, 262–64
    goal pattern framework, 250–51
multinomial regression analysis, 168–70, 169t
mut'ah weddings, 261

Narcissistic Personality Inventory, 10–11
narrative accounts
    authorship, 144–45
    parental support, 193–97
narrative continuity, 133
narrative identity, 132–34, 145–46, 256
Natalie (study participant), 88–89
National Longitudinal Study of Adolescent
        Health, 125, 220
Natti (study participant)
    authorship, 136–37, 144–45, 146
    depressive trajectory, 227–28
    personality assets, 164–65
NEETs (not in employment, education, or
        training), 236
Netta (study participant), 140
Network of Relationship Inventory (NRI), 19–20, 187–88, 202
Noach (study participant), 118
Noam (study participant), 38, 39t
No career, frustrated mother pattern, 160–61
non-commitment, 9–10, 95. See also
        intimacy status
non-heterosexual young adults, 82, 89–90
Non-intimate Commitment intimacy pattern,
        99, 102–3, 104–5, 106t, 110–11
Non-stable intimacy pattern, 99, 100, 105,
        106–9, 106t
Nora (study participant)
    authorship, 145
    career adaptability, 71–72, 138
    career pathway, 55–56, 138, 196
    dependency, 175–77
    efficacy, 171–72

floundering behavior, 164–65
goals, 27–28, 35–36, 36t, 44–45
intimacy status, 110, 111
mental health patterns, 214, 215–16, 218
romantic pathway, 84–86, 138
North African emerging adults, 241–45, 246
not in employment, education, or training
        (NEETs), 236
NRI (Network of Relationship Inventory), 19–20, 187–88, 202
Nurit (study participant), 175
Nurmi, J. E., 21–22, 50

Obama, Barack, 134
OECD (Organisation for Economic Co-
        operation and Development), 18
Oren (study participant), 195
Organisation for Economic Co-operation and
        Development (OECD), 18
Orlofsky, J. L., 98
Osgood, D. W., 126–27
outcomes. See future outcomes

parental support, 6
    career pathways and, 191–93
    maternal support, 192–93, 200, 203, 203t, 204, 206–7
    narrative accounts, 193–97
    overview, 188
    paternal support, 190–91, 200, 203, 206–7
    reflective capacity and, 198–204
parent-child relationship, 15–16
Parent Development Interview (PDI), 199–200, 201–2
paternal support, 190–91, 200, 203, 206–7
pattern constellations, 34–42
Paulsen, Jacob, 11–12
PDI (Parent Development Interview), 199–200, 201–2
peer support, 13, 15–16, 204–5
personal capacities, 263
personality attributes
    Brief Symptom Inventory, 181
    Brief Young Adult Life Events Scale, 180
    Client Motivation for Therapy Scale, 168
    Connectedness subscale, 181
    data analysis, 181–84
    dependency, 167–68, 175–77
    Depressive Experience Questionnaire, 167–68, 180
    depressive symptoms, 181
    developmental outcomes and future
        well-being, 177–79

personality attributes (*cont.*)
  efficacy, 166, 167–68, 170–72, 175–77
  life satisfaction and, 181
  motivation, 167, 168, 170–72
  multinomial regression analysis, 168–70, 169*t*
  overview, 164–65
  personality maturity, 177–79
  Personal Project Analysis, 180
  psychological outcomes, 180–81
  role in career life stories, 170–72
  role in romantic life stories, 175–77
  Romantic pathways and, 172–75
  school-to-work transition, 165–66
  self-acceptance, 180–81
  self-criticism, 14, 166, 167–68, 170–72, 179–84, 182*f*, 183*f*
  self-definition, 14
  self-determination theory, 166–67
personality maturity, 146, 216–19, 253, 254–55
  self-criticism and, 183–84
  well-being and, 178–79, 216–17
Personal Project Analysis, 20, 59, 92–93, 180, 200, 202
personal resources
  goal attainment and, 21
  measuring, 19–20
  role in effective functioning, 13
Piscedda, Valter, 239
postmodern societies, 125–26
Pratt, M. W., 133
Pre-intimate status, 99
priorities
  gendered pathways and, 149–50
  goals and plans, 30–34
  prioritization of career, 128–30
Pseudo-intimate status, 99
psychological assets. *See also* authorship
  grow out of difficulties, 4, 133–34, 256
  learning from experiences, 4, 133–34, 256
  overcoming difficulties, 4, 133–34, 256
psychological outcomes, 180–81
psychopathology. *See also* depressive affect
  developmental deviation, 210
  group-based trajectory model, 219–20, 229
  normative development and, 229
  overview, 208–9
  personality maturity, 216–19
  role in understanding adaptive and maladaptive courses and outcomes, 209–11
  scar model, 6, 226–28
  theory of personality, 14, 150–51, 166, 172, 184, 222–23
  vulnerability model, 219–20

psychosocial functioning, 143*t*
Purpose of Life inventory, 142–43
Pursuit of goals accompanied by underlying insecurities and concerns goals pattern, 37–38

qualitative approach
  goals and plans, 27
  Intimacy Status Interview, 98–99
  romantic history interview, 81–82
quantitative approach, authorship, 142–44

Racheli (study participant)
  intimacy status, 102, 103, 110–11
  romantic pathway, 85–86, 93
Rauer, A. J., 91–92
Realistic and orderly career and family goals pattern, 38–40
reflective capacity and career-related outcomes, 203*t*
  about parents' career and work, 199–201
  Brief Young Adult Life Events Scale, 200
  goal achievement and attainment and, 201, 203–4
  interpersonal dimension, 254–55
  intrapersonal dimension, 254–55
  overview, 198–204
  parental support and, 198–204
  Personal Project Analysis, 200
  regarding parents' marital and family relationships, 201–4
  Vocational Identity Status Assessment, 200
rejection sensitivity, 253–54
reproductive strategies, 125–26, 128
resilience, 13, 210–11
Reuben (study participant)
  career adaptability, 66–68
  career pathway, 54–55
Rina (study participant), 119, 120
Rivka (study participant), 69–70, 71
romantic authorship. *See also* authorship
  achievement of, 140–41
  failure to achieve, 137–38
romantic development, 259. *See also* intimacy status; work-family balance
  attainment of romantic goals and, 92–94, 93*t*
  casual sexual encounters, 9–10
  Casual to steady pathway, 86–88, 89–91, 93, 93*t*, 94*f*, 94, 148–49, 173–74, 174*t*, 214–15, 215*f*, 258
  cohabitation, 9–10, 79–97, 233
  Conflictual but Committed intimacy status, 99

depressive affect and, 94f
fluidity and progression, 90–92
gendered pathways, 148–49
identifying, 82–83
intimacy status and, 105–6, 106t
Intimate but not Committed intimacy pattern, 99, 101–2, 103, 106t, 111–13
Intimately Committed intimacy pattern, 99, 100, 104–5, 106t
Lengthy Relationships but Absence of Experiential Learning pathway, 84–86, 91, 93–94, 93t, 94f, 110–11, 148–49, 173–74, 174t, 192, 215f, 215–16, 258
Mergers/Committed intimacy status, 99
non-heterosexual young adults, 89–90
Non-intimate Commitment intimacy pattern, 99, 102–3, 104–5, 106t, 110–11
Non-stable intimacy pattern, 99, 100, 105, 106–9, 106t
overview, 79–81
personality attributes and, 172–75
relationship between work status and marital status, 231–35
romantic history interview, 81–82
Sporadic pathway, 83–84, 90, 93, 93t, 94f, 94, 106–9, 148–49, 214–15, 215f, 258
Steady relationships pathway, 88–89, 90–91, 93–94, 93t, 94f, 148–49, 151–52
Stereotype intimacy status, 99
romantic partners, as support system, 189
Ronen (study participant), 72
Roni (study participant)
  career adaptability, 67–68
  career pathway, 53–55
  goals, 37–38, 38t
  mental health patterns, 218–19
  support systems, 195–97, 205
Rothbard, N. P., 122–23
Rothermund, K., 40
Roy (study participant), 117, 129
Ryan, Richard, 14
Ryff, C. D., 180–81

Salemla-Aro, Katarina, 30–31
Salvatore, J. E., 172
Sarah (study participant)
  career pursuit and romantic development, 127
  intimacy status, 102–3
Sardinian emerging adults, 238–41, 246
Sasha (study participant), 100
scar model, psychopathology, 6, 226–28
Schmitt, D. P., 152

school-to-work (STW) transition, 13, 165–66
Schulenberg, John, 208
SDT (self-determination theory), 14–15, 166–67, 184
Seasons of a Man's Life, The (Levinson), 163
Seasons of a Woman's Life, The (Levinson), 163
self-acceptance, 180–81
Self-Acceptance inventory, 142–43
self-actualization, 64–65, 217
self-concordance model, 14–15
self-continuity, 132–33, 256
self-criticism, 14, 166, 170–72, 179, 181–84, 222–23
  changes in, 179–84
  defined, 19, 167–68
  goal attainment and, 21
  perception of self and others, 172
  role in career life stories, 170–72
  univariate linear growth curve analysis, 181–84, 182f, 183f
self-definition, 14, 166, 172–73, 222–23
self-determination theory (SDT), 14–15, 166–67, 184
self-goals, 20–21
self-regulation, 73–74, 166–67
self-socialization, 12–13, 23–24
sexual strategies theory, 152–53
Shahar, G., 20–21, 167
Shiner, R. L., 216–17
Shulman, S., 20–22
Sideridis, G., 235–36
Slaughter, Anne-Marie, 149–50
Smith, L. B., 81, 92, 251–52
Snarey, J. R., 193
Sneed, J. R., 33, 123–24
social acceleration theory, 240
social capital, 263
socialization theory
  gendered pathways, 150–52
  support systems, 189–90
sociocultural context, 17–19
socioeconomic risks/difficulties, 125, 128, 130
Sporadic romantic pathway, 90, 94f, 94, 258
  goal attainment, 93, 93t
  level of depressive affect among members of, 214–15, 215f
  men vs. women, 148–49
  multinomial regression analysis predicting membership in, 173–74, 174t
  Non-stable intimacy pattern and, 106–9
  overview, 83–84
Sroufe, L. A., 189–210
Stabelou, Areti, 237

Steady Relationships romantic pathway, 90–91, 93–94, 258
    changes in depressive affect, 94f
    goal attainment, 93t
    level of depressive affect among members of, 214–15, 215f
    men vs. women, 148–49, 151–52
    overview, 88–89
    parental support and, 192
Stereotype intimacy status, 99
stereotypes, gendered pathways, 161–62
STW (school-to-work) transition, 13, 165–66
subsistence economy, Sardinia, 238–39
support systems, 13, 19–20, 188f, See also parental support
    attainment of developmental tasks and, 189–91
    goal attainment and, 21
    mentors, 205–6
    Network of Relationship Inventory, 187–88
    overview, 186–87
    peer support, 13, 15–16, 204–5
    romantic partners, 189
    socialization theory, 189–90
    vocational psychology, 190
Survivors pathway, 53–55, 57–58, 59, 60t, 257–58
    career adaptability and, 66–68
    level of depressive affect among members of, 213f, 214
    men vs. women, 168–69, 258–59
    parental support and, 191–92, 195–97

Tami (study participant), 196–97
te Riele, K., 52–53
Thelen, E., 81, 92, 251–52
theoretical and research frameworks for emerging adulthood study, 9–26
    conceptualization, 10–12
    gendered pathways, 150–53
    general discussion, 9–10
    goal management an adaptability, 24–25
    initial findings, 20–23
    lessons learned from earlier youth studies, 12–13
    measuring developmental outcomes, 20
    measuring personal resources, 19–20
    motivational theory of life-span development, 24
    participants, 16–17
    personality development, 26
    qualitative approach, 25–26
    quantitative approach, 25

    role of personality and social resources in meeting developmental challenges, 14–16
    self-socialization, 23–24
    sociocultural context, 17–19
    success and failure in meeting developmental tasks, 16–20
    support systems, 19–20
theory of personality, 14, 166, 184, 222–23
    dependency, 223
    gendered pathways and, 150–51
    self-criticism, 172
    self-definition, 222–23
"time-out" periods, 24
Tippett, L. J., 133
Tomi (study participant), 175
Twenge, Jean, 10–11

unattainable goals, 24
unemployment, 231–33, 232f
    Arab and North African emerging adults, 241–42, 243
    Greek emerging adults, 236–38
    NEETs, 236
    Sardinian emerging adults, 238–41

Vague pattern of career adaptability, 75–78, 77t
Varda (study participant), 119
Vocational Identity Status Assessment, 142–43, 200
vocational psychology, 190
vulnerability model, 219–20

waithood, 6–7, 241
Ward, K., 156
well-being, 76–78
Whiston, S. C., 190
"Why Women Still Can't Have It All" article (Slaughter), 149–50
Williams, V. A., 189
Winkles, J. K., 107, 128–29
Wolf-Wendel, L., 156
women
    Career-focused combined with investment in motherhood and family pattern, 158–59, 162
    Compromised pattern of career adaptability, 157–58, 162
    maternal identity, 156–57
    No career, frustrated mother pattern, 160–61
    overview, 156–61
work authorship, 136–40. See also authorship
work-family balance
    dating, 116–21

evolutionary approach, 124–28
life-course approach, 122
life-cycle approach, 121–24
overview, 115–16
prioritization of career, 128–30
Work–Family Spillover Scale, 202
Wynne, L. C., 104–5

Yafa (study participant), 227
Yair (study participant), 89
Yaron (study participant), 127
Yehoshua (study participant)
   authorship, 145
   intimacy status, 101–2, 112–13
Yochanan (study participant)
   career and romance, 115
   gendered pathways, 154

Yonit (study participant), 160–61
Yoram (study participant)
   authorship, 139–40, 145
   gendered pathways, 154–55
   mental health patterns, 218
   work-family balance, 118, 129–30
Yori (study participant), 117–18
Yossi (study participant), 84, 129
youth unemployment, 231–33, 232*f*
   Arab and North African countries, 241–42, 243
   Greece, 236–38
   Sardinia, 238–41
"yo-yo" structure, 9
Yuri (study participant), 101

Zarrett, Nicole, 208